Tafsīr al-Qurṭubī

Vol. 1

Juz' 1: Al-Fātiḥah & Sūrat al-Baqarah 1-141

Tafsīr al-Qurṭubī

The General Judgments of the Qur'an and Clarification of what it contains of the Sunnah and *Āyahs* of Discrimination

Abū 'Abdullāh Muḥammad ibn Aḥmad ibn Abī Bakr ibn Farḥ al-Anṣārī al-Khazrajī al-Andalusī al-Qurṭubī

Vol. 1

Juz' 1: Al-Fātiḥah & Sūrat al-Baqarah 1-141

translated by
Aisha Bewley

DIWAN PRESS
Classical and Contemporary Books on Islam and Sufism

Published by: Diwan Press Ltd.

Website: www.diwanpress.com
E-mail: info@diwanpress.com

By: Abu 'Abdullah Muhammad ibn Ahmad al-Qurtubi
Translated by: Aisha Abdarrahman Bewley
Edited by: Abdalhaqq Bewley

A catalogue record of this book is available from the British Library.

ISBN13: 978-1-908892-60-7 (Paperback)
978-1-908892-61-4 (Casebound)
978-1-908892-59-1 (Hardback)
978-1-908892-73-7 (ePub & Kindle)

CONTENTS

Translator's note **vii**

1. Sūrat al-Fātiḥah 1

Topic One: its virtues and names 2

Topic Two: its revelation and its rulings 7

Topic Three: Saying 'Āmīn' 19

Topic Four: the meanings of the Fātiḥah, its recitations and syntax, and the excellence of those who praise 22

2. Sūrat al-Baqarah – The Cow 1 – 141 **38**

Table of Contents for *Āyats* **335**

Glossary **339**

Table of Transliterations

ء	’	ض	ḍ
ا	a	ط	ṭ
ب	b	ظ	ẓ
ت	t	ع	‘
ث	th	غ	gh
ج	j	ف	f
ح	ḥ	ق	q
خ	kh	ك	k
د	d	ل	l
ذ	dh	م	m
ر	r	ن	n
ز	z	ه	h
س	s	و	w
ش	sh	ي	y
ص	ṣ		

Long vowel		Short vowel	
ا	ā	ـَ	a [*fatḥah*]
و	ū	ـُ	u [*ḍammah*]
ي	ī	ـِ	i [*kasrah*]
أَوْ	aw		
أَيْ	ay		

Translator's note

There are minor omissions in the text. Some poems have been omitted which the author quotes to illustrate a point of grammatical usage or as an example of orthography or the usage of a word, often a derivative of the root of the word used in the *āyah*, but not the actual word used. Often it is difficult to convey the sense in English. Occasionally the author explores a grammatical matter or a tangential issue, and some of these may have been shortened. English grammatical terms used to translate Arabic grammatical terms do not have exactly the same meaning, sometimes rendering a precise translation of them problematic and often obscure.

The end of a *juz'* may vary by an *āyah* or two in order to preserve relevant passages.

1. *Sūrat al-Fātiḥah*

بِسْمِ اِ۬للَّهِ اِ۬لرَّحْمَٰنِ اِ۬لرَّحِيمِ

In the name of Allah, All-Merciful, Most Merciful

اَ۬لْحَمْدُ لِلَّهِ رَبِّ اِ۬لْعَٰلَمِينَ ۝١ اَ۬لرَّحْمَٰنِ
اِ۬لرَّحِيمِ ۝٢ مَلِكِ يَوْمِ اِ۬لدِّينِ ۝٣

1 Praise be to Allah, the Lord of all the worlds,
2 the All-Merciful, the Most Merciful,
3 the King of the Day of Repayment.

إِيَّاكَ نَعْبُدُ وَإِيَّاكَ نَسْتَعِينُ ۝٤

4 You alone we worship. You alone we ask for help.

اِ۪هْدِنَا اَ۬لصِّرَٰطَ اَ۬لْمُسْتَقِيمَ ۝٥
صِرَٰطَ اَ۬لَّذِينَ أَنْعَمْتَ عَلَيْهِمْ ۝٦
غَيْرِ اِ۬لْمَغْضُوبِ عَلَيْهِمْ وَلَا اَ۬لضَّآلِّينَ ۝٧

5 Guide us on the Straight Path,
6 the Path of those You have blessed,
7 not of those with anger on them, nor of the misguided.

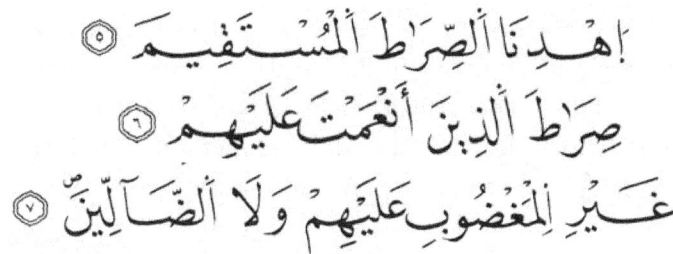

It contains four topics.

Topic One: its virtues and names

There are seven points in it.

At-Tirmidhī related from Ubayy ibn Ka'b that the Messenger of Allah ﷺ said, 'Allah has not revealed anything like the Mother of the Book either in the Torah or the Gospel. It is the Seven *Mathānī* (Oft-repeated). "It is divided between Me and My slave, and My slave has what he asks for."' Mālik transmitted this from al-'Alā' ibn 'Abd ar-Raḥmān ibn Ya'qūb who said that Abū Sa'īd, the freedman of 'Abdullāh ibn 'Āmir ibn Kurayz, reported that the Messenger of Allah ﷺ called to Ubayy ibn Ka'b while he was praying and he mentioned the hadith. Ibn 'Abd al-Barr said, 'No further name is known for Abū Sa'īd. He is counted as one of the people of Madīnah.' He transmitted from Abū Hurayrah and this hadith is *mursal.* The hadith is related from Abū Sa'īd ibn al-Mu'allā from one of the Companions whose name is also not known. Ḥafṣ ibn 'Āṣim and 'Ubayd ibn Ḥunayn related it from him. This is how it is stated in *at-Tamhīd*: 'His name is not found.' He mentioned the disagreement about his name in the Book of the Companions. Al-Bukhārī transmitted the hadith from Abū Sa'īd ibn al-Mu'allā: 'I was praying and the Messenger of Allah ﷺ called me but I did not answer until I had finished praying. Then I went to him and he asked, "What kept you from coming to me? Does not Allah say, *'Respond to Allah, and to the Messenger, when He calls you'* (8:24)?" Then he said to me, "I will teach you a *sūrah* which is the greatest of the *sūrahs* in the Qur'an before you leave the mosque." Then he took my hand. When the Prophet ﷺ was about to leave, I said to him, "Did you not say, 'I will teach you a *sūrah* which is the greatest of the *sūrahs* in the Qur'an'?" He said, "*Praise be to Allah, the Lord of all the worlds*, it is the Seven Oft-Repeated ones and the Immense Qur'an that I have been given."' Ibn 'Abd al-Barr and others said that Abū Sa'īd ibn al-Mu'allā was one of the esteemed men and masters of the Anṣār. Al-Bukhārī alone has him, and his name was Rāfi'. It is also said that it was al-Ḥārith ibn Nufay' ibn al-Mu'allā. It is also said that it was Aws ibn al-Mu'allā and Abū Sa'īd ibn Aws ibn al-Mu'allā. He died in 74 AH at the age of sixty-four. He was the first to pray towards the qiblah when it was changed as will be mentioned. There is an *isnād* of the hadith of Abū Yazīd ibn Zuray' from Rawḥ ibn al-Qāsim from al-'Alā' ibn 'Abd ar-Raḥmān from his father from Abū Hurayrah who said, 'The Messenger of Allah ﷺ came out to Ubayy while he was praying.' He mentioned the gist of the hadith.

Ibn al-Anbārī mentioned in his *Kitāb ar-radd* from his father from Abū

'Ubaydullāh al-Warrāq from Abū Dāwūd from Shaybān from Manṣūr that Mujāhid said, 'Iblīs, may Allah curse him, lamented four times: when he was cursed, when he fell from the Garden, when Muḥammad ﷺ was sent, and when the *Fātiḥah* of the Book was revealed, and it was revealed in Madīnah.'

Scholars disagree about the relative excellence of some *sūrah*s and *āyah*s over others, and some of the Beautiful Names of Allah over others. Some people say that none of them are better than any other because all are the Speech of Allah, and the same lack of preference applies to His Names. Shaykh Abu-l-Ḥasan al-Ash'arī, Qāḍī Abū Bakr ibn aṭ-Ṭayyib, Abū Ḥātim Muḥammad ibn Ḥibbān as-Sibtī and a group of *fuqahā'* believed this, and something to that effect is related from Mālik. Yaḥyā ibn Yaḥyā said that it is an error to consider one part of the Qur'an better than other parts. Similarly Mālik disliked the repetition of one particular *sūrah* rather than others. In reference to the words of Allah Almighty: *'We bring one better than it or equal to it'* (2:106), Mālik says that this means 'one containing judgment rather than one subject to abrogation.' Ibn Kinānah related the same as all that from Mālik.

Some of them use the following argument: 'The best is only recognised by comparison with what might be considered slightly less excellent, but the essential nature of all *āyah*s is one and the same. They are all part of the Speech of Allah and there can be no deficiency in the Speech of Allah.' As-Sibtī stated: 'The meaning of the words "Allah has not revealed anything like the Mother of the Qur'an either in the Torah or the Gospel" is that Allah Almighty does not give those who recite the Torah or the Gospel a reward like the one He gives to someone who recites the Mother of the Qur'an, since Allah has favoured this community over other communities and He has given a greater excellence to the recitation of His Words in His Revelation than He gave to others for reciting His Words. It is a favour from Him to this Community. The words of the Prophet ﷺ, "the greatest of the *sūrah*s", means that it is the greatest in reward. His words do not mean that some parts of the Qur'an are better than other parts.'

Some people have said that there is a certain kind of superiority which may be seen in such *āyah*s as in the words of the Almighty, *'Your God is One God. There is no God but Him, the All-Merciful, the Most Merciful'* (2:163), the Throne Verse, the end of *Sūrat al-Ḥashr*, and *Sūrat al-Ikhlāṣ*, which are among the proofs of His Oneness and His attributes, and that does not exist, for instance, in such *āyah*s as *'Perish the hands of Abū Lahab'* (111:1). Superiority occurs through the wondrous meanings and how numerous they are, not in respect of the quality of the language. This is the truth. Those who said that there was preference included Isḥāq ibn Rāhawayh as well as other scholars and *mutakallimūn*. It is the position preferred by Qāḍī Abū Bakr ibn al-'Arabī and Ibn al-Ḥaṣṣār who go by the hadith of Ubayy ibn Ka'b, in which he said, 'The Messenger of Allah ﷺ asked me, "Ubayy, which of the *āyahs* of the Book is the greatest?" I replied. *"Allah, there is no god but Him, the Living, the Self-Sustaining"* (2:255) [i.e. the Throne Verse.] He struck my chest and said, "May Allah give you joy, Abū al-Mundhir!"' Al-Bukhārī and Muslim transmitted it. Ibn al-Ḥassār said, 'I am surprised at those who differ when such texts exist.'

Ibn al-'Arabī said, 'He says, "Allah has not revealed its like in the Torah, the Gospel or the Qur'an." He was silent about other Scriptures, like the Revealed Scrolls, the Psalms and other things because this mentions the best of them. When something is the best of the best, then it is the best of all. It is as you say, "Zayd is the best of scholars," and so he is the best of all.'

The *Fātiḥah* possesses attributes which other *sūrahs* do not possess, to the extent that it is said that the entire Qur'an is contained in it. It consists of twenty-five words which embrace all the sciences of the Qur'an. Part of its distinction is that Allah has divided it between Himself and His slaves, and the prayer is only valid with it, and no action is necessary to gain a reward for it. It is in this sense that it is the Mother of the Immense Qur'an. *Sūrat al-Ikhlāṣ* is considered to be equivalent to a third of the Qur'an. The *Fātiḥah* contains *tawḥīd*, judgments and admonition and *Sūrat al-Ikhlāṣ* contains all of *tawḥīd*. It also explains the words of the Prophet ﷺ to Ubayy, 'Ubayy, which of the *āyahs* of the Book is the greatest?' to which he replied, *'Allah, there is no god but Him, the Living, the Self-Sustaining.'* (2:255) It is the greatest *āyah* because it contains every aspect of *tawḥīd*. In the same way the Prophet's words, 'The best of what I and the Prophets before have said is "There is no god but Allah alone with no partner", indicate that that is the best form of *dhikr* because they are words which contains all the knowledge of *tawḥīd*. The *Fātiḥah*, on the other hand, contains *tawḥīd*, worship and admonition. That is not impossible in Allah's power.

'Alī ibn Abī Ṭālib related that the Messenger of Allah ﷺ said, 'The *Fātiḥah* of the Book, the Throne Verse, *"Allah bears witness that there is no god but Him"* (3:18) and *"Say: 'O Allah, Master of the Kingdom'"* (3:26): these *āyahs* are suspended from the Throne. There is no veil between them and Allah.' Abū 'Amr ad-Dānī has this in his *Kitāb al-bayān*.

The *Fātiḥah* has twelve names:

1. ***Ṣalāt* (the Prayer).** Allah Almighty says in a hadith: 'I have divided the prayer between Myself and My slave.'

2. ***Sūrat al-Ḥamd* (*Sūrah* of Praise)**, because praise is mentioned in it.

This is similar in the way that other *sūrahs* are named, such as 'The *Sūrah* of the Battlements', 'Booty', 'Repentance' and the like.

3. **The *Fātiḥah* (Opener) of the Book**. This name is undisputed among scholars. It is called that because it opens the recitation of the Qur'an and the writing of every copy of the Qur'an opens with it, and the prayers also open with it.

4. ***Umm al-Kitāb* (Mother of the Book).** There is some disagreement concerning this name. Some allow it while Anas, al-Ḥasan and Ibn Sīrīn disliked it. Al-Ḥasan said, 'The *Umm al-Kitāb* is the lawful and unlawful. Allah Almighty says, "*Āyahs containing clear judgments – they are the* Umm al-Kitāb – *and others are open to interpretation.*" (3:7)' Anas and Ibn Sīrīn said that the *Umm al-Kitāb* is the name of the Preserved Tablet. Allah Almighty says, '*It is in the* Umm al-Kitāb *with Us.*' (43:4)

5. ***Umm al-Qur'ān* (The Mother of the Qur'ān).** There is also disagreement about this. The majority allow it while Anas and Ibn Sīrīn dislike it. Firm hadiths refute these two opinions. At-Tirmidhī transmitted from Abū Hurayrah that the Messenger of Allah ﷺ said, '"*Praise belongs to Allah*" is the Mother of the Qur'an, the Mother of the Book and the Seven *Mathānī*.' He said that this hadith is *ḥasan ṣaḥīḥ*. We find in al-Bukhārī: 'It is called the Mother of the Book because it begins the writing of copies of the Qur'an and one begins with its recitation in the prayer.' Yaḥyā ibn Ya'mar said, 'The Mother of Towns is Makkah, the Mother of Khorasan is Marv, the Mother of the Qur'an is the *Sūrah* of Praise.' It is said that it was called the Mother of the Qur'an because it is the beginning of it and contains all its sciences. It is for that reason that Makkah is called the Mother of the Towns because it was the first on the earth and the earth spread out from it. A mother is called 'mother' because she is the root of progeny. Earth is a 'mother'. Umayyah ibn Abī aṣ-Ṣalt said:

'The earth is our stronghold and our mother.
Our graves are in it and we were born from it.'

A banner of war is called '*Umm*' because it precedes it and the army follows it. The root of *umm* is *ummahah* which is why the plural is *ummahāt.*

6. ***Al-Mathānī* (the Oft-Repeated).** It is called that because it is repeated in every *rak'ah* of the prayer. It is said that it is called that because it is exclusively for this Community and it was not revealed to anyone before because it was a treasure stored up for this Community.

7. **The Immense Qur'an**. It is called that because it contains all the sciences

of the Qur'an. That is because it contains praise of Allah Almighty with the qualities of His Perfection and Majesty, the command to perform acts of worship and to be sincere in them, acknowledgement of the inability to do any of it except with Allah's help, entreaty to Him for guidance to the Straight Path and being spared the states of those who violate the contract, and clarification of the final state of the deniers.

8. ***Ash-Shifā'* (Healing).** Ad-Dārimī related from Abū Sa'īd al-Khudrī that the Messenger of Allah ﷺ said, 'The *Fātiḥah* of the Book is healing for every poison.'

9. ***Ar-Ruqyah* (the Charm).** This name is taken from a hadith of Abū Sa'īd al-Khudrī in which the Messenger of Allah ﷺ said to a man who had recited it as a charm for someone with a snake-bite, 'What taught you that it was a charm?' He replied, 'Messenger of Allah, something that came into my heart.' The *imāms* transmitted it.

10. ***Al-Asās* (the Core).** A man complained to ash-Sha'bī of abdominal pain and he said, 'You must have the Core of the Qur'an, the *Fātiḥah* of the Book. I heard Ibn 'Abbās say, "Everything has a core. The core of this world is Makkah because the world spread out from it. The core of the heavens is *'Arīb*, which is the seventh heaven. The core of the earth is *'Ajīb*, and it is the lowest of the seven earths. The core of the Gardens is the Garden of *'Adn*, and it is the navel of the Gardens and on it the Garden is founded. The core of the Fire is Jahannam, which is the lowest level on which the other levels are based. The core of creatures is Ādam. And the core of the Prophets is Nūḥ. The core of the tribe of Israel is Ya'qūb. The core of the Qur'an is the *Fātiḥah* and the core of the *Fātiḥah* is *'In the Name of Allah, the All-Merciful, Most Merciful'*. When you are ill, you should recite the *Fātiḥah* and you will be healed."'

11. ***Al-Wāfiyah* (the Complete).** Sufyān ibn 'Uyaynah said that it is because it may not be halved or broken up. In the case of other *sūrahs*, if one reads half in one *rak'ah* and half in the other *rak'ah*, that is allowed. If the *Fātiḥah* is divided between two *rak'ahs*, that does not satisfy the legal requirement.

12. ***Al-Kāfiyah* (the Sufficient).** Yaḥyā ibn Abī Kathīr said that it is because it suffices for others while others do not suffice for it. This is indicated by what Muḥammad ibn Khallād al-Iskandāranī mentioned that the Prophet ﷺ said, 'The *Umm al-Qur'ān* is a substitute for other than it but other than it is not a substitute for it.'

Al-Muhallab said, 'The locus of the charm is in the words *"You alone we worship and You alone we ask for help."*' It is also said that the entire *sūrah* is a charm, based on the words of the Prophet ﷺ to the man, 'What taught you that it is a charm?' He did not say that there is a charm in it. This indicates that the entire *sūrah* is a charm because it is the *Fātiḥah* of the Book and its beginning and contains all of its sciences, as has already been stated. Allah knows best.

The fact that it bears the names *al-Mathānī* and *Umm al-Kitāb* does not prevent other things from having those names as well. Allah Almighty says, *'A Book consistent in its frequent repetitions* (mathānī)' (39:23) and so He called His whole Book '*mathānī*' because things are repeated in it. The seven long *sūrahs* are also *mathānī* because of the obligations and stories repeated in them. Ibn 'Abbās said, 'The Messenger of Allah ﷺ was given the Seven *Mathānī*.' He said that they are the seven long *sūrahs*. An-Nasā'ī mentioned that and said that the six extend from *al-Baqarah* to *al-A'rāf*, but they disagree about the seventh. Some people say that it is *Yūnus*, some that it is *al-Anfāl*, and some that it is *at-Tawbah*. The last is the position of Mujāhid and Sa'īd ibn Jubayr. A'shā Hamdān said:

Stay in the mosque and pray to your Lord.
Study these *Mathānī* and the long *sūrahs* (*ṭuwal*).

Mathānī is the plural of *mathnā*, which is that which comes after the first. *Ṭuwal* is the plural of *aṭwal* (longest). *Al-Anfāl* is called one of the *Mathānī* because it follows the longest *sūrahs* in length. It is said that it is that whose *āyahs* are more than those of the *Mufaṣṣal* and less than the Hundreds. The Hundreds are *sūrahs* which have more than a hundred *āyahs*.

TOPIC TWO: ITS REVELATION AND ITS RULINGS

There are twenty points regarding this.

The Community agree that the *Fātiḥah* of the Book has seven *āyahs* except for a report from Ḥusayn al-Ju'fī that it only has six, which is unusual. There is also a report from 'Amr ibn 'Ubayd that *'You alone we worship'* is an *āyah*, and so it is eight *āyahs*, but this is aberrant. Allah's words, *'We have given you the Seven Oft-repeated'* (15:87), and the hadith *qudsī*, 'I have divided the prayer...' refute these two statements.

The Community also agree that it is part of the Qur'an. There are those who counter this by saying that if it were truly part of the Qur'an, then 'Abdullāh ibn Mas'ūd would have written it in his copy of the Qur'an, and the fact that he did not write it indicates that it is not part of the Qur'an, nor indeed are the two *Sūrahs* of Refuge. The answer to that was given by Abū Bakr al-Anbārī. He related from al-Ḥasan ibn al-Ḥubbāb from Sulaymān ibn al-Ash'ath from Abū Qudāmah from Jarīr that al-A'mash said, "Abdullāh ibn Mas'ūd was asked, "Why have you not written the *Fātiḥah* of the Book in your copy of the Qur'an?" He replied, "If I had written it, I would have written it with every *sūrah*."' Abū Bakr said, 'He was referring to the way that every *rak'ah* is begun with the *Umm al-Qur'ān* before the *sūrah* is recited after it.' He said, 'I made things shorter by omitting it. It is safely preserved because all the Muslims memorise it and so I did not write it anywhere to avoid having to write it with every *sūra* since it precedes all of them in the prayer.'

There is disagreement about whether it is Makkan or Madinan. Ibn 'Abbās, Qatādah, Abu-l-'Āliyah, ar-Riyāḥī Rufay' and others said that it is Makkan. Abū Hurayrah, Mujāhid, 'Aṭā' ibn Yasār, az-Zuhrī and others said that it is Madinan. It is said that half of it was revealed in Makkah and half in Madīnah, as is related by Abū al-Layth Naṣr ibn Muḥammad ibn Ibrāhīm as-Samarqandī in his commentary. The first position is considered sounder because of the words of the Almighty, *'We have given you the seven Oft-repeated and the Magnificent Qur'an'* from the end of *al-Ḥijr* and it is agreed that *al-Ḥijr* is a Makkan *sūrah* and there is no disagreement that the prayer was made obligatory in Makkah. It has not been recorded anywhere that the prayer in Islam was ever performed without reciting *'Praise be to Allah, the Lord of the worlds.'* This is backed up by the words of the Prophet ﷺ, 'There is no prayer without the *Fātiḥah* of the Book.' This is a report about a ruling.

Qāḍī Ibn aṭ-Ṭayyib mentioned people's disagreement about the first part of the Qur'an to be revealed. It is said that it was *al-Muddaththir* (74) or *al-'Alaq* (96) or the *Fātiḥah*. Al-Bayhaqī mentioned in the *Proofs of Prophethood* from Abū Maysarah 'Amr ibn Sharaḥbīl that the Messenger of Allah ﷺ said to his wife Khadījah, 'When I was alone, I heard a voice calling and, by Allah, I fear that this is an affliction.' She said, 'We seek refuge with Allah! Allah would not do that to you. By Allah, you return people's trusts, maintain ties of kinship and give *ṣadaqah*...' When Abū Bakr entered when the Messenger of Allah ﷺ was not there, Khadījah mentioned the matter to him and said, "Atīq, go with Muḥammad to Waraqah ibn Nawfal.' When the Messenger of Allah ﷺ came in, Abū Bakr took his hand and said, 'Let us go to Waraqah.' He asked, 'Who told you?' 'Khadījah,' he answered.

So they went to him and told him the story. He said, 'When I was alone, I heard a voice calling behind me, "O Muḥammad, O Muḥammad!" and I began to run away from that place.' He said, 'Do not do that. When it comes to you, be firm so that you can hear what it says. Then come and tell me.' When he was alone, he was called and told: 'O Muḥammad! Say: *"In the Name of Allah, the All-Merciful,*

Most Merciful. Praise be to Allah, the Lord of the worlds ... to ... *misguided.*" Say: "There is no god but Allah."' So he went and told Waraqah and Waraqah said to him, 'Good news and good news again! I testify to you that you are the one about whom 'Īsā son of Maryam gave the good news and you have received the like of the *Nāmūs* of Mūsā and you are a sent Prophet. You will be commanded to do jihād at some future date. If I am alive, I will strive with you.' When Waraqah died, the Messenger of Allah ﷺ said, 'I have seen the priest in the Garden wearing a silk garment because he believed in me and affirmed me.' He meant Waraqah. Al-Bayhaqī said, 'This hadith is *munqaṭi'*.' If it is guaranteed safe from corruption (*maḥfūẓ*) it may be a report about the revelation of the *Fātiḥah* after the revelation of '*Read in the name of your Lord*' (96:1) and *al-Muddaththir* (74).

Ibn 'Aṭiyyah said that some scholars think that Jibrīl did not bring down the *Sūrah* of Praise because of the hadith in which Muslim related that Ibn 'Abbās said, 'While Jibrīl was sitting with the Prophet ﷺ, he heard a crack above him. He lifted his head and said, "This is a door of heaven being opened today which has not been opened before now." An angel descended from it and he said, "This is an angel who has descended to Earth who has not descended before today." He greeted them and said, "Good news of two lights which you have been given which no Prophet before you was given: the *Fātiḥah* of the Book and the Seals of *Sūrat al-Baqarah* (2:285-286). You will not read a single letter of them without being rewarded for it."' Ibn 'Aṭiyyah said, 'It is not as they think. This hadith indicates that Jibrīl came before the other angel to the Prophet ﷺ to inform him of it and of what he brought down. Accordingly Jibrīl participated in its revelation, but Allah knows best.'

It is clear that this hadith indicates that Jibrīl did not teach the Prophet ﷺ any of the *Fātiḥah*. We explained that it was revealed in Makkah and that Jibrīl brought it down since Allah says: '*The Faithful* Rūḥ *brought it down.*' (26:193) This means all of the Qur'an. So Jibrīl brought down its recitation in Makkah and the angel brought down its reward in Madīnah, but Allah knows best. It is said that it is Makkan/Madinan and that Jibrīl brought it down twice, as ath-Tha'labī related. What we mentioned is more likely since it combines the Qur'an and the *Sunnah*. Praise and favour belongs to Allah.

It has already been made clear that the *basmalah* is not an *āyah* of the *Fātiḥah* according to the sound position. Given that, the ruling for those doing the prayer is that, after the *takbīr*, they begin straight away with the *Fātiḥah* and are not silent, and do not recite any *tawjīh* (the *du'ā*, '*I have turned my face...*') or *tasbīḥ*. This is verified by the hadith of 'Ā'ishah, Anas and others. There are other hadiths which contain the *tawjīh*, *tasbīḥ*, and silence, and a group of scholars follow that position. It is related that, when they began the prayer, 'Umar ibn al-Khaṭṭāb and 'Abdullāh ibn Mas'ūd used to say: 'Glory be to You, O Allah, and by Your praise. Blessed is Your Name and exalted is Your Majesty. There is no god but You.' Sufyān, Aḥmad, Isḥāq and the people of opinion follow that. Ash-Shāfi'ī used to say what is related from 'Alī from the Prophet ﷺ, which is that when he began the prayer, he said the *takbīr* and then *'I have turned my face...'* (6:79). Muslim mentioned it and it will come in full at the end of *Sūrat al-An'ām*. At this point what we have said here is enough concerning this matter, Allah willing.

Ibn al-Mundhir said, 'It is verified that when the Messenger of Allah ﷺ said the *takbīr* for the prayer, he was silent for a time before starting the recitation, during which time he said, "O Allah, put as much distance between me and my errors as You have put between the east and the west. O Allah, cleanse me of my errors as a white garment is cleansed of dirt. O Allah, wash me of my errors with snow, ice and hail." Abū Hurayrah acted according to that.' Abū Salamah ibn 'Abd ar-Raḥmān said, 'The imām is silent twice, so take advantage of them with recitation.' Al-Awzā'ī, Sa'īd ibn 'Abd al-'Azīz and Aḥmad ibn Ḥanbal inclined to the hadith of the Prophet ﷺ regarding this matter.'

Scholars disagree about the exact nature of the obligation of reciting the *Fātiḥah* in the prayer. Mālik and his people say that it is incumbent on the imām and anyone praying alone in every *rak'ah*. Ibn Khuwayzimandād al-Baṣrī al-Mālikī said, 'There is no disagreement about the position of Mālik in respect of someone forgetting it in one *rak'ah* of a two-*rak'ah* prayer: the prayer is then invalid and does not satisfy the obligation. There is disagreement about his position regarding someone who forgets it in one *rak'ah* of a three or four-*rak'at* prayer. Once he said that he must repeat the prayer and another time that he should perform the prostration of forgetfulness. This is transmitted by Ibn 'Abd al-Ḥakam and others from Mālik.' Ibn Khuwayzimandād said, 'It is said that he repeats that *rak'ah* and then performs the prostration of forgetfulness after the *salām*.' Ibn 'Abd al-Barr said, 'The sound position is that he discounts that *rak'ah* and does another to replace it, like someone who omits a prostration out of forgetfulness. That is what Ibn al-Qāsim preferred.'

Al-Ḥasan al-Baṣrī, most of the people of Basra, and al-Mughīrah ibn 'Abd ar-Raḥmān al-Makhzūmī al-Madanī said, 'If someone recites the *Umm al-Qur'ān* once during the prayer, it satisfies the obligation and he does not have to repeat it because it is a prayer in which the *Umm al-Qur'ān* was recited. It is complete according to the words of the Prophet ﷺ: "The prayer of anyone who does not recite the *Umm al-Qur'ān* is invalid," and he recited it.' It is possible that the prayer of anyone who does not recite it in every *rak'ah* is invalid, which is sound as will be mentioned, and it is also possible that the prayer of someone who does not recite it in most of the *rak'ahs* is invalid. This is the reason for the disagreement, and Allah knows best.

Abū Ḥanīfah, ath-Thawrī and al-Awzā'ī said, 'If it is omitted intentionally throughout the entire prayer and something else is recited instead, that satisfies the requirements,' although al-Awzā'ī had some disagreement about that. Abū Yūsuf and Muḥammad ibn al-Ḥasan said, 'Its minimum is three *āyahs* or a long *āyah*, like the *Āyah* of Debt (2:282).' Muḥammad ibn al-Ḥasan said, 'Discretion is allowed regarding the size of the *āyah* and the size of understood words, like "Praise be to Allah." What is not allowed is a single letter which is not a word.'

Aṭ-Ṭabarī said, 'Someone who prays should recite the *Umm al-Qur'ān* in every *rak'ah*. If he does not recite it, the requirement is only satisfied by reciting its equivalent in the Qur'an in respect of the number of *āyahs* and the letters it contains.' Ibn 'Abd al-Barr stated, 'This makes no sense because the specification of it and the text on it specify it and nothing else. It is not permissible for the one for whom it is obliged to do something else in its place and to leave it when he is able to recite it. He must do it and repeat it, just as he must fulfil all other specific obligations in acts of worship.'

If someone following the imām catches the *rukū'* with the imām, the recitation of the imām is considered sufficient for him since there is consensus that when someone catches the *rukū'* he just says his *takbīr al-iḥrām* and bows without reciting anything else. If he finds the imām standing, he should recite. This is one point.

No one should fail to recite behind the imām in one of the silent prayers. If he does so, he has acted badly but, according to Mālik and his people, he owes nothing. When the imām recites aloud, those following the imām do not recite the *Fātiḥah* or anything else according to the well known position from the school of Mālik since Allah Almighty says: *'When the Qur'an is recited, listen to it and be quiet.'* (7:204) The Messenger of Allah ﷺ said, 'Why am I being contended with in the Qur'an.' He said about the imām, 'When he recites, be silent,' and 'If someone has an imām, the recitation of the imām is his recitation.'

Ash-Shāfi'ī said in what al-Buwayṭī and Aḥmad ibn Ḥanbal reported, 'No one's prayer is satisfied unless he recites the *Fātiḥah* of the Book in every *rak'ah*, be he an imām or follower, and whether the imām recites aloud or silently.' In Iraq ash-Shāfi'ī used to say about the follower, 'He recites when it is silent but not when it is aloud,' like the well-known position of the school of Mālik. In Egypt he said that there are two positions about when the imām recites aloud. One is that the follower should recite, and the other is that the requirements of the prayer are satisfied if he does not recite, the recitation of the imām being sufficient. Ibn al-Mundhir related this view while Ibn Wahb, Ashhab, Ibn 'Abd al-Ḥakam, Ibn Ḥabīb and the Kufans said that the follower should not recite anything, whether the imām recites aloud or silently, since the Prophet ﷺ said, 'The recitation of the imām in his recitation.' This is general, It is also because Jābir said, 'Whoever prays a *rak'ah* in which he does not recite the *Umm al-Qur'ān* has not prayed – except behind an imām.'

What is sound of these views is the position of ash-Shāfi'ī, Aḥmad, and Mālik in his final view: the *Fātiḥah* is incumbent in every *rak'ah* on everyone in general by the words of the Prophet ﷺ: 'There is no prayer for the one who does not recite the *Fātiḥah* of the Book in it,' and his words: 'If anyone prays a prayer in which he does not recite the *Umm al-Qur'an*, it is incomplete,' three times. Abū Hurayrah said, 'The Messenger of Allah ﷺ commanded me to call out: "There is no prayer except with the recitation of the *Fātiḥah* of the Book."' Abū Dāwūd transmitted it. As the prostration or *rukū'* of a *rak'ah* does not replace that of another *rak'ah*, so the recitation of one *rak'ah* does not replace that of another. That is stated by 'Abdullāh ibn 'Awn, Ayyūb as-Sakhtiyānī, Abū Thawr and others among the people of ash-Shāfi'ī and Dāwūd ibn 'Alī. The same thing is reported from al-Awzā'ī and Makḥūl also stated that.

It is related that 'Umar ibn al-Khaṭṭāb, 'Abdullāh ibn 'Abbās, Abū Hurayrah, Ubayy ibn Ka'b, Abū Ayyūb al-Ansārī, 'Abdullāh ibn 'Amr ibn al-'Āṣ, 'Ubāda ibn aṣ-Ṣāmit, Abū Sa'īd al-Khudrī, 'Uthmān ibn Abī al-'Āṣ and Khawwāt ibn Jubayr said, 'There is no prayer except with the *Fātiḥah* of the Book.' That is the position of Ibn 'Amr, and is famous in the school of al-Awzā'ī. Those Companions are models and examples and all of them made the *Fātiḥah* obligatory in every *rak'ah*.

Imām Abū 'Abdullāh Muḥammad ibn Yazīd ibn Mājah al-Qazwīnī transmitted something in his *Sunan* which removes any disagreement or ambiguity. He reported from Abū Kurayb from Muḥammad ibn Fuḍayl, from Suwayd ibn Sa'īd and from 'Alī ibn Mushar, all from Abū Sufyān as-Sa'dī from Abū Naḍrah that Abū Sa'īd al-Khudrī said that the Messenger of Allah ﷺ said, 'There is no prayer for someone who does not recite the *Fātiḥah* and another *sūrah* in every *rak'ah*, be it a *farḍ* prayer or any other.' We find in *Ṣaḥīḥ Muslim* from Abū Hurayrah that the Prophet ﷺ told someone to whom he taught the prayer: 'Do that throughout all your prayer.'

Another proof of that is what Abū Dāwūd related that Nāfi' ibn Maḥmūd ibn ar-Rabī' al-Anṣārī said, "Ubādah ibn aṣ-Ṣāmit was late for the *Ṣubḥ* prayer and the *mu'adhdhin*, Abū Nu'aym, did the *iqāmah* for the prayer and Abū Nu'aym led the people in the prayer. 'Ubādah ibn aṣ-Ṣāmit came forward and I along with him until we were in a line behind Abū Nu'aym. Abū Nu'aym was reciting aloud. 'Ubādah began to recite the *Umm al-Qur'ān*. When he finished, I said to 'Ubādah, "Did I hear you reciting the *Umm al-Qur'ān* while Abū Nu'aym was reciting aloud?" "Yes," he answered, "The Messenger of Allah ﷺ led us in some prayers in which recitation was aloud and it was confusing for him. When he finished, he faced us and said, 'Do you recite when I am reciting aloud?' Some of us said, 'We do that.' He said, 'No, I tell you not to contend with me in the Qur'an. When I recite aloud, do not recite anything except the *Umm al-Qur'ān*.'"" This is a clear text about someone following the imām. Abū 'Īsā at-Tirmidhī transmitted the same from the hadith of Muḥammad ibn Isḥāq and said that it is a *ḥasan* hadith.

The practice is based on this hadith regarding recitation behind the imām among most of the people of knowledge among the Companions of the Prophet ﷺ and the Tābi'ūn. It is the position of Mālik ibn Anas, Ibn al-Mubārak, ash-Shāfi'ī, Aḥmad, and Isḥāq. They think that one recites behind the imām. Ad-Dāraquṭnī also transmitted it and said that it has a good *isnād* and all its men are trustworthy. He mentioned that Maḥmūd ibn ar-Rabī' used to live in Jerusalem and Abū Nu'aym was the first to give the *adhān* in Jerusalem. Abū Muḥammad 'Abd al-Ḥaqq said, 'Al-Bukhārī did not mention Nāfi' ibn Maḥmūd in his *History* nor did Ibn Abī Ḥātim. Neither al-Bukhārī nor Muslim transmitted anything from him.' Abū 'Umar said that he is unknown.

Ad-Dāraquṭnī mentioned that Yazīd ibn Sharīk said, 'I asked 'Umar about reciting behind the imām and he ordered me to recite. I asked, "Even if it is you?" "Even if it is me," he answered. I said, "Even if you are reciting aloud?" He replied, "Even if I am reciting aloud."' Ad-Dāraquṭnī said that it is a sound *isnād*. It is related that Jābir ibn 'Abdullāh said that Messenger of Allah ﷺ said, 'The imām is a guarantor, so do what he does.' Abū Ḥātim said, 'This is sound for those who believe that one recites behind the imām. Abū Hurayrah al-Fārisī used it to give a legal decision that he recites to himself when he says, "Sometimes I am behind the imām." Then he cited as evidence the words of the Almighty, "I have divided the prayer between me and Myself. My slave will have what he asks for" and the Messenger ﷺ said, "Recite. The slave says, '*Praise belongs to Allah, the Lord of the worlds…*'"'

As for the evidence that the former use, taking the words of the Prophet ﷺ:

'When he recites, be silent,' Muslim transmitted it from the hadith of Abū Mūsā al-Ash'arī. He said that there is an addition in it from Qatādah in the hadith of Jarīr ibn Sulaymān: 'When he recites, be silent.' Ad-Dāraquṭnī said, 'Sulaymān at-Taymī does not follow these words from Qatādah. The memorisers of the people of Qatādah opposed him and did not mention it. They include Shu'bah, Hishām, Sa'īd ibn Abī 'Arūba, Hammām, Abū 'Awānah, Ma'mar, and 'Adī ibn Abī 'Ammārah.' Ad-Dāraquṭnī said, 'Their consensus indicates that it is weak.' It is related from 'Abdullāh ibn 'Āmir from Qatādah, following at-Taymī, but he is not strong and al-Qaṭṭa'ān abandoned him. Abū Dāwūd also transmitted this addition from the ḥadīth of Abū Hurayrah. He said, 'This addition, "when he recites, be silent," is not preserved.' Abū Muḥammad 'Abd al-Ḥaqq mentioned that Muslim considered the hadith of Abū Hurayrah sound, saying, 'I consider it sound.'

Part of what indicates its soundness in his view is its inclusion in his book from the hadith of Abū Mūsā even if there is no consensus about it. Imām Aḥmad ibn Ḥanbal and Ibn al-Mundhir considered it to be sound. The words of the Almighty: *'When the Qur'an is recited, listen to it and be silent'* (7:204) were revealed in Makkah and the prohibition against speaking in the prayer was revealed in Madīnah, as Zayd ibn Arqam said. So it is not an argument. It is the idolators who were meant according to what Sa'īd ibn al-Musayyab said. Ad-Dāraquṭnī related from Abū Hurayrah that it was revealed about raising the voice when behind the Messenger of Allah ﷺ. 'Abdullāh ibn 'Āmir said that it is weak.

As for his words, 'Do not contend with me in the Qur'an,' Mālik transmitted that from Ibn Shihāb from Ibn Ukaymah al-Laythī. According to Mālik, his name is 'Amr, and others said that his name was 'Āmir, Yazīd, 'Ammārah or 'Ubbād. His *kunyah* was Abu-l-Walīd. He died in 101 AH at the age of ninety-nine. Az-Zuhrī only related one hadith from him. He is trustworthy. Muḥammad ibn 'Amr and others related from him. The meaning of his hadith is: 'Do not recite aloud when I recite aloud. That is contending and vying. Recite it inside yourselves.' It is made clear by the hadith of 'Ubādah, the legal decisions of 'Umar al-Fārūq and Abū Hurayrah who related both hadiths. If his words ﷺ, 'Do not contend with me in the Qur'an', had been understood to entail a total prohibition, he would not have given a legal decision contrary to it and to the words of az-Zuhrī in the hadith of Ibn Ukaymah. So people stopped reciting with the Messenger of Allah ﷺ when the Messenger of Allah ﷺ recited aloud when they heard that from him.

As for the words of the Prophet ﷺ, 'If someone has an imām, the imām recites on his behalf,' the hadith is weak. Al-Ḥasan ibn 'Ammārah gives its *isnād*, and he is abandoned, and Abū Ḥanīfah, who is weak, both relating from Mūsā ibn Abī 'Ā'ishah from 'Abdullāh ibn Shaddād from Jābir. Ad-Dāraquṭnī transmitted it and said, 'Sufyān ath-Thawrī, Shu'bah, Isrā'īl ibn Yunus, Sharīk, Abū Khālid ad-Dālānī, Abu-l-Aḥwaṣ, Sufyān ibn 'Uyaynah, Jarīr ibn 'Abd al-Ḥamīd and others related it from Mūsā ibn Abī 'Ā'ishah from 'Abdullāh ibn Shaddād *mursal* from the Prophet ﷺ. That is correct.' As for the statement of Jābir, 'Whoever prays a *rak'ah* in which he did not recite the *Umm al-Qur'ān* has not prayed', it is related by Mālik from Wahb ibn Kaysān from Jābir, and Jābir has it from the Prophet ﷺ. Ibn 'Abd al-Barr said that Yaḥyā ibn Salām, the author of the *Tafsīr*, related it from Mālik from Abū Nu'aym Wahb ibn Kaysān from Jābir from the Prophet ﷺ. What is correct is that it is *mawqūf*, stopping with Jābir, as is stated in the *Muwaṭṭa'*. Part of the *fiqh* taken from it is that a *rak'ah* in which the *Umm al-Qur'ān* is not recited is invalid. It attests to the soundness of what Ibn al-Qāsim believed. He related it from Mālik regarding the invalidation of the *rak'ah* and building on other *rak'ah*s and the person praying does not repeat a *rak'ah* in which he did not recite the *Fātiḥah* of the Book. Also part of that is that the imām recites on behalf of those behind him. This is the school of Jābir and others disagreed with him about it.

Ibn al-'Arabī said, 'He said, "There is no prayer for the one who does not recite the *Fātiḥah* of the Book." People disagree about this principle and whether the negation applies to the entire prayer or to a part. The fatwā varies according to the different states of those who investigate. The best-known and strongest opinion is that the negation is general. The strongest comes from the transmission of Mālik that the prayer of someone who does not recite the *Fātiḥah* is invalid. Then we look at its repetition in every *rak'ah*. Whoever reflects on the words of the Prophet ﷺ, "Do that in all your prayer" obliges him to repeat the recitation as he repeats the *rukū'* and prostration, but Allah knows best.'

The hadiths and ideas mentioned about this that specify the *Fātiḥah* refute the statement of the Kufans about the *Fātiḥah* not being specified and other *āyah*s of the Qur'an being the same as it. The Prophet ﷺ specified it when he said what we mentioned. It is clear from Allah Almighty that it is meant in His words, 'Establish the prayer.' Abū Dāwūd related that Abū Sa'īd al-Khudrī said, 'We were commanded to recite the *Fātiḥah* of the Book and what is easy.' This hadith indicates that the words of the Prophet ﷺ to the Bedouin, 'Recite what is easy for you of the Qur'an,' mean not more than the *Fātiḥah*. It explains the words of the Almighty: *'Recite as much of the Qur'an as is easy for you.'* (73:20) Muslim related from 'Ubādah ibn aṣ-Ṣāmit that the Messenger of Allah ﷺ said, 'There is no prayer for the one who does not recite the *Umm al-Qur'an*,' and added 'and more', and that he ﷺ said, 'it is incomplete' three times. This means that it does not satisfy the legal requirement by the aforementioned proofs. '*Khidāj* (incomplete)' means deficient and unsound. Al-Akhfash said that the verb *khadija* is used of a she-camel miscarrying before the foetus is completely formed.

Investigation makes it clear that the prayer is not permitted with that deficiency because the prayer is not complete. If someone leaves his prayer without completing it, he must repeat it as he is commanded according to its ruling. If someone claims that it is allowed while affirming that it is incomplete, then he must provide evidence, but there is no way to do so in a binding way. Allah knows best.

It is related from Mālik that recitation is not obliged in any part of the prayer. That is like what ash-Shāfi'ī used to say in Iraq in respect of someone who forgets it. Then he retracted that position in Egypt and said, 'If someone can recite the *Fātiḥah* of the Book well, the prayer is only achieved by it and he is not allowed to omit a single letter of it. If he does not recite it or omits a single letter of it, then he must repeat the prayer, even if he recited something else.' This is the sound view regarding this question. As for what is related about 'Umar praying *Maghrib* and not reciting in it and when that was mentioned to him, he asked, 'How were the *rukū'* and prostration?' 'Good,' they answered. He said, 'There is no harm then.' The hadith is *munkar* in its words and its *isnād* is broken because it is related from Ibrāhīm ibn al-Ḥārith at-Taymī from 'Umar, but sometimes Ibrāhīm related it from Abū Salamah ibn 'Abd ar-Raḥmān from 'Umar. Both are broken and provide no evidence. Mālik mentioned it in the *Muwaṭṭa'*. Some transmitters have it, but it is not found with Yaḥyā and a group along with him because Mālik removed it from his book at the end. He said, 'There is no action based on it because the Prophet ﷺ said, 'Any prayer in which the *Umm al-Qur'ān* is not recited is incomplete.'

It is related that 'Umar repeated that prayer, and that is sound. Yaḥyā ibn Yaḥyā an-Naysābūrī related from Abū Mu'āwiyah from al-A'mash from Ibrāhīm an-Nakha'ī from Hammām ibn al-Ḥārith that 'Umar forgot to recite in *Maghrib* and repeated the prayer with them. Ibn 'Abd al-Barr said, 'This hadith is connected and Hammām was witness to it from 'Umar. That was related by various paths.' Ashhab related what Mālik said: 'Mālik was asked about someone who forgot to recite, "Do you approve of what 'Umar said?" He answered, "I do not acknowledge what 'Umar did," and he did not acknowledge the hadith. He said, "People relate that 'Umar did this in *Maghrib* and they did not say, 'Glory be to Allah!' I think that someone who does that repeats the prayer."'

Scholars agree that there is no prayer without recitation and they agree that there is no particular amount specified beyond the *Fātiḥah* of the Book, although they recommend that only one *sūrah* should be recited with the *Fātiḥah* because that is the maximum which has come from the Prophet ﷺ. Mālik said, 'The *sunnah* of recitation is to recite the *Umm al-Qur'ān* and a *sūrah* in the first two *rak'ahs* and only the *Fātiḥah* in the last two.' Al-Awzā'ī said, 'You should recite the *Umm al-Qur'ān*. If you do not recite *Umm al-Qur'ān* and recite something else instead, that satisfies the requirements.' He said, 'If he forgets to recite in three *rak'ahs*, he repeats it.' Ath-Thawrī said, 'In the first two *rak'ahs*, you recite the *Fātiḥah* and a *sūrah*, and you can glorify in the last two if you wish, or if you wish, you may recite. If you neither recite nor glorify your prayer is still allowed.' That is the position of Abū Ḥanīfah and the rest of the Kufans. Ibn al-Mundhir said, 'We related that 'Alī ibn Abī Ṭālib said, "Recite in the first two and glorify in the last two."'

An-Nakha'ī reported that Sufyān said, 'If someone does not recite in three *rak'ahs*, he must repeat the prayer because the recitation in a single *rak'ah* is not sufficient.' He said, 'The same applies if someone forgets to recite in one *rak'ah* in the *Fajr* prayer.' Abū Thawr said, 'A prayer is only satisfied by the recitation of the *Fātiḥah* in every *rak'ah*, which was the Egyptian position of ash-Shāfi'ī, and a group of the people of ash-Shāfi'ī also say that.' Ibn Khuwayzimandād al-Mālikī said the same. He said, 'We consider recitation of the *Fātiḥah* to be mandatory in every *rak'ah*. This is the sound position regarding this question.' Muslim related that Abū Qatādah said, 'The Messenger of Allah ﷺ used to lead us in the prayer and he would recite the *Fātiḥah* of the Book and two *sūrahs* in the first two *rak'ahs* of *Ẓuhr* and *'Aṣr*. Sometimes we would hear the *āyah*. He was long in the first *rak'ah* of *Ẓuhr* and short in the second, and did the same in *Ṣubḥ*.' One variant has: 'He used to recite the *Fātiḥah* in the last two *rak'ahs*.' This is a clear text and sound hadith supporting what Mālik believed and a text for specifying that the *Fātiḥah* is recited in every *rak'ah*. The definitive proof is in the *Sunnah*, not in what opposes it.

The majority believe that what is additional to the *Fātiḥah* in the recitation is not mandatory according to what Muslim related from Abū Hurayrah. He said, 'There is recitation in every prayer. What the Prophet ﷺ made us hear, we make you hear, and what he hid from us we hide from you. If anyone recites the *Umm al-Qur'ān*, it is enough for him. If someone recites more, that is better.' Al-Bukhārī said, 'If there is more, it is good.' Many of the people of knowledge reject abandoning reciting the *sūrah*, with or without necessity, including 'Imrān ibn Ḥusayn, Abū Sa'īd al-Khudrī, Khawwāt ibn Jubayr, Mujāhid, Abū Wā'il, Ibn 'Umar, Ibn 'Abbās and others. They said, 'There is no prayer for the one who does not recite the *Fātiḥah* in it and something of the Qur'an along with it.' Some of them stipulate two *āyahs*, or one *āyah*, and some do not set a limit. He said, 'Something of the Qur'an with it.' In any case, all of this obliges learning what is feasible of the Quran along with the *Fātiḥah* of the Book based on the *ḥadīth* of 'Ubādah, Abū Sa'īd al-Khudrī and others. We find in *al-Mudawwanah*: 'Wakī' related from al-A'mash that Khaythama said that someone heard 'Umar ibn al-Khaṭṭāb say, "The requirement of the prayer is not satisfied if someone does not recite the *Fātiḥah* of the Book and something with it." The School has three different positions about the recitation of the *sūrah*: *sunnah*, meritorious and mandatory.'

If someone finds it impossible, after his best efforts, to learn the *Fātiḥah* or anything of the Qur'an, he should mention Allah in place of the recitation using whatever formula he can: *takbīr*, *'lā ilaha illā'llāh'*, praise, glorification, magnification or '*lā hawla walā quwwata illā bi'llāh*' when he prays alone or with an imām in a silent prayer. Abū Dāwūd and others reported that 'Abdullāh ibn Abī Awfā said, 'A man came to the Messenger of Allah ﷺ and said, "I cannot learn any of the Qur'an, so teach me what will compensate that for me." He said, "Say: 'Glory be to Allah and praise be to Allah. There is no god but Allah and there is no strength or power except by Allah.'" He said, "Messenger of Allah, this is for Allah. What is for me?" He answered, "Say: 'O Allah, show mercy to me, protect me, guide me and provide for me.'"'

If someone is unable even to learn any of these expressions, he should not fail to try to pray with the imām. The imām will bear that responsibility for him if Allah wills. He must, however, always persevere in trying to memorise the *Fātiḥah* of the Book and more of the Qur'an until death intervenes. He is engaged in striving and so Allah will excuse him. If someone cannot speak Arabic, the Arabic supplication is translated for him into a language which he understands so he can perform his prayer. That will satisfy the requirement, Allah willing.

If someone recites the prayer in Persian when he has good Arabic, it is not allowed according to the position of the majority. Abū Ḥanīfah said, 'Recitation in Persian satisfies it, even if he is good in Arabic, because the goal is to grasp the meaning.' Ibn al-Mundhir said, 'That does not satisfy it because it is contrary to what Allah commanded and contrary to what the Prophet ﷺ taught, and contrary to what the Community of the Muslims do. We do not know of anyone agreeing with this statement of his.'

If someone begins the prayer as he is commanded without knowing Arabic and then he suddenly knows Arabic while in the prayer – and that is conceivable if he hears someone reciting it and he retains it by simply hearing it – he does not start the prayer anew because he performed in the past according to what he was commanded and there is no way to invalidate it. That is said in the book of Ibn Saḥnūn.

Topic Three: Saying 'Āmīn'

There are eight points connected with it.

It is *sunnah* for the reciter of the Qur'an to say '*āmīn*' when he finishes the *Fātiḥah*, after a moment of silence following the *nūn* of '*ḍāllīn*' to distinguish what is part of the Qur'an from what is not part of it.

It is established in the primary sources from the hadith of Abū Hurayrah that the Messenger of Allah ﷺ said, 'When the imām says "*āmīn*", say "*āmīn*". If someone's *āmīn* coincides with that of the angels, he will be forgiven his past wrong actions.' Our scholars say that the forgiveness of wrong actions is dependent on four conditions which are contained in this hadith. The first is the imām saying *āmīn*, the second is those with him saying *āmīn*, the third is the *āmīn* of the angels, and the fourth is the coinciding of the *āmīn*s. Some say that the coinciding refers to the answer, some that it is about the time, and some say that it is about sincerity in supplication as is made clear by the words of the Prophet ﷺ, 'Call on Allah and be certain of the answer. Know that Allah does not answer the supplication of a heedless negligent heart.'

Abū Dāwūd related that Abū Muṣabbaḥ al-Maqrānī said, 'We used to sit with Abū Zuhayr an-Namīrī, one of the Companions, and he related the best statement about this. When one of us made a supplication, he said, "End it with *āmīn*. *Āmīn* is like the seal on the page." Abū Zuhayr continued, "Shall I tell you how I know that? One night we went out with the Messenger of Allah ﷺ and came to a man who was intense in asking [of Allah]. The Prophet ﷺ stood listening to him and said, "It is guaranteed if he seals it." Someone there asked him, "With what is it sealed?" He answered, "With *āmīn*. If he seals with it with *āmīn*, it is guaranteed." The man who asked the Prophet ﷺ went to the man and asked, "Did you seal it, so-and-so" and he gave him the good news.' Ibn 'Abd al-Barr said, 'The name of Abū Zuhayr an-Namīrī was Yaḥyā ibn Nufayr. He related from the Prophet ﷺ: "Do not kill locusts. They are the greatest army of Allah."'

Wahb ibn Munabbih said, '*Āmīn* consists of four letters. Allah creates an angel from every letter which says, "O Allah, forgive the one who said *āmīn*!"' In a report we also find: 'Jibrīl taught me *āmīn* when I finished the *Fātiḥah* of the Book and said that it is like a seal on the Book.' We find in another hadith: '*Āmīn* is the seal of the Lord of the worlds.' Al-Harawī said that Abū Bakr said, 'Its meaning is that Allah puts a seal on His servants because by it He averts from them ruin and afflictions. So it is like the seal of the book which protects it and prevents it from being ruined and showing what it contains.' We find in another hadith: '*Āmīn* is a degree in the Garden.' Abū Bakr said, 'It means that it is a letter by which the one who utters it obtains a degree in the Garden.'

The meaning of *āmīn* according to the people of knowledge is: 'O Allah, give us an answer!' which acts as a kind of supplication. Some people say that it is one of the Names of Allah. That is related from Ja'far ibn Muḥammad, Mujāhid and Hilāl ibn Yasāf. Ibn 'Abbās is also said to have related it from the Prophet ﷺ, but the transmission is not sound. Ibn al-'Arabī said that as well. It is said that the meaning of *āmīn* is 'Let it be like that.' Al-Jawharī said that. Al-Kalbī related from Abū Ṣāliḥ that Ibn 'Abbās said, 'I asked the Messenger of Allah ﷺ about the meaning of *āmīn*. He answered, "Lord, do it!"' Muqātil said, 'It strengthens the supplication and asks for the descent of blessing.' At-Tirmidhī said, 'It means: "Do not disappoint our hopes."'

There are two ways of pronouncing *āmīn*: with both vowels long like Yāsīn, and with the first vowel short like *yamīn*. Doubling the *mīm* is an error, according to al-Jawharī. The doubling is related from al-Ḥasan and Ja'far aṣ-Ṣādiq. It is the position of al-Ḥusayn ibn al-Faḍl, who derived it from *amma* meaning to aim for something, which gives it the meaning, 'we aim for You.' This occurs in Allah's words: *'or those heading* (āmmīn) *for the Sacred House…'* (5:2). Abū Naṣr 'Abd ar-Raḥīm ibn 'Abd al-Karīm al-Qushayrī related it. Al-Jawharī said, 'It is based on the *fatḥah* as is "*ayna*" and "*kayfa*" because of joining of two silent letters.'

Scholars disagree about whether the imām says it at all and, if he does, whether he says it out loud. Ash-Shāfi'ī and Mālik believe in the transmission of the Madinans regarding that whereas the Kufans and some Madinans say that it should not be said out loud. That is the view of aṭ-Ṭabarī. Among our scholars, Ibn Ḥabīb said that. Ibn Bukayr said that there is a choice. Ibn al-Qāsim related from Mālik that the imām does not say *āmīn* but those behind him do. That is the position of Ibn al-Qāsim and the Egyptians among Mālik's followers. Their evidence is the hadith of Abū Mūsā al-Ash'arī: 'The Messenger of Allah ﷺ addressed us, made our *sunnah* clear to us and taught us our prayer. He said, "When you pray, then make your rows straight. Then let one of you lead the prayer. When he says the *takbīr*, say the *takbīr*. When he says, *'not of those with anger on them nor of the misguided,'* say *āmīn* and Allah will answer you."'" Muslim transmitted it. It is like the hadith of Sumayy from Abū Hurayrah that Mālik transmitted. The first is sound because of the hadith of Wā'il ibn Hujr who said, 'When the Messenger of Allah ﷺ recited, "*nor of the misguided,*" he said, "*Āmīn,*" raising his voice.' Abū Dāwūd and ad-Dāraquṭnī transmitted it. He added that Abū Bakr said that only the people of Kufa have this *sunnah.* This is sound. Al-Bukhārī has a chapter on 'The imām saying *āmīn* out loud.'

'Aṭā' said that *āmīn* is a supplication. Ibn az-Zubayr and those behind him said it until the mosque reverberated. At-Tirmidhī said, 'That is the position of more than one of the people of knowledge among the Companions of the Prophet ﷺ and those after them. They related that a man should raise his voice with *āmīn* and not say it silently.' Ash-Shāfi'ī, Aḥmad and Isḥāq said that. In the *Muwaṭṭa'* and the two *Ṣaḥīḥ* Collections Ibn Shihāb said that the Messenger of Allah ﷺ used to say, '*Āmīn.*' We find in the *Sunan* of Ibn Mājah that Abū Hurayrah said, 'People have abandoned the *āmīn.* When the Messenger of Allah ﷺ said, "*not of those with anger on them nor of the misguided,*" he would say, "*Āmīn*" so that the people of the first row heard it and the mosque would reverberate with it.' The point in the hadith of Abū Mūsā and Sumayy is defining the place where *āmīn* is said. It is when the imām says, '*nor of the misguided*' so that they say it together and do not get ahead of it by saying '*Āmīn*' as we mentioned. Allah knows best. The Prophet ﷺ also said. 'When the imām says, "*Āmīn*", then say "*Āmīn*".' Ibn Nāfi' said in the book of Ibn al-Ḥārith: 'The one following the imām does not say it unless he hears the imām say, "*nor of the misguided.*" When he is so far away that he does not hear it, he does not say it.' Ibn 'Abdūs said, 'He estimates the amount of the recitation and then says, "*Āmīn*".'

The people of Abū Ḥanīfah said that it is more appropriate to say *āmīn* silently rather than out loud because it is supplication and Allah Almighty says, '*Call on your Lord humbly and secretly.*' (7:55) They said, 'The evidence for it is what is related about the interpretation of the words of the Almighty: "*Your request is answered.*" (19:89)' They said, 'Mūsā and Hārūn used to make supplication using *āmīn* and so Allah called them both supplicators.' The answer is that making supplication silently is better in order to avoid any showing-off. As for the group prayer, attending it is in order to publicise an outward obligation and to promote a duty which people are recommended to observe. The imām has to articulate the recitation of the *Fātiḥah,* which contains supplication and *āmīn* at the end of it. When supplication is of the sort which it is *sunna* to say aloud, then *āmīn* follows at the end of the supplication and is also *sunnah.* This is clear.

The word '*Āmīn*' was not found before us except with Mūsa and Hārūn. At-Tirmidhī al-Ḥakīm related in *Nawādir al-uṣūl* from 'Abd al-Wārith ibn 'Abd aṣ-

Ṣamad from Razīn, the *mu'adhdhin* of the mosque of Hishām ibn Ḥassān, from Anas ibn Mālik that the Messenger of Allah ﷺ said, 'Allah has given three things to my Community that He did not give to anyone before them: the greeting of the people, the rows of the angels, and *Āmīn*, except for what was said by Mūsa and Hārūn.' Abū 'Abdullāh said, 'It means that Mūsa prayed against Pharaoh and Hārūn said, *"Āmīn."*'' Allah – blessed is His Name – said when He mentioned the supplication of Mūsa in the Revelation: *'Your request is answered.'* (10:89) He did not mention what Hārūn said. Mūsa said, 'Our Lord' and Hārūn said, *'Āmīn.'* So he is called a supplicator in the Revelation because that amounted to a supplication on his part.

It is said that *'Āmīn'* is particular to this community since it is related that the Prophet ﷺ said, 'The Jews do not envy you for anything as they envy you for the *salām* and saying *āmīn*.' Ibn Mājah transmitted it from Ḥammād ibn Salamah from Suhayl ibn Abī Ṣāliḥ from his father from 'Ā'ishah that the Prophet ﷺ said…' It is also transmitted from the ḥadīth of Ibn 'Abbās that the Prophet ﷺ said, 'The Jews do not envy you for anything as much as they envy you for the *amīn*. So say *"Āmīn"* often.' Our scholars say that the People of the Book envy us because the beginning of the *Fātiḥah* is praise of Allah, lauding Him, then humility and humbleness to Him, and then praying to guide us to the Straight Path and then invocation against them with saying *'Āmīn.'*

TOPIC FOUR: THE MEANINGS OF THE *FĀTIḤAH*, ITS RECITATIONS AND SYNTAX, AND THE EXCELLENCE OF THOSE WHO PRAISE

There are thirty-six points in it.

Praise be to Allah.

Abū Muḥammad 'Abd al-Ghanī ibn Sa'īd related from Abū Hurayrah and Abū Sa'īd al-Khudrī that the Prophet ﷺ said, 'When someone says, "*Praise be to Allah*," Allah says, "My slave has praised Me."' Muslim related from Anas ibn Mālik that the Messenger of Allah ﷺ said, 'Allah is pleased with the slave who eats and praises Him for it or takes a drink and praises Him for it.' Al-Ḥasan said, 'There is no blessing but that the words, "Praise be to Allah" are better than it.' Ibn Mājah related from Anas ibn Mālik that the Messenger of Allah ﷺ said, 'When Allah gives someone a blessing and he says, "Praise be to Allah", what he says is better than what he receives.'

In *Nawādir al-uṣūl*, Anas ibn Mālik reported that the Messenger of Allah ﷺ said, 'If the entire world, lock, stock and barrel, were to be in the hand of a man of my

Community and then he said, "Praise be to Allah," his praise of Allah would be greater than everything he possessed.' Abū 'Abdullāh said, 'We find that its meaning is that he has been given this world and then is given these words to say after it. Then the words are better than all of this world because this world will end while the words will remain, being one of the enduring good actions. Allah says: *"In your Lord's sight, right actions which are lasting are better both in reward and end result."* (19:76) It is said in some variants, 'What he was given was greater than what he took.' So 'was given' refers to the slave and this world is taken from Allah. This is about management. That is how this statement is said to be from the slave and this world is from Allah while, in reality, both are from Allah. This world is from Allah and the words of Allah are also from Him. He gave him this world and made him rich, and He gave him the words and honoured him by them in the Next World.'

Ibn Mājah related from Ibn 'Umar that the Messenger of Allah ﷺ said to them, 'One of the slaves of Allah said, "O Lord, praise is Yours as befits the majesty of Your face and the immensity of Your power." His two recording angels were perplexed by it. They did not know how to record it, so they rose to heaven and said, "Our Lord, Your slave said something we do not know how to record." Allah Almighty, Who knows better what His slave said, asked, "What did My slave say?" They replied, "O Lord, he said, 'O Lord, praise is Yours as befits the majesty of Your face and the immensity of Your power.'" Allah said to them, "Continue to write it as My slave said it until He meets Me and I will replay him for it."'

Scholars disagree about which is better: the words, 'Praise be to Allah, the Lord of all the worlds,' or the words, 'There is no god but Allah'. One group said that 'Praise be to Allah, the Lord of all the worlds' is better because it incorporates the *tawḥīd* contained in 'There is no god but Allah'. It thus contains both *tawḥīd* and praise whereas 'There is no god but Allah' contains *tawḥīd* alone. Another group say that 'There is no god but Allah' is better because it repels disbelief and idolatry and because people are fought for refusing to say it. The Messenger of Allah ﷺ said, 'I was commanded to fight people until they say, "There is no god but Allah."' Ibn 'Aṭiyyah preferred this and said that this view is entailed by the words of the Prophet ﷺ: 'The best of what I and the Prophets before me said is, "There is no god but Allah alone with no partner."'

The Muslims agree that Allah is praised for all His blessings and that one of Allah's blessings is faith. This indicates that faith is both an action and a creation. The evidence for that is found in His words, '*Lord of all the worlds.*' '*Ālamīn* (worlds)' is the total of all creatures, and faith is part of that whole. The Qadariyyah claim of it being their own creation is false, as will be explained.

The word 'praise (*ḥamd*)' in the Arabic language means comprehensive praise. The definite article is used since the category includes all forms of praise. Allah deserves all praise since He has the Most Beautiful Names and Sublime Attributes. The expression '*ḥamd*' has a plural of paucity as in the words of the poet:

I have singled out the brightest of the praised
with my best words and best praise (*aḥmadī*).

Praise is the opposite of blame. You say, 'I praised the man' and he is praiseworthy (*ḥamīd, maḥmūd*). *Taḥmīd* from Form II is more extensive than *ḥamd*. Praise is more universal than gratitude. The name 'Muḥammad' which is derived from it means the one who has many praiseworthy qualities. That is why the Messenger of Allah ﷺ is called that. A poet said:

It is derived for him from His Own Name to esteem him.
The Possessor of the Throne is praised (*maḥmūd*)
and this is Muḥammad.

Praiseworthy is the opposite of blameworthy.

Abū Ja'far aṭ-Ṭabarī and Abū al-'Abbās al-Mubarrad believed that praise and gratitude have the same meaning and that it does not mean 'approval'. Abū 'Abd ar-Raḥmān as-Sulamī related that in his *Kitāb al-ḥaqā'iq*, quoting Ja'far aṣ-Ṣādiq and Ibn 'Aṭā' 'llāh. Ibn 'Aṭā' 'llāh said, 'It means "Thanks be to Allah" since there is a blessing from Him in teaching it to us so that we praise Him.' Aṭ-Ṭabarī deduced that they mean the same by the validity of the words, 'Praise be to Allah in gratitude.' Ibn 'Aṭā' 'llāh said, 'In reality, it is evidence for other than what he believed because the word "gratitude" is specific to praise because it is one of the blessings. Some scholars say that "gratitude" is more general than praise because it is shown with the tongue, the limbs, and the heart whereas praise is made only with the tongue. It is said that praise is more general because it contains the meaning of gratitude and the meaning of praise and is therefore more universal than gratitude because praise can include gratitude but gratitude does not include praise.'

It is related that Ibn 'Abbās said, '"Praise be to Allah" is the statement of every grateful person. When he sneezed, Ādam said, "Praise be to Allah." Allah said to Nūḥ, *"Then say: 'Praise be to Allah Who has rescued us from the people of the wrongdoers!'* (23:28)" Ibrāhīm said, *"Praise be to Allah Who, despite my old age, has given me Ismā'īl and Isḥāq!*" (27:15) Dāwūd and Sulaymān said, *"Praise be to Allah Who has favoured us over many of His slaves who are believers.* (27:15)" He said to His Prophet ﷺ, *"Say: 'praise be to Allah Who has no son.'* (17:111)" The people of the Garden will say, *"Praise be to Allah Who has removed all sadness from us* (35:34)" and *"The end of their call is: 'Praise be to Allah, the Lord of all the worlds!'* (10:10)" These are the words of everyone who is grateful.'

The sound position is that the word 'praise' is used for the qualities of a person praised without the need of any prior act of charity on that person's part. Thanks is praise for the one thanked because of some good that he has done. Based on this definition, our scholars say that praise is more universal than gratitude because it comprises both praising and thanking. Thanks is particular, being directed towards someone who did good to you. So the word 'praise' is more general and is used in the *āyah* because it is more than thanks. 'Praise' is also used with approval. It is said, 'I tested him and approved (*ḥamdatu*) of him.' Part of that is the words of the Almighty: *'A praiseworthy (maḥmūd) station.'* (17:79) The Prophet ﷺ said, 'I approve (*aḥmadu*) of you washing the urethra.'

It is mentioned that Ja'far aṣ-Ṣādiq said, '"Praise be to Allah" is a way of praising Him with the attributes with which He has described Himself, and the word *ḥamd* is used because it is made up of the letters *ḥā'*, *mīm*, and *dāl*. *Ḥā'* is from oneness (*wa**ḥ**dāniyyah*), *mīm* is from dominion (***m**ulk*), and *dāl* is everlastingness (***d**aymūmiyah*). This is the real meaning of *"al-ḥamdu lillāh"*.' Shaqīq ibn Ibrāhīm said in the explanation of 'Praise be to Allah' that it has three aspects. The first is that when Allah gives you something, you acknowledge the One Who gave it to you. The second is that you show you are pleased with what He has given you. The third is that, as long as there us still strength in your body you do not disobey Him. These are the preconditions of praise.

Allah Almighty praised Himself and began His Book with praise of Himself and did not allow that for anyone but Himself. Indeed, He forbade that in His Book and on the tongue of His Prophet ﷺ. The Almighty says: *'Do not claim purity for yourselves. He knows best those who are godfearing.'* (52:32) The Prophet ﷺ said, 'Throw dust in the faces of those who praise.' Al-Miqdād related it and it will be discussed in *al-Mā'idah*, Allah willing.

The meaning of the words *'Praise be to Allah, the Lord of all the worlds'* is 'My prior praise of Myself before any created being praises Me. My praise of Myself before time does not have a cause while praise of Me by My creatures is sullied by causes.' Our scholars said, 'It is repugnant for a creature who has not been given perfection to praise himself for bringing benefits and repelling harms.' It is said that since

He knew His slaves' inability to praise Him, He praised Himself by Himself for Himself before time. No matter how much His slaves try, they are unable to praise Him sufficiently. Do you not see how the Master of the Messengers ﷺ displayed inability when he said, 'I cannot number Your praises.' They said:

When we praise You for good,
You are as You are praised and above the one who praises.

It is said that Allah praised Himself before time because He knew the great number of His blessings would be more enjoyed by them since He removed the burden of praising Him from them.

All seven readings and the majority of people agree that there is a *ḍammah* on the *dāl* of *ḥamd*, making it *ḥamd**u***. *Ḥamd**a*** is related from Sufyān ibn 'Uyaynah and Ru'bah ibn al-'Ajjāj. This is based on an implied elided verb. Sībuwayh says that, grammatically, if someone uses the nominative *ḥamd**u***, it has the meaning of "I praise Allah greatly." Praise is from Him and from all of creation for Allah. If someone uses the accusative *ḥamd**a***, he is saying praise is from him alone for Allah. Those other than Sībuwayh say that saying this is alluding to Allah's pardon and forgiveness and proclaiming Him great and magnifying Him. So it has a different meaning than a report: it is a request. We find in a hadith: 'If someone is distracted from asking of Me by remembering Me, I will give him more than I give those who ask.' It is said that His praise of Himself is to inform His slaves of it. What is implied, according to this, is: 'Say: "Praise be to Allah."' Aṭ-Ṭabarī said, '"Praise be to Allah" is praise by which He praises Himself. It contains a command for His slaves to praise Him and so it is as if He were saying, "Say: 'Praise be to Allah.'"'

The Lord of all the Worlds

'The Lord of all the Worlds' is their Master. Every kingdom has its lord and the Lord is the Master (*mālik*). We find in *aṣ-Ṣiḥāḥ*: '"Lord" (*rabb*) is one of the Names of Allah Almighty. It is only used of someone else in a relative sense. They used to use it to designate a king in the *Jāhiliyyah* period.'

The word '*Rabb*' means 'master'. That is demonstrated by the words of the Almighty in *Sūrat Yūsuf*: *'Mention me when you are with your lord.'* (12:42) We find in a hadith: 'When the slave-girl gives birth to her mistress (*rabbah*).' We have explained it in *Kitāb at-tadhkirah*. The Lord is the one who puts things right, manages, compels and preserves. Al-Harawī and others said that it is used of the one who tries to put a thing right and complete it. He sees to its fulfilment (*rabba*) and so he is a lord (*rabb, rābb*) to it. *Rabbāniyyūn* (divines) are so called because of their guarding of the Revealed Books. We find in a hadith: 'Do you have a blessing which you tend to (*tarubbuhā*)?' i.e. to which you attend and put in order. The Lord is the One Who is worshipped. Part of that is the words of a poet:

Is he a lord on whose head
the male fox urinates?

Some scholars say that *Rabb* is the greatest name of Allah because of the large number of those who make supplication using it. Consider its use in the Qur'an as at the end of *al-Baqarah* and *Āl 'Imrān*, and in *Sūrat Ibrāhīm* and other *sūrahs*. By this quality of Lordship we are made aware of the quality of the relationship between the Lord and the slave which involves kindness, mercy, and need in every state.

There is disagreement about the derivation of the word *rabb*. Some say that it is derived from *tarbiyah* (upbringing). So Allah Almighty manages His creation and nurtures them. We find that borne out in the words of the Almighty: *'Your foster daughters in your care.'* (4:23) He called a foster daughter *rabībah* because the husband cares for her. On the basis that Allah manages His creation and nurtures it, *Rabb* reflects an attribute connected to Divine Action, and, in as far as *Rabb* means king and master, it is an attribute of the Divine Essence.

When the definite article is affixed to 'Lord' on its own it can only mean Allah Almighty because it is defined, but if it is elided, it can be shared between Allah and His slaves. It is said, 'Allah is the Lord of the slaves, Zayd is the lord of the house, and Allah is the Lord of the lords.' Allah owns both the owner and what is owned. He created him and provides for him. No lord except for Allah can be either a creator or provider. A slave can become an owner after he was not an owner and ownership can also be removed from him. He can own one thing and not own another. The attribute of lordship when it is applied to Allah is different from this. He everlastingly knows and owns everything in existence. This is the difference between the attribute of the Creator and the created.

There is great disagreement among interpreters about he meaning of the word 'worlds (*'ālamīn*)'. Qatādah said that it is the plural of *'ālam*, and means every existent thing except Allah. It has no singular form, like *raht* (group) and *qawm* (people). It is said that the people of every age are 'a world'. Al-Ḥusayn ibn al-Faḍl said that, based on the words of Allah: *'Of all beings* ('ālamīn), *do you lie with males'* (26:165), he means people. Al-'Ajjāj said:

Khindif is the head of this world.

Ibn 'Abbās said that *'ālamīn* means the jinn and human beings. The evidence for his position is the words of the Almighty: *'So that he can be a warner to all beings* ('ālamīn)'. (25:1) He was not a warner to animals. Al-Farrā' and Abū 'Ubaydah said, 'The word "world (*'ālam*)" designates all who have understanding and they constitute four communities: mankind, jinn, angels and shayṭāns. "World" is not used for beasts, because it is a word only used for those with intelligence.'

Zayd ibn Aslam said, 'They are those who are provided for.' It is like what Abū 'Amr ibn al-'Alā' said: 'They are those with a *rūḥ*.' That is the same idea that Ibn 'Abbās expressed: 'It means everything with a *rūḥ* crawling on the earth.' Wahb ibn Munabbih said, 'Allah has eighteen thousand worlds. This world is just one of them.' Abū Sa'īd al-Khudrī said, 'Allah has forty thousand worlds, and this world from east to west is just one of them.' Muqātil said, 'There are eighty thousand worlds, forty thousand are on the land and forty thousand on the sea.' Ar-Rabī' ibn Anas related that Abu-l-'Āliyah said, 'The jinn are a world and mankind is a world. Beyond that the earth has four corners and there are fifteen hundred worlds in each corner. He created them to worship Him.'

The first view is the soundest of these, because it includes every creature and existent thing. Evidence for it is found in the words of the Almighty: *'Pharaoh said, "What is the Lord of all the worlds?" He said, "The Lord of the heavens and the earth and everything between them."'* (26:23-24) The word is derived from *'alam* (sign) and *'alamah* (token) because it indicates the One Who brought it into existence. That is like what az-Zajjāj said: 'The word "worlds" refers to all that Allah created in this world and the Next.' Al-Khalīl said, '*'Alam*, *'alāmah* and *ma'lam* are what indicates a thing, so *'ālam* indicates that it has a Creator and Director. This is clear.' It is mentioned that a man said in the presence of al-Junayd, 'Praise be to Allah.' He told him, 'Complete it as Allah did. Say: "the Lord of all the worlds."' The man said, 'What are these worlds that they should be mentioned with the Real?' He said, 'Say it, my brother. When the temporal is connected to the timeless, no trace of it remains.'

Although the word 'Lord' is usually considered to be genitive (*Rabb**i***) in this context, it can also be read as nominative (*Rabb**u***) or accusative (*Rabb**a***). If it is read as accusative, it becomes the object of the praise, and if it is as read as nominative it is the beginning of a new sentence, implying, 'He is the Lord of all the worlds.'

The All-Merciful, Most Merciful

After calling Himself 'the Lord of all the worlds' Allah then describes Himself as 'the All-Merciful, Most Merciful'. Because His description as 'the Lord of all the worlds' causes fear, He follows it by 'the All-Merciful, Most Merciful' since that contains reassurance, so that His qualities induce both awe of Him and the desire for Him. This helps people in their obedience to Him. He does the same in several places in His Book. He says: *'Tell My slaves that I am the Ever-Forgiving, the Most Merciful, but also that My punishment is the painful punishment.'* (15:49-50) He says elsewhere: *'The Forgiver of wrong action, the Accepter of repentance, the Severe in retribution, the Possessor of abundance.'* (40:3) In *Ṣaḥīḥ Muslim* we find a hadith in which Abū Hurayrah reported that the Messenger of Allah ﷺ said, 'If the believers knew the punishment of Allah, no one would hope for His Garden. If the unbelievers knew the mercy of Allah, no one would despair of His Garden.' The meanings of these two Names have already been given in the introduction.

The King of the Day of Repayment.

Muḥammad ibn as-Samayqa' has 'King' in the accusative, and there are four readings of it: *mālik*, *malik*, *malk* and *malīk*. It is related from Nāfi' that there is *ishbā'* on the *kasrah* of *malik* and so he recited, *malikī*. Scholars disagree about which is the more comprehensive: *malik* (king) or *mālik* (master). Both readings are transmitted from the Prophet ﷺ, Abū Bakr, and 'Umar ﷺ. At-Tirmidhī mentioned both readings. It is said that 'King (*malik*)' is more general and intensive than 'Master (*mālik*)' since every king is a master but not every master is a king, and because a king has authority over the property of a master so that he can only dispose of it according to the directives of the king. Abū 'Ubaydah and al-Mubarrad also held that opinion. It is said that 'Master is more comprehensive because He is the Master of people and other creatures and so it is more far reaching and greater in His power of disposal since He sees to the imposing of the laws of the Sharī'ah. So he has greater mastery.'

Abū 'Alī said that Abū Bakr ibn as-Sirāj transmitted from some of those who preferred to recite *mālik* that Allah describes Himself as being the Master of everything in His words, 'Lord of all the worlds', so there is no point in the recitation *mālik* because that would be a repetition. Abū 'Alī said, 'This is not a valid argument because the Revelation contains many similar instances, where the general comes first and then the particular. One example is Allah's words: *"He is Allah, the Creator, the Maker, the Giver of Form."* (59:24) Creator is general, and the Giver of Form is mentioned because it calls attention to what is created and the existence of wisdom. Another instance is when the Almighty says: *"They are certain about the Next World'* after saying *'those who believe in the Unseen."* (2:3) The Unseen contains the Next World and other things, but He mentioned it because of its immensity and to call attention to the obligation to believe in it and to refute the unbelievers who deny it. Yet another example, of particular relevance to the *Fātiḥah* is the formula, *"the All-Merciful, Most Merciful"* when *Raḥmān* is general for all existence and *Raḥīm* is mentioned after it to make it specific to the believers in the Next World, something made explicit by His words, *"merciful to the believers"* (33:43).'

Abū Ḥātim said that *mālik* is more intensive when praising the Creator than *malik*, and *malik* is more intensive when praising creatures than *mālik*. The difference between them is that a master in the case of creatures can be other than a king. But when Allah is master, He is also a king. This position was chosen by Qāḍī Abū Bakr ibn al-'Arabī. He mentioned three reasons. One is that it can be applied to both the particular and the general and so you can say 'master of a house, land and garment', in the same way that you say 'master of a kingdom'. The second is that it is applied to the master of a little or a lot. When you reflect on these two statements, you find that they are the same. The third is that you say, 'Master of the Kingdom (*mālik al-mulk*)', not 'King of the Kingdom (*malik al-mulk*)'. Ibn al-Ḥaṣṣār said that that is the case because the word 'master' indicates property (*milk*) and does not necessarily entail a kingdom (*mulk*). Property comprises both matters and so it is more intensive. It also entails completeness. That is why *malik* is more entitled than others.

Have you not seen the words of the Almighty: *'Allah has chosen him over you and increased him greatly in knowledge and physical strength'* (2:247)? And that is why the Prophet ﷺ said, 'The imamate is in Quraysh,' and Quraysh is the best of the Arab tribes and the Arabs are better and nobler than the non-Arabs. It contains power and choice, which is something which is necessary for a king. If he were not powerful, possessing choice and having his judgments and commands carried out, then his enemies would overpower him and his subjects would be held in contempt. It also contains force, promise and threat. Do you not see that Sulaymān said: *'How is it that I do not see the hoopoe? Or is it absent without leave? I will certainly punish it most severely'* (27:20-21)? There are other extraordinary matters and sublime meanings which are not found in *mālik*. Some of them argue that *mālik* is more intensive because it has an extra letter and so its reciter receives ten more good actions than the one who reads *malik*. This is looking at form rather than meaning. The recitation of *malik* is established and it has meanings that *mālik* does not have, and Allah knows best.

It is said that it is not permitted to give anyone the name nor to call other than Allah Almighty by it. Al-Bukhārī and Muslim related from Abū Hurayrah that the Messenger of Allah ﷺ said, 'Allah will seize the earth on the Day of Rising and roll up heaven in His right hand and then say, "I am the King. Where are the kings of the earth?"' Abū Hurayrah also reported that the Messenger of Allah ﷺ said, 'The most abased man in the sight of Allah is a man who calls himself "the King of Kings".' Muslim added, 'There is no king except Allah Almighty.' Sufyān said, 'Like the Persian title *Shahanshah*.' Aḥmad ibn Ḥanbal said, 'I asked Abū 'Amr ash-Shaybānī about the meaning of *"akhna'"* and he said, "lowly".' He said that the Messenger of Allah ﷺ said, 'The man with whom Allah will be angriest is a man who calls himself "the king of kings." There is no king except Allah.' Ibn al-Ḥaṣṣār said, 'It is like that with "King of the Day of Judgment" and "Master of the Kingdom."' There is no disagreement that this title is forbidden to all creatures in the same way that 'king of kings' is forbidden. It is, however, permitted to be described as king or master if what is intended is what is customarily understood by those terms. Allah Almighty says: *'Allah sent you Ṭālūt as a king.'* (2:247) The Prophet ﷺ said, 'Some people from my community were shown to me raiding in the way of Allah, riding the middle of this sea like kings on thrones.'

It may be asked why does Allah say *'Master of the Day of Repayment'* when the Day of Judgment has not yet arrived? How can He describe Himself as being the Master of something He has not yet brought into existence? The response to this is that the word used is an active participle from the verb *malaka*, and the active participle in Arabic can be used to indicate something which is still to come. That is a correct, sound, intelligible use of language, like 'I will hit (*ḍārib*) Zayd tomorrow,' using the active participle. The form can be used for the future, and that is the case in the words, *'Master of the Day of Repayment,'* meaning that He will be the Master on the Day when it comes.

A second point is that the interpretation of the phrase refers to power, meaning that Allah has power on the Day of Judgment or over the Day of Judgment and is bringing it about because the king of a thing can dispose of a thing as He wills and has power over it. Allah Almighty is the King of all things and disposes of them as He wills. Nothing is impossible for Him. The first aspect is close to Arabic and more effective. Abū al-Qāsim az-Zajjāj said that.

A third point is to ask why Allah singled out the Day of Repayment when He is King of that Day and all other days. The answer is because, in this world, there is contention about who has sovereignty, as is displayed in what Pharaoh, Nimrod and other tyrants did. On that Day no one will contend with Him for sovereignty and all of them will be humbled to Him, as He says: *'To whom does the kingdom belong today?'* (40:16) The answer of all creatures will be: *'To Allah, the One, the Conqueror.'*

(40:16) Glory be to Him! There is no god but Him.

If the reading *malik* (King) is employed, it is one of the attributes of the Divine Essence. If *mālik* (Master) is used, it is one of the attributes of Divine Action.

The word 'day' normally designates the time from the rising of dawn until the moment when the sun sets. It is used metaphorically here for the time from when the Resurrection takes place until the time when the people of the Next World take up their respective abodes. The word 'day' can apply to a time in it, as when Allah Almighty says: *'Today I have completed your* dīn *for you.'* (5:3) The plural of *yawm* is *ayyām*. The root is *awyām* and there is assimilation. Sometimes they describe hardship as 'a day'.

*'Repayment (*dīn*)'* here means requital for actions and reckoning for them. That is what Ibn 'Abbās, Ibn Mas'ūd, Ibn Jurayj, Qatādah and others said. This understanding is related from the Prophet ﷺ. It is indicated by the words of the Almighty: *'On that Day Allah will repay them what is due to them.'* (24:25) This is their reckoning. He says: *'Every self will be repaid today for what it earned.'* (40:17) *'Today you will be repaid for what you did.'* (45:28) *'Will we face a reckoning?'* (37:53)

Linguists report that *dayn* is debt and *dīn* is repayment. Another aspect of it is the term *ad-Dayyān* as an attribute of the Lord, meaning 'the Repayer'. A ḥadīth states: 'The clever one is he who calls himself to account (*dāna*).' It is said that it means judgment and this is also related from Ibn 'Abbās. These three meanings are similar. *Dīn* can also mean obedience. So the word is one which has several meanings. Tha'lab said, 'The verb *dāna* is used for a man when he obeys, when he disobeys, when he is exalted, when he is abased, and when he is overcome, and so it is one of the words with opposite meanings, also used for custom and affair. *Dīn* can be used for the policy of a king. *Dayn* can be a malady.'

You alone we worship and You alone we ask for help

With *'You alone we worship'* the third person changes to the second person based on a grammatical shift (*talwīn*). From the beginning to this point the *sūrah* has been a description of Allah and praise for Him as is the case in other examples in Allah's Book: *'Their Lord will give them a pure drink'* which then changes to *'This is your reward.'* (76:21-22) We find the reverse in *'When some of you are on a boat, running before a fair wind'* which changes to *'and then a violent squall comes upon them.'* (10:22)

'We worship' means 'We obey'. Worship is obedience and humility. A smooth (*mu'abbad*) road is one which is easy for travellers to travel on. Al-Harawī said, 'When those subject to the Sharī'ah say this they are acknowledging Allah's Lordship and affirming the worship of Allah alone since other people worship

other than Him in the form of idols and other things.' The meaning of 'ask for help' (*ista'āna*) is to seek aid, support and success. As-Sulamī says in *al-Ḥaqā'iq*: 'I heard Muḥammad ibn 'Abdullāh ibn Shādhān say that he heard Abu Ḥafṣ al-Farghānī say, "Whoever recites *'You alone we worship and You alone we ask for help'* cannot be considered guilty of espousing either the doctrine of fatalism or that of absolute free will."'

If it is asked why the object is put before the verb, the answer is that it is put first because of its importance. The Arabs tend to put the most important thing first. It is mentioned that a Bedouin cursed another and so the cursed man turned away from him and the curser exclaimed, 'You (*iyyāka*) from me!' And the other replied, 'From you I turn.' They put the object of emphasis first. It also ensures that the created slave and worship is not put before the object of worship. So it is not permitted to say '*na'buduka*' and '*nasta'īnuka*', nor is it permitted to say '*na'budu iyyāka*' and '*nasta'īnu iyyāka*', putting the verb first before the object. One follows the wording of the Qur'an.

Most reciters and scholars double the *yā'* in *iyyāka* in both places, although 'Amr ibn Fā'id recited it as *iyāk*. That is because he disliked the doubling of the *yā'* since it is heavy and because there is a *kasra* before it. One turns away from this reading. *'You alone we ask for help'* is adding one sentence to a prior one. Yaḥyā ibn Waththāb and al-A'mash recite '*nista'īn*'. That is the dialect of the tribes of Tamīm, Asad, Qays and Rabī'ah.

Guide us on the Straight Path

The words 'guide us' are a supplication, implying that this is something desired by the speaker from their Lord. It means: 'Direct us to the Straight Path and guide us to it. Show us Your guidance which will lead us to intimacy with You and nearness to You.' Some scholars say that Allah made this *sūrah* a model for all supplication. Half of it comprises His praise and half comprises our needs. The supplication which is in the *sūrah* is the best which one can use for supplication because these are words spoken by the Lord of the worlds. When you use it you make supplication using His words which He spoke. We find in a hadith: 'There is nothing Allah considers more noble than supplication.'

It is said that it means: 'Guide us to follow the *Sunnah* in performing all the obligations we owe you.' It is said that the root of the word 'guide' is inclination towards something. That can be seen in the words of the Almighty: *'We have truly turned* (hudnā) *to you'* (7:156), meaning 'we have inclined towards You,' and the Prophet ﷺ went out leaning (*yatahādī*) between two men. Another facet of its meaning can be gleaned from the word *hadiyah* (gift) because it moves from one owner to another. Yet another aspect of its meaning can be inferred from the word *hady* which is the term used for an animal driven to the *Ḥaram*. From all this we can see that the meaning is: 'Incline our hearts to the Truth.'

Al-Fuḍayl ibn 'Iyāḍ said the the Straight Path is the path of the *ḥajj*. This is a very specific meaning and a general meaning is far more likely. Muḥammad ibn al-Ḥanafiyyah said about the words, *'Guide us to the Straight Path'*, that they mean to the *dīn* of Allah and that no other kind of worship is accepted. 'Āṣim al-Aḥwal said that Abu-l-'Āliyah said, 'The Straight Path is the Messenger of Allah ﷺ and his two companions after him.' 'Āṣim said, 'I said to al-Ḥusayn that Abu-l-'Āliyah said that the Straight Path was the Messenger of Allah ﷺ and his two companions after him. He said, "He spoke the truth and was faithful."'

The root meaning of *ṣirāṭ* (path) in Arabic is 'a way'. 'Āmir ibn aṭ-Ṭufayl said:

> We chased through their land with horses
> until we left them more abased than the way (*ṣirāṭ*).

An-Naqqāsh said that *ṣirāṭ* means road in Greek. Ibn 'Aṭiyyah said, 'This is very weak indeed.' It is also sometimes recited with a *sīn* rather than a *ṣād*, from *istirāṭ*, meaning 'swallowing', implying the swallowing up of the Path by the one who travels on it, and it is enunciated between a *zāyy* and *ṣād*. It is also recited as a pure *zāyy*, but *sīn* is the root. Salamah related that al-Farrā' said that *zirāṭ* with a pure *zāyy* is the dialect of 'Udhrah, Kalb and Banū al-Qayn. He mentioned that they say '*azdaq*' instead of '*aṣdaq*' as they say '*azad*' instead of '*asad*'.

Ṣirāṭ is in the accusative as a second object because the verb "guide' is transitive, taking a second object either with the particle '*bi*' or without the particle. 'Straight" is an adjective describing 'Path' and it is one which has no crookedness or deviation in it. We find it used in the words of the Almighty: *'This is My Path and it is straight, so follow it.'* (6:153)

The Path of those whom You have blessed

This 'Path' is the same as the first and the meaning is: 'continue to guide us'. Someone may be guided to the path and then be prevented from going along it. It is also said that it is another path and means knowledge of Allah Almighty and recognition of Him. Ja'far ibn Muḥammad said that.

There are ten readings of the word normally recited as *'alayhim* used in this phrase. Most recite it as *'alayhum*. It can be recited as *'alayhum*, *'alayhim*, *'alayhimī*, *'alayhimū*, *'alayhumū*, *'alayhumu*. These are the six forms related from the imāms among the reciters. There are four other possibilities transmitted from the Arabs, but not related from the reciters.

'Umar ibn al-Khaṭṭāb and Ibn az-Zubayr recited *ṣirāṭa man* (the path of **him** who) instead of *ṣirāṭa alladhīna* (the path of **those** who). People disagree about the identity of those who are blessed. The majority of commentators say that it means the Prophets, the people of truth, the martyrs and the righteous. They deduce that from the *āyah* in *Sūrat an-Nisā'* which says: *'Whoever obeys Allah and the Messenger will be with those whom Allah has blessed: the Prophets and the true, the martyrs and the righteous. What excellent company such people are!'* (4:69) It is clear from this *āyah* that these are the people who have been blessed by Allah and therefore those who are referred to in the *Fātiḥah* as following the Straight Path. Everything that has been said on this subject boils down to this and so there is no sense in mentioning all the different positions, and Allah is the One whom we ask for success.

This *āyah* becomes a refutation of the Qadariyyah, Mu'tazilites and Shi'ah because they all believe that the will of a human being alone is enough to initiate his actions, obedience or disobedience. They believe that man is the creator of his own actions and so he does not need his Lord to originate them. Allah refutes them in this *āyah* since in it we ask Him for guidance to the Straight Path. If the matter had really been theirs and not their Lord's, they would not need to ask Him for guidance and to repeat that request in every prayer. They also pray to Him to avert from them what is disliked which are those things contrary to guidance. They say, *'the path of those whom You have blessed, not of those with anger on them nor of the misguided.'* As they ask Him to guide them, they also ask Him not to misguide them. That is how they pray, saying, *'Our Lord, do not make our hearts swerve aside after You have guided us.'* (3:8)

not of those with anger on them nor of the misguided

There is also disagreement about the identity of *'those with anger on them'* and the *'misguided'*. The majority say that *'those with anger on them'* are the Jews and *'the misguided'* are the Christians. That was explained by the Prophet ﷺ in the hadith of 'Adī ibn Ḥātim and the story of how he became Muslim, transmitted by Abū Dāwūd aṭ-Ṭayālisī in his *Musnad* and at-Tirmidhī in his *Collection*. That explanation is also attested to by the Almighty who says about the Jews: *'They brought down anger from Allah on themselves'* (2:61, 3:112) and He says: *'Allah is angry with them.'* (48:6) He says about the Christians that they *'were misguided previously and have misguided many others, and are far from the right way.'* (5:77)

It is also said that *'those with anger on them'* are the idolaters and that the misguided are the hypocrites. It is said that those with anger on them are those who omit the obligation of reciting this *sūrah* in the prayer, and the misguided are those who lose the blessing of its recitation. In *al-Ḥaqā'iq*, as-Sulamī said – as did al-Māwardī in his commentary – that this is nonsense. Al-Māwardī said that this view is rejected because reports contradict it and a different view about it is widespread. Therefore it is not permitted to apply this judgment to it. It is said that *'those with anger on them'* refers to people who follow innovations and that the misguided are those who lose the *sunnahs* of guidance.

This is good. The explanation of the Messenger of Allah ﷺ is more appropriate, higher and better. *'On them'* is in the nominative because it means: 'anger is on them.' Linguistically *'ghaḍab'* (anger) means intensity of feeling. A man who is described as *ghaḍūb* has a harsh character. *Ghaḍūb* is also a foul malignant because of its severity. *Ghaḍbah* is a shield made of camel-hide, one part which is folded over the other. It is called that because of its strength. The meaning of anger when it is attributed to Allah is the will to punish; it is an attribute of the Essence since the will of Allah is one of the attributes of the Essence. It is also said to mean the punishment itself. A corroboration of that view is the ḥadīth: *'Ṣadaqah* extinguishes the anger of the Lord.' It describes the action.

The word "misguidance" (*ḍalāl*) in Arabic means 'missing the target and straying from the path of Truth.' One way the word is used is to describe when milk dissolves (*ḍalla*) in water. It is also used in the *āyah*: *'When we have been absorbed* (ḍalalnā) *into the earth'* (32:10), i.e. we disappear by death and become dust. It is said:

Did you not ask so that the houses inform you
about where the disappeared (*muḍallal*) has gone?

Ḍalḍala is a smooth stone which swater has turned over again and again in a valley. Similarly *ghaḍbah* is a stone found in the mountains which has various colours.

'Umar ibn al-Khaṭṭāb and Ubayy ibn Ka'b inserted a second *ghayri* before *ḍāllīn*. It is related from the two of them with the *rā'* in the accusative and genitive on both letters. If it is in the genitive, it is an appositive for 'those' or for '*hum*' in 'on them' or as an adjective of 'those' which is definite. Definite nouns do not have indefinite adjectives just as indefinite nouns do not have definite adjectives. However, 'those' here can be undefined and general and so the words are like your words, 'I passed by someone like you and showed honour to him,' or it is because the word *'ghayr'* makes something definite because it can only be one of two things without any other possibility, as you say, 'The living is not (*ghayr*) the dead'; 'the one who is still is not (*ghayr*) the one who is moving'; and 'the one who is standing is not (*ghayr*) the one who is sitting.'

There is disagreement about the '*lā*' in '*nor* (walā) *of the misguided*'. It is said that it is redundant as aṭ-Ṭabarī says. It is also said that it is for stress and is added so that no one will suppose that 'misguided' is added to 'those'. Makkī and al-Mahdawī related it. The Kufans said that '*lā*' means '*ghayr*' and that is the reading of 'Amr and Ubayy. The root of '*ḍāllīn*' is '*ḍālilīn*' and the vowel of the first *lām* has been elided and then the *lām* assimilated into the other *lām*.

2. Sūrat al-Baqarah – The Cow 1 – 141

We will first mention its revelation, excellence and summarise its contents. We will do that with each *sūrah*.

Sūrat al-Baqarah is Madinan and different parts of it were revealed at various times. It is said that it was the first *sūrah* to be revealed in Madīnah except for Allah's words *'Have fear of a Day when you will be returned to Allah'* (2:281). That was the last *āyah* to be revealed and it was revealed on the Day of Sacrifice during the Farewell Ḥajj at Minā. The *āyah*s about usury were also numbered among the last *āyah*s to be revealed of the Qur'an.

The excellence of this *sūrah* is unsurpassed and the reward for reciting it is immense. It is called the Pavilion (*fusṭāṭ*) of the Qur'an. Khālid ibn Ma'dān said that. That is due to its greatness, splendour and the great number of rulings and warnings it contains. 'Umar spent twelve years learning it, its *fiqh* and contents and his son spent eight years doing that. Ibn al-'Arabī said, 'I heard one of our shaykhs say, "It contains a thousand commands, a thousand prohibitions, a thousand wisdoms and a thousand reports."' The Messenger of Allah ﷺ sent out an expedition, consisting a number of men, and he put the youngest of them in charge of it because he knew *Sūrat al-Baqarah*. He told him, "Go! You are their commander." At-Tirmidhī transmitted this from Abū Hurayrah and said that it is sound. Muslim related from Abū Umāmah al-Bāhilī: 'I heard the Messenger of Allah ﷺ say, "Read *Sūrat al-Baqarah*. Learning it is a blessing, abandoning it is a cause of regret, and sorcerers (*baṭalah*) are impotent before it."' Mu'āwiyah said that he heard that '*baṭalah*' are sorcerers.

It is also related from Abū Hurayrah that the Messenger of Allah ﷺ said, 'Do not turn your houses into graveyards. Shayṭān flees from a house in which *Sūrat al-Baqarah* is recited.' Ad-Dārimī related that Ibn Mas'ūd said, 'There is no house, in which *Sūrat al-Baqarah* is recited, but that Shayṭān leaves it breaking wind.' The Prophet ﷺ also said, 'Everything has a hump, and the hump of the Qur'an is *Sūrat al-Baqarah*. Everything has a core, and the core of the Qur'an is the *Mufaṣṣal*.' In *Ṣaḥīḥ* of al-Bustī, Sahl ibn Sa'd reported that the Messenger of Allah

ﷺ said, 'Everything has a hump, and the hump of the Qur'an is *Sūrat al-Baqarah*. If someone recites it in his house at night, Shayṭān will not enter his house for three nights. If someone recites it during the day, Shayṭān will not enter his house for three days.' Al-Bustī says what is meant are the rebellious shayṭāns.

Ad-Dārimī reported in his *Musnad* from ash-Sha'bi that 'Abdullāh ibn Mas'ūd said, 'If anyone recites ten *āyahs* of *Sūrat al-Baqarah* in the night, Shayṭān will not enter that house that night until morning. They are: the four at the beginning of it, the *Āyat al-Kursī* and the two following it, and the three at the end, which begin *"Everything in the heavens and everything in the earth belongs to Allah"* (2:284).' Ash-Sha'bī said that neither Shayṭān nor anything he dislikes will come near him or his family that day. They are not recited over a mad person without him recovering. Al-Mughīrah ibn Subay', one of the companions of Ibn Mas'ūd, said, 'And he will not forget the Qur'an.' Isḥāq ibn 'Īsā said, 'He will not forget what he has memorised.'

We read in the *Kitāb al-Isti'āb* of Ibn 'Abd al-Barr: 'Labīd ibn Rabī'ah was one of the poets of the *Jāhiliyyah*. He lived until the time of Islam and became a good Muslim and abandoned his poetry after entering the *dīn*. While he was caliph, 'Umar asked him about his poetry and asked him to recite some of it. He recited *Sūrat al-Baqarah* and 'Umar said, "I asked about your poetry." He said, "I have not uttered a line of poetry since Allah taught me *al-Baqarah* and *Āl 'Imrān*." 'Umar liked what he said, and gave him a stipend of 2000 and then added 500 more.' Many historians say that Labīd did not utter any poetry from the time he became Muslim. Some say that after he was Muslim he only said:

"Praise be to Allah, since the end of my life did not come
before I had put on the trousers of Islam!"

Ibn 'Abd al-Barr said that this verse was actually uttered by Qaradah ibn Nufāthah as-Salūlī. I believe that to be sounder. Someone else said that the verse Labīd uttered in Islam was:

No one criticizes a person as he does himself.
A person is put right by a righteous companion.

الٓمٓ ۝

1 Alif. Lam. Mim.

Interpreters disagree about the letters at the beginnings of the *sūrahs*. 'Āmir ash-Sha'bī, Sufyān ath-Thawrī and a group of hadith scholars say that Allah has a secret in each of His Books and these letters are Allah's secret in the Qur'an. They form part of the *mutashābih* (open to interpretation) *āyahs* in the Qur'an about which only Allah knows. It is not necessary to discuss them but one should simply believe in them and recite them as they have come. This position was related from Abū Bakr aṣ-Ṣiddīq and 'Alī ibn Abī Ṭālib. Abū al-Layth as-Samarqandī related that 'Umar, 'Uthmān, and lbn Mas'ūd said, 'The "separated letters" are a branch of hidden knowledge which cannot be explained.' Abū Ḥātim said, 'We only find the "separated letters" in the Qur'an at the beginning of the *sūrahs*. We do not know what Allah Almighty means by them.'

This was also stated by Abū Bakr al-Anbari, who reported from al-Ḥasan ibn al-Ḥubāb from Abū Bakr ibn Abī Ṭālib from Abu-l-Mundhir al-Wāsiṭī from Mālik ibn Mighwal from Sa'īd ibn Masrūq that ar-Rabī' ibn Khuthaym said, 'Allah Almighty revealed this Qur'an and He has kept the knowledge of whatever He wishes for Himself and He has acquainted you with what He wishes. As for what He has kept to Himself, you will not acquire it, so do not ask about it. As for what He has acquainted you with, it is that which you can ask and report about. You do not know the entire Qur'an and you will not teach all that you know.' Abū Bakr said, 'This tells us that He concealed the meanings of the letters of the Qur'an from everyone as a test from Allah Almighty. Anyone who believes in them is rewarded and is fortunate. Anyone who rejects and doubts them sins and is far from Allah's mercy.' 'Abdullāh ibn Mas'ūd said, 'A believer does not have any belief in anything better than belief in the Unseen.' Then he recited, *'those who believe in the Unseen.'* (2:3)

This is the basic position and ruling about the *mutashābih*. It is sound according to the evidence, which will be presented when the matter is again addressed at the beginning of *Āl 'Imrān*, Allah willing. The position of a large group of scholars, however, is that we should speak about this matter and search out the benefits it contains and the ideas that can be deduced from it. People disagree about the letters and say many different things. It is related from Ibn 'Abbās and 'Alī that the 'separated letters' in the Qur'an are the greatest Name of Allah, though we do not know how it is composed from them.

Quṭrub, al-Farrā' and others say that it is simply a question of the letters of the alphabet — and Allah knows best — so that when the Arabs were challenged by the Qur'an to produce something like it, it would be clear that it is composed of the same letters which are the basis of their normal language. That would make their inability to duplicate it all the more apparent in the proof against them since there is nothing in it outside of the letters they use in their everyday speech.

Quṭrub said, 'They used to run away when they heard the Qur'an. When they heard, *"Alif Lām Mīm"* and *"Alif Lām Mīm Ṣād"*, they did not know this expression and so they stopped to listen to him ﷺ and he then presented the familiar Qur'an to them so that it would be firm in their hearing and ears and would be evidence against them.' Some people say as corroboration for this, 'It is related that, when the idolaters refused to listen to the Qur'an in Makkah and said, *"Do not listen to this Qur'an. Drown it out"* (41:26), these letters were revealed so that they would find it odd and start to listen. So they began listening to the Qur'an and the evidence against them was clearly established.'

Another group said that they are letters which indicate the names of things from which they are taken. Ibn 'Abbās and others said that *Alif* is from Allah, *Lām* from Jibrīl and *Mīm* from Muhammad ﷺ. It is said that *alif* is the beginning of the Divine Name Allah, *lām* is the beginning of the Divine Name *Laṭīf*, and *mīm* is the beginning of the Divine Name *Majīd*. Abu-ḍ-Ḍuḥā related from Ibn 'Abbās that *'Alif Lām Mīm'* means: 'I, Allah, know best.' *'Alif Lām Rā"* means: 'I, Allah, see.' And *'Alif Lām Mīm Ṣād'* means: 'I, Allah, bestow.' So the *alif* indicates the idea 'I', *lām* indicates the name Allah, and *mīm* indicates the meaning 'I know.' Az-Zajjāj preferred this position and said, 'I believe that each letter has a meaning.' The Arabs have spoken by these letters in verse and used them instead of words.

Zayd ibn Aslam said, 'They are the names of the *sūrahs*.' Al-Kalbī said, 'They are oaths which Allah Almighty swore by due to their excellence and honour. They are an aspect of His Names.' Ibn 'Abbās also said that. Some scholars refute this position saying that it is not valid for them to be oaths because an oath is always connected to a particle, such as *inna*, *qad*, *laqad* or *mā*. None of these is used here and so it is not correct to say that they are oaths. The reply to that is that the object of the oath is His words: *'without any doubt'*. If a man were to swear, saying, 'By Allah, there is no doubt in this Book,' then the words would be correct. '*Lā*' [no] is the complement of the oath. So the position of al-Kalbī and what is reported from Ibn 'Abbās is confirmed as being both correct and valid.

If it is asked what is the wisdom in an oath from Allah Almighty, when people in that time were in two groups – those who accepted and those who denied – since those who accept do so without an oath and those who deny will not believe even with an oath, the answer is that the Qur'an was revealed in the language of the Arabs and when one of the Arabs wanted to stress his words, he would swear to what he said. Allah Almighty wanted to stress the proof to them and so He swore that the Qur'an was from Him.

Some say that *'Alif Lām Mīm'* means: 'This Book was revealed to you from the Preserved Tablet.' Qatādah said, '*Alif Lām Mim* is one of the Names of the Qur'an.' It is related that Muḥammad ibn 'Alī at-Tirmidhī said, 'Allah Almighty summed up all the rulings and stories which are in that *sūrah* in the letters which are mentioned at the beginning of it. That can only be understood by a Prophet or a *walī*. Then He made that clear throughout the entire *sūrah* so that all people would understand it.' Other things are said as well, and Allah knows best.

The stop on these letters is with a *sukūn* since they are incomplete, except when they are reported about or connected. Then they are inflected. There is disagreement about their position in respect of inflection.

ذَٰلِكَ ٱلْكِتَٰبُ لَا رَيْبَ ۛ فِيهِ ۛ هُدًى لِّلْمُتَّقِينَ ۝٢

2 That is the Book, without any doubt. In it is guidance for the godfearing:

That is the Book

It is said that *'That is the Book'* really means 'This is the Book'. The word 'that' (*dhālika*) is used here to indicate what is present, even if its normal usage is to indicate something absent, just as Allah says about Himself: *'That* (dhālika) *is the Knower of the Unseen and the Visible, the Almighty, the Most Merciful.'* (32:6) So the word 'that' indicates the Qur'an. In short the meaning is: *'Alif Lām Mīm.* This Book is without any doubt.' That is the position of Abū 'Ubaydah, 'Ikrimah and others. We find support for it in the words of the Almighty: *'That* (tilka) *is the argument We gave to Ibrāhīm.'* (6:83) and *'Those* (tilka) *are Allah's Signs which we recite to you with truth.'* (2:252). But when they become as if they were distant, the word 'that' is used. In al-Bukhārī we find, 'Ma'mar said, '"That Book" is the Qur'an.' It is *'guidance for the godfearing'* in its clarification and evidence, just as He says: *'That is Allah's judgment. Allah will judge between you.'* (60:10) This is Allah's judgment. 'This' can mean 'that'.

There are a number of different things said about the meaning of these words. It is said that *'That is the Book'* refers to the Book which accompanies all human beings, containing the information about whether they will be happy or wretched in the Next World, their lifespan and their provision, and the whole phrase means that there is no way of altering it. It is said that *'That is the Book'* means: 'That which I wrote for Myself before time: "My mercy precedes My anger."' In *Ṣaḥīḥ Muslim*, Abū Hurayrah reported that the Messenger of Allah ﷺ said, 'When Allah finished creating creation, He wrote in His Book which is with Him, "My mercy predominates over (or precedes) My anger."'

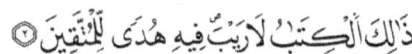

It is said that Allah Almighty promised His Prophet ﷺ that He would send down on him a Book which water would not erase. It indicates the promise which is referred to in *Ṣaḥīḥ Muslim* in the hadith of 'Iyāḍ ibn Ḥimār al-Majāsha'ī that the Messenger of Allah ﷺ said, 'Allah looked at the people of the earth and hated men, both Arabs and non-Arabs, except for the remainder of the People of the Book. He said to His Prophet ﷺ, "I sent you to test you and to test others by you. I sent down to you a Book which cannot be washed away by water. You recite it asleep and awake."'

It is said that this phrase indicates the part of the Qur'an which was promised in Makkah. It is said that when Allah Almighty revealed to His Prophet ﷺ: *'We will impose a weighty Word upon you'* (73:5), the Messenger of Allah ﷺ continued to wait for this promise to be fulfilled by his Lord. When *'Alif. Lām. Mim. That is the Book, without any doubt'* (2:2) was revealed to him in Madīnah, it had the meaning: 'This Qur'an which was revealed to you in Madīnah is that Book which you were promised and which I revealed to you in Makkah.'

It is said that the word 'That' indicates what was revealed in the Torah and Gospel concerning the Qur'an. The implication is that it is that Book which was foretold by the Torah and Gospel. The Gospel and Torah testify to its soundness and it deals with what is in them as well as containing things which are not in them. It is said that *'That is the Book'* is a reference to the Torah and Gospel themselves, so that the meaning is *'Alif Lām Mim.* Those two Books' or the like of those two Books, meaning that this Qur'an contains what is in those two Books. So the word 'that' indicates 'two', the possibility of which is attested to in the Qur'an when Allah Almighty says: *'A cow, not old or virgin, but somewhere between the two* (dhālika)' (2:68), making it clear that the word 'that' can refer to two things.

It is said that *'That is the Book'* refers to the Preserved Tablet – that Book in which the destinies of all existent things are recorded. Al-Kisā'ī said that it refers to the Qur'an in heaven which had not yet been revealed. It is said that Allah Almighty promised the People of the Book that He would send down a Book to Muhammad ﷺ and so it indicates that promise. Al-Mubarrad said that the meaning is that this Qur'an is that Book by which you seek victory against the unbelievers.

It is also said that it means all the letters of the alphabet, out of which all books are composed. This is somewhat borne out by the derivation of the word *kitāb* (book) which is a verbal noun from *kataba, yaktubu*. From it comes *katībah* (squadron), so called because it is composed of horsemen gathered together and *takattaba* is used when horses are deployed in squadrons. *Kutbah* is a seam, and the plural is *kutab.* So *kitāb* is the writing by the scribe of the letters of the alphabet joined together in words. It is called a Book, even if it is just writing. The word *kitāb* also denotes obligation, judgment, prescription and the decree.

without any doubt.

The word 'doubt' (*rayb*) has three meanings. One is doubt, the second is suspicion, and the third is need. So there is no doubt and no suspicion about the Book of Allah Almighty. It means that it is true in itself and it is revealed from Allah and is one of His qualities, uncreated and not within time, even if the unbelievers doubt that. It is said that the phrase is a prohibition, meaning 'Do not doubt.' The words end as if He were saying, 'That Book is true.' The verb *rāba* is used when you have doubt and fear about something. *Arāba* means to become full of doubt.

In it is guidance

The word *hudā* (guidance) in Arabic means right guidance and clarification, in other words it involves unveiling, guidance and increased clarification for the people who follow it.

There are two types of guidance. Guidance can mean pointing out the way and this is what the Messengers and their followers are able to do. Allah says: *'Every people has a guide.'* (13:7) He says: *'You are guiding to a straight path.'* (42:52) So he ﷺ has given us that aspect of guidance which entails direction, calling to the truth and admonition. The aspect of guidance, however, which involves people actually following the path and reaching the goal is the business of Allah alone. He says to his Prophet ﷺ: *'You cannot guide those you would like to.'* (28:56) Guidance here means filling the heart with faith. Further examples of this are when Allah says: *'They are the people guided by their Lord'* (2:5) and *'He guides whoever He wills'* (35:8) where guidance means being actually moved to and on the path of guidance.

Abu-l-Ma'ālī said, 'Guidance means "bringing to" and it entails guiding the believers to the paths of the Garden and the roads which lead to it, as in the words of Allah describing those who do *jihād*: *"He will not let their actions go astray. He will guide them...* " (47:4-5) or in the case of the unbelievers to the Fire, as in His words: *"Guide them to the Path of the Blazing Fire"* (37:23).' It is said that '*hudā*' is one of the names for a river because people are guided in it to their livelihood and all their hopes.

for the godfearing:

Allah Almighty singled out the godfearing for His guidance, even though the Qur'an is, in fact, guidance for all creatures, in order to honour them because they believe and affirm what it contains. It is related that Abū Rawq said, "'*Guidance for the godfearing*" means honour for them. It is ascribed to them out of esteem and honour for them and to show their excellence.'

The word 'godfearing (*muttaqīn*)' is derived from *taqwā* whose linguistic root is said to mean to be sparing of words. Ibn Fāris related that. That is indicated by the hadith, 'The godly (*taqī*) is sparing in his words and the godfearing (*muttaqī*) is above both the believers and those who are obedient.' He is someone who protects himself, by his righteous actions and sincere supplication, from Allah's punishment. It is derived from guarding yourself against the disliked by putting a barrier between you and it.

It is reported that Ibn Mas'ūd said one day to his nephew, 'Nephew, do you see how many people there are?' 'Yes,' he replied. He said, 'There is no good in any of them except those who turn to Allah or are godfearing.' Then he added, 'Nephew, do you see how many people there are?' 'Yes,' he replied. He said, 'There is no good in them except for a man of knowledge or a student.' Abū Yazīd al-Bisṭāmī said, 'A godfearing person is someone whose words are for Allah when he speaks and whose actions are for Allah when he acts.' Abū Sulaymān ad-Dārānī said, 'The godfearing are those from whose hearts love of appetites has been stripped away.' It is said that a godfearing person is one is protected from *shirk* and free of hypocrisy. Ibn 'Aṭiyyah said, 'This is false because someone could be like that and still be a deviator.' In relation to *taqwā* 'Umar ibn al-Khaṭṭāb asked Ubayy, 'Have you ever taken a path between thorny bushes?' 'Yes,' he replied. He asked, 'What did you do?' He said, 'I gathered in my clothes and was careful.' He said, 'That is *taqwā*.'

Taqwā comprises all good. It is Allah's directive to all human beings and it is the best acquisition a person can acquire. Abu-d-Dardā' was asked, "Your companions utter poetry but you do not memorise any of it." He refuted them, declaiming:

A man wants to be given his desire
    but Allah only gives him what He wills.
A man says, 'My profit and my property,'
    but *taqwā* of Allah is the best thing that can be acquired.

Ibn Mājah related in his *Sunan* that the Prophet ﷺ said, 'After *taqwā*, nothing benefits a believer more than a righteous wife. When he commands her, she obeys him. When he looks at her, she delights him. When he swears by her, she carries out the oath. When he is absent from her, she is faithful to him in her person and his property.'

ٱلَّذِينَ يُؤْمِنُونَ بِٱلْغَيْبِ وَيُقِيمُونَ ٱلصَّلَوٰةَ وَمِمَّا رَزَقْنَـٰهُمْ يُنفِقُونَ ۝٣

3 those who believe in the Unseen and establish the prayer and spend from what We have provided for them;

those who believe

The word 'believe' here means to hold to be true. Linguistically *īmān* (faith, belief) is affirmation. In the Revelation the words of the brothers of Yūsuf: *'You will not believe us'* (12:17) mean 'believe that we are telling the truth'. Qatādah is reported as saying, 'Son of Ādam, if the only time you want to do good is when you are feeling enthusiastic, you should know that it is the nature of the self to incline to ennui, indifference and boredom; the believer, however, is the one who spurs himself on; the believer is the one who takes heart; the believer is the one who remains strong. The believers are those who cry out to Allah night and day. By Allah, a true believer continues to say, 'O Lord', secretly and openly until it is answered secretly and openly.'

In the Unseen

In the language of the Arabs, the word *ghayb* (Unseen) denotes everything which is hidden from you. It is used for the setting of the sun. *Mughībah* is used for a woman when her husband is absent. We fall into a *ghaybah*, meaning a hole in the ground. *Ghayābah* is a forest, which is a group of trees into which one disappears. It is also used for low-lying ground, because it is out of sight.

Scholars disagree about the meaning of the word here. Some say that what is meant by 'Unseen' in this *āyah* is Allah Himself. Ibn al-'Arabī said that this is weak. Others have said that it is the Decree; others that it is the Qur'an and the unseen things it contains; others that the Unseen are those matters about which the Messengers report which are beyond the scope of human intellect: the signs of the Last Hour, the punishment of the grave, the Gathering, the Resurrection, the *Sirāt*, the Scales, the Garden and the Fire. Ibn 'Aṭiyyah said that these statements are not mutually exclusive. The Unseen refers to all of them.

It is, in fact, the prescribed faith indicated in the hadith of Jibrīl when he said to the Prophet ﷺ, 'Tell me about faith (*īmān*)' He replied, 'It is to believe in Allah, His angels, His Books, His Messengers, and the Last Day, and to believe in the decree, both its good and its evil.' He said, 'You have spoken the truth.' 'Abdullāh ibn Mas'ūd said, 'There is no faith better for the believer than faith in the Unseen.' Then he recited, *'Those who believe in the Unseen.'* (2:3)

In the Qur'an we find: *'We are never absent* (ghā'ibīn)' (7:7), and also: *'Those who fear their Lord in the Unseen.'* (21:49). Allah cannot be seen by the eyes and cannot be seen in this dimension of existence but He is not absent to investigation and deduction. The believers believe that they have a powerful Lord who will repay all their actions. They fear Him in their hearts and fear Him when they are alone, where others cannot see them, through their knowledge that He is aware of them. These *āyahs* agree and there is no contradiction in them. Praise be to Allah!

'Unseen' is also said to mean their consciences and hearts. According to this understanding, the words *'they believe in the Unseen'* mean 'they believe in their hearts'. In other words, their hearts are filled with faith in contradistinction to the hearts of the hypocrites which are empty of faith. That is what al-Ḥasan said. A poet said:

We believed in the Unseen when our people
were praying to idols before Muḥammad came.

and establish

Establishing the prayer means performing it together with its pillars, *sunnahs* and positions at the correct time as will be explained. *Qāma* here does not have the normal meaning of 'stand' but rather means to continue with and firmly establish.

The call known as the *iqāmah* of the prayer is well-known. It is *sunnah* with the majority so that, if someone fails to recite it, he does not have to repeat the prayer. Al-Awza'ī, 'Aṭā', Mujāhid, and Ibn Abi Laylā, however, made it obligatory and anyone who forgets it has to repeat the prayer. The literalists said that. It is related from Mālik, and Ibn al-'Arabī preferred that because, he said, it is found in the hadith about the Bedouin, 'Do the *iqāmah*.' So he ﷺ commanded him to do the *iqāmah* as he commanded the *takbīr*, facing the qiblah and *wuḍū'*. He said, 'You now have the hadith and it supports you in repeating one of the two transmissions from Mālik that agree with the hadith: the *iqāmah* is a *farḍ*.' Some scholars say that if someone abandons it intentionally, he should repeat the prayer. That is not because it is obligatory since, if it that were the case, those who forget and those who abandon it deliberately would be subject to the same ruling. It is on account of making light of the *Sunnah*. Allah knows best.

Scholars disagree about whether someone who hears the *iqāmah* should hurry to the prayer or not. Most believe that he should not hurry, even if he fears that he will miss a *rak'ah*, because the Prophet ﷺ said, 'When the *iqāmah* for the prayer is given, do not come running to it. Come walking. You must be tranquil. Pray what you catch and complete what you miss.' Abū Hurayrah related it and Muslim transmitted it. The Messenger of Allah ﷺ also said, 'When the prayer is called, none of you should run to it. He should walk. He must be sedate and grave. Pray what you catch and finish what you missed.' This is a text. Part of the reason for this is that when someone hurries, he is breathless and his entry into the prayer, recitation and humility are disordered. A group of the Salaf, including Ibn 'Umar and Ibn Mas'ūd, disagree about hurrying when someone fears they will miss the prayer. Isḥāq said, 'He hurries when he fears that he will miss the *rak'ah*.' Something similar is related from Mālik. He said, 'There is no harm in someone on a horse making the horse go faster.' Some of them interpret it as the difference between someone walking and someone sitting because a rider does not become breathless in the same way that someone on foot does.

It is more appropriate to follow the sunnah of the Messenger of Allah ﷺ in every case. As in the hadith, you should walk and be sedate and grave because you are in the prayer. It is impossible for the report of the Prophet ﷺ to be different to what he reported. Just as someone who enters the prayer must be grave and still, so the one who is walking to it must be like that so that he obtains its reward. Part of what indicates the soundness of this is what we mentioned of the Sunnah and what ad-Dārimī transmitted in the *Musnad* from Muḥammad ibn Yūsuf from Sufyān from Muḥammad ibn 'Ajlān from al-Maqbarī from Ka'b ibn 'Ujrah that the Messenger of Allah ﷺ said, 'When you have done *wuḍū'*, go to the mosque. Do not entangle your fingers together. You are in the prayer.' In this hadith, which is sound, the Prophet ﷺ forbade what is less than hurrying. He made him like someone in prayer. These sunnahs clarify the meaning of His words: *'hasten to the remembrance of Allah'* (62:9). It does not just mean getting there quickly. This is about action. This is how Mālik explained it. It is what is correct regarding that. Allah knows best.

Scholars disagree about the interpretation of 'complete what you missed' and 'finish what you missed' and whether they mean the same thing. It is said that they mean the same and that 'finish' is undefined and 'completion' is meant by it. Allah says: *'When the prayer is finished'* (63:10) an:d *'When you have completed your rites'* (2:200). It is said that they have different meanings, and that is sound. The difference depends on whether the person joins at the beginning or end of the prayer. The first view is held by a group of the people of Mālik, including Ibn al-Qāsim. The person concerned finishes what he missed of the *Fātiḥah* and *sūrah* and so it is about building on actions and finishing words. Ibn 'Abd al-Barr said that this is well known in the School. Ibn Khuwayzimandād said, 'That is the view of our people. It is the view of al-Awzā'ī, ash-Shāfi'ī, Muḥammad ibn al-

Ḥasan, Aḥmad ibn Ḥanbal, aṭ-Ṭabarī and Dāwūd ibn 'Alī. Ashhab, who is the one Ibn 'Abd al-Ḥakam mentioned, related it from Mālik.'

'Īsā related from Ibn al-Qāsim from Mālik that what the person catches is the end of his prayer and he finishes the actions and words. That is the view of the Kufans. Qāḍī Abū Muḥammad 'Abd al-Wahhāb said, 'It is the well known position of the school of Mālik.' Ibn 'Abd al-Barr said, 'I think that those who make what he caught the beginning of his prayer take account of *takbir al-iḥrām* because that only happens at the beginning of the prayer, and the *tashahhud* and *taslīm* are only at the end of it. So they say that what he caught is the beginning of his prayer, supported by the Sunnah in his words, "Complete". "Completion" is the end.' Others cite 'finish' and someone who finishes something has missed it. The reading of 'complete', however, is more common.

The *iqāmah* precludes you from beginning any supererogatory prayers. The Messenger of Allah ﷺ said, 'When the *iqāmah* for the prayer is given, there is no prayer except the prescribed one.' Muslim and others transmitted it. If someone has started a supererogatory prayer, he does not break it off because Allah says: *'Do not make your actions of no worth.'* (47:33) That is especially the case if he has prayed a *rak'ah* of it. It is also said that he stops it because of the general meaning of the hadith. Allah knows best.

Scholars disagree about someone who enters the mosque without having prayed the two *rak'ahs* of *fajr* and then the *iqāmah* is given. Mālik says that he should join the prayer with the imam without praying them. If he has not entered the mosque and does not fear missing a *rak'ah* of it, he may pray them outside the mosque. He should not pray them in any of the courtyard connected to a mosque in which the *Jumu'ah* is prayed. If he fears that he will miss the first *rak'ah* of the communal prayer, he should enter and pray with the imam and then pray the two *rak'ahs* after sunrise if he wishes. I think that it is better to pray them after sunrise than to leave them. Abū Ḥanīfah and his people say that if someone fears that he will miss both *rak'ah*s and not catch the imam before he rises from *rukū'* in the second *rak'ah*, he should join the prayer. If he hopes to catch one *rak'ah*, he should pray *fajr* outside the mosque and then join with the imam.

That is also what al-Awzā'ī said, although he permits praying the *rak'ah*s in the mosque if the person is not afraid of missing the final *rak'ah*. Ath-Thawrī said, 'If he fears missing a *rak'ah*, he should join the imam and not pray them. Otherwise he should pray them in the mosque.' Al-Ḥasan ibn Ḥayy (or Ḥayyān) said, 'Once the *iqāmah* has started, there are no voluntary prayers except for the two *rak'ahs* of *fajr*.' Ash-Shāfi'ī said, 'If someone enters the mosque when the *iqāmah* for the prayer has been given, he joins with the imam. He does not pray the two *rak'ahs* of *fajr* either in the mosque or outside of the mosque.' Aṭ-Ṭabarī said the same. Aḥmad ibn Ḥanbal also said that, relating from Mālik, and it is the sound position concerning that since the Prophet ﷺ said, 'When the *iqāmah* for the prayer is given, then there is no prayer except the prescribed one.' The two *rak'ahs* of *fajr* are either sunnah, excellent or meritorious. When there is a dispute, one takes the proof of the Sunnah.

Part of the evidence for the well known position of Mālik and that of Abū Ḥanīfah is what is related from Ibn 'Umar who once arrived when the imam was praying the *Ṣubḥ* prayer: he prayed *fajr* in Ḥafṣah's room and then prayed with the imam. The argument of ath-Thawrī and al-Awza'ī is what is related about 'Abdullāh ibn Mas'ūd. He entered the mosque when the *iqāmah* had been given and he prayed *fajr* behind a pillar and then joined the prayer in the presence of Ḥudhayfah and Abū Mūsā. They said, 'If it is permitted to perform the supererogatory apart from the prayer outside the mosque, one is likewise permitted to do it inside the mosque.' Muslim related that 'Abdullāh ibn Mālik ibn Buḥaynah said, 'The *iqāmah* for the *Ṣubḥ* prayer had been given and the Messenger of Allah ﷺ saw a man praying while the *mu'adhdhin* was giving the *iqāmah*. He said, "Are you praying *Ṣubḥ* with four *rak'ahs*?"' This was the Messenger of Allah ﷺ objecting to the man praying the two *rak'ahs* of *fajr* inside the mosque while the imām was praying. It is possible that it is evidence that if the two *rak'ahs* of *fajr* are done in that situation they are sound, because he did not stop him praying while he was able to do so. Allah knows best.

the prayer

Linguistically the root of the word '*ṣalāh*' (prayer) means supplication. Evidence for that is the words of the Prophet ﷺ, 'When one of you is invited for food, he should accept. If he is not fasting, he should eat, and if he is fasting, he should make supplication (*ṣallā*).' When Asmā' gave birth to 'Abdullāh ibn az-Zubayr, she sent him to the Prophet ﷺ. Asma' said, 'He wiped his head and prayed (*ṣallā*) for him,' meaning made supplication. Some scholars say that the obligatory prayer is meant and that he prayed two *rak'ahs* and left, but the first opinion is better known. It is the view of most scholars. Allah Almighty says: *'Pray* (ṣalla) *for them'* (9:103), meaning to make supplication for them.

Some people say that it is derived from the word *ṣalā*, which is the cord in the middle of the back which separates at the base of the spine and goes round it. From it is also derived the word *muṣallā* for the second horse in a horse race, because at the end of the race, his head is at the rump (*ṣalwān*) of the horse in front. So the derivation of the *ṣalāh* from this is either because it is the second pillar after the declaration of faith, and so it resembles someone coming second immediately behind another horse, or because the back of the one who bows in the prayer is bent, in which case *ṣalā* refers to the bending of the horse's back. 'Alī said, using the word with this meaning, 'The Messenger of Allah ﷺ came first, Abū Bakr second (*sallā*) and 'Umar third.'

It is also said that it comes from the idea of abiding in something, as *'roasting in a red-hot fire'* in 88:4. According to this, it means holding to worship to the extent which Allah has commanded. It is also said to be taken from the idea of warming a branch with fire to straighten it and make it supple by heat since *ṣilā'* means roasting by fire, thus referring to how the one who prays straightens himself by his efforts and makes himself supple and humble. *Ṣalāh* can also mean supplication and mercy, as in 'O Allah, bless (*ṣalli*) Muḥammad.' *Ṣalāh* is also an undefined act of worship. Allah says: *'Their prayer* (ṣalāh) *at the House'* (8:35), meaning their worship. *Ṣalāh* can also mean supererogatory prayer as in *'Instruct your family to do the prayer (ṣalāh).'* (20:132) It can also mean glorification. *Ṣalāh* can also mean recitation as in 17:110. So it is a word with several meanings. *Ṣalāh* is also a house in which one prays as Ibn Fāris said. It is also said that *ṣalāh* is a name simply for this act of worship. Allah would not leave a time without a Law and would not leave a Law without a prayer. Abū Naṣr al-Qushayrī narrated that. According to this position, it has no derivation.

According to the position of the majority, those who study the roots disagree about whether it remains connected to its original linguistic root, and the same is true of *īmān*, *zakāt*, *ṣiyām*, *ḥajj* and *shar'*, which are subjected to legal preconditions and rulings, or whether that addition acts in the same way as it did before the Sharī'ah was revealed. The first is sounder because the Sharī'ah is confirmed in Arabic and the Qur'an was revealed in clear Arabic. But the Arabs do have an arbitrary usage where nouns are concerned, such as the word *dābbah,* which is used for everything that crawls (*dabba*), and then the Arabs apply it specifically to animals. That is also the custom with nouns in the Sharī'ah. Allah knows best.

There is disagreement about what is meant by 'the prayer' in this instance. It is said that it is both the obligatory and voluntary prayers, and that is the sound position because the expression is undefined.

The prayer is also cause for provision. Allah says: *'Instruct your family to do the prayer'* (20:132) as will be explained in *Ṭaha*, Allah willing. It is healing for stomach pain and other things. Ibn Mājah related that Abū Hurayrah said, 'The Prophet ﷺ rested at midday as I did and I prayed and sat down. The Prophet ﷺ turned to me and said in Persian, "Is your stomach bothering you?" "Yes, Messenger of Allah," I answered. He said, 'Get up and pray. There is healing in the prayer."'

The prayer is only valid if all its preconditions and obligatory elements are fulfilled. Purity is one of its preconditions. Its rulings will be explained in *Sūrat an-Nisā'* and *Sūrat al-Mā'idah.* The private parts must be covered, which will be dealt with in *Sūrat al-A'rāf,* Allah willing. Its obligatory elements are facing the qiblah, the intention, the *takbīr al-iḥrām* and standing for it, reciting the *Fātiḥah* and standing for it, *rukū'* and being still in it, rising from *rukū'* and standing up straight, prostration and being still in it, rising from prostration, sitting between the two prostrations and being still in it, the second prostration and being still in it, and the final sitting and being still in it.

The source for all this is the hadith of Abū Hurayrah about the man who had prayed incorrectly and whom the Prophet ﷺ then taught. He told him, 'When you stand for the prayer, perform *wuḍū'* thoroughly and then face the qiblah. Say the *takbīr* and then recite what is easy of the Qur'an. Then bow and remain still in it and then come up until you are standing straight. Then prostrate until you are still in prostration. Then come up until you are still in sitting. Then do the like of that in all your prayer.' Muslim transmitted it. Something similar is found in the hadith of Rifā'ah ibn Rāfi' transmitted by ad-Dāraquṭnī and others.

Our scholars said that the Prophet ﷺ explained to us the pillars of the prayer. He said nothing about the *iqāmah*, raising the hands, the amount of recitation, the *takbīrs* for the movements, the glorification in *rukū'* and prostration, the middle sitting, the *tashahhud* for the final sitting and the *salām.* As for the *iqāmah* and the specific requirement of the *Fātiḥah*, they have already been discussed. As for raising the hands, a group of scholars and most *fuqahā'* say that it is not mandatory based on the hadith of Abū Hurayrah and Rifā'ah ibn Rāfi'. Dāwūd and some of his people say that it is mandatory for the *takbīr al-iḥrām,* and some of his people said it is mandatory to raise the hands in *iḥrām, rukū'* and coming up from *rukū',* and if someone does not raise his hands, his prayer is invalid. That is the view of al-Ḥumaydī and it is related from al-Awzā'ī. They cite as evidence the words of the Prophet ﷺ: 'Pray as you saw me praying' which al-Bukhārī transmitted. They said, 'It is obligatory for us to act as we saw him acting because he conveys Allah's desire.'

As for *takbīrs* other than the *takbīr al-iḥrām*, Most say that they are sunnah based on the hadith. Ibn al-Qāsim, Mālik's companion, said, 'If someone omits three or more *takbīrs* in the prayer, he should prostrate before the *salām.* If he does not prostrate, then the prayer is invalid. If he forgets one or two *takbīrs*, he also prostrates for forgetfulness, but owes nothing if he forgets.' It is related from him that omitting one *takbīr* does not amount to forgetfulness. This indicates that he thinks that all the *takbīrs* are obligatory but omitting a few is overlooked. Aṣbagh ibn al-Faraj and 'Abdullāh ibn 'Abd al-Ḥakam, 'There is nothing due from anyone who does not say any of the *takbīrs* in the prayer including the *takbīr al-iḥrām*. If he omits it out of forgetfulness, then he prostrates for forgetfulness. If he does not prostrate, he owes nothing. However one must not omit the *takbīr al-iḥrām* deliberately because it is one of the sunnahs of the prayer. If someone does so, he has acted badly, but owes nothing and his prayer is valid.'

This is sound and it is the position of most of the *fuqahā'* of the cities among the Shāfi'īs and Kufans, a group of the people of hadith and the Mālikīs except for the position of Ibn al-Qāsim. Al-Bukhārī has a 'Chapter on completing the *takbīr* in *rukū'* and prostration'. He includes the hadith of Muṭarrif ibn 'Abdullāh who said: "Imrān ibn Ḥusayn and I prayed behind 'Alī ibn Abī Ṭālib. When he went into *sajdah* he said the *takbīr* and when he raised his head, he said the *takbīr*. When he got up after two *rak'ahs*, he said the *takbīr*. When he finished the prayer, 'Imrān ibn Ḥusayn took hold of my hand and said, "This man reminded me of the prayer of Muhammad ﷺ," or he said, "He prayed the prayer of Muḥammad with us."'

'Ikrimah said, 'I saw a man at the *Maqām* saying the *takbīr* every time he did *rukū'* and rose, when he stood up, and when he went down. I told Ibn 'Abbās and he said, "If that is not indeed the prayer of the Prophet, you have no mother!"' By this chapter al-Bukhārī indicated to you that the *takbīr* was not done by them. Abū Isḥāq as-Sabī'ī related from Yazīd ibn Abī Maryam that Abū Mūsā al-Ash'arī said, 'On the day of the Battle of the Camel, 'Alī led us in a prayer which reminded us of the prayer of the Prophet ﷺ. He said the *takbīr* every time he went down and came up, stood and sat.' Abū Mūsā said, 'Either we forgot it or abandoned it deliberately.'

Do you see them repeating the prayer? So how can it be said that omission of the *takbīr* invalidates the prayer? If that had been the case, there would have been no difference between sunnah and *farḍ*. When the thing on its own is not mandatory, then all of them are not mandatory. Success is by Allah.

According to the majority, *tasbīḥ* in *rukū'* and prostration are not mandatory based on the ḥadīth already mentioned. Isḥāq ibn Rāhawayh made them mandatory and said that someone who omits them must repeat the prayer since the Prophet ﷺ said, 'Exalt the Lord in *rukū'* and entreat in supplication in prostration. It is fitting that it be answered.'

Scholars disagree about the sitting and *tashahhud*. Mālik and his people say that the first sitting and its *tashahhud* are sunnahs. A group of scholars consider the first sitting to be mandatory and say that it is singled out among other obligations since prostration represents it, just as *'arāyā* do with *muzābanah* and *qirāḍ* does with wages [types of business transactions] and like standing for the *takbīr al-iḥrām* when someone finds the imām bowing. They argue that if it had been sunnah, then someone who abandons it would not invalidate his prayer as the prayer is not invalidated by abandoning sunnahs of the prayer. Those who do not consider it mandatory say that if it had been one of the obligatory elements of the prayer, someone who forgot it would return to it and perform it, as is the case if he misses a prostration or *rukū'*, and he would observe in it what he observes in *rukū'* and prostration in order. Then he would prostrate for forgetting it as is done by someone who omits a *rukū'* or prostration and then performs them. We find in the hadith of 'Abdullāh ibn Buḥaynah that the Messenger of Allah ﷺ stood up from two *rak'ahs* and forgot the *tashahhud*. People behind him said, 'Glory be to Allah!' He remained standing and they stood. When he finished the prayer, he did the two prostrations of forgetfulness before the *salām*. If sitting had been obligatory, forgetfulness would not cancel it because the obligations of the prayer are the same when they are omitted out of forgetfulness or deliberately.

There are five different positions about the ruling of the final sitting in the prayer. The first is that sitting is obligatory, the *tashahhud* is obligatory and the *salām* is obligatory. Those who said that include ash-Shāfi'ī and Aḥmad ibn Ḥanbal in one transmission. Abū Muṣ'ab related it from Mālik and the people of Madīnah in his *Mukhtaṣar.* Dāwūd also stated that. Ash-Shāfi'ī said, 'If someone omits the first *tashahhud* and the prayer on the Prophet ﷺ, he does not have to repeat the prayer, but he does the two prostrations of forgetfulness for omitting it. If he omits the final *tashahhud* out of forgetfulness or deliberately, he should repeat the prayer.' They cite as evidence the fact that the Prophet ﷺ made the obligatory clear in the prayer because the basis of its obligation is undefined and requires clarification except for that which has a proof. The Prophet ﷺ said, 'Pray as you saw me praying.'

The second view is that sitting, the *tashahhud* and the *salām* are not mandatory. They are all sunnahs. This is the view of some of the Basrans. It was the position of Ibrāhīm ibn 'Ulayyah and he stated that the final sitting is analogous with the first. He differs from the majority and is aberrant, although he thought that anyone who omits any of that must repeat the prayer. Part of their argument is the hadith of 'Abdullāh ibn 'Amr ibn al-'Āṣ that the Prophet ﷺ said, 'When the imam raises his head from the final prostration in the prayer and then breaks his *wuḍū'*, his prayer is complete.' It is a hadith which is not sound according to Abū 'Amr.

We explained it in *Kitāb al-muqtabis*. This wording omits the *salām*, not the sitting.

The third view is that sitting for the amount of time needed for the *tashahhud* is obligatory, but neither the *tashahhud* nor the *salām* are obligatory. Abū Ḥanīfah and his people and a group of Kufans said that. They use as evidence the hadith of Ibn al-Mubarak from 'Abd ar-Raḥmān ibn Ziyād al-Ifrīqī which is weak. In it the Prophet ﷺ said, 'When one of you sits at the end of his prayer and then breaks his *wuḍū'* before saying the *salām*, his prayer is complete.'

The fourth view is that sitting is obligatory and the *salām* is obligatory, but the *tashahhud* is not mandatory. Those who said that include Mālik ibn Anas and his people and Aḥmad ibn Ḥanbal in one variant. Their argument is that no remembrance is mandatory except the *takbīr al-iḥrām* and recitation of the *Umm al-Qur'ān*.

The fifth view is that *tashahhud* and sitting are mandatory, but not the *salām*. The group took that view included Isḥāq ibn Rāhawayh. Isḥāq cited as proof the hadith of Ibn Mas'ūd when the Messenger of Allah ﷺ taught him the *tashahhud*. He told him, 'When you have finished this, your prayer is complete. Make up what you owe.' Ad-Dāraquṭnī said that these words were inserted by Zuhayr into the hadith and then connected to the words of the Prophet ﷺ. Shabābah separated it from Zuhayr and made it part of the words of Ibn Mas'ūd. His words are more likely to be correct than saying that it is interpolated into the hadith. Shabābah is trustworthy. It is corroborated by Ghassān ibn ar-Rabī' who makes the end part of the words of Ibn Mas'ūd rather than the Prophet ﷺ.

Scholars disagree about the *salām*. It is said that it is mandatory and also that it is not mandatory. What is sound is that it is mandatory based on the hadith of 'Ā'ishah and the sound hadith of 'Alī that Abū Dāwūd and at-Tirmidhī transmitted. Sufyān ath-Thawrī related from 'Abdullāh ibn Muḥammad ibn 'Aqīl ibn al-Ḥanafiyyah from 'Alī that the Messenger of Allah ﷺ said, 'The key to the prayer is purification. Its *taḥrīm* is the *takbīr*. Its release is the *salām*.' This hadith is the basis for the obligation of the *takbīr* and the *salām* and it is agreed that nothing else satisfies them just as nothing else satisfies purification.' 'Abd ar-Raḥmān ibn Mahdī said, 'If a man were to begin his prayer with seventy of the names of Allah Almighty without saying the *takbīr al-iḥrām*, it would not satisfy the requirement. If he breaks *wuḍū'* before the *salām*, it does not satisfy it.' This is sound from 'Abd ar-Raḥmān ibn Mahdī by the hadith of 'Alī. He is an imam in the science of hadith, knowing the sound from the weak. He is enough for you.

Scholars disagree about the obligation of the *takbīr* at the beginning of the prayer. Ibn Shihāb az-Zuhrī, Sa'īd ibn al-Musayyab, al-Awzā'ī, 'Abd ar-Raḥmān and a group said that the *takbīr al-iḥrām* is not mandatory. What is related from Mālik about someone following the imam indicates this view. What is sound in the School is that the *takbīr al-iḥrām* is mandatory and it is an obligation and one of the pillars of the prayer. It is correct. Most agree on it. The evidence is found in the Sunnah for all those who oppose that.

Scholars disagree about the wording used to enter into the prayer. Mālik and his people and a group of scholars say that only the *takbīr* satisfies it. It is not satisfied by the *shahādah, tasbīḥ*, proclaiming Allah great or praising Him. This is the position of the Hijazīs and most Iraqīs. According to Mālik, only the expression *'Allāhu akbar'* satisfies it and nothing else. That is similar to what ash-Shāfi'ī said. He said that it is satisfied by *'Allāhu akbar'* and *'Allāhu'l-Kabīr'*. Mālik's proof is the hadith of 'Ā'ishah who said, 'The Messenger of Allah ﷺ used to begin the prayer with the *takbīr* and reciting *"Praise be to Allah, the Lord of the Worlds"*', the hadith of 'Alī, 'His *taḥrīm* was the *takbīr,'* and the hadith of the Bedouin, 'he said the *takbīr.'* According to the *Sunan* of Ibn Mājah, Abū Bakr ibn Abī Shaybah and 'Alī ibn Muḥammad aṭ-Ṭanāfisī related from Abū Usāmah from 'Abd al-Ḥamīd ibn Ja'far from Muḥammad ibn 'Amr ibn 'Aṭā' who heard Abū Ḥamīd as-Sā'idī say, 'When the Messenger of Allah ﷺ rose for the prayer, he faced the qiblah, raised his hands and said, *"Allāhu akbar".'* This is a clear text and sound hadith specifying the words of the *takbīr.*

Abū Ḥanīfah said, 'If someone begins the prayer with "*lā ilaha illā 'llāh*", it does not satisfy the requirement. If he says, "O Allah, forgive me," that does not satisfy it.' That is what Muḥammad ibn al-Ḥasan said. Abū Yūsuf said that it does not satisfy it when he can articulate the *takbīr* well. Al-Ḥakam ibn 'Uyaynah said that the requirement is satisfied if he mentions Allah in place of the *takbīr.* Ibn al-Mundhir said, "I do not know of any disagreement between them that if someone can recite well and says the *shahādah* and *takbīr* but does not recite, his prayer is unsound. If someone holds this position, then he is obliged to say that nothing else satisfies the *takbīr* just as nothing else can satisfy recitation. Abū Ḥanīfah said, 'The requirement is satisfied by saying "Allah is greater" in Persian, even if someone speaks Arabic well.' Ibn al-Mundhir said, 'It does not satisfy it because it is different to what the groups of Muslims believe and differs from what the Prophet ﷺ taught his community. We do not know of anyone who agrees with what he said.' Allah knows best.

The community agree that the intention is obligatory at the time of the *takbīr al-iḥrām* except for something related from some of our people who discuss it in the *Āyah* of Purification. Its reality is to intend to approach the business by doing what is commanded in the recommended manner. Ibn al-'Arabī said, 'The basis for every intention is to formulate it in direct proximity with the intended action, or before that, provided that it accompanies that action. If the intention is made earlier and then the person concerned becomes heedless of it and starts the act of worship in that state, it is not counted when he makes it after starting the action. There is an allowance for putting it earlier in the case of fasting because of the great need for it to be connected to its beginning.'

Ibn al-'Arabī said, 'Abu-l-Ḥasan al-Qarawī told us at the port of 'Asqalan that he heard the Imam of the two Ḥarams say, 'A man should make the intention when beginning the prayer and remove his thought from the Maker, the Knower and Prophethoods so that he considers only the intention of the prayer.' He said that it does not require a long time. That can be in an instant because teaching a camel takes a long time but remembering it can be in an instant. An element of having a full intention is for it to continue right through the whole prayer. However, since that is extremely difficult for a person, the Sharī'ah allows for the intention to slip during the prayer. He said, 'I heard our Shaykh Abū Bakr al-Fihrī say in Jerusalem that Muḥammad ibn Saḥnūn said, "I sometimes saw my father Saḥnūn finish the prayer and then repeat it. I asked him about that and said, 'I lost my intention during it. That is why I repeated it.'"'

These are some of the rulings of the prayer. All its rulings will come in their proper place in this book by Allah's strength. We will mention *rukū'*, the group prayer, qiblah, doing it early in the time and something about the Fear Prayer in this *sūrah*. Shortening the prayer and the Fear Prayer proper will be mentioned in *an-Nisā'*, the times in *Hūd, al-Isrā'* and *ar-Rūm*, the night prayers in *al-Muzzammil*, the prostration of the recitation in *al-A'rāf*, and the prostration of thankfulness in *Ṣād*, each in its proper place, Allah willing.

and spend from what We have provided for them;

The word 'provided' means 'given to'. Provision, according to the people who follow the Sunnah, refers to everything which can be used, *ḥarām* or *ḥalāl*, as opposed to the Mu'tazilites who say that the *ḥarām* is not provision because it is not valid for a person to own it. According to them Allah does not 'provide' the *ḥarām*; He only 'provides' the *ḥalāl*; only something which is validly owned can properly be called provision. So, according to them, if a child grows up with thieves and only eats what the thieves eat until he is adult and strong and then himself becomes a thief and remains a thief and eats what he steals until he dies, Allah has not provided him with anything, since everything he ever consumed was *ḥarām* and he did not validly own it. He dies, therefore, without having consumed any of Allah's provision. This is false and the evidence for it is that, if provision had meant legally valid ownership, it would mean that no child could receive provision, nor could any animal which grazes in the wilderness, nor could a lamb because its mother's milk belongs to its owner and not to the lamb!

The Community agree that children, lambs and beasts are provided for and that Allah Almighty provides for them, even though they are not the owners of anything, because it is known that nourishment is an aspect of provision. The Community also agree that slaves are provided for and that Allah Almighty provides for them although they are not owners. So it is clear that provision is what we have said, not what the Mu'tazilites say.

All nourishment is provision and there is no provider except Allah: *'Is there any creator other than Allah providing for you from what is in heaven and the earth?'* (35:3) He says: *'Allah is the Provider, the Possessor of Strength, the Sure.'* (51:58) He says: *'There is no creature on the earth which is not dependent upon Allah for its provision.'* (11:6) This is definitive. Allah Almighty is the true Provider in every instance. The son of Ādam is a mere recipient because his ownership of property is, in fact, only metaphorical as we have made clear in our commentary on the *Fātiḥah*. He is provided for, like the animals, which truly own nothing. If the thing is something he is permitted to obtain, it is *ḥalāl* for him, and if it is not permitted, then it is *ḥarām* for him, but nevertheless all of it is provision. One great man of knowledge explained the words of Allah, *'Eat of your Lord's provision and give thanks to Him, a bountiful land and a forgiving Lord'* (34:15) by saying the adjective 'forgiving' (*ghafūr*) used in it indicates that provision may contain what is unlawful.

Rizq is a verbal noun derived from the verb *razaqa*. *Razq* is the verbal noun and *rizq* is a noun whose plural is *arzāq*. *Razq* is giving. *Rāziqiyyah* is a cotton garment. Form VIII is used for an army taking its provisions. *Razqah* is a single time. Ibn as-Sakīt said that *rizq* means thankfulness in the dialect of Arzdishanu'ah as in 56:82 where it means 'thanks'.

The word for 'those who spend' (*yunfiqūn*) means 'to bring something out'. 'Spending' is to give out money with the hand. The verb *nafaqa*, with regard to a sale, means to transfer money from the hand of the seller to the hand of the buyer. *Nafaqa* is used for an animal when its life leaves it. From the same root comes *nāfiqā'*, the second entrance of the hole of the jerboa from which it emerges when it is attacked from the other entrance. We also have the word *munāfiq* (hypocrite), so called because he leaves belief or belief leaves his heart. *Nayfaq* is used for trousers because the legs emerge from them. *Nafaqa* is also used for something which is spent, used up or comes to an end. An example of that usage is in the words of Allah: *'You would still hold back out of the fear it would run out* (infāq).*'* (17:100)

Scholars disagree about what is meant by the giving of provision in this instance. It is said that it refers to obligatory *zakāt*. That is related from Ibn 'Abbās and is because the prayer accompanies it. It is said that it refers to what a man spends on his family. That is related from Ibn Mas'ūd because that is the best type of expenditure. Muslim related from Abū Hurayrah that the Messenger of Allah ﷺ said, 'Out of a dinar which you spend in the way of Allah and a dinar which you spend on freeing a slave and a dinar which you give to a poor person and a dinar which you spend on your family, the one with the greatest reward is the one which you spend on your family.' It is related from Thawbān that the Messenger of Allah ﷺ said, 'Is not the best dinar a man spends the dinar which he spends on his family and the dinar which he spends on his mount in the way of Allah and the dinar which he spends on his companions in the way of Allah?' Abū Qilābah said, 'He began with the family,' and then he continued, 'What man could have a greater reward than someone who spends on a young family to keep them virtuous, or Allah gives them the benefit of him and he enriches them?'

It is also said that what is meant here is voluntary *ṣadaqah*. That is related from aḍ-Ḍaḥḥāk in reference to the fact that obligatory *zakāt* is only referred to with the expression particular to it, which is the word *zakāt*. When a word other than *zakāt* is used, it may be obligatory or voluntary. When the word 'spend' is used, it is only voluntary. Aḍ-Ḍaḥḥāk said, 'Spending was, at first, a kind of sacrifice by which a person drew near to Allah Almighty according to his effort in it until Allah revealed the obligations of *zakāt* in *Sūrat at-Tawbah* which abrogated that.' It is said that it refers to obligatory rights on wealth other than *zakāt* because by connecting it to the prayer, Allah Almighty is indicating that they are obligatory, and the fact that He uses another expression shows that this is an obligation other than *zakāt*.

It is said that its meaning is general and that is a sound position because Allah praises all kinds of spending out from what we are provided with. In that case the meaning is that they pay the *zakāt* obliged by the Sharī'ah and also spend in other ways in which it is recommended for them to spend. It is said that *'believe in the Unseen'* is the portion of the heart, *'establish the prayer'* is the portion of the body and *'spend from what they are provided with'* is the portion of wealth. This is evident. Some early scholars said in their interpretation of the words of Allah Almighty: *'they spend from what We have provided them,'* that they refer to people teaching others some of what Allah has taught them. Abū Naṣr 'Abd ar-Raḥīm ibn 'Abd al-Karīm al-Qushayrī related that.

وَالَّذِينَ يُؤْمِنُونَ بِمَا أُنزِلَ إِلَيْكَ وَمَا أُنزِلَ مِن قَبْلِكَ وَبِالْآخِرَةِ هُمْ يُوقِنُونَ ﴿٤﴾

4 those who believe in what has been sent down to you and what was sent down before you, and are certain about the Next World.

It is said that what is meant here are believers from the People of the Book, such as 'Abdullāh ibn Sallām, and that it was revealed about him. The previous *āyah* was revealed about believers among the Arabs. It is also said that both this *āyah* and the previous one are about believers in general.

Allah's words *'what has been sent down to you,'* refer to the Qur'an and His words *'and what was sent down before you'* refer to previous Books, so this differs from what the Jews and Christians did, since they only believed in their own Books as Allah tells us later in this *sūrah*: *'When they are told, "Believe in what Allah has sent down," they say, "We believe in what was sent down to us."'* (2:91)

It is said that when this *āyah* was revealed and the words *'those who believe in the Unseen'* came, the Jews and Christians said, 'We believe in the Unseen.' When Allah said: *'establish the prayer'* (2:3), they said, 'We establish the prayer.' When He said: *'and spend from what We have provided for them,'* they said, 'We spend and give alms.' When He said: *'those who believe in what has been sent down to you and what was sent down before you,'* they were averse to that. We find in a hadith that Abū Dharr asked, 'Messenger of Allah, how many Books have been sent down?' He answered, 'One hundred and four Books. Allah sent down fifty scrolls to Seth, thirty scrolls to Enoch, ten scrolls to Ibrāhīm, and ten scrolls to Mūsā before the Torah, and He sent down the Torah, the Gospel, the Zabūr and the Furqān.' Al-Ḥusayn al-Ujurrī and Abū Ḥātim al-Bustī transmitted it.

There is a question which arises here. How can one believe in all the various Revelations when it is clear that their rulings conflict? Two answers are given. One is that one believes that all of them came from Allah. This is the position of those who abolish all the acts of worship prescribed by prior *sharī'ahs*. The second is that one believes in those things in them which have not been abrogated. This is the position of those who say it is obligatory to abide by prior *sharī'ahs*, a judgment which will be explained in the proper place.

and are certain about the Next World

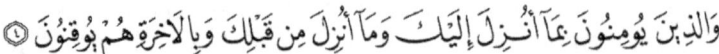

The words *'and are certain about the Next World'* refer to the Resurrection after death. Certainty is knowledge free from all doubt. Various forms of this verb (*yaqina*) can be used to express this idea. Sometimes it is possible for this word to indicate the opposite meaning of 'conjecture', and we find it in this sense elsewhere in the Qur'an and in many poems. *Ākhirah* (Next World) is derived from *ta'akhkhur* (delay) because it is later for us, as *dunyā* (this world) is derived from *danuw* (nearness)

أُوْلَٰٓئِكَ عَلَىٰ هُدٗى مِّن رَّبِّهِمۡۖ وَأُوْلَٰٓئِكَ هُمُ ٱلۡمُفۡلِحُونَ ٥

5 They are the people guided by their Lord. They are the ones who have success.

Our scholars say that the words *'by their Lord'* refute the Qadariyyah who say that they themselves are the creators of their own faith and their own guidance. Allah is too exalted for their position to be true. If that had been the case, Allah would have said, 'by their own selves'. The meaning of the word 'guidance' (*hudā*) has already been discussed in the commentary on the second *āyah* of this *sūrah.*

They are the ones who have success.

The linguistic root of '*falāḥ*' (success) is *falḥ*, which has the meaning of splitting or cleaving. From it comes *filāḥah*, tillage of the earth when it is ploughed for cultivation. Abū 'Ubayd said that. That is why a ploughman is called a *fallāḥ*. Someone with a split lower lip is called *aflaḥ*. It is as if the one with success cuts through adversity until he reaches his goal. The word is used for success and continuation, which is also another aspect of its linguistic root.

The meaning of *'the ones who have success'* in this context is those who win the Garden and remain in it. Ibn Abī Isḥāq said, 'Those who are successful are those who attain what they seek and are saved from the evil from which they flee.' The meaning is the same. The word *falāḥ* is also used for *saḥūr* (the pre-dawn meal in Ramadan), as in the hadith recorded by Abū Dāwūd: 'Until we almost missed *falāḥ* with the Messenger of Allah ﷺ.' It was asked, 'What is *falāḥ*?' The answer was, '*Saḥūr*.' *Falāḥ* normally means to gain one's goal and to be delivered from what one fears.

إِنَّ ٱلَّذِينَ كَفَرُواْ سَوَآءٌ عَلَيۡهِمۡ ءَأَنذَرۡتَهُمۡ أَمۡ لَمۡ تُنذِرۡهُمۡ لَا يُؤۡمِنُونَ ٦

6 As for those who disbelieve, it makes no difference to them whether you warn them or do not warn them they will not believe.

As for those who disbelieve,

After mentioning the believers and their states, Allah then mentions the unbelievers and their end. *Kufr* (disbelief) is the opposite of *īmān* (belief) and that is what is meant in this *āyah. Kufr* can also mean ingratitude for blessings and gifts received. The Prophet ﷺ used it in that way when he spoke about women in the eclipse hadith: 'Then I saw the Fire – and I have never seen anything more hideous than what I saw today – and I saw that most of its inhabitants were women.' They asked, 'Why, Messenger of Allah?' He replied, 'For their *kufr*.' It was asked, 'Do they reject Allah [or 'Are they ungrateful to Allah']?' He said, 'They are ungrateful to their husbands, and they are ungrateful for good behaviour (towards them). Even if you were to behave well to one of them for a whole lifetime and she were to see you do something (that she did not like) she would say that she had never seen anything good from you.' Al-Bukhārī and others transmitted it.

The root of the verb *kafara* in Arabic indicates covering and hiding. Part of that usage is found in the words of a poet:

In the night its clouds cover (*kafara*) the stars.

Night is called *kāfir* because it covers everything in darkness. *Kāfir* can also mean a sea or huge river and is also used with the meaning of cultivator – someone who covers seeds with earth. Its plural in that case is *kuffār* rather than *kāfirūn*. Allah Almighty says, *'Like the plant-growth after rain which delights the cultivators* (kuffār)' (57:20). Ashes are called *makfūr* when the wind has swept the dust so that it has covered them. 'Land which is *kāfir* is that which is so far off the beaten track that people almost never stop in it or pass by it. Those who do stop in such places are people of *kufūr*. It is also said that *kufūr* means isolated villages.

A point is made about why Ḥamza recites "*alayhum*', '*ilayhum*' and '*ladayhum*' and does not recite '*rabbihum*', '*fīhum*' or '*jannatayhum*,' the answer is that in the first examples, a *yā'* has replaced an *alif* and the root is "*alāhum*', '*ladāhum*' and '*ilāhum*' and therefore the *hā'* keeps its *ḍammah*. That is not the case with the other examples.

it makes no difference to them

The words *'it makes no difference to them'* mean that it is the same to them whether or not you warn them.

whether you warn them

His words: *'whether you warn them'* mean to announce and convey warning. The word used here for 'warn' (*andhara*) is almost only ever used to alarm people when there is time for them to take measures to avoid the thing they are being warned about. If the situation does not allow for such a time of preparation, it is called announcement (*ish'ār*) and not warning.

Scholars disagree about the interpretation of this *āyah*. It is said to refer to people in general, indicating those against whom the decree of punishment will be carried out. It is an established fact that Allah already knows that these people will die in *kufr*. Allah wanted to tell people about those whose state is like that without being specific.

Ibn 'Abbās and al-Kalbī said that the *āyah* was revealed about the leaders of the Jews in Madīnah, including Ḥuyayy ibn al-Akhṭab, Ka'b ibn al-Ashraf and those like them. Ar-Rabī' ibn Anas said, 'It was revealed about the leaders of the idolaters who were killed at Badr.' The first position is sounder. Anyone who says it was revealed about a particular person can only be referring to someone whose *kufr* was revealed from the Unseen after his death. That is one aspect of the *āyah*.

خَتَمَ ٱللَّهُ عَلَىٰ قُلُوبِهِمْ وَعَلَىٰ سَمْعِهِمْ وَعَلَىٰٓ أَبْصَٰرِهِمْ غِشَٰوَةٌ وَلَهُمْ عَذَابٌ عَظِيمٌ ۝٧

7 Allah has sealed up their hearts and their hearing and over their eyes is a blindfold. They will have a terrible punishment.

Allah has sealed up

The words, *'Allah has sealed up,'* make it clear that in this *āyah* Allah debars such people from having faith. The word '*khatama*' (sealed up) means covering a thing and fastening it up so that nothing can enter it. It is used for letters and other such things so that what is inside them cannot be reached or replaced.

Interpreters say that, in His Book, Allah describes the hearts of the unbelievers as having ten qualities: as being sealed up, stamped, constricted, sick, rusted up, dead, hard, turning away, fanatically enraged and in denial. On being in denial, He says: *'Their hearts are in denial and they are puffed up with pride.'* (16:22) On fanatical rage: *'When those who disbelieve filled their hearts with fanatical rage.'* (48:26) On turning away: *'Then they turn away. Allah has turned their hearts away because they are people who do not understand.'* (9:127) On being hard: *'Woe to those whose hearts are hardened against remembrance of Allah'* (39:22) and: *'Then your hearts became hardened after that.'* (2:74) On being dead: *'Someone who was dead and whom We brought to life.'* (61122) and: *'Only those who can hear respond. As for the dead, Allah will raise them up.'* (6:36) On being rusted up: *'No indeed! Rather what they have earned has rusted up their hearts.'* (83:14) On being sick:

'Those with sickness in their hearts.' (47:29) On being constricted: *'When He desires to misguide someone, He makes his breast narrow and constricted.'* (6:125) On being stamped: *'Their hearts have been stamped so that they do not understand'* (9:87) and: *'Allah has stamped them with* kufr.' (4: 155) On being sealed up, He says: *'Allah has sealed up their hearts.'* (2:7) All will be explained in their proper place, Allah willing.

Sealing up can be physical, as we have made clear, and also spiritual as in this *āyah*. In respect of the heart, being sealed up entails the inability to absorb Allah's words, understand what He says and reflect on His *āyah*s. In respect of hearing, it entails the inability to understand the Qur'an when it is recited or to respond to the call to believe in the Oneness of Allah. The blindfold over the eyes entails the inability to be guided by means of reflecting on His creatures and the wondrous things He has made. This is what Ibn 'Abbās, Ibn Mas'ūd, Qatādah and others have said about this.

We find in this *āyah* definitive proof of the fact that it is Allah Who is the author of guidance and misguidance, *kufr* and *īmān*. So we can only be amazed at the obtuseness of the minds of the Qadariyyah who say that they are the authors of their own faith and guidance. The 'sealing up' referred to in the *āyah* is the stamp of *kufr* so how could someone subject to that come to have *īmān*, no matter how hard his striving was? Allah has sealed up their hearts and hearing and a blindfold has been placed over their eyes. How they going to be guided and who is going to guide them after Allah, when He has misguided them, made them deaf, and blinded their eyes. *'And no one can guide those whom Allah misguides.'* (39:23) That action of Allah is nevertheless just, since He does not place any real impediment in the way of those He misguides and disappoints preventing them from fulfilling those things which are obligatory for them. So the attribute of justice is not negated. He denies them His grace, He does not prevent them doing what was obliged for them.

Some say that the words *'khatm'* (sealing), *'ṭab''* (stamping) and *'ghishāwah'* (covering) are used metaphorically and are really a way of designating them as unbelievers, judging them to be unbelievers, and reporting that they are unbelievers and are not to be taken as retaining their literal meaning. We say that this is not the case because the reality of this sealing and stamping is an action by which the heart actually becomes sealed and stamped, so it is not correct to take it metaphorically. Do you not see that when it is said, 'So-and-so stamped the book and sealed it,' it means that the book in question is actually stamped and sealed, not designated or judged. There is no disagreement concerning this among people with knowledge of the language, and the whole community agree that Allah Almighty has described Himself as sealing and stamping the hearts of the unbelievers to repay them for their disbelief, as He says: *'Allah has stamped them with disbelief.'* (4:155) So the sealing and stamping are something that Allah does to a heart which prevents faith entering it. There is evidence for this in His words: *'In that way We insert it into the evildoers' hearts. They do not believe in it'* (15:12) and He says: *'We have placed covers on their hearts, preventing them from understanding it.'* (6:25)

their hearts

Putting the heart first indicates the excellence of the heart over all other limbs and faculties. The core and the noblest part of anything is its heart. The heart is the locus of reflection. The Arabic word for heart, *qalb*, is a verbal noun meaning to turn something over completely so that it is returned to how it was at the beginning. '*Qalaba*' (to turn) a vessel is to turn it upside down. Then this image is transferred and used for this organ, the noblest part of the creature, owing to the speed with which thoughts revolve in it. It is as is said by the poet:

The heart is only called '*qalb*' because of its revolving (*taqallub*),
so beware of turning and change in the heart.

Ibn Mājah reported from Abū Mūsā al-Ash'arī that the Prophet ﷺ said, 'The metaphor of the heart is that of a feather moved by the winds in the desert.' This is the meaning which the Prophet ﷺ expressed when he said, 'O Allah, Who makes hearts firm, make our hearts firm in Your obedience.' If the Prophet ﷺ, in spite of his immense worth and exalted station, said that, then it is even more fitting for us to say it in imitation of him. Allah Almighty says: *'Know that Allah intervenes between a man and his heart.'* (8:24)

Even though the limbs follow the heart and it is their leader and master, they nevertheless affect it, because the actions they perform make a connection between the outward and the inward. The Prophet ﷺ said, 'A man gives *ṣadaqah* and a white spot is engraved in his heart. A man lies and his heart goes black.' At-Tirmidhī reports as a sound hadith from Abū Hurayrah: 'A man may commit a sin and his heart becomes black. If he repents, his heart is polished.' He said, 'That is the rust which Allah mentions in the Qur'an when He says: *"No indeed! Rather what they have earned has rusted up their hearts."* (83:14)' Mujāhid said, 'The heart is like a hand which holds a sin with every finger and then is sealed.' The Prophet ﷺ said, 'There is a lump of flesh in the body. When it is sound, the entire body is sound, and when it is corrupt, the entire body is corrupt – it is the heart.' This indicates that 'sealing' is real, and Allah knows best.

Muslim relates a hadith from Ḥudhayfah: 'The Messenger of Allah ﷺ related two hadiths to us. I have seen one of them come true and am still waiting for the other. He related to us that the quality of trustworthiness had descended into the hearts of men. Then the Qur'an came down and they knew it from the Qur'an and they knew it from the Sunnah. Then he related that trustworthiness would be removed and he said, "A man will go to sleep and trustworthiness will be taken from his heart and its trace will remain like a small scar. Then he will go to sleep and trustworthiness will be taken from his heart and its trace will remain like a superficial blister, such as you see when an ember rolls onto someone's foot and it blisters up." Then he took some pebbles and rolled them onto his foot. "And people will continue to trade but practically no one will fulfil his trust to such a point that it will be said, 'There is a trustworthy man among the Banū so-and-so!' and until it will be said of a man 'How tough he is! How elegant! How intelligent!' when he does not have even a speck of belief in his heart." There was a time when I did not care whom I did business with. If he was a Muslim, his *dīn* was sufficient assurance for me, and if he was a Christian or a Jew, his Muslim patron was sufficient assurance for me. Today I only do business with so-and-so and so-and-so among you.'

Ḥudhayfah said that he heard the Messenger of Allah ﷺ say, 'Trials will come upon the hearts, following one after another like the reeds in a woven mat. Any heart which opens the door to them will have a black mark put in it. A heart which rejects them will have a white mark put in it. Thus hearts will be of two kinds: those which are white like marble, which will not be harmed by trial as long as the heavens and the earth endure, and those which are black and dust-coloured like an upset earthen jug, not recognising what is right or rejecting what is wrong, totally permeated by base desires.'

The heart is sometimes referred to by the word *fu'ād* and also the term *ṣadr* (breast). Allah Almighty says: *'It is so that We can fortify your heart* (fu'ād) *by it.'* (25:32) He says: *'Did We not expand your breast* (ṣadr) *for you?'* (94:1). In both places it is the heart which is meant. The heart is also often equated with the intellect. Allah Almighty says: *'There is a reminder in that for anyone who has a heart'* (50:37) meaning intelligence, because the heart is the locus of the intellect according to most authorities. *Fu'ād* is the locus of the *qalb* and the breast is the locus of the *fu'ād*. Allah knows best.

and their hearing

The fact that hearing comes before sight in this *āyah* is used as evidence by those who say that hearing is better than vision. Allah also says: *'Say: "What do you think? If Allah took away your hearing and your sight..."'* (6:46) He says: *'He gave you hearing, sight and hearts.'* (32:9) This is said to be because hearing is always receptive from every direction, both in light and darkness, while sight is only effective in one direction at a time and needs light to function. However, most people put sight above hearing because hearing only perceives sounds and words, while sight perceives bodies, colours and all forms. They said, 'Something which embraces more things is better.'

If it is asked why 'sight' is in the plural and 'hearing' in the singular, the answer is that it is in the singular because '*sam*'' (hearing) is a verbal noun which can be used for both a little and a lot. It is also used as a noun for the part of the body that hears. When it is used in the plural, it indicates the individual hearing of a group of people. It is possible that it means 'the sites of their hearing' because 'hearing' is not sealed up, but the site of hearing is sealed up. '*Sam*'' can also mean the function of hearing. *Sim'* is mentioning someone well. It is also a wolf born from a hyena.

and over their eyes is a blindfold.

The pronoun 'their' applies to those whom Allah knows will not believe among the unbelievers of Quraysh, or to the hypocrites or the Jews, or to all unbelievers, which is more correct because it is universal. The seal is what covers hearts and hearing and the blindfold covers the eyes. The word used for blindfold is *ghishā'* which simply means a covering. From it comes *ghāshiyah*, a saddle cover, so-called because it goes right over it.

Some commentators say that the covering applies to the hearing and the eyes and that it is only the hearts which are sealed. Others say that the seal covers all of them and that blindfold is another way of saying seal.

They will have a terrible punishment.

'They' here refers to the unbelievers who deny the 'terrible punishment' they are going to receive. The word 'punishment' *('adhāb)* includes things like whipping, burning with fire, cutting with steel and other things which inflict pain and suffering on a person. In the Qur'an we find: *'A number of believers should attend their punishment.'* (24:2) The word is derived from a root meaning imprisonment and prevention. Linguistically one can say, 'I will punish him,' meaning restrain him. The same root is used for the sweetness *('adhūbah)* of water because it becomes sweet by being confined in a vessel so that it is pure and separated from what it is mixed with. We also find it used in the words of 'Alī, 'Keep (*a'dhibū*) your women from going out.' Punishment is called that because the person being punished is held and kept from everything which is conducive to his comfort and afflicted with the opposite.

وَمِنَ ٱلنَّاسِ مَن يَقُولُ ءَامَنَّا بِٱللَّهِ وَبِٱلْيَوْمِ ٱلْءَاخِرِ وَمَا هُم بِمُؤْمِنِينَ ۝٨

8 Among the people there are some who say, 'We believe in Allah and the Last Day,' when they do not believe.

Ibn Jurayj related that Mujahid said, 'Four *āyah*s were revealed in *Sūrat al-Baqarah* about the believers, two about the unbelievers, and thirteen about the hypocrites. As-Suddī said that 'people' here refers to the hypocrites.' Sufi scholars say that the word 'people' is a generic noun and one does not use the generic to address friends.

Grammarians disagree about the derivation of the word 'people' (*an-nās*). It is said that it is the plural of *insān* (human being). In this case the word *nās* comes from *naws*, which means movement. The word is used to mean moving about and it is found with that meaning in hadith. It is also said that the word comes from the word 'forget' (*nasī*), in which case its root would be *nasiya*. Ibn 'Abbās said, 'Ādam forgot (*nasiya*) the covenant with his Lord and so was named *insān*.' He ﷺ said, 'Ādam forgot and so his descendants forgot.' This is borne out in the Qur'an when Allah says: *'We made a contract with Ādam before, but he forgot.'* (20:115)

Allah Almighty mentions the believers first because of their nobility and excellence. Then He mentions the unbelievers next because disbelief and belief are two opposites. Then after that He mentions the hypocrites and connects them to the unbelievers to deny that they have faith with the words, '*They do not believe*.' This refutes the Karramite thesis that faith is confirmed by affirmation of it on the tongue even if the heart does not believe. Their evidence is the words of Allah: *'Allah will reward them for what they say.'* (5:85). He does not say 'for what they say and their belief in it.' They also used as evidence the words of the Prophet ﷺ, 'I was commanded to fight people until they say, "There is no god but Allah." When they have said it, their blood and property are protected from me.'

This is wrong and fails to look into what the Qur'an and Sunnah actually say about acting by both statement and belief. The Messenger of Allah ﷺ said, 'Faith is recognition in the heart, articulation by the tongue and acting according to the pillars.' Ibn Mājah transmitted it in the *Sunan*. That which Muḥammad ibn

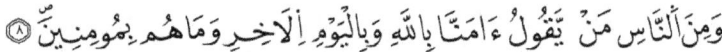

Karrām as-Sijistānī and his people state is hypocrisy and schism. We seek refuge with Allah from disappointment and corrupted belief!

Our scholars say that there are two types of believer: a believer whom Allah loves and protects and a believer whom Allah loves and does not protect, but with whom He is angry and towards whom He is hostile. Allah loves and protects all those whom He knows will end up as believers. Allah hates and is angry with and hostile towards all those whom He knows will end up as unbelievers – not, of course, on account of their belief but because of the disbelief and misguidance which will overpower them. Likewise there are two types of unbeliever: an unbeliever who will be punished and an unbeliever who will not be punished. The one who will be punished is the one who ends up with disbelief and so Allah is angry with him and hostile towards him. The one who will not be punished is the one who ends up with belief: Allah is not angry with this one nor does he hate him. He loves him and protects him, not for his disbelief, but for the belief which will overtake him.

This means that it is not permitted to make the following general statement: a believer deserves the reward and an unbeliever deserves the punishment. Rather such a statement must be made conditional on the end result. Because of this we say that Allah was pleased with 'Umar even while he was worshipping idols and meant to reward him and admit him to the Garden, not, of course, for his worship of idols, but for his ultimate belief. On the other hand, Allah was angry with Iblīs even while he was worshipping because of his ultimate disbelief.

The Qadariyyah differed regarding this matter. They said that Allah was not angry with Iblīs when he worshipped Him nor pleased with 'Umar when he was worshipping idols. This is false since it is confirmed that Allah knew how Iblīs would end up and how 'Umar would end up even though this had not yet happened. So it is confirmed that He was angry with Iblīs and loved 'Umar. The consensus of the Community indicates that Allah would never show love for anyone He knew was going to be one of the people of the Fire. He would be angry with him. He does, however, love the one He knows will be one of the people of the Garden.

The Messenger of Allah ﷺ said, 'Actions are revealed by their final seals.' That is why Sufi scholars say that faith is not what the slave is adorned with in word and deed, but faith is the preordainment of happiness before time. As for its outward appearance on individuals, that may be either empty of reality or actually true.

This is confirmed in *Ṣaḥīḥ Muslim* and elsewhere by the hadith from 'Abdullāh ibn Mas'ūd in which the Messenger of Allah ﷺ said, 'The way that each of you is created is that you are gathered in your mother's womb for forty days as a sperm-drop and then for a similar length of time as a blood-clot and then for a similar length of time as a lump of flesh. Then an angel is sent and he breathes the spirit into you and is encharged with four commandments: to write down your provision, your life-span, your actions, and whether you will be wretched or happy. By Him, apart from Whom there is no god, one of you can do the actions of someone destined for the Garden until there is only an armspan between him and it, and then what is written will overtake him and he will do the actions of someone destined for the Fire and enter it. And one of you can do the actions of someone destined for the Fire until there is only an armspan between him and it, and then what is written will overtake him and he will do the actions of someone destined for the Garden and enter it.'

Abū Muḥammad 'Abd al-Ghanī ibn Sa'īd al-Misrī transmitted a hadith about the *zindīq*s from Muḥammad ibn Sa'īd ash-Shāmī, who was crucified for being a *zindīq*, from Sulaymān ibn Mūsā al-Ashdaq from Mujājid ibn Jabr from Ibn 'Abbās that Abū Razīn al-'Uqaylī said, 'The Messenger of Allah ﷺ told me, "Abū Razīn, you and I will drink from a milk whose taste is unaltered." Then I asked, "How will Allah bring the dead to life?" He said, "Have you passed by a land which is barren and then you pass by it and it is lush, and then you pass by it again and it is barren and you pass by it again and it is lush?" I replied, "Yes." He said, "That is how the Resurrection is." I asked, "How will I know that I am a believer?" He said, "None of this Community (or My Community) does an action and knows that it is good and that Allah will reward it, or does an evil action and knows that it is bad and that Allah will either punish it or forgive it, without that showing that he is a believer."'

Even if the *isnād* of this hadith is not strong, its meaning is sound. It does not contradict the hadith of Ibn Mas'ūd. That depends on the seal as the Prophet ﷺ said, 'Actions are defined by their final seals.' This indicates that he is actually a believer, and Allah knows best.

Linguists say, 'A hypocrite (*munāfiq*) is called a hypocrite when he displays outwardly something different from what he is concealing inside himself, like the jerboa whose hole is called a *nāfiqā'*. That is because it burrows into the earth leaving some fine soil near the surface. When it is alarmed, it covers the mouth of its hole with dirt and leaves, so the outside of its hole seems to be solid earth whereas the inside is really hollow. Thus the outside of the hypocrite has the appearance of faith while inwardly it is really disbelief.'

يُخَٰدِعُونَ ٱللَّهَ وَٱلَّذِينَ ءَامَنُوا۟ وَمَا يُخَٰدِعُونَ إِلَّآ أَنفُسَهُمْ وَمَا يَشْعُرُونَ ﴿٩﴾

9 They think they deceive Allah and those who believe. They deceive no one but themselves but they are not aware of it.

They think they deceive Allah and those who believe.

Our scholars have said that their imagined deceit of Allah is in themselves and in their thinking. It is said that it is by their actions, which are those of a deceiver. It is said that there is something elided here and that what is really meant is deceit of the Messenger of Allah ﷺ. Al-Ḥasan and others said that. Allah has made their deceit of His Messenger equivalent to deceit of Himself because the Prophet ﷺ called them using Allah's Words. The same applies to their deceit of the believers as a whole: in reality they are trying to deceive Allah. Their deceit lies in their display of faith which differs from the disbelief they conceal. This results in their lives and property being spared and makes them think that they are safe and have been successful in deceiving the believers. Some interpreters said that.

Linguists say that the root of the verb '*khadā'a*' (deceit) means corruption. So the meaning is that they corrupt their faith and actions, in respect of what is between them and Allah, by showing off. This is explained by the Prophet ﷺ. Its root is also said to signify concealment, from which comes *mikhda'*, a cabinet in which something is kept in the house. One form of the word is used of a hyena concealing itself in its den.

They deceive no one but themselves

The words, '*They deceive no one but themselves,*' mean that the result of what they do is that only they are deceived. There is a saying: 'Whoever tries to deceive someone who is not deceived has deceived himself.' This is true because deceit can only occur in respect of someone who does not know the inward reality. Any attempt to deceive someone who knows what is really going on is inevitably self-deceit. This is proof that the hypocrites do not recognise Allah since they do not know that He is not deceived. The Prophet ﷺ said, 'Do not deceive Allah. If anyone deceives Allah, Allah deceives him and his self deceives him while he is not aware.' They asked, 'Messenger of Allah, how can Allah be deceived?' He replied, 'By your doing what Allah has commanded while seeking the pleasure of another by it.' The full extent of this deception will be seen in the interpretation of Allah's words: '*Allah is mocking them.*' (2:15)

Nāfi', Ibn Kathīr and Abū 'Amr read, *yukhādi'ūna* for 'deceive' both times it occurs, whereas 'Āṣim, Ḥamzah, al-Kisā'ī and Ibn 'Āmir read *yakhda'ūna*, without the middle *alif* the second time.

but they are not aware of it.

This means that they do not understand that the evil of their deception will come back on them; they think that they will be saved and win by their deceit. That may seem to be the case in this world but in the Next World they will be told, *'Go back and look for light.'* (57:13) Linguists say that 'being aware of a thing' is to comprehend it.

فِي قُلُوبِهِم مَّرَضٌ فَزَادَهُمُ ٱللَّهُ مَرَضًا وَلَهُمْ عَذَابٌ أَلِيمٌۢ بِمَا كَانُوا۟ يَكْذِبُونَ ﴿١٠﴾

10 There is a sickness in their hearts and Allah has increased their sickness. They will have a painful punishment on account of their denial.

There is a sickness in their hearts

In the words *'a sickness in their hearts'*, sickness is a metaphor for the corruption caused by their lack of faith. That is either doubt and hypocrisy or denial and repudiation. The meaning is that their hearts are sick since they lack the protection, success and support which come from true faith. Ibn Fāris, the linguist, says that sickness is anything which removes a person from good health such as illness, hypocrisy, or shortcoming in something.

and Allah has increased their sickness

This is a supplication against them. The meaning of these words is that Allah has increased them in doubt and hypocrisy on top of their disbelief and lack of support and lack of power. So this *āyah* indicates the permission to pray against the hypocrites and expel them because they are the worst of Allah's creatures. Indeed one possibility is that the words actually are a supplication against them with the meaning, 'May Allah increase their sickness'. It is said that the phrase is simply information from Allah about their increased sickness, meaning sickness on top of their sickness. He says in another *āyah*: *'It adds defilement to their defilement.'* (9:125)

Those with knowledge of the precise use of language say that the first *'sickness in their hearts'* is because of their reliance on this world and their love for it and their neglect of the Next World and their turning away from it. Then Allah's words *'Allah has increased their sickness'* mean that He has thrown them back on themselves and loaded them with the cares of this world, so that they are unable to break through them and turn to concern for the Next World. Al-Junayd said, 'Sickness of the heart comes from following the lower desires, and sickness of the limbs comes from the sickness of the body itself.'

on account of their denial.

This refers to their denial of the Messengers and rejection of Allah. It is their denial of His *āyahs*. 'Āṣim, Ḥamzah and al-Kisā'ī recite *'yakdhibūna'* meaning 'because of their lying'.

Scholars disagree about why the Prophet ﷺ left the hypocrites alone even though he knew that they were hypocrites. There are basically four positions.

Some scholars say that he did not kill them because he was the only one who knew their state. Without exception, scholars agree that a qāḍī may not issue a sentence of execution on the basis of personal knowledge. They disagree about lesser sentences.

Ibn al-'Arabī said, 'This is contradictory. Al-Mujadhdhir ibn Ziyād was killed by al-Ḥārith ibn Suwayd ibn aṣ-Ṣāmit because al-Mujadhdhir had killed his father, Suwayd, in the Battle of Bu'āth. Al-Ḥārith became Muslim and was ignored during the Battle of Uḥud and he killed al-Mujadhdhir. Jibrīl informed the Prophet ﷺ and he had him killed because he had murdered him, and treacherous murder incurs one of the *hudūd* of Allah.' This is negligence on the part of this imam because if this consensus is confirmed, it is not contradictory with what he mentioned because consensus was only established after the death of the Prophet ﷺ and the end of Revelation. That case was a specific one based on Revelation and so it is not used as a proof nor is it superseded by consensus. Allah knows best.

The people of ash-Shāfi'i say that he did not kill the hypocrites because a *zindīq*, who is someone who conceals disbelief and shows faith, is asked to repent and is not killed. Ibn al-'Arabī said, 'This is weak. The Prophet ﷺ did not ask them to repent and no one transmits that and no one says that it is obligatory to ask *zindiqs* (heretics) to repent. The Prophet ﷺ left them alone in spite of his knowledge of them.'

He did not kill them in order to bring hearts closer to him and so that people would not be alienated. The Prophet ﷺ indicated this when he said to 'Umar, 'I seek refuge with Allah from people saying that I kill my Companions.' Al-Bukhārī and Muslim transmitted it. He used to give people things to bring their hearts closer although he knew about their weak belief. This is the position of our scholars and others. Ibn 'Aṭiyyah said that this is the approach of the people of Mālik when talking about the Messenger of Allah ﷺ refraining from the hypocrites, as stated by Muḥammad ibn al-Jahm, Qāḍī Ismā'īl, al-Abharī and Ibn al-Mājishūn.

As for those who use the words of Allah Almighty: *'If the hypocrites and those with sickness in their hearts do not desist'* to the words *'mercilessly put to death'* (33:60-61) as justification for killing hypocrites, Qatādah said that this only applies when they make their hypocrisy public. Mālik said, 'Hypocrisy in the time of the Messenger of Allah ﷺ is like heresy among us today. If there is firm evidence against him, a *zindīq* is killed without being asked to repent.' This is one of the positions of ash-Shafi'ī.

Mālik said that the Messenger of Allah ﷺ refrained from killing hypocrites to make it clear to his Community that a ruler is not permitted to judge by personal knowledge when there is no other clear evidence against someone. Qāḍī Ismā'īl said, 'There was no witness against 'Abdullāh ibn Ubayy, except for Zayd ibn Arqam alone, nor against al-Julās ibn Suwayd, except 'Umayr ibn Sa'd, his foster son. If two men had testified to the disbelief and hypocrisy of either of the two men, they would have been killed.'

Ash-Shāfi'ī gave the evidence for the other position when he said, 'The sunnah about someone against whom there is evidence of heresy and who then denies it and proclaims his faith and that he is free of every *dīn* except Islam is that it is forbidden to shed his blood.' That is what was stated by the people of opinion (*ra'y*), Aḥmad, aṭ-Ṭabarī and others. Ash-Shāfi'ī and his people said, 'The Messenger of Allah ﷺ forbade killing hypocrites as long as they display Islam, even when it is known that they are hypocrites, because what they display outwardly must be accepted.'

Aṭ-Ṭabarī said, 'Allah Almighty made the rulings between his slaves dependent on the outward and entrusted judgment about their secret beliefs to none of His creation. No one can judge against what is apparent because that would be judgment by supposition. If anyone had been entitled to do that, the most entitled would have been the Messenger of Allah ﷺ. He judged the hypocrites to be Muslims because of what they displayed outwardly and left their secrets to Allah.' Allah says that their outward appearance is false: *'Allah bears witness that the hypocrites are certainly liars.'* (63:1)

There is debate about this distinction. The Prophet ﷺ used to know them – or many of them – by their names and persons by Allah's informing him of who they were. Ḥudhayfah also knew who they were since the Prophet ﷺ told him so that

'Umar used to ask him, 'Ḥudhayfah, who are they?' He refused to answer.

Allah preserved the Companions of his Prophet since he made them firm against the efforts of the hypocrites to corrupt them or corrupt their *dīn* and for this reason there was no harm in their remaining. That is not the case today because we are not safe from the heretics corrupting our common people and the ignorant among us.

وَإِذَا قِيلَ لَهُمْ لَا تُفْسِدُوا فِي الْأَرْضِ قَالُوا إِنَّمَا نَحْنُ مُصْلِحُونَ ﴿١١﴾

11 When they are told, 'Do not cause corruption on the earth,' they say, 'We are only putting things right.'

Corruption is the opposite of rightness. Its reality is turning from rectitude to its opposite. The meaning in the *āyah* is: 'Do not cause corruption on the earth through disbelief and friendliness with unbelievers and making people abandon their faith in Muḥammad ﷺ and the Qur'an.' It is said that the earth, before the Prophet ﷺ was sent, was full of corruption and many acts of disobedience were done in it. When the Messenger of Allah ﷺ was sent, the corruption was eliminated and the earth put right. Then, when people again perpetrated acts of disobedience, they corrupted the earth after it had been put right, as Allah says in another *āyah*: *'Do not corrupt the earth after it has been put right.'* (7:56)

The word for earth (*arḍ*) is feminine and is a generic term so that it means the earth in general. Everything under the sky is earth. The word *arīḍ* means wide. A common curse is, 'May you have no land (*arḍ*)'. *Arḍ* also means the shakes and shaking. It also means catarrh. One derived word means a young palm-tree which is an off-shoot. *Irāḍ* is a large carpet of wool or hair. A man who is *arīḍ* is humble and disposed to do good.

they say, "We are only putting things right."

'Putting things right' (*ṣalāḥ*) is the opposite of corruption. They say this because they are under the illusion that their corruption is putting things right. One aspect of it is what they do for unbelievers under the false impression that they are setting things right between them and the believers.

أَلَا إِنَّهُمْ هُمُ الْمُفْسِدُونَ وَلَٰكِن لَّا يَشْعُرُونَ ﴿١٢﴾

12 No indeed! They are the corrupters, but they are not aware of it.

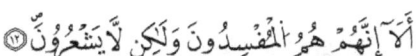

No indeed! They are the corrupters,

These words are to refute their claims and to deny what they said. Those with knowledge of the precise use of language say that it shows that their claim is a lie. Do you not see that Allah says: *'They are corrupters'*? This is the truth.

but they are not aware of it

There are two opinions about this. One is that they do corruption secretly and display righteousness and are not aware that what they were doing was known by the Prophet ﷺ. The other aspect is that they consider their corruption to be righteousness and are not aware that it is corruption and that they have disobeyed Allah and His Messenger by not making the truth clear and then following it.

وَإِذَا قِيلَ لَهُمْ ءَامِنُوا۟ كَمَآ ءَامَنَ ٱلنَّاسُ قَالُوٓا۟ أَنُؤْمِنُ كَمَآ ءَامَنَ ٱلسُّفَهَآءُ ۗ أَلَآ
إِنَّهُمْ هُمُ ٱلسُّفَهَآءُ وَلَٰكِن لَّا يَعْلَمُونَ ﴿١٣﴾

13 When they are told, "Believe in the way that the people believe," they say, "What! Are we to believe in the way that fools believe?" No indeed! They are the fools but they do not know it.

When they are told,

'They' refers to the hypocrites, according to Muqātil and others.

"Believe in the way that the people believe,"

This means to affirm Muhammad ﷺ and his Sharī'ah in the same way that that the Muhājirūn and the people of Yathrib who had become Muslim affirmed them.

They say, "What! Are we to believe in the way that fools believe?"

This was said by the hypocrites who used to say it when they mocked and made fun of Islam, referring to the Companions of Muḥammad ﷺ. Ibn 'Abbās said that, and he also said that it was the believers of the People of the Book who were intended by their words. Allah acquainted His Prophet ﷺ and the believers with what they said.

No indeed! They are the fools,

Allah confirmed that they possess foolishness, lack of understanding and lack of insight, and they are the ones properly described by that. He reported that they are the fools but they do not realise that they are because of the rust covering their hearts.

Al-Kalbī related from Abū Ṣāliḥ from Ibn 'Abbās that this *āyah* was revealed about the Jews so that when it was said to them, 'Believe in the way that the people believe,' i.e. 'Abdullāh ibn Sallām and his companions, they said, 'What! Are we to believe in the way that fools believe?' meaning the ignorant and superstitious Arabs.

The root of *safah* (foolishness) is lightness and shallowness. It is used of woven cloth when it is flimsy and badly woven and suggests shabbiness. It is used for the wind which makes the branches of a tree move. It is used to disparage a person. *Safah* is the opposite of *ḥilm* (forbearance).

But they do not know it.

These words are like 'They are not aware of it.' Knowledge is recognising and knowing something for what it is.

وَإِذَا لَقُوا۟ ٱلَّذِينَ ءَامَنُوا۟ قَالُوٓا۟ ءَامَنَّا وَإِذَا خَلَوْا۟ إِلَىٰ شَيَٰطِينِهِمْ قَالُوٓا۟ إِنَّا مَعَكُمْ إِنَّمَا نَحْنُ مُسْتَهْزِءُونَ ﴿١٤﴾

14 When they meet those who believe, they say 'We believe.' But then when they go apart with their shayṭāns, they say, 'We are really with you. We were only mocking.'

This *āyah* was revealed about the hypocrites.

When they go apart with their shayṭāns,

Commentators disagree about the meaning of shayṭāns here. Ibn 'Abbās and as-Suddī said that they are the leaders of the hypocrites. Al-Kalbī said that they are the shayṭāns of the jinn. A group of commentators said that they are the soothsayers. 'Shaytāns' means people distant from faith. The best course is to combine all of these meanings. Allah knows best.

they say, 'We are really with you. We were only mocking.'

This is the proof against them because, with these words, they negate their claim to be believers. It is said that it means making fun of the believers. *Haz'* is mockery and playing about.

ٱللَّهُ يَسْتَهْزِئُ بِهِمْ وَيَمُدُّهُمْ فِى طُغْيَٰنِهِمْ يَعْمَهُونَ ﴿١٥﴾

15 But Allah is mocking them, and drawing them on, as they wander blindly in their excessive insolence.

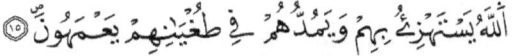

But Allah is mocking them,

This means taking revenge on them and punishing them. He mocks them and repays them for their mocking. The punishment they receive has the same name as the wrong action they commit. This is the statement of the majority of scholars and is a common Arabic usage.

Al-Kalbī related from Abū Ṣāliḥ from Ibn 'Abbās that this *āyah* refers to the hypocrites of the People of the Book. He mentioned them and their mocking and that when they withdraw to their shayṭāns, meaning their leaders in disbelief, they said, 'We are with you in your religion. We were only mocking the Companions of Muḥammad.' Allah will mock them in the Next World and open for them a door between Hell and the Garden and they will be told, 'Come,' and they will come swimming in the Fire while the believers are on beds in alcoves looking at them. When they reach the door, it will be shut against them and the believers will laugh at them. According to this understanding the words *'Allah is mocking them'* refer to something which happens in the Next World. The believers will laugh at them when the doors are locked against them. That is confirmed by the words of the Almighty: *'those who believe are laughing at the unbelievers, on couches, gazing in wonder'* (83:34-35) at the people of the Fire. *'Have not the unbelievers been rewarded for what they did?'* (83:36)

Some people say that Allah's mocking takes the form of drawing them on by degrees in allowing them to experience the blessings of this world. Allah Almighty shows them kindness in this world, contrary to the reality of their situation which is hidden from them, and veils them from the punishment of the Next World so that they think that He is pleased with them when, in fact, the Almighty has foreordained their punishment. A human being considers this to be mocking, deceit, and tricking.

The Prophet ﷺ indicated this interpretation by his words: 'When you see Allah Almighty, giving a person what he wants when he continues to perform acts of disobedience, that is part of drawing on.' Then he finished with this *āyah*: *'When they forgot what they had been reminded of, We opened up for them the doors of everything, until, when they were exulting in what they had been given, We suddenly seized them and at once they were in despair. So the last remnant of the people who did wrong was cut off. Praise belongs to Allah, the Lord of the worlds.'* (6:44-45). Some scholars say that the meaning of the *āyah*, *'We will lead them on from where they do not know'* (7:182), is that when they commit a sin, they receive a blessing.

and drawing them on,

This phrase means allowing them a long period of respite, as we find in Allah's words: *'We only allow them more time so that they will increase in evildoing.'* (3:178) The verbal root means increase. Yūnus ibn Ḥabīb said, 'It is said that Allah gives to them when they commit evil in just the same way that He gives to them when they do good. Allah Almighty says: *"We supplied you with property and sons."* (17:6) He says: *"We will supply them with fruit and meat they desire."* (52:22)' Al-Akhfash said, 'It means to give.' Al-Farrā' and al-Lahyānī said, 'It is to give more of the same. It is used giving support, as when you reinforce an army.' Allah says: *'with seven seas more.'* (31:27)

they wander blindly

Mujāhid said, 'They go to and fro, confused in disbelief.' The scholars of language use it for when someone is confused and vacillates. It is used for camels that do not know which way to go. *'Amā* signifies blindness of the eyes and *'amah*, as is used here, signifies blindness of the heart. We find in Revelation: *'It is not eyes that are blind but hearts in breasts that are blind.'* (22:46)

in their excessive insolence.

Their disbelief and misguidance. The basic meaning of the words 'excessive insolence' comes from the idea of overflowing or going over the limits of something. We find the same root used in the words of the Almighty: *'When the waters rose'* (69:11), meaning rose high and overflowed the banks of the reservoir. It is also used of Pharaoh when Allah says: *'He overstepped'* (20:24), meaning that he was excessive in his claim when he said, *'I am your Lord Most High.'* (79:24) The meaning in the *āyah* is to extend the length of their lives so that they increase in insolence and so that their punishment will in turn be increased.

أُوْلَٰٓئِكَ ٱلَّذِينَ ٱشْتَرَوُاْ ٱلضَّلَٰلَةَ بِٱلْهُدَىٰ فَمَا رَبِحَت تِّجَٰرَتُهُمْ وَمَا
كَانُواْ مُهْتَدِينَ ١٦

16 Those are the people who have sold guidance for misguidance. Their trade has brought no profit; they are not guided.

Those are the people who have sold guidance for misguidance.

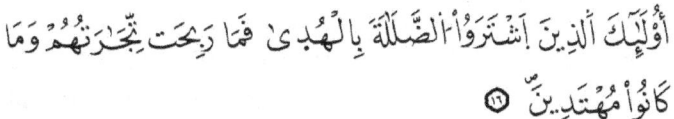

Selling here is a metaphor. It means that these people have preferred disbelief to belief, because the act of buying and selling only occurs when someone desires one thing rather than another. No real exchange is involved here, however, because the hypocrites are not really believers in the first place so in fact they have no faith to sell. Ibn 'Abbās said, 'They take misguidance and abandon guidance.' It means that they choose disbelief over belief. The business metaphor is appropriate because buying and selling refer to replacing one thing with another and the Arabs used it in this way.

Misguidance (*ḍalāl*) is bewilderment. Forgetfulness is called misguidance because of the confusion it entails. It can mean being forgotten. Death is also sometimes called misguidance as in Allah's Words: *'They said, "When we have been absorbed (*ḍalāl*) into the earth."'* (32:10)

Their trade has brought no profit.

Allah ascribed profit to trade since it is the custom of the Arabs to use terms related to commerce metaphorically in this context. It means that they have made no profit in the transaction they have made.

They are not guided.

There is misguidance in the transaction they have made. It is said that is in the prior knowledge of Allah. Guidance is the opposite of misguidance.

مثلهم كمثل الذي استوقد نارا فلما أضاءت ما حوله ذهب الله بنورهم
وتركهم في ظلمات لا يبصرون ﴿١٧﴾

17 Their likeness is that of people who light a fire, and then when it has lit up all around it, Allah removes their light and leaves them in darkness, unable to see.

Some of this *āyah* is in the singular and some in the plural. Some people say that the word *alladhī*, which is usually singular, has a plural meaning here and means people who light, and this is borne out by the fact that the *āyah* begins and ends with the plural usage of 'their' and 'them'. Others say that the singular is used because it only takes one person to actually light the fire among the group who undertake to do it. When the light is gone, the effect is the same for all of them and so Allah says: '*their light*'. The pronoun 'their' refers to the hypocrites and this depicts their state in the Next World, as Allah does in another place when He says: *'A wall will be erected between them with a gate in it.'* (57:13) Someone who lights a fire in darkness can only see a short distance, just as the hypocrite remains lost in his confusion and vacillation.

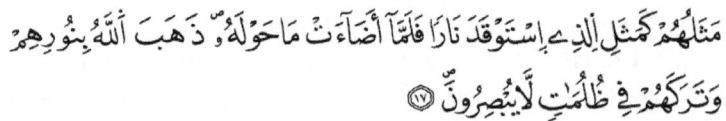

The *āyah* is a metaphor which illustrates the true reality of the hypocrites. They make a show of faith taking advantage of the judgments of Islam in respect of marriage, inheritance, booty, and other such things and giving security to themselves, their children and their property. This is like someone who lights a fire on a dark night and it gives him just enough light to see what he needs to protect himself. But when it goes out he is no longer safe from harm and he becomes confused. That is how the hypocrites are when they imagine that they are deceiving the believers by uttering the Words of Islam. Then, after they die, they will go to the painful punishment since, *'The hypocrites are in the lowest level of the Fire'* (41:45) and their light vanishes. They say, *'Let us borrow some of your light.'* (57:13). It is said that the approach and words of the hypocrites to the Muslims are like fire and their turning from love of them and their reversal is like its extinguishing. Others things are said. The word for fire (*nār*) is derived from the word for light (*nūr*), as fire gives light. The plural of *nūr* is *anwār* and that of *nār* is *nīrān*. *Ẓulumāt* is the plural of *ẓulmah* (darkness).

صُمٌّۢ بُكۡمٌ عُمۡيٞ فَهُمۡ لَا يَرۡجِعُونَ ١٨

18 Deaf, dumb, blind. They will not return.

It means that they are deaf. The reading of 'Abdullāh ibn Mas'ūd and Ḥafṣah has it in the accusative which can be for censure. The word for deafness in Arabic (*ṣimām*) comes from a word which means to be blocked, like a canal which is silted up or like a vial with a stopper in it. So a deaf person is someone whose hearing is blocked up. The word for dumb (*bukm*) used here refers to those who cannot speak or understand. If someone can understand, the word used is *akhras*. It is also said that they mean the same thing. The word *'umy* (blind) is used of those who have lost their sight. It is also said that someone is 'blind' when he is confused. What is meant here is not the actual senses themselves, rather what is intended is the negation of the ability to perceive the truth. Qatādah said of this that they are deaf to hearing the truth, dumb to speaking it and blind to seeing it. This meaning was used by the Prophet ﷺ in describing the ruler when the Final Hour is near in the hadith of Jibrīl. Allah knows best.

They will not return.

They will not return to the truth. Allah says this from the position of His prior knowledge of them.

أَوْ كَصَيِّبٍ مِّنَ ٱلسَّمَآءِ فِيهِ ظُلُمَٰتٌ وَرَعْدٌ وَبَرْقٌ يَجْعَلُونَ أَصَٰبِعَهُمْ فِىٓ
ءَاذَانِهِم مِّنَ ٱلصَّوَٰعِقِ حَذَرَ ٱلْمَوْتِ ۚ وَٱللَّهُ مُحِيطٌۢ بِٱلْكَٰفِرِينَ ﴿١٩﴾

19 Or that of a storm-cloud in the sky, full of darkness, thunder and lightning. They put their fingers in their ears against the thunderclaps, fearful of death. Allah encompasses the unbelievers.

Or that of a storm-cloud in the sky

At-Ṭabarī says that the 'or' here, in fact, means 'and', and it is also said that the 'or' is in order to give a choice between the two neighbours so as not to confine the description of the hypocrites to just one of them.

The word for sky, *samā'*, which means sky or heaven, is everything that is above you and covers you. So the roof of a house is sometimes called *samā'*. The word can also designate the rain because rain descends from the sky. Herbage is also sometimes called *samā'* in Arabic because it covers the ground. Heaven is what is above and the earth is what is underneath.

full of darkness, thunder and lightning.

The word *ẓumulāt* (darkness) is in the plural, indicating both the darkness of night and the darkness of the clouds which are piled up.

Scholars disagree about what thunder is. At-Tirmidhī reports that Ibn 'Abbās said, 'The Jews asked the Prophet ﷺ what thunder was. He said, "One of the angels is entrusted with the clouds and wields a fiery sword with which he drives the clouds wherever he wishes." They asked, "What is this sound we hear?' He answered, "He hits the clouds when he pushes them until they go wherever Allah has commanded." They said, "You have spoken the truth."' It is a long hadith. Many scholars accept this explanation. Thunder is the name of the sound heard. 'Alī said that. It is reported from Ibn 'Abbās that it is a wind caught between the clouds which causes that sound.

They also disagree about lightning. It is reported from 'Alī, Ibn Mas'ūd and Ibn 'Abbās that lightning comes from the iron bar in the hand of an angel with which he drives the clouds. This is the literal meaning of the hadith of at-Tirmidhī. Ibn 'Abbās also said that it is a whip of fire in the hand of an angel with which he drives the clouds.

Scientists say that thunder is the sound of the collision of the clouds and lightning is what is sparked by their collision. This is rejected and not transmitted and

Allah knows best. It is said that the root of thunder (*ra'd*) means movement. Hence *ri'dīd* is used for a coward. One form of the word means to tremble. The root of the word for lightning, *barq*, means 'glittering' and 'a bright light'. Associated with that is Burāq, the animal that the Messenger of Allah ﷺ rode in the Night Journey and which the Prophets before him rode. The sky trembles from thunder and flashes light with lightning

Ibn 'Abbās reported, 'We were with 'Umar ibn al-Khaṭṭāb on a journey between Madīnah and Syria with Ka'b al-Aḥbār. There was a wind and then rain, strong wind and hail. The people separated. Ka'b told me, "If someone hears the thunder and then says, 'Glory be to the One *'whom the thunder glorifies His praise and the angels from fear of Him'* (13:13), he is safe from what is in these clouds, hail and thunderclaps." I said it as did Ka'b. In the morning the people gathered and I said to 'Umar, "Amīr al-Mu'minīn, we were in a different situation to everyone else." "And why is that?" he asked. I told him the hadith of Ka'b. He said, "Glory be to Allah! Why didn't you tell us so that we could say the same as you said!"' Ibn 'Umar reported about the Prophet ﷺ, 'When he heard thunder and lightning, he said, "O Allah, do not kill us with Your anger or destroy us with Your punishment, and protect us from them."'

They put their fingers in their ears

So that they will not hear the Qur'an and thereby believe in it and in Muḥammad ﷺ. That was disbelief for them and disbelief is death.

against the thunderclaps,

To protect them from the thunderclaps. Ibn 'Abbās, Mujāhid and others said that, when the force of the thunder is very strong, there is an angel who wields the fire from within, which is the lightning. Al-Khalīl said, 'It is the strong event arising from the sound of the thunder which is accompanied by flashes of fire which burn what they strike.' Abū Zayd said, 'The fire that falls from the sky is strong thunder.' The word 'thunderclaps' is also used for the blast and 'the Shout' which is a punishment with which Allah strikes the unbelievers. Allah says: *'The lightning-bolt of the humiliating punishment seized them.'* (41:17) The verb *ṣu'iqa* means to faint as in 7:143. And Allah says: *'those in the earth will lose consciousness'* which means that they will die.

In this *āyah* Allah likens the states of the hypocrites to the darkness, lightning and thunderclaps which are found in a cloudburst. Darkness resembles their disbelief, and thunder and lightning is like what they fear. Blindness is also darkness. It contains a threat and rebuke, which is the thunder, and radiant proofs, which can be dazzling like the lightning. The thunderclaps represent what the Qur'an contains of being summoned to fight and the threat of the punishment in the Hereafter. It is said that the 'thunderclaps' are the burdens of the Sharī'ah which they hate, such as *jihād*, *zakāt* and other things.

Allah encompasses the unbelievers.

They cannot evade Him. This linguistic term is used when someone is hemmed in on all sides. Allah encompasses all creatures, meaning they are in His grasp and under His power. This means that He knows everything about them. It is said that it means He will destroy them and bring them all together. The unbelievers are singled out because they were mentioned earlier in the *āyah*, and Allah knows best.

يَكَادُ ٱلْبَرْقُ يَخْطَفُ أَبْصَٰرَهُمْ كُلَّمَآ أَضَآءَ لَهُم مَّشَوْاْ فِيهِ وَإِذَآ أَظْلَمَ
عَلَيْهِمْ قَامُواْ وَلَوْ شَآءَ ٱللَّهُ لَذَهَبَ بِسَمْعِهِمْ وَأَبْصَٰرِهِمْ إِنَّ ٱللَّهَ عَلَىٰ كُلِّ
شَىْءٍ قَدِيرٌ ٢٠

20 The lightning all but takes away their sight. Whenever they have light, they walk in it but whenever darkness covers them, they halt. If Allah wished, He could take away their hearing and their sight. Allah has power over all things.

The lightning all but takes away their sight.

The word for 'take away' (*khaṭafa*) used here means taking extremely quickly or snatching. It is used of birds of prey because of their speed. If one takes the Qur'anic metaphor of lightning as indicating alarm, the expression means that their fear of what will happen to them almost takes away their sight. If one takes it as indicating the Qur'anic commands to the believers, it means that it is those which nearly blind them. '*Yakhṭafu*' and '*yakhṭifu*' are two dialectical forms that are recited. *Abṣār* (sight) is the plural of *baṣar*, the faculty of sight. If 'lightning' is metaphorical, then it means that their fear at what befalls them almost removes their sight.

Whenever they have light, they walk in it but whenever darkness covers them, they halt.

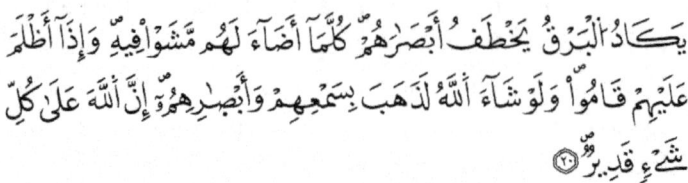

Al-Mubarrad says that what is implied is: 'Whenever the lightning lights up the road for them.' The meaning is that when they hear *āyahs* of the Qur'an which they understand and agree with, they accept them and act by them. But when some *āyahs* are revealed about which they are confused and which they do not understand or find burdensome, they 'halt', in other words they remain fixed in their hypocrisy, as Ibn 'Abbās said. It is said that the meaning is that, when their crops and cattle were flourishing and they had continuous blessings, they said, 'The *dīn* of Muḥammad is a blessed *dīn*.' But when hardship befell them and difficulties afflicted them, they became angry and remained fixed in their hypocrisy, as Ibn Mas'ūd and Qatādah said. The soundness of this is indicated by the words of the Almighty: *'Among the people there is one who worships Allah right on the edge. If good befalls him, he is content with it, but if trial befalls him, he reverts to his former ways.'* (22:11)

Sufi scholars say that this is a metaphor which Allah made for someone whose initial state is made unsound by a self-seeking intention and who, because of that, lays claim to the states of the great. His initial state would have continued to give him illumination if it had remained sound by being accompanied by correct manners. But when he adulterates it with false claims, Allah removes its light from him and he remains in the darkness of his false claims, not seeing any way to emerge from them.

It is also related from Ibn 'Abbās that the people meant here are the Jews since, when the Prophet ﷺ was victorious at Badr, they were greedy and said, 'This, by Allah, is the Prophet of whom Mūsā gave good news. There is no banner which will resist him.' When he suffered a reverse at Uḥud, they went back on that and were full of doubt. This is weak. The *āyah* is about the hypocrites, and this is sounder from Ibn 'Abbās. The meaning can apply to all.

If Allah wished, He could take away their hearing and their sight.

This means that, if Allah had wished, he could have informed the believers about them and removed the protection and power of Islam from them by overwhelming them, killing them and expelling them from their homes. Hearing and sight are specifically mentioned since they were already mentioned in the *āyah* or because they are the noblest senses of the human body.

Allah has power over all things.

This is general. According to the *mutakallimūn,* it means that it is permitted to describe Allah with the attribute of power. The Community agree that Allah has the name *al-Qadīr,* the Powerful. He is described as *Qadīr, Qādir* and *Muqtadir. Qadīr* is more intensive than *Qādir.* Az-Zajjājī said that. Al-Harawī said that they mean the same. Allah has power over every possibility whether it is brought into existence or remains non-existent. All responsible people are obliged to know that Allah possesses the power to act as He wills and He does whatever He wishes according to His knowledge and choice. They must also know that human beings possess a certain limited power through which they obtain what Allah has decreed for them by the use of normal means, but this power is not self-generated.

Allah singled out the attribute of power in this instance because He already mentioned the action which results from the threat and intimidation contained in the *āyahs*, and so power is fitting here. Allah knows best.

The *āyahs* up to this point form an introductory section to the Book of Allah. The first four describe the believers, the next two describe the unbelievers and the rest are about the hypocrites. This transmission was already mentioned from Ibn Jurayj. Mujāhid said that.

يَٰٓأَيُّهَا ٱلنَّاسُ ٱعْبُدُوا۟ رَبَّكُمُ ٱلَّذِى خَلَقَكُمْ وَٱلَّذِينَ مِن قَبْلِكُمْ لَعَلَّكُمْ تَتَّقُونَ ﴿٢١﴾

21 Mankind! worship your Lord, Who created you and those before you, so that hopefully you will be godfearing.

Mankind!

'Alqamah and Mujāhid said that every *āyah* which begins with 'Mankind!' was revealed in Makkah and every one which begins with 'You who believe!' was revealed in Madīnah. That is refuted by the fact that this *sūrah* and *Sūrat an-Nisā'* are definitely Madinan and both contain *āyahs* beginning 'Mankind!'. But what they said about 'You who believe' is true. 'Urwah ibn az-Zubayr said, 'All *ḥudūd* and legal obligations were revealed in Madīnah and what is mentioned about Divine punishment was revealed in Makkah.' This is clear.

There is disagreement about who is meant by 'mankind'. There are two positions. One is that it refers to the unbelievers who do not worship Allah, which is indicated by His words: *'If you have doubts...'* (2:23) The second is that it is all people, in which case the believers are being told to remain constant in their worship and the unbelievers to begin it.

worship your Lord,

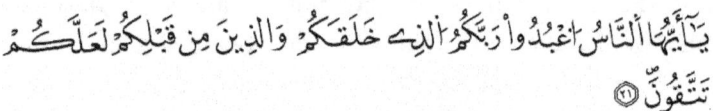

The word 'worship' here designates affirming Allah's unity and holding to laws of His *dīn*. The root of *'ibādah* (worship) means humility and abasement. The word *mu'abbadah* is used for a path made by people's feet. *'Ibādah* also means obedience, devotion and religious practices.

Who created you

Allah mentions His quality as Creator since the Arabs acknowledged that Allah created them. He mentioned that as an argument against them and to rebuke them. It is said that by that He reminded them of His blessings to them. There are two aspects to the basic meaning of creation. The first is determination and the second is origination and genesis.

and those before you,

If it is said that if they admit that He created them, they must also admit that He created others, the answer is that the words are notification and reminding so that it will be more extensive in warning. He reminds them about those before them so that they will know that the One who made those before them die, having created them, will also make them die. They should reflect on the circumstances of those before them and how they died. They know that they will be tested as those others were tested. Allah knows best.

and hopefully you will be godfearing.

This is clearly connected to *'worship your Lord,'* not to *'created you'* because if Allah created someone for Hell, He obviously did not create him to be godfearing.

There are three interpretations of the term *la'alla* (hopefully). The first is its usual meaning of hope and anticipation. Such qualities are within the scope of human beings. It is as if He were saying: 'Do that with the hope and desire that you will be godfearing.' This is the position of Sībuwayh and leading grammarians. The second is that Arabs often use the term to mean 'in order to' and so that it would mean 'in order for you to be godfearing'. Aṭ-Ṭabarī says this. The third is that it means to bring a thing within reach. It is as if He were saying, 'Do that because by accepting Allah's command you will have protection from the Fire.'

ٱلَّذِى جَعَلَ لَكُمُ ٱلْأَرْضَ فِرَٰشًا وَٱلسَّمَآءَ بِنَآءً وَأَنزَلَ مِنَ ٱلسَّمَآءِ مَآءً فَأَخْرَجَ بِهِۦ
مِنَ ٱلثَّمَرَٰتِ رِزْقًا لَّكُمْ فَلَا تَجْعَلُوا۟ لِلَّهِ أَندَادًا وَأَنتُمْ تَعْلَمُونَ ٢٢

22 It is He who made the earth a couch for you and the sky a dome. He sends down water from the sky and by it brings forth fruits for your provision. Do not, then, knowingly make others equal to Allah.

It is He who made the earth a couch for you

The word 'made' (*ja'ala*) can mean create as in the *āyah*: *'He who created/appointed* (ja'ala) *the darkness and the light'* (6:1) and can also mean 'designate' as in: *'We have made* (ja'alnā) *it an Arabic Qur'an'* (43:3) and *'They have assigned* (ja'alū) *to Him a portion'* (43:15).

A 'couch' is something on which people lie and rest. So the description cannot apply to mountains, wild areas and seas, because one of the characteristics of a couch is that it is something on which one reclines. The mountains, however, are described pegs, as we find in: *'Have We not made the earth a flat carpet and the mountains its pegs?'* (78:6-7) and other places, and the seas as something on which one travels to gain benefit as in: *'the ships which sail the seas to people's benefit'* (2:164) and elsewhere.

and the sky a dome.

The sky is to the earth like a roof is to a house Allah says elsewhere: *'We made the sky* (samā') *a preserved and protected roof.'* (21:32). *Samā'* is used for everything which is high and gives shade, as was mentioned earlier.

He sends down water from the sky and by it brings forth fruits for your provision.

The root of *mā'* (water) is *mawh* and the *wāw* has been changed to an *alif* by its vowelling. The words *'and by it brings forth fruits for your provision'* mean that Allah produces various kinds of fruits and plants for us. 'Provision' means food for us and fodder for our animals. This is clear from His words: *'We pour down plentiful water. Then split the earth into furrows. Then We make grain grow in it, and grapes and herbs, and olives and dates, and luxuriant gardens, and orchards and meadows, for you and your livestock to enjoy.'* (80:25-32) We have already discussed the meaning of provision. If it is asked how provision can be used for fruits before they are owned by any owner, the reply is that they are ready to be owned and sound for use and so they constitute provision.

This *āyah* indicates that Allah spares the human being from being dependent on any other creature. The Prophet ﷺ indicated this when he said, 'It is better for one of you to take a rope and carry firewood on his back than for him to go to a man and beg from him who then may give to him or refuse to do so.' Muslim transmitted it. All forms of work are meant by this. Anyone who makes himself dependent on another human being like himself out of laziness, hope and desire for the things of this world has taken the path of someone who makes another equal to Allah.

A Sufi scholar said, 'In this *āyah* Allah speaks about the path of poverty, which is that you make the earth your bed, the sky your cover, water your perfume and grass your food, and do not worship anyone in this world of creatures for the sake of this world. Allah Almighty has given you what you need without owing anything to anyone.' Nawf al-Bikālī said, 'I once saw 'Alī ibn Abī Ṭālib go out and look at the stars. He asked, "Nawf, are you asleep or awake?" I replied, "Awake, Amīr al-Mu'minīn." He said, "Blessed are those who make do with little of this world and desire the Next World. Those are the people who take the ground as a bed, its soil as a mattress, its water as a perfume, and the Qur'an and supplication as a blanket. They reject this world, taking the path of the Messiah."'

Do not then, knowingly, make others equal to Allah.

This means His likes and peers. A poet said:

We praise Allah Who has no equal.
All good is with Him and He does whatever He wills.

Ibn 'Abbās said that the word 'knowingly' is addressed to the unbelievers and hypocrites. It might be asked, 'How can they be described as knowing when Allah has already described them with the attributes of sealing, deafness and blindness?' The answer has two facets. One is that 'knowingly' means the specific knowledge that Allah Almighty created creatures sent down the rain and made provision grow. So they know that He is their Blesser without any equal. The second is that the meaning is that you, in fact, have the strength and ability to know His concern if you were only to reflect and consider. Allah knows best.

This *āyah* contains evidence for the command to use the evidence of the intellect and invalidates blind imitation. Ibn Fūrak said, 'It is possible to apply this *āyah* to the believers in which case it means, 'O believer, do not apostatise and make others equal to Allah when you know that Allah is One.'

وَإِن كُنتُمْ فِي رَيْبٍ مِّمَّا نَزَّلْنَا عَلَىٰ عَبْدِنَا فَأْتُوا بِسُورَةٍ مِّن مِّثْلِهِ وَادْعُوا
شُهَدَاءَكُم مِّن دُونِ اللَّهِ إِن كُنتُمْ صَادِقِينَ ﴿٢٣﴾

23 If you have doubts about what We have sent down to Our slave, produce another sūrah equal to it, and call your witnesses, besides Allah, if you are telling the truth.

If you have doubts about what We have sent down

This refers to the Qur'an and is addressed to the idolaters who are being challenged by Allah. When they heard the Qur'an, they said, 'This does not seem to us like the words of Allah. We have doubts about it.' So *the āyah* was revealed.

It is connected to the previous *āyah* since in that Allah has mentioned evidence of His power and now gives evidence for the Prophethood of His Prophet, showing that what he brings is not a forgery.

our slave

'Our slave' (*'abd*) is Muḥammad ﷺ. *'Abd* is derived from *ta'abbud*, meaning abasement. A slave is so-called because he is submissive. Some people said that *'ibādah* is the noblest of qualities and that being called *"abd'* is the noblest of designations, and so Allah calls His Prophet a slave.

produce another sūrah equal to it,

Ibn Kaysān said that this is a command which, in fact, means that they lack the power to do so, because Allah knew that they would be unable to do it. In the words *'equal to it'* the *'it'* refers to the Qur'an according to the majority, while some say that it refers to the Torah and Gospel. Some say that *'it'* should be read *'him'* and refers to the Prophet ﷺ, meaning "produce a mortal like him, unable to read or write, who is able to produce such words."

and call your witnesses, besides Allah,

This means your helpers and supporters. Al-Farrā' says it means 'your gods'. Ibn Kaysān said, 'If someone asks why witnesses are mentioned here when witnesses testify to a matter, or inform about the matter to which they have witnessed, yet here they are told "to produce a *sūrah*", the answer is that they are ordered to seek the help of their scholars and summon them to witness what they bring. So the *āyah* will refute all of them and be a stronger proof.' Mujāhid said that it means, 'summon people to be your witnesses,' in other words to testify that you are against it.

if you are telling the truth.

This is regarding what you say about being able to match it, since they said elsewhere, *'If we wanted we could say the same thing.'* (8:31) Truthfulness is the opposite of lying. The root meaning of *ṣidq* (truthfulness) is the firmness of a spear. *Ṣiddīq* is someone who is devoted to truthfulness. *Ṣadāqah* (friendship) is derived from the same root and indicates truthfulness in counsel and love.

فَإِن لَّمْ تَفْعَلُوا۟ وَلَن تَفْعَلُوا۟ فَٱتَّقُوا۟ ٱلنَّارَ ٱلَّتِى وَقُودُهَا ٱلنَّاسُ
وَٱلْحِجَارَةُ ۖ أُعِدَّتْ لِلْكَٰفِرِينَ ٢٤

24 If you do not do that – and you will not do it – then fear the Fire whose fuel is people and stones, made ready for the unbelievers.

If you do not do that – and you will not do it –

You will not be able to produce another *sūrah* equal to it. Some commentators say that the *āyah* is about not being able to call witnesses. This is one of the unseen things about which the Qur'an reported before it could happen. Ibn Kaysān said that they were not telling the truth when they said that it was lies, forged, magic, poetry or myths of earlier peoples, as we find elsewhere in the Qur'an. They claimed to have knowledge but could not produce anything like it

then fear the Fire whose fuel is people and stones,

Fear and safeguard yourself against the Fire by believing the Prophet ﷺ and obeying Allah. The word *waqūd* (fuel) refers to firewood and *wuqūd* is burning. The word 'people' is usually general, but its meaning here is particular to those who have been decreed to be the fuel of the Fire. May Allah protect us from it! The 'stones' in this *āyah* are said by Ibn Mas'ūd and al-Farrā' to be black sulphur. It is singled out because it has five qualities of punishment which other minerals do not: speed of burning, foul smell, much smoke, clinging strongly to bodies, and great intensity of heat when it is burned. It is also said that 'stones' means idols since Allah says elsewhere: *'You and what you worship besides Allah are fuel for Hell.'* (21:98)

This *āyah* does not mean that only people and stones are in the Fire. There are indications elsewhere that the jinn and shayṭāns will be in it as well. It is a warning that the Fire is so hot that it burns stones as well as burning people. According to one interpretation, the stones are part of the punishment and the people of the Fire are punished with fire and stones.

A ḥadīth of the Prophet ﷺ says: 'Every harmful thing will be in the Fire.' This has two interpretations. One is that everyone who harms others in this world will be punished by Allah in the Next World with the Fire. The second is that everything which harms people in this world – wild animals, vermin and other things – will be in the Fire to punish the people of the Fire. Some interpreters believe that this fire with stones is particular to the Fire of the unbelievers. Allah knows best.

Muslim related from 'Abbās, 'I said, "Messenger of Allah, Abū Ṭālib used to protect you and support you. Will that benefit him?" He replied, "Yes. I found him in the midst of the Fire and I brought him to a shallow part. If it were not for me, he would have been in the lowest level of the Fire."'

made ready for the unbelievers.

The literal meaning of this phrase would seem to imply that only the unbelievers will enter the Fire but that is not the case, as is mentioned in the threat to wrongdoers and in the firm hadiths about intercession.

It also contains an indication of what the people who hold the true position say about the Fire being already created and in existence, which differs from innovators who state that it has not yet been created. Muslim reported that 'Abdullāh ibn Mas'ūd said, 'We were with the Messenger of Allah ﷺ when he heard something fall. He said, "Do you know what that was?" We said, "Allah and His Messenger know best." He said, "It was a stone which was thrown into the Fire seventy years ago, and it has been falling through the Fire right up until now when it hit the bottom."'

Al-Bukhārī related from Abū Hurayrah that the Messenger of Allah ﷺ said, 'The Garden and the Fire argued and the Fire said, "I have the tyrants and the arrogant." The Garden said, "I have the weak and poor people." Allah Almighty said to the Fire, "You are My punishment by which I punish whomever I will," and He said to the Garden, "You are My mercy by which I show mercy to whomever I will. Each of you will have its fill."' Muslim also transmitted that idea. The Prophet ﷺ saw them both during the Eclipse prayer and in his Night Journey and entered the Garden, and this is irrefutable. Success is by Allah.

وَبَشِّرِ ٱلَّذِينَ ءَامَنُوا۟ وَعَمِلُوا۟ ٱلصَّٰلِحَٰتِ أَنَّ لَهُمْ جَنَّٰتٍ تَجْرِى مِن
تَحْتِهَا ٱلْأَنْهَٰرُ ۖ كُلَّمَا رُزِقُوا۟ مِنْهَا مِن ثَمَرَةٍ رِّزْقًا ۙ قَالُوا۟ هَٰذَا ٱلَّذِى رُزِقْنَا
مِن قَبْلُ ۖ وَأُتُوا۟ بِهِۦ مُتَشَٰبِهًا ۖ وَلَهُمْ فِيهَآ أَزْوَٰجٌ مُّطَهَّرَةٌ ۖ وَهُمْ
فِيهَا خَٰلِدُونَ ﴿٢٥﴾

25 Give the good news to those who believe and do right actions that they will have Gardens with rivers flowing under them. When they are given fruit there as provision, they will say, 'This is what we were given before,' But they were only given a simulation of it. They will have there spouses of perfect purity and will remain there timelessly, for ever.

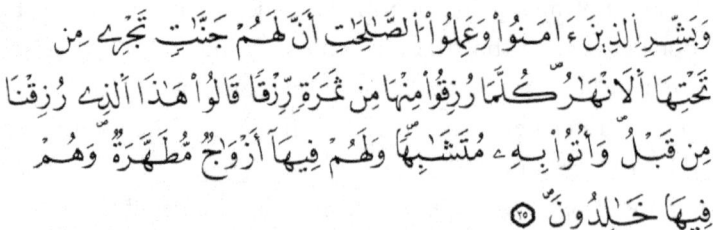

Give the good news to those who believe

Whenever Allah mentions the repayment of the unbelievers, He also mentions the repayment of the believers. Good news (*bushrā*) means a report about something which produces an effect which is seen on the outer skin (*basharah*). It is usually used for joy connected to the news of some good occurrence but can also be used for news of a sorrowful or evil type. Allah says, using the same word: *'Give him the news of a painful punishment.'* (45:8)

and do right actions

This refutes those who say that faith alone is sufficient to gain Divine reward, because if that had been the case, Allah would not have added right actions. The Garden is obtained by faith and right actions. It is also said that the Garden is obtained by faith and the different degrees in it by right actions. Allah knows best.

that they will have Gardens.

The 'Gardens' are given that name because they shade those in them with their trees.

with rivers flowing under them.

It is related that the rivers of the Garden are not in channels, but flow on the surface, held in place by Divine power, flowing wherever its inhabitants wish. They flow under those trees.

When they are given fruit there as provision, they will say, 'This is what we were given before.'

'Before' means in this world. There are two aspects to this. One is that their words mean, 'This is what we were promised in the world below,' and the second is that they actually mean, 'This is what we were given in the world below' because the colour of the fruits they receive there resembles the colour of the fruits of this world. But when they eat it, they find the taste different. It is said that 'before' refers to earlier during their time in the Garden because they were given provision there and then later are given more provision. They are given food and fruit at the beginning of the day and eat it and then, when they are given it at the end of the day, they say this, but then they find that the taste is different.

But they were only given a simulation of it.

This means that it is similar in appearance but differs in taste. Ibn 'Abbās, Mujāhid, al-Ḥasan and others said that. 'Ikrimah said that it resembles the fruit of this world but differs from it in almost every way. Ibn 'Abbās said, 'This is an expression of wonderment. There is nothing of this world which is in the Garden except the names of things. So it is as if they wonder when they see the excellence of the fruit and its great size.' Qatādah said that all of it is the best and there is nothing inferior in it, unlike fruits in this world.

They will have there spouses of perfect purity

'Spouse' in Arabic can refer to husband or wife. 'Purity' means that they are free of menstruation, phlegm and all human impurities. Mujāhid said that they do not urinate, defecate, give birth, menstruate, ejaculate or expectorate.

and will remain there timelessly, for ever.

Remaining timelessly, forever (*khulūd*) means staying for time without end, from which comes 'the Garden of Eternity'. It is used metaphorically for something which is of extremely long duration.

إِنَّ ٱللَّهَ لَا يَسْتَحْىِۦٓ أَن يَضْرِبَ مَثَلًا مَّا بَعُوضَةً فَمَا فَوْقَهَا ۚ فَأَمَّا
ٱلَّذِينَ ءَامَنُوا۟ فَيَعْلَمُونَ أَنَّهُ ٱلْحَقُّ مِن رَّبِّهِمْ ۖ وَأَمَّا ٱلَّذِينَ
كَفَرُوا۟ فَيَقُولُونَ مَاذَآ أَرَادَ ٱللَّهُ بِهَٰذَا مَثَلًا ۘ يُضِلُّ بِهِۦ كَثِيرًا
وَيَهْدِى بِهِۦ كَثِيرًا ۚ وَمَا يُضِلُّ بِهِۦٓ إِلَّا ٱلْفَٰسِقِينَ ﴿٢٦﴾

26 Allah is not ashamed to make an example of a gnat or of an even smaller thing. As for those who believe, they know it is the truth from their Lord. But as for those who disbelieve, they say, 'What does Allah mean by this example?' He misguides many by it and guides many by it. But He only misguides the deviators.

Allah is not ashamed to make an example of a gnat

Ibn 'Abbās said, 'When Allah Almighty made the two earlier metaphors for the hypocrites (2:17 and 2:19), people said. "Allah is too high and exalted to make metaphors." Therefore Allah revealed this *āyah*.'

In the transmission of 'Aṭā' from Ibn 'Abbās we find: 'When Allah mentioned the gods of the idolaters, and said: *"If a fly steals something from them, they cannot get it back,"* (22:73), and He mentioned the stratagems of their gods and compared them to a spider's web (cf. 29:41), they said, "Do you see that Allah mentions flies and spiders in the Qur'an He revealed to Muḥammad? How can He possibly do that?" So Allah revealed this.' Al-Ḥasan and Qatādah said that when Allah mentioned flies and the spider in the Book, the Jews laughed and said, 'This has got nothing to do with Divine Revelation,' and so Allah revealed this *āyah.*

Commentators disagree on the meaning of the word '*yastaḥyī*' (ashamed) in this *āyah.* It is said that it means, 'does not fear,' which aṭ-Ṭabarī prefers. Others say that it means, 'does not fail to' or 'does not refuse to'. The root means to withdraw from doing a thing and refuse to do it out of fear of the occurrence of something ugly. This is impossible for Allah. In *Ṣaḥīḥ Muslim,* Umm Salamah mentioned that Umm Sulaym came to the Prophet ﷺ and said, 'Messenger of Allah, Allah is not ashamed of the truth,' meaning that He commanded people not to be to embarrassed to ask about it.

or of an even smaller thing.

'*Wa mā fawqahā*' (lit. 'what is above it') means linguistically – and Allah knows best – what is smaller than it. Qatādah and Ibn Jurayj, however, said that it means what is larger.

they know it is the truth from their Lord.

The pronoun 'it' refers to the example, meaning that the example is the truth and the truth is the opposite of the false.

they say, 'What does Allah mean by this example?'

This is not really a question; they are just denying it.

He misguides many by it and guides many by it.

It is said that these are the words of the unbelievers, who say, 'What does Allah means by this example by which people are divided between guidance and misguidance?' It is also said that it is a reply from Allah Almighty and this interpretation is more likely because they affirm that guidance is from Him. In this case it is: 'Say: "He misguides many by it and guides many by it,"' meaning He gives success to some and disappoints others. This is a refutation of the position of the Mu'tazilites and others who say that Allah did not create misguidance or guidance. They said that the meaning of 'misguides many' is only descriptive, in other words He describes such a person as being misguided because in reality Allah Himself does not misguide anyone. This understanding is in fact an example of their misguidance, differs from the statements of the commentators and is linguistically improbable.

But He only misguides the deviators.

He does not misguide anyone except the deviators whom He already knew He would not guide. Nawf al-Bikālī says, "Uzayr said, when speaking to his Lord, "My God, You create creatures and then misguide whomever You wish and guide whomever You wish?" A voice said, "'Uzayr, turn from this! You should turn from this or I will remove your Prophethood from you. I will not be asked about what I do but they will be asked.'"

The basic meaning of *'ḍalāl'* (misguidance) is disintegration. It is used when milk is dispersed in water and Allah says, using that meaning of the word: *'When we have been absorbed into the earth.'* (32:10). The root of *'fisq'* (deviation) is to come out from something and it is used, for instance, to describe a date-stone coming out of its skin and a mouse leaving its hole. In a hadith we find, 'Five animals are all deviant (*fawāsiq*) and can be killed in the Ḥaram and out of it: snakes, crows, mice, rabid dogs and kites.' 'Ā'ishah related it in Muslim. One variant has scorpions instead of snakes. The Prophet ﷺ used the word *fisq* for them because of the harm they do. When a man is *fāsiq* he is impious. In the usage in the Sharī'ah, someone who is *fāsiq* has ceased to obey Allah. It is used both for those who do so in disbelief and those who do so in disobeying Allah.

ٱلَّذِينَ يَنقُضُونَ عَهْدَ ٱللَّهِ مِنۢ بَعْدِ مِيثَٰقِهِۦ وَيَقْطَعُونَ مَآ أَمَرَ ٱللَّهُ
بِهِۦٓ أَن يُوصَلَ وَيُفْسِدُونَ فِى ٱلْأَرْضِ ۚ أُو۟لَٰٓئِكَ هُمُ ٱلْخَٰسِرُونَ ﴿٢٧﴾

27 Those who break Allah's contract after it has been agreed, and sever what Allah has commanded to be joined, and cause corruption on the earth, it is they who are the lost.

Those who break Allah's contract

'Those' refers back to the 'deviators' in the previous *āyah*. The word used here for 'break' (*naqada*) means to nullify what has been concluded of a marriage contract, treaty or other agreement. *Naqada* means unravelled when applied to a rope and *munāqadah*, when used in respect of words, means that they contradict one another.

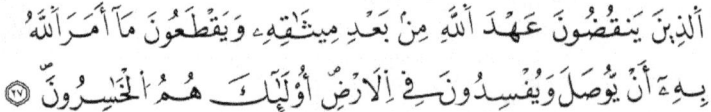

People disagree about the nature of the 'contract' alluded to here. It is said that it is the one which Allah made with all the descendants of Ādam when He brought them forth from his loins. (cf. 7:172) It is said that it is Allah's directive to His creatures, commanding them to obey His commands and forbidding them to disobey Him. This is found in His Books, revealed on the tongues of all His Messengers. 'Breaking it' is to abandon acting by it. It is said that the clear evidence of His Oneness in the heavens and the earth constitutes the contract and breaking it is not grasping it. It is also said that it is Allah's contract with those given the previous Books to make the Prophethood of Muḥammad ﷺ clear and not to conceal it. In this case, the *āyah* is about the People of the Book. Abū Isḥāq az-Zajjāj said, 'The contract is the one He made with the Prophets and those who follow them not to reject the Prophet ﷺ.' The evidence for that is found in: *'When Allah made a covenant with the Prophets … undertake my commission that condition?'* (3:81) The most likely position is that the *āyah* refers to the unbelievers.

after it has been agreed,

The word for 'agreed' (*mithāq*) used here is employed when a contract has been confirmed by oath. It implies firmness in the strength of the contract.

and sever what Allah has commanded to be joined,

Scholars disagree about what Allah has commanded to be joined. It is said that it means to maintain the ties of kinship. It is said that He commanded that words must be joined to action and their severing is by speaking without acting. It is said that the 'joining' refers to Allah's command to affirm all His Prophets but they severed this by affirming some of them and denying others. It is said that it refers to the *dīn* of Allah and His worship on earth, establishing His laws and observing the limits He has imposed. It is general, in that case, to everything that Allah Almighty commanded be joined. This is the statement of the majority. Kinship is, of course, a part of that.

and cause corruption on the earth

This refers to the fact that they worship other than Allah Almighty and commit injustice in what they do in order to fulfill their lower appetites. This is extreme corruption.

it is they who are the lost.

They have lost their fortunes and their honour. This is misguidance and destruction. One who is lost will find he has lost himself and his family on the Day of Rising and will be denied a place in the Garden.

This *āyah* directs people to be trustworthy in their contracts and to hold to that. It is not permitted to break any permissible contract to which you commit yourself, whether it is with a Muslim or anyone else, since Allah Almighty censured those who break their contracts. He says: *'Fulfil your contracts'* (5:1), and He said to His

Prophet ﷺ: *'If you fear treachery on the part of a people, then revoke your treaty with them mutually.'* (8:58). He forbade treachery and that is nothing other than the breaking of a contract, as will be made clear in its proper place.

كَيْفَ تَكْفُرُونَ بِاللَّهِ وَكُنتُمْ أَمْوَٰتًا فَأَحْيَاكُمْ ثُمَّ يُمِيتُكُمْ
ثُمَّ يُحْيِيكُمْ ثُمَّ إِلَيْهِ تُرْجَعُونَ ﴿٢٨﴾

28 How can you reject Allah, when you were dead and then He gave you life, then He will make you die and then give you life again, then you will be returned to Him?

How can you reject Allah

This question conveys amazement. It is extraordinary how anyone can disbelieve when the proof has been established. If it is asked how this can be addressed to the People of the Book when they have belief, the answer is that, although they have not rejected Allah, they did not affirm the Prophethood of Muḥammad ﷺ and accept what he brought. So then they associated something else with Allah because they did not acknowledge that the Qur'an was from Him. Anyone who asserts that the Qur'an is the words of a mortal has associated something else with Allah and therefore broken his contract. It is said that the rebuke means: 'How can you be ungrateful for His blessings to you and reject His power to do this?' Al-Wāsiṭī said that this is used to rebuke them because dead things and inanimate things cannot contend with their Maker in any way at all. Dispute only issues from bodies which possess a *rūḥ*.

and then give you life again,

There is disagreement among the people of interpretation on the order of these two deaths and lives and how many deaths and lives a human being has. Ibn 'Abbās and Ibn Mas'ūd said that it means that you were dead and non-existent before you were created and then He gave you life by creating you. Then He will make you die when your term comes to an end. Then He will bring you to life on the Day of Rising. Ibn 'Aṭiyyah said, 'This is what is meant by the *āyah*. It is a position which the unbelievers must hold since they acknowledge their life and previous non-existence. When the selves of the unbelievers concede that they were dead and non-existent and are now alive in this world, the fact that they will be made to die should make them more open to the possibility of another revivification. Yet they still deny that it has any valid relevance to them.'

Someone else said, 'According to this interpretation, the life in the grave has the same judgment as the life of this world.' It is also said that it means that you were dead in the loins of Ādam and then Allah brought you out from him like atoms and then He made you die the death of this world and then He will resurrect you.

Another interpretation is that it means that you were dead as sperm in the loins of a man and the womb of a woman and then He took you out of the womb and gave you life. Then He will make you die after that in this life and give you life in the grave for the questioning. Then He will make you die in the grave and then give you the life of the resurrection for the Gathering, which is the life after which there is no more death. According to this interpretation, there are three deaths and three lives. If they were dead in Ādam's loins and He brought them out from his back and made them testify before they were sperm in the loins of men and wombs of women, then there are four deaths and four lives.

It is even said that Allah Almighty brought them into existence before He created Ādam, in a dust-like form, and then made them die. According to this, there are five deaths and five lives. There is a sixth death for the rebels of the Community of Muhammad ﷺ when they enter the Fire, based on the hadith of Abū Sa'id al-Khudrī in which the Messenger of Allah ﷺ stated, 'As for the true people of the Fire, who are its eternal inhabitants, they do not die in it nor live. The Fire, however, will smite some people for their wrong actions and Allah will make them die until they are coals. Then He will grant intercession on their behalf and they will be brought out group by group. They will be scattered by the rivers of the Garden and it will be said to the people of the Garden, "Pour water on them." And they will grow like seeds which are carried by a flood.' A man of the people remarked, 'It seems as if the Messenger of Allah ﷺ must have grazed sheep in the desert!' Muslim transmitted it.

Then He will make you die

These words indicate a real death because they are stressed by the use of the verbal noun. That is to honour them. It is said that it is permitted for the words '*make you die*' to be a metaphor about their being absent from its pains by sleep and not a real death. The first is sounder. Grammarians agree that, when a verb is intensified by a verbal noun, it is not a metaphor, but indicates a reality, as when Allah says: '*Allah spoke directly to Mūsā.*' (4:164). It is said that the meaning of '*you were dead*' means you were obscure and then He brought you to life by making you mentioned and honoured by this *dīn* and the Prophet who came to you. Then He will make you die and your fame will die and then He will bring you to life for the resurrection.

Then you will be returned to Him.

You will be returned to His punishment on account of your disbelief. It is said it is to return to life and to the questioning as the Almighty says: *'As We originated the first creation, so We will regenerate it.'* (21:104). So their return is like their beginning. Most recite *'turja'ūna'* while Yaḥyā ibn Ya'mar, Ibn Abī Isḥāq, Mujāhid, Ibn Muḥayṣin and Salām ibn Ya'qūb recite *'tarji'ūna'*.

هُوَ ٱلَّذِى خَلَقَ لَكُم مَّا فِى ٱلْأَرْضِ جَمِيعًا ثُمَّ ٱسْتَوَىٰٓ إِلَى ٱلسَّمَآءِ
فَسَوَّىٰهُنَّ سَبْعَ سَمَٰوَٰتٍ وَهُوَ بِكُلِّ شَىْءٍ عَلِيمٌ ﴿٢٩﴾

29 It is He who created everything on the earth for you and then directed His attention up to heaven and arranged it into seven regular heavens. He has knowledge of all things.

It is He who created everything on the earth for you

'Created' means originated and brought into existence after non-existence. All of this was created for our sake. The word *'everything'* means that all of the earth's blessings are for us. It is said that this fact indicates the Divine Unity and demands reflection on our part.

Those who say that the basic position, in respect of things which are useful, is that they are all permissible use this *āyah* and those like it as evidence. Another example is: *'He has made everything in the heavens and everything on the earth subservient to you.'* (45:13) This applies until there is specific evidence that something is forbidden. The holders of this view support this by saying that tasty foods were created while it was possible that they would not be created. They were not created to no purpose and so they must have a use. That cannot be for Allah because He has no need of anything and so they must be for our benefit. That benefit consists either in our enjoying them, or in our avoiding them because they are a test for us, or in our reflecting on them. Those things can only come about through our tasting them and therefore they must be permissible.

This is unsound reasoning because we cannot accept as true the proposition that something, which is not created to give benefit, is of no purpose. Allah created things as they are and the principle of bringing benefit is not compulsory for Him. He is the only One Who can make things compulsory. So we cannot require the imposition of some benefit as such people claim, nor can we state that some of those benefits can only be obtained by means of taste. Other matters can also be deduced from foods, as is done by biologists. Another objection to their position is found in the case of substances which are feared to be lethal poisons. So those who espouse this position are countered by those people who forbid certain things. Others do not come down on either side, saying that there is no action about which we know either good or bad but that it is possible for it to be good in itself without that being specified before the Sharī'ah came and therefore its ruling had to wait for the arrival of the Sharī'ah. These are three statements made by the Mu'tazilites.

Abu-l-Ḥasan [al-Ash'arī] and his adherents, most Mālikīs and aṣ-Ṣayarifī say that one suspends judgment about this question. That means that there is no judgment about the thing in that case and that the Sharī'ah will judge whatever it wishes when it comes. The intellect cannot judge something to be obligatory or not. Its portion in the matter is simply to recognise matters for what they are.

The sound meaning of *'created everything on the earth for you'* is that it means that it is food for reflection. That is indicated by the lessons which precede and follow it: giving life, making die, creation, direction to the heaven and arranging it. The One who does such things does not lack the power to bring you back to life again.

It is said that the meaning of *'for you'* is 'all for your use'. What is meant by it is 'for you to reflect upon' because of what we mentioned. If one were to ask what the benefit of reflecting on scorpions and snakes is, we reply that by means of harmful things a person is reminded of the punishments which Allah has prepared for the believers in the Fire, and that induces him to believe and abandon disobedience. This is the greatest consideration. Ibn 'Arabī said, 'There is nothing in this phrase which involves prohibition, permission or suspension of judgment. This *āyah* is evidence and clarification of Allah's Oneness.'

Those with a firm grasp of meanings say about *'It is He Who created everything on the earth for you'* that it implies that people should use these things to strengthen their obedience to Allah and not use them in ways that involve disobedience. Abū 'Uthmān said, 'He gave it all to you and subjected it to you as proof of the vastness of His generosity and so that you would have confidence in the generous gifts He has guaranteed to you in the Hereafter. But do not allow His great kindness to lead you to be content with few actions simply because He showed you immense blessings before any action on your part. That is *tawḥīd*.'

'Umar said that a man came to the Messenger of Allah ﷺ and asked him to give to him. The Messenger of Allah ﷺ said, 'I do not have anything, but buy in my name and when something comes to me, we will pay it.' 'Umar said to him, 'You give something when you have something to give! Allah has not obliged you to do what you are unable to do.' The Prophet ﷺ disliked what 'Umar said. Then a man of the Anṣār said, 'Messenger of Allah! Spend and do not fear diminution from the Master of the Throne!' The Messenger of Allah ﷺ smiled and joy could be seen in his face at the words of the Anṣārī. Then the Messenger of Allah ﷺ said, 'That is what I am commanded to do.'

Our scholars say that fear of diminution is having a bad opinion of Allah because Allah Almighty created the earth and what is in it for the sons of Ādam, quoting the phrase, *'He created everything on the earth for you.'* All these things are subjected to the human being absolutely as evidence against him so that he will be Allah's slave as he was created to be. When the slave has a good opinion of Allah, he does not fear diminution because he knows that Allah will replace it. *'Anything you expend will be replaced by Him. He is the Best of Providers,'* (34:39) and: *'My Lord is Rich Beyond Need, Generous.'* (27:40) The Messenger of Allah ﷺ said, 'Allah Almighty said, "My mercy precedes My anger. Son of Ādam, spend and I will spend on you." The right hand of Allah is full and pouring forth, not decreased by any of the night or day.' The Messenger of Allah ﷺ also said, 'There is no day which dawns on the slaves of Allah without two angels descending and one of them saying, "O Allah, refund those who give money" and the other saying, "O Allah, ruin those who withhold it." The same happens in the evening.' This is all sound and related by the Imams, praise be to Allah.

If someone has an illuminated breast and knows that his Lord is wealthy and generous, he spends and does not fear diminution. That is how it is with someone whose appetites are dead to this world and is content with a little nourishment to keep him alive and whose desires for himself are cut off. This person gives in both wealth and constriction and does not fear diminution. The person who relies on himself fears diminution. When he gives today and has a desire for something tomorrow, he fears that he will not get it tomorrow and the business of the expenses of the day worry him because of fear of diminution.

Muslim reported that Asmā' bint Abi Bakr said, 'The Messenger of Allah ﷺ told me, "Spend (or give out or expend) and do not hold back, or Allah will hold back from you. Do not refuse to spend your surplus or Allah will deny you His."' An-Nasā'ī reported that 'Ā'ishah said, 'Once a beggar came to me while the Messenger of Allah ﷺ was with me and I gave instructions for something to be given to him and then summoned him and looked at him. The Messenger of Allah ﷺ said, "Do you want nothing to enter or leave your house except with your knowledge." "Yes," I replied. He said, "Do not worry, 'Ā'ishah. Do not hold back, or Allah will hold back from you."'

and then directed His attention up to heaven

In His words *'then directed'*, the word 'then' is simply a narrative aid and does not imply any time sequence in the matters referred to. Linguistically the word 'directed' (*istawā'*) means to ascend to and be on top of something, as in: *'When you and those with you settled in the ship.'* (23:28). It is used for the sky over your head and the birds over your head.

This *āyah* is one of those which are considered problematic. Regarding it and others of a similar nature people take three views. One of them is that we should read it and believe in it and not try to explain it, which is the position of most of the Imams. An example of this attitude is what is related from Mālik when a man asked him about the words of Allah: *'The All-Merciful was established firmly on the throne.'* (20:5) Mālik said, 'The meaning of *istawā* (established firmly) is not unknown but the how of it is not intelligible; belief in it is mandatory; and asking about it is an innovation. I think you are an evil man!' Others say that we should read it and understand it literally. This is the position of the anthropomorphists. Yet others say that we should read it and interpret it metaphorically and cannot take it literally.

Al-Farrā' said about this *āyah*, '*Istawā* in Arabic has two usual meanings. One refers to people reaching full maturity. The second is being free from crookedness. A third possibility is someone directing himself to something. This is its meaning in this *āyah* and Allah knows best.' Ibn 'Abbās said that *istawā* here means to ascend. All these things are possible in Arabic. Abū Bakr Aḥmad ibn 'Alī ibn al-Ḥusayn al-Bayhaqī said that it is sound for *istawā* to mean to direct oneself because here directing Himself is to aim for creating heaven and aiming for something is a question of will. That is permitted in respect of the Attributes of Allah Almighty. So 'then' is connected to creation, not will. What is related from Ibn 'Abbās is taken from the commentary of al-Kalbī who is weak. Sufyān ibn 'Uyaynah said that it means 'to aim for it', in other words its creation. This is one view. It is said that the meaning of the word is without limitation or definition, as aṭ-Ṭabarī preferred. Abū al-'Āliyah ar-Riyāḥī said, 'It means "to rise".' Al-Bayhaqī said, 'Allah knows best, but what is meant by that is its elevation. It is the vapour of the water from which the sky was created.' It is said that '*mustawā*' means smoke. Ibn Aṭiyyah said that the words do not accept that interpretation. It is said that it means to take control, and Ibn Aṭiyyah said that this comes from His words: *'The All-Merciful was established firmly on the throne.'* (20:5)

It would appear from this *āyah*, if you take the word 'then' as having a temporally sequential meaning, that Allah created the earth before the heavens whereas in *Sūrat an-Nāzi'āt* (79) He describes the heavens being created before the earth. This was the position of Qatādah: heaven was created first. Aṭ-Ṭabarī related it from him. Mujāhid and other commentators say that Allah dried the water on which His Throne rested and turned it into the earth and made smoke rise from it and made heaven. Thus earth was created before heaven. I believe that what Qatādah said is sound, Allah willing: that Allah first created the smoke of heaven and then created the earth and directed Himself to heaven, which was smoke and arranged it and then He smoothed out the earth.

Part of what indicates that smoke was created before the earth is what is related by as-Suddī from Abū Mālik from Abū Ṣāliḥ from Ibn 'Abbās, and from Murrah al-Hamdānī from Ibn Mas'ūd and some Companions about this *āyah*: the Throne of Allah Almighty was on the water and He did not create anything before water. When He desired to bring about creation, He produced smoke from the water and it rose above it and was high above it (*samā*) and so He called it heaven (*samā'*). Then He dried the water and made it earth and then split it up made it into seven earths over two days, Sunday and Monday. The earth was placed on the Fish which is the *Nūn* which Allah mentioned in the Qur'an in *al-Qalam*. The fish was in the water and the water was on a stone. The stone was on the back of an angel and the angel was on a large stone. The stone, which is the one Luqmān mentioned, was in the wind, neither in heaven nor on earth. The fish moved and was agitated and so the earth quaked. So He sent down mountains on it and it became firm. The mountains vaunt themselves over the earth. That is His words: *'He cast firmly embedded mountains on the earth so it would not move under you.'* (16:15)

He created the mountains and the provision and trees and its inhabitants and what it needs over two days, Tuesday and Wednesday. That is when He says: *'Say: "Do you reject Him Who created the earth in two days, and make others equal to Him? That is the Lord of all the worlds." He placed firmly embedded mountains on it, towering over it, and blessed it and measured out its nourishment in it, laid down for those who seek it – all in four days.'* (41:9-10) That is the answer for someone who asks. *'Then He turned to heaven when it was smoke'*. That smoke came from the respiration of water. He made it one heaven. Then He split it open and made it seven heavens in two days, Thursday and Friday. It is called 'Jumu'ah' because in it the creation of the heavens and earth were combined.' *'He revealed, in every heaven, its own mandate.'* (41:12)

Then in every heaven He created the angels and creatures in it of vapour and mountains of hail and what is not known. Then He adorned the lower heaven with stars and made them an adornment and protection from shayṭāns. When he finished creating what He wished, He settled on the Throne. That is: *'It is He Who created the heavens and the earth in six days'* (57:1) and: *'they were sewn together and then We unstitched them.'* (21:30)

Wakī' mentioned from Abū Ẓabyān that Ibn 'Abbās said, 'The first thing that Allah Almighty created was the Pen. "Write," He told it. It said, "Lord, what shall I write?" He said, "Write the Decree." So it wrote what would be on the day until the coming of the Final Hour. Then He created the Nūn and flattened the earth on it and made it firm with the mountains. The mountains will vaunt themselves over the earth until the Day of Rising.' One variant states that He created the earth before elevating the vapour of the water, which is the smoke, differing from the first variant. The views about this differ and there is scope for independent judgment regarding it.

The basic element of the creation of all things is water as is reported by Ibn Mājah and Abū Ḥātim al-Bustī from Abū Hurayrah. He said to the Messenger of Allah ﷺ, 'When I see you my self is happy and my eye delighted. Tell me about the origin of all things.' He replied, 'All things were created from water.' He asked, 'Tell me about something by virtue of which, I will enter the Garden.' He said, 'Feed people, extend the greeting, maintain ties with your kin, and stand in prayer at night when people are asleep, and you will enter the Garden in peace.'

Ibn 'Abbās said that the Messenger of Allah ﷺ said, 'The first thing that Allah created was the Pen and He commanded it to write down all that would be.' Al-Bayhaqī said, 'Allah knows best, but he meant that the first thing that Allah created after water, wind and the Throne was the Pen.' Ṭāwus said that a man came to 'Abdullāh ibn 'Amr ibn al-'Āṣ and asked 'What was creation created from?' He said, 'From water, fire, darkness, wind and earth.' The man asked, 'And from what were these created?' He replied, 'I do not know.' Then the man went to 'Abdullāh ibn az-Zubayr and asked him and he gave the same answer as 'Abdullāh ibn 'Amr. Then he went to 'Abdullāh ibn 'Abbas and he answered the same. When he asked the second question, Ibn 'Abbās recited: *'He has made everything in the heavens and everything on the earth subservient to you.'* (45:13) The man said, 'This could only come from a man of the people of the House of the Prophet!' Al-Bayhaqī said, 'He means that it is the source of all in its creation and origination. He created water first, or water and whatever He willed of His creation, not from a root or prior model. Then He made it the root for what He created afterwards. He is the Originator and He is the Creator. There is no god but Him and no Creator but Him. Glory be to Him! He is Mighty and Exalted!'

and arranged it into seven regular heavens.

Allah mentions seven heavens but does not give a clear number of earths in the Revelation. The only possible reference to seven earths is found in His words: *'and of the earth the same number* (mithlahunna)' (65:12). There is disagreement about the meaning of that but it is said that it is referring to their number (literally 'their like'), and the number is also used in several hadiths reference to the number of earths. Their quality and description varies, as it is said that 'the same number' can mean 'the same density'. It is said that there are seven heavens, but they are not unstitched. Ad-Dāwūdī said that. The first is the sound view: there are seven heavens. Muslim related that Sa'īd ibn Zayd said that he heard the Messenger of Allah ﷺ say, 'If someone takes a span of land unjustly, his neck will be encircled with it through the seven earths.' 'Ā'ishah has something similar as does Abū Hurayrah. An-Nasā'ī related from Abū Sa'īd al-Khudrī that the Messenger of Allah ﷺ said, 'Mūsā said, "Lord, teach me something by which I can remember you and by which I can pray to you." He said, "Mūsā, say: 'There is no god but Allah.'" Mūsā said, "Lord, all of Your slaves say that." He said, "Say: 'There is no god but Allah." He said, "There is no god but You. I want something especially for me." He said, "Mūsā, if the seven heavens and their inhabitants other than Me, and the seven earths, were put in one pan, and 'There is no god but Allah' in the other pan, 'There is no god but Allah' would outweigh them."'

At-Tirmidhī related that Abū Hurayrah said, 'Once while the Prophet of Allah ﷺ and his Companions were sitting, clouds came over them, and the Prophet of Allah ﷺ asked, "Do you know what this is?" "Allah and His Messenger know best," they answered. He said, "These are the clouds. These are the water-bearers of the earth which Allah drives to people who are not grateful to Him and do not call on Him." He asked, "Do you know what is above you?" "Allah and His Messenger know best," they answered. He said, "It is the firmament, a protected ceiling and waves that are held back." Then he asked, "Do you know what is between you and it?" "Allah and His Messenger know best," they answered. He said, "Between you and it is the distance of five hundred years." Then he asked, "Do you know what is above that?" "Allah and His Messenger know best," they replied. He said, "Above that are two heavens with a distance of five hundred years between them." He continued in that manner until he had mentioned seven heavens, the distance between every two heavens being like that which is between heaven and earth. Then he asked, "Do you know what is above that?" "Allah and His Messenger know best," was the reply. He said, "Above that is the Throne and the distance between it and the [final] heaven is like what is between a pair of heavens." Then he asked, "Do you know what is below you?" "Allah and His Messenger know best," they answered. He said, "It is the earth." Then he asked, "Do you know what is under that?" They replied, "Allah and His Messenger know best." He said, "Under that is another earth, and the distance between them is five hundred years," and he continued until he had counted seven earths with a distance of five hundred years between each two. Then he said, "By the One Who has the soul of Muḥammad in His hand, if you were to drop a rope to the lowest earth, it would fall on Allah." Then he recited: *"He is the First and the Last, the Outward and the Inward. He has knowledge of all things."* (57:3)' Abū 'Īsā said, "The fact that the Prophet ﷺ recited this *āyah* indicates that it means "it would fall in the knowledge, power and authority of Allah. He is on His Throne as He described in His Book." It is a *gharīb* hadith. Al-Ḥasan did not hear directly from Abū Hurayrah.

There are many reports about there being seven earths. We have mentioned enough that about that.

He has knowledge of all things.

He has knowledge of all He created. Since He created things, He must know them. He says: *'Does He who created not then know?'* (67:14). He knows all known things with timeless pre-eternal knowledge which He alone possesses. He has described Himself with knowledge in various *āyahs*.

وَإِذْ قَالَ رَبُّكَ لِلْمَلَـٰٓئِكَةِ إِنِّى جَاعِلٌ فِى ٱلْأَرْضِ خَلِيفَةً ۖ قَالُوٓا۟ أَتَجْعَلُ فِيهَا
مَن يُفْسِدُ فِيهَا وَيَسْفِكُ ٱلدِّمَآءَ وَنَحْنُ نُسَبِّحُ بِحَمْدِكَ وَنُقَدِّسُ لَكَ ۖ
قَالَ إِنِّىٓ أَعْلَمُ مَا لَا تَعْلَمُونَ ﴿٣٠﴾

30 When your Lord said to the angels, 'I am putting a caliph on the earth,' they said, 'Why put on it one who will cause corruption on it and shed blood when we glorify You with praise and proclaim Your purity?' He said, 'I know what you do not know.'

When your Lord said to the angels,

It is possible that there is an elided word here in which case the meaning would be, 'Remember when ...' It is also said that it goes back to His words: *'Worship your Lord who created you'* (2:21), in which case the meaning would be: 'When the One who created you said to the angels.'

The fact that Allah addressed the angels indicates that they existed and understood. He addressed them not to consult them or to ask for their opinion but simply to inform them. This is the case with Allah's commands and prohibitions. The 'Lord' is the Master, Controller, the One Who puts right and compels. The singular of 'angels' (*malā'ikah*) is *malak*.

I am putting a caliph on the earth,'

'Putting' in this context means 'creating' as aṭ-Ṭabarī said. The 'earth' means Makkah. The Prophet ﷺ said, 'The earth was smoothed out from Makkah,' which is why it is called 'the Mother of Cities'. *Khalīfah* (caliph) has the form of an active participle, meaning 'the one who replaced the angels before him on the earth', or other than the angels, according to what has been reported. It is also possible that it is in the passive mode, in which case it means someone who is sent as a representative.

According to Ibn 'Abbās, Ibn Mas'ūd and all the people of interpretation, the caliph is Ādam ﷺ. He was the caliph of Allah in carrying out His commands and prohibitions because he was the first Messenger to the earth as we find in the hadith of Abū Dharr. He said, 'I asked, "Messenger of Allah, was he a Prophet and a Messenger?" "Yes," he answered.' If it were to be asked to whom was he a Messenger when there was no one on earth, the answer is that he was a Messenger to his children. He had forty children over twenty pregnancies, each pregnancy having a male and a female. They reproduced until they became numerous as Allah says: *'He created you from a single self and created its mate from it and then disseminated many men and women from the two of them.'* (4:1) He revealed to them the prohibition of carrion, blood and pork. He lived for 930 years according to the Torah. Wahb ibn Munabbih related that he lived for a thousand years. Allah knows best.

This *āyah* is sound evidence for having a leader and a caliph who is obeyed so that he will be a focus for the cohesion of society and the rulings of the caliphate will carried out. None of the Imams of the Community disagree about the obligatory nature of having such a leader, except for what is related from al-Aṣamm (lit. the Deaf), who lived up to the meaning of his name and was indeed deaf to the Sharī'ah, and those who take his position who say that the caliphate is merely permitted rather than mandatory if the Community undertakes all their obligations on their own without the need for a ruler to enforce them. Our evidence is found in the words of Allah Almighty: *'I am putting a caliph on the earth'* as well as other *āyahs* (38:26, 24:55)

...

The Companions agreed to make Abū Bakr caliph after the disagreement about the selection which took place between the Muhājirūn and the Anṣār in the veranda of the Banū Sā'idah. The Anṣār said, 'We will have a leader and you will have a leader.' Abū Bakr, 'Umar and the Muhājirūn dissuaded them from that, telling them, 'The Arabs will only take their *dīn* from this tribe of Quraysh,' and so the Anṣār retracted and obeyed Quraysh. If it had been a definite obligation that the ruler had to be from Quraysh, there would have been no point in the argument and debate which took place. It would have been said, 'The obligation for appointing the leader does not have to be from Quraysh or anyone else, so why are you arguing with us by a pointless issue that is not mandatory?' When Abū Bakr died, he delegated the office of caliph to 'Umar and no one claimed that it was not mandatory. That indicates that it is mandatory and that it is one of the pillars of the *dīn* which support the Muslims. Praise be to Allah, the Lord of the worlds.

The Rāfidite Shi'ites say that the appointment of a leader should be based on logic. Obedience then follows what is logically decided. Recognition of the leader is achieved by obedience rather than logic. This is false because logic does not make something mandatory or forbidden, or ugly or good. It is confirmed that it is mandatory by the Sharī'ah, not by logic. This is clear.

If one were to accept that the means to the mandatory nature of leadership (*imāmah*) is obedience, then tell us whether obedience is obliged by designation (*naṣṣ*) about the leader (imam) from the Messenger ﷺ, or from the choice of the people who make binding decisions of community, or by the existence of all the qualities of the imams in him so that when he calls on them to obey, that is sufficient?

The answer is that people disagree about this topic. The Imāmiyyah and others believe that the means by which the imam is known is by designation from the Messenger ﷺ and that choice has no part in it. We believe that investigation is the path to acknowledging the ruler, along with the consensus of the people of *ijtihād* who reach that conclusion. Those who say that the only way to it is by designation base that on their fundamental position that analogy, opinion and *ijtihād* are false and nothing at all is known by those means. They say that analogy is invalid, root and branch. Then they fall into three different groups. One group claim that the designation of appointment was to Abū Bakr, one group say al-'Abbās, and one group that it was 'Alī ibn Abī Ṭālib.

The proof of the absence and non-existence of a text of designation naming a specific imam is that, if the Prophet ﷺ had imposed on his community obedience to a particular imam so that it would not be possible to turn away from him to someone else, that would have been known since it is impossible to obligate the entire community to obey Allah in something which is unspecified and when there is no way to know that obligation. Since knowledge of who he is is mandatory, then that knowledge must come by way of multiple transmission which necessarily demands that it be known or deduced, or that it come from single reports. It is not possible for that to have the same authority as multiple transmission which demands a priori knowledge or by evidence, since if that had been the case, every responsible person would find in himself knowledge entailing obedience to that specific person and that would be part of the *dīn* of Allah which is obliged for him, just as every responsible person knows from the *dīn* of Allah what is obliged for him regarding the five prayers, fasting Ramadan, ḥajj and the like. No one knows that from himself necessarily, so this claim is false.

It is false that it is known by single reports since it is impossible for definitive knowledge to occur by that means. Furthermore, had it been mandatory to go to the transmission of the designation of an imam by any manner, it would be obliged to confirm the leadership of Abū Bakr and al-'Abbās because each of them had people who transmitted a designation by text explicitly stating his imamate. Then since it is false for the three to be confirmed by designation at the same time, as we will explain, the same is true of one of them, since one of the three must be more entitled than the other. When confirmation of the designation is false because of the absence of a path connected to it, then choice and *ijtihād* are confirmed.

If someone claims the existence of multiple transmission and necessary knowledge of the designation, then they must be confronted immediately by the demolishment of their claim through the designation of Abū Bakr and the numerous reports about that which, as a whole, take the place of a text. Then there will be no doubt about the determination of those other than the Imāmiyyah in denying the designation. They are huge in number. Necessary knowledge does not agree on denying it by less than a tenth of those who oppose the Imāmiyyah. If the refutation of what is necessary had been permitted in that way, it would be permitted for a group to deny Baghdad, furthest China and other things.

Refutation will be given of hadith which the Imāmiyyah use as evidence for the designation of 'Alī and their position that any of the community who reject that designation are apostates and oppose the command of the Messenger ﷺ out of obstinacy. One of them is his words ﷺ, 'Those of whom I am the master (*mawlā*), 'Alī is his master. O Allah, befriend whomever befriends him and oppose whomever opposes him.' They said, 'Linguistically *mawlā* means more entitled, and so when he said, "'Alī is his master" with the *fā'* of consequence, it is known that what is meant by "*mawlā'* is that he is more entitled and so it is clear that what is meant by that is the imamate and that it demands obedience.' There are also his words to 'Alī, 'In relation to me, you are as Hārūn was to Mūsā, but there will be no Prophet after me.' They said that the position of Hārūn is known, and he shared with him in being a Prophet, and 'Alī was not that. He was his brother, but 'Alī was not that. He was a khalīfah and so it is known that what is meant by that is the caliphate. There are other things that they cited as evidence as will be mentioned, Allah willing.

The first answer to the hadith is that it is not transmitted by multiple sources and there is disagreement about its validity. It was attacked by Abū Dāwūd as-Sijistānī and Abū Ḥātim ar-Rāzī. They deduced that it was false because the Prophet ﷺ said, 'Muzaynah, Juhaynah, Ghifār and Aslam are my *mawlā*s rather than others and they have no *mawlā* other than Allah and His Messenger.' They said, 'If the first report had been as he said, then one of the two reports must be false.'

Secondly, even if this report is sound and related from someone trustworthy to someone trustworthy, there is nothing in it that indicates his imamate. Rather it indicates his excellence. That is because *mawlā* means *walī* and so the meaning of the report is: 'If I am the *walī* of someone, 'Alī is his *walī*.' Allah says: *'Allah is his Mawlā'* (66:4) and *mawlā* means Protector (*walī*). What is meant in the report is to inform people that 'Alī was the same both inwardly and outwardly. That is an immense virtue of 'Alī.

This report came for a reason, which was that Usāmah and 'Alī had a quarrel. 'Alī said to Usāmah, 'You are my *mawlā*.' He retorted, 'I am not your *mawlā*! I am the *mawlā* of the Messenger of Allah ﷺ!' The Prophet ﷺ was informed about that and said, 'If I am the *mawlā* of someone, 'Alī is his *mawlā*.'

Another point is found in the Story of the Lie. 'Alī said to the Prophet ﷺ about 'Ā'ishah, 'There are many women besides her.' That was hard on her and the hypocrites found an opening and attacked him and said that they were free of him. Then the Prophet ﷺ said this to refute what they said and denied their offering to be free of him and attack him. That is why it is related that a group of the Companions said, 'We did not recognise the hypocrites in the time of the Messenger of Allah ﷺ except by their hatred for 'Alī.'

As for the second hadith, there is no disagreement that when he referred to the position of Hārūn in respect of Mūsā, the Prophet ﷺ did not mean the caliphate after him. There is no disagreement that Hārūn died before Mūsā ﷺ as will be made clear in *Sūrat al-Mā'idah*. He was not the *khalīfah* after him: the *khalīfah* after him was Yūsha' ibn Nūn. If he had meant the caliphate by what he said, he would have said, 'In relation to me, you are as Yūsha' ibn Nūn was to Mūsā.' Since he did not say that, it indicates that it was not what he meant. He meant: 'I have put you in charge of my people during my lifetime and in my absence from my people.' Hārūn was the khalīfah of Mūsā over his people when he went to speak to his Lord.

It is said that this hadith has a reason behind it, which was that when he went out on the Tabūk expedition, he put 'Alī in charge of his family and people in Madīnah. So the hypocrites spread lies about him and said, 'He left him behind because he hates him.' 'Alī went out and joined the Prophet ﷺ. He said, 'The hypocrites have said this and said that!' He answered him, 'They lied. I appointed you as Mūsā appointed Hārūn.' He added, 'Are you not content to be in relation to me as Hārūn was to Mūsā?'

If it were to be confirmed that he meant the caliphate, as they claim, then 'Alī shared with others in this virtue because the Prophet ﷺ appointed one of his Companions as *khalīfah* in every expedition he made. They included: Ibn Umm Maktūm, Muḥammad ibn Maslamah and others, although this report centres on Sa'd ibn Abī Waqqāṣ and it is a single report. Abū Bakr and 'Umar are mentioned in a way that is more appropriate that that. It is related that when the Prophet ﷺ appointed Mu'ādh ibn Jabal to Yemen, he was asked, 'Why not send Abū Bakr and 'Umar?' He answered, 'I cannot do without them. Their position is relation to me is that of hearing and sight to the head.' He said, 'They are my two wazīrs among the people of the earth.' It is related that the Prophet ﷺ said, 'Abū Bakr and 'Umar are in the position that Hārūn was to Mūsā' This report came on its own [without a cause], and that of 'Alī came because of a cause, and so it means that Abū Bakr is more entitled to the imamate. Allah knows best.

There is disagreement about the method by which someone is made the imam. There are three ways. The first is by designation, and the disagreement about that has already been mentioned. That position was also taken by some Ḥanbalīs, a group of the People of Hadith, al-Ḥasan al-Baṣrī, Bakr, the son of the sister of 'Abd al-Wāḥid and his people, and a group of Khārijites. That view is that the Prophet ﷺ designated Abū Bakr by indication and Abū Bakr designated 'Umar. Then someone may appoint someone specific by designation as Abū Bakr did, or a group as 'Umar did, which is the second method. Then they choose which of them should be selected as the Companions did in appointing 'Uthmān ibn 'Affān.

The third method is the consensus of the people who can appoint and dismiss. That is that when the leader of a group in one of the cities of the Muslims dies and they have no leader and he did not appoint anyone, then the community of the people of that city, which is the base of the imam, undertake that themselves and agree about someone and are satisfied with him. All the Muslims before and after them in all regions must obey that leader when that leader is not known for impiety and corruption because it is an invitation which includes them to which they must respond. No one should absent himself from it since the establishment of two rulers entails division and corruption of unity. The Messenger of Allah said, 'If the heart of a believer possesses three qualities, it will not be filled with rancour: sincere action for Allah, holding to the community and giving good counsel to those in power.'

If one of the people who can appoint and dismiss does that, it is confirmed and his action binds others, although some people disagree and say that that it can only be done by a group of the people who can appoint and dismiss. Our evidence is that 'Umar gave allegiance to Abū Bakr and none of the Companions objected to him doing that. It is also because it is a contract and it does not require a number to contract it as is the case with other contracts. Imām Abu-l-Ma'ālī said, 'If a contract for leadership is made by one contract, it is binding, and it is not permitted to dismiss him without a reason or change of affairs. This is agreed upon.'

If someone who possesses the qualifications for leadership seizes the imāmah and takes it by force and conquest, it is said that that is a fourth method. Sahl ibn 'Abdullāh at-Tustarī was asked, 'What is obliged for us in the case of a ruler who conquers our land?' He answered, 'To respond to him and give him what he demands of you of his right, not to object to his actions nor flee from him. When he entrusts you with a secret concerning the *dīn*, do not disseminate it.' Ibn Khuwayzimandād said, 'If someone suited for command seizes it without consultation or choice and people give him allegiance, then allegiance to him is complete. Allah knows best.'

There is disagreement about having witnesses to the contract of leadership. Some of our people said that it does not require witnesses because testimony is only established by definitive hearing. Here there is no definitive hearing to confirm the witnessing. Some of them said that it requires witnesses. Those who say that argue that if there were no witnessing to it, that would lead to every claimant claiming that he had a secret contract and that would lead to bloodshed and civil war. Therefore it is obliged that witnessing be taken into account. Two witnesses are enough for it. Al-Jubbā'ī is an exception to that. He said that one considers four witnesses, the contractor and the one contracted because 'Umar made the Council consist of six, and so that is what is indicated. Our evidence is that there is no disagreement between us and him that the testimony of two is considered. There is disagreement about a larger number. No evidence indicates it and so it should not be considered.

There are eleven preconditions which a ruler (imam) must meet. He should be from Quraysh since the Prophet ﷺ said, 'The rulers are from Quraysh.' There is disagreement about this. He should be someone who is able to be one of the *qāḍīs* of the Muslims and capable of *ijtihād* so that he does not need to consult others for a legal decision about things that happen. This is agreed upon. The third is that he should possess experience, sound judgment regarding war, management of armies, protecting frontiers, guarding territory, deterring the community, enforcing retribution on those who do wrong and recompensing those who are wronged. He should be someone who is not preventing by softness from carrying out the *ḥudūd*, not alarmed by execution or amputation. The proof for all of this is the consensus of the Companions because there was no disagreement between them that all of that was agreed upon. That is also necessary because the ruler is the one who undertakes judgment and legal decisions and he must settle disputes and judge. He must also investigate the affairs of his representatives and judges. That can only be fulfilled by someone who knows all of that and carries it out. Allah knows best.

He must be a free man and Muslim. He must be male and have sound limbs. There is a consensus that a woman cannot be the imam although there is disagreement about her acting as *qāḍī* concerning matters in which her testimony is permitted. He must be adult and intelligent. There is no disagreement about that. He must be of good character. There is no disagreement among the Community that it is not permitted to give the leadership to a deviant. He should be the best of them in knowledge since the Prophet ﷺ said, 'Your imams are your intercessors, so look to those whom you ask to intercede.' Ṭālūt (Saul) is described in Revelation: *'Allah has chosen him over you and increased him greatly in knowledge and physical strength.'* (2:247) He began with knowledge and then mentioned what indicated his strength and sound limbs. It is not a precondition that he be protected from slips and errors or that he should know the Unseen. He does not have to be the most discriminating or most courageous of people nor must he come from the Banū Hāshim or any other clan of Quraysh. There is consensus on the validity of the leadership of Abū Bakr, 'Umar and 'Uthmān, and they were not from the Banū Hāshim.

It is permitted to appoint a less excellent candidate when there is someone better if there is fear of civil unrest and that the affairs of the community will not be in order. That is when the ruler is appointed to repel enemies, protect territory, block gaps, deliver rights, establish the *ḥudūd*, and collect revenue for the Treasury and distribute it to its people. If it is feared that appointing the better person will result in bloodshed and unrest and that things will be disordered because of the appointment of that leader, that is a clear excuse for turning away from the better man for the lesser one. That is also indicated by the knowledge shown by 'Umar and the rest of the Community at the time of the Shūrā. The six of them included those who were better and those who were less qualified. It was permitted to give the leadership to any of them when the best interest lay in that choice. They agreed on that and none of them objected to it. Allah knows best.

When a ruler is appointed and then becomes deviant after having taken his position, most say that his leadership is voided and, in the case of well known apparent deviance, that he should be deposed, because it is confirmed that the ruler is responsible for establishing the *ḥudūd*, fulfilling rights, preserving the property of orphans and mad people, and looking into their affairs in the areas we have already mentioned. Deviance in him would prevent him from undertaking these things. If it were to be permitted for him to be deviant, that would lead to the invalidation of what he undertakes.

Others say that he may only deposed on account of unbelief, abandoning establishing the prayer, or abandoning calling to it or something else in the Sharī'ah, since 'Ubādah said that the Prophet ﷺ said, 'Do not contend for authority with its people unless you see open unbelief for which you have a proof from Allah.' There is also the hadith of 'Awf ibn Mālik: '...not as long as they establish the prayer among you.' Muslim transmitted both. Umm Salamah reported that the Prophet ﷺ said, 'Rulers will be appointed over you. Some you approve of and some you disapprove of. Anyone who hates that is innocent. Anyone who disapproves is safe. But those who are content and follow [are destroyed].' They said, 'Messenger of Allah, should we not fight them?' 'No,' he answered, 'not as long as they pray.' It means those who hated and disapproved in their hearts. Muslim also transmitted it.

If a leader finds in himself an impediment which would impair his leadership, he should retire. If he does not find any impediment, is he permitted to dismiss himself and appoint someone else? People disagree about that. Some people say that he may not do that, and if he does it, then he is not deposed. Some say that he may do that. The evidence that when a ruler dismisses himself he can retire is found in what Abū Bakr aṣ-Ṣiddīq said when he said, 'Dismiss me! Dismiss me!' The Companions replied, 'We will not dismiss you or let you be dismissed. The Messenger of Allah ﷺ advanced you among us, so who would be better than you?

The Messenger of Allah ﷺ was pleased with you, so should we not be pleased with you?' If he could not do that then the Companions would not have objected to it and told him that he could not say or do that. When the Companions affirmed in that, it is known that he could do that.

When leadership is given by the agreement of the people of influence or by one of them as was already mentioned, then all people are obliged to give their allegiance to hear and obey and to establish the Book of Allah and the Sunnah of His Messenger ﷺ. If someone refuses to give allegiance with a valid excuse, he is excused, but if someone refuses without an excuse, he is compelled to accept so that there will be no division among the Muslims. If allegiance is given to two caliphs, then the true caliph is the first one and the other is killed. In respect of killing him, there is disagreement about whether it is actual execution or metaphorical and so that his dismissal is tantamount to his killing and death. The first is clearer. The Messenger of Allah ﷺ said, 'When allegiance is given to two caliphs, kill the second of them.'Abū Sa'īd al-Khudrī related it and it is transmitted by Muslim.

We find in the hadith of 'Abdullāh ibn 'Umar who heard the Prophet ﷺ say, 'If someone gives allegiance to a ruler with the clasp of his hand and the fruit of his heart, he should obey to the best of his ability. If another comes to dispute with him, then strike the neck of the other.' Muslim also related that. 'Arfajah has: 'Strike him with a sword, whoever he is.' This is the strongest evidence forbidding there being two rulers. Another reason is because that can lead to hypocrisy, conflict, division, civil strife and removal of blessings. If, however, regions are far apart and separate, like Andalusia and Khorasan, then that is permitted as will be explained, Allah willing.

If a Khārijite rebels against a ruler known for justice, then people are obliged to fight him. If the ruler is impious, and the Khārijite shows his justice, people should not hurry to help the Khārijite until his business is clear with regard to his justice or the community agree to depose the first. That is because anyone who seeks that might make a show of righteousness in himself until he is well established and then he reverts to his normal behaviour which is not what he was showing.

As for there being two or three rulers at the same time in the same land, the consensus is that that is not permitted. Imam Abu-l-Ma'ālī said, 'Our people believe that it is forbidden to give rule to two individuals at the opposite ends of the world. Then they say that if leadership is given to two individuals, that is like marriage in which two guardians give a woman in marriage to two husbands without either of them being aware of the contract of the other. That which I believe is that giving leadership to two people in one region with narrow territory is not permitted, and there is consensus on that. When there is a great distance between the two rulers, then there is scope for that and it is not absolutely prohibited.'

Abū Isḥāq said, 'It is permitted when the two regions are far apart so that people's rights and rulings will not be neglected.' The Karrāmites believe that it is permitted to have two rulers and do not give any detail and so they must allow that in the same land and believe that both Mu'āwiyah and 'Alī were rulers. They said that if there are two in two lands or regions, each of them carries out what he is in charge of. That is because it is permitted for two Prophets to be sent at the same time and that does not lead to the invalidation of Prophethood. Therefore it is even more likely to apply to leadership and that does not lead to the invalidation of leadership. The answer to this is that it would be permitted had not the Sharī'ah forbidden it because the Prophet ﷺ said, 'Kill the second of them' and because the Community agree on that. Mu'āwiyah did not claim leadership for himself. He claimed to be governor of Syria because he was appointed by the prior ruler. This indicates the consensus of the Community in their time that there is only one leader. Neither of them said, 'I am a ruler and opposite me is a ruler.' That is even though it is not logically impossible. The consensus is stronger.

They said, 'Why put on it one who will cause corruption on it and shed blood,

We know definitely that the angels only know what they are informed about and have no foreknowledge. That applies to all angels because Allah says in praise of them: *'They do not precede Him in speech'* (21:27).

As to why they asked this question, it is said that it means that when they heard the word "*khalīfah*", they understood that the sons of Ādam would cause corruption since the task of the caliph is to put things right. They, however, made the label of disobedience apply to all human beings. So to cheer their hearts, Allah made it clear to them that some humans would cause corruption and some would not. That was confirmed when Allah taught Ādam the names and unveiled knowledge to him, which had previously been hidden. It is also said that they asked the question because they had seen the corruption and bloodshed of the jinn who had inhabited the earth before the creation of Ādam. So Allah sent Iblīs against them with an army of angels and they killed them and drove them into the seas and to the tops of the mountains. That was when pride entered Iblīs's heart. Their words, 'Why put...?' is thus a simple question. 'Is this caliph going to be like the jinn or not?"'

Ibn Zayd and others said that Allah informed them that the caliph's descendants would cause corruption and shed blood and so they asked this, either from astonishment that Allah was appointing a species who would disobey him or because they considered both the appointment and the disobedience terrible.

when we glorify You with praise

Its meaning is 'We disassociate You from any attribute which is not appropriate for You.' By their glorification they disassociate Him from all defects through His exaltation. Ṭalḥah ibn 'Ubaydullāh said, 'I asked the Messenger of Allah ﷺ about the meaning of "Glory be to Allah", and he answered, "It is disassociating Allah from every defect."' It is derived from the verbal root *sabḥ*, which means swimming and travelling a long distance.

Interpreters disagree about the interpretation of the glorification of the angels. Ibn Mas'ūd and Ibn 'Abbās said that it is their prayer, as in the words of Allah: *'If it had not been that he was a man who glorified Allah'* (37:143), meaning 'one of those who pray'. It is said that their glorification is raising their voices with *dhikr*, as al-Mufaḍḍal says. Qatādah said that it is their saying of *'subhānallāh'* as is usual linguistically. That is confirmed according to what is related by Abū Dharr from the Messenger of Allah ﷺ who, when he was asked 'Which words are best?', replied, 'Those which Allah chose for His angels and slaves: "Glory be to Allah with His praise."' Muslim transmitted it. 'Abd ar-Raḥmān ibn Qurṭ reported that the Messenger of Allah ﷺ said during the Night Journey, 'Glory be to the High, the Most High. Glory be to Him and exalted is He!' Al-Bayhaqī mentioned it.

and proclaim Your purity?'

'We exalt You, praise You and purify Your Name from those things which are not appropriate for You which heretics have ascribed to You,' as Mujāhid, Abū Ṣāliḥ and others said. Aḍ-Ḍaḥḥāk and others said that it means: 'We purify ourselves for You, seeking Your pleasure.' Some people said that Qatādah said it means 'pray' and that *taqdīs* is prayer, but this is weak according to Ibn 'Aṭiyyah. I say that it is a sound meaning. Prayer contains exaltation, proclamation of purity and glorification. The Messenger of Allah ﷺ used to say in his *rukū'* and prostration, 'Glorious, Pure, Lord of the angels and the *Rūḥ*'. Ā'ishah related it and Muslim transmitted it. It means purification as is seen elsewhere in the Qur'an. The prayer is purification from wrong actions. Someone who performs the prayer enters the prayer in the most perfect state because it is the best of actions. Allah knows best.

He said, 'I know what you do not know.'

Scholars disagree about the meaning of the words *'what you do not know'*. Ibn 'Abbās said, 'Iblīs was proud when He was honoured and made the treasurer of heaven. He believed that it was his prerogative and he despised the potential for disbelief and disobedience inherent in Ādam. The angels said this, not knowing what Iblīs had inside him, which was different to what they had. Then Allah told them, "I know what you do not know," meaning that He knew what Iblīs really felt about Ādam.' Qatādah said that it refers to the Prophets, men of virtue and people of obedience who Allah would place on earth. It is also possible that the meaning is general and includes all of that.

وَعَلَّمَ ءَادَمَ ٱلْأَسْمَآءَ كُلَّهَا ثُمَّ عَرَضَهُمْ عَلَى ٱلْمَلَٰٓئِكَةِ فَقَالَ أَنۢبِـُٔونِى بِأَسْمَآءِ
هَٰٓؤُلَآءِ إِن كُنتُمْ صَٰدِقِينَ ﴿٣١﴾

31 He taught Ādam the names of all things. Then He arrayed them before the angels and said, 'Tell me the names of these if you are telling the truth.'

He taught Ādam the names of all things.

'Teaching' here means 'inspiring with the necessary knowledge'. It is possible that it took place by means of the angel Jibrīl. Sufi scholars say, 'He knew them when Allah taught him and remembered them when He made him do so but forgot the contract he had made because, in it, he relied on himself. Allah says: *"We made a contract with Ādam before, but he forgot. We did not find that he had a firm resolve."* (20:115)' Ibn 'Aṭā' said, 'If those names had not been unveiled to Ādam, he would not have been able to tell them to the angels.'

Ādam's *kunyah* (familiar name) is Abū al-Bashar, which means 'the father of humanity'. Abū Muḥammad is also used since Muḥammad is the Seal of the Prophets, as as-Suhaylī said. It is said that his *kunyah* was Abū Muhammad in the Garden and Abu-l-Bashar on the earth.

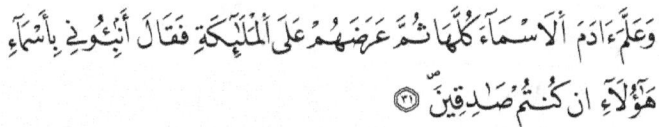

There is disagreement about the derivation of the name Ādam. It is said that it is derived from the crust (*ādam*) and surface (*adīm*) of the earth and he was called that because he was created from it. Ibn 'Abbās stated that. It is said that it is derived from *admah*, which is brownness. Aḍ-Ḍaḥḥāk claimed that it is duskiness. An-Naḍr claimed that it is whiteness and that Ādam was white, since they use this word for a white camel. I believe that the sound view is that it is derived from the surface of the earth. Sa'īd ibn Jubayr said, 'Ādam received his name because he was created from the surface of the earth and he was called *insān* (human being) because he forgot (*nasā*).' Ibn Sa'd mentioned that in the *Ṭabaqāt*.

As-Suddī related from Abū Mālik, from Abū Ṣāliḥ from Ibn 'Abbās and from Murrah al-Hamdānī from Ibn Mas'ūd about the creation of Ādam. He said, 'Allah sent Jibrīl to the earth to bring him some of its mud. The earth said, "I seek refuge with Allah from your diminishing or marring me!" He returned without taking anything. He said, "Lord, it sought refuge from me with You and so I gave it refuge." He sent Mīkā'īl and it sought refuge from him and he gave it. He returned and said the same as Jibrīl said. So he sent the Angel of Death and it sought refuge from him and the angel said, "I seek refuge with Allah from returning without what He commanded me to carry out." So he took from the surface of the earth and mixed it, not taking it all from one place. He took red, white and black mud, and that is why the sons of Ādam emerge as different colours. That is also why he is named Ādam: because he took from the surface (*adīm*) of the earth. He ascended with it and Allah Almighty said to him, "Did you not show mercy to the earth when it entreated you?" He answered, "I saw that Your command was more binding that its words." He said, "You are fit for taking the souls of his children." He moistened the earth until it became sticky mud whose parts cling to one another. Then he left it until it became fetid. That is His words: *"formed from fetid black mud."* (15:26) Then He said to the angels: *"I am going to create a human being out of clay, When I have formed him and breathed My* Rūḥ *into him, fall down in prostration to him!"* (38:71-72)

'Allah created him with His own hand so that Iblīs would not vaunt himself over him. He said, "Do you vaunt yourself over what I have created with my own hand when I am not?" So He created him as a human being and it was a body of forty years on Friday. The angels passed by him and were alarmed at him when they saw him. Iblīs had the greatest fear. He would pass by him and hit him and the body would make a noise like clay that had a ringing sound. That is His words, "*earth like dried clay.*" (55:14) He entered by his mouth and emerged from his anus and Iblīs said to the angels, "Do not fear this thing. It is hollow. If I have control over him, I will destroy him."' It is said that when he passed by him with the angels he said, 'Do you see this being whose like you have not seen among creatures? If he is preferred to you and you are commanded to obey him, do not do it!' They replied. 'We will obey our Lord's command.' So Iblīs concealed inside himself: 'If he is preferred to me, I will not obey him. If preference is given to him, I will destroy him!'

When the time came when He wanted to breathe the *rūḥ* into him, He said to the angels, 'When I breathe some of My *Rūḥ* into him, then prostrate to him.' When he breathed the *rūḥ* into him and it entered into his head, he sneezed. The angels told him, 'Say: "Praise belongs to Allah."' So he said, 'Praise belongs to Allah.' Allah said to him, 'May your Lord have mercy on you.' When the *rūḥ* entered into his eyes, he looked at the fruits of the Garden. When it entered his belly, he desired food and jumped up before the *rūḥ* had reached his feet, hastening for the fruit of the Garden. That is when He says: *'Man was created hasty.'* (21:37) *'Then the angels prostrated all together, every one of them – except Iblīs. He disdained to be one of the prostrators.'* (15:30)

At-Tirmidhī related that Abū Mūsā al-Ash'arī said that he heard the Messenger of Allah ﷺ say, 'Allah Almighty created Ādam from a handful that He took from all over the earth. So the sons of Ādam come according to that earth: some of them are red, some white and some black, and colours between that, easy-tempered and rough, foul and good.' Abū 'Īsā said that it is a sound *ḥasan* ḥadīth.

'Names' here means expressions. *'Ism'* can be undefined and mean something named as you say, 'Zayd is standing' and the 'The lion is standing.' 'Naming' means their essence. It is also said that 'essence' (*dhāt*), 'self' (*nafs*), 'source' (*'ayn*) and *'ism'* mean the same. That is true of many of its usages in the Qur'an.

The people of interpretation disagree about the meaning of the names mentioned in this *āyah*. Ibn 'Abbās, 'Ikrimah, Qatādah, Mujāhid and Ibn Jubayr said that He taught him the names of all things, large and small. 'Āṣim ibn Kulayb related that Sa'd, the freedman of al-Ḥasan ibn 'Alī, said, 'I was sitting with Ibn 'Abbās when they mentioned the noun for vessel and the noun for whip. Ibn 'Abbās said, "He taught Ādam all the names."' This idea is related by a *marfū'* transmission and the words demands all these meanings since it is a word which is comprehensive and unspecified. We find in al-Bukhārī from Anas that the Prophet ﷺ said, 'The believers will be gathered on the Day of Rising and will say, "We should ask someone to intercede with our Lord." They will go to Ādam and say, "You are the father of mankind. Allah created you with His hand, the angels prostrated to you and He taught you the names of all things."'

Ibn Khuwayzimandād said, 'This *āyah* contains evidence that language is learned by being informed of it and that Allah Almighty taught it to Ādam in detail and in general.' That is like what Ibn 'Abbās said: 'He taught him the names of all things, even the bowl and milk-pan.' Shaybān related that Qatādah said, 'He taught Ādam the names of His creation which He had not taught to the angels. He gave the names of every thing and use of all things and their species.' An-Naḥḥās said, 'This is the best of what has been related regarding this. It means that He taught him the names of the species and informed him of their uses.' Aṭ-Ṭabarī said, 'He taught him the names of the angels and his descendants.' He preferred this. Ibn Zayd said, 'He taught him the names of all his descendants.' Ar-Rabī' ibn Khuthaym said that it was the names of the angels in particular. Al-Qutabī said that it was the names of what He created in the earth. It is said that it is the names of the species and categories. The first view is sounder, Allah willing.

Then He arrayed them before the angels

Interpreters disagree about whether the presentation of the names involved the presentation of the things themselves, or simply their names, to the angels. Ibn Mas'ūd says that it means to display the actual things. Others say that it just means the names. The verb *'araḍa* means to show or display something. It is used for displaying goods for sale. Ibn 'Abbās and others said that it means He displayed the names. The variant reading of Ibn Mas'ūd has: "*araḍahunna'*, referring to the names, not the persons because '*hunna'* is used for the feminine. The variant of Ubayy has "*araḍahā*'. Mujāhid said, 'those with names'. The second reading would indicate that they are the names and the second that it is the individuals. That would also be the case with '*hum'* (them). Ibn 'Aṭiyyah said, 'It is clear that Allah Almighty taught Ādam the names and presented them to him with those individual species. Then He arrayed them before the angels and asked them for their names if they knew them. Then Ādam told them their names. Al-Māwardī said that the presentation refers to those names named.

Two things are said about the time of the arraying. One is that it was after they were created and the second is that He made the hearts of the angels give them form and then arrayed them.

There is disagreement about the first person to speak Arabic. It is related from Ka'b al-Aḥbār that Ādam was the first to use Arabic and Syriac writing and books in all languages. Others besides Ka'b have said that. It is said that it is related by another path that Ka'b al-Aḥbār said, 'Jibrīl was the first to speak Arabic, He is the one who taught it to Nūḥ and Nūḥ taught it to his son Shām.' That is related from Thawr ibn Zayd from Khālid ibn Ma'dān from Ka'b. It is related that the Prophet ﷺ said, 'The first to speak clear Arabic was Ismā'īl when he was ten years old.' It is also related that the first to speak Arabic was Ya'rub ibn Qaḥṭān. Other things are related. We say that the sound position is that the first to speak all human languages was Ādam. The Qur'an bears witness to this as Allah Almighty says: *'He taught Ādam the names of all things.'* All languages are names and so they are included in this and the Sunnah states this. The Prophet ﷺ

said, 'He taught Ādam the names of all things even bowls.' It is mentioned that it is possible that Ismā'īl was the first of Ibrāhīm's children to speak Arabic. If other things are sound, it is possible that he was the first of his tribe to speak Arabic. Allah knows best.

and said, 'Tell Me the names of these if you are telling the truth.'

'If the sons of Ādam are simply going to cause corruption on the earth, then show Me that you have the same knowledge that I have taught this new creature.' In other words there is far more to a human being than the angels were able to perceive. Al-Mubarrad says that. '*Ṣādiqīn*' (telling the truth) means 'truly knowing'. That is why the angels were unable to try and answer and instead said, '*Glory be to You!*' as an-Naḥḥās related. If truthfulness had not been stipulated, they could have made an effort to answer.

قَالُوا سُبْحَانَكَ لَا عِلْمَ لَنَا إِلَّا مَا عَلَّمْتَنَا إِنَّكَ أَنْتَ الْعَلِيمُ الْحَكِيمُ ٣٢

32 They said, 'Glory be to You! We have no knowledge except what You have taught us. You are the All-Knowing, the All-Wise.'

'"*Glory be to You*" beyond anyone but You knowing the Unseen.' This is their response to '*Tell me.*' They answered that they only know what Allah has taught them and do not concern themselves with what they do not know as the ignorant do. From this comes the obligation for someone who is asked for knowledge he does not possess to say, 'Allah knows best, I do not know,' in imitation of the angels, Prophets, and virtuous scholars. The Prophet ﷺ told us, however, that, when the scholars died, true knowledge would disappear and we would be left with ignorant people who would be asked for fatwas and give fatwas according to their own opinion. So they will be misguided and also misguide others.

As for the reports related from the Prophet ﷺ, his Companions and the Tābi'ūn after them about the meaning of the *āyah*, it is related by al-Bustī in his *Musnad* from Ibn 'Umar that a man asked the Messenger of Allah ﷺ, 'What place is worst?' He replied, 'I do not know until I ask Jibrīl.' He asked Jibrīl who replied, 'I do not know until I ask Mīkā'īl.' He said, 'The best of places are the mosques and the worst of places are the markets.' Abū Bakr said to a grandmother, 'Come back later so that I can consult the people.' 'Alī said three times, 'It is most cooling for the liver.' 'What is that, *Amīr al-Mu'minīn*?' they asked. He said, 'That a man is asked about what he does not know and says, "Allah knows best."' Ibn 'Umar was asked about something and said, 'I have no knowledge of it.' When the man turned back, Ibn

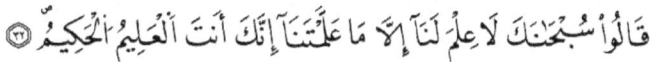

'Umar said, 'Excellent is what Ibn Umar said! He was asked about what he did not know and said, "I have no knowledge of it"!' Ad-Dārimī mentioned it in his *Musnad*.

We find in *Ṣaḥīḥ Muslim* that Abū 'Aqīl Yaḥyā ibn Al-Mutawakkil, the companion of Buhayyah said, 'I was sitting with al-Qāsim ibn 'Ubaydullāh and Yaḥyā ibn Sa'd and Yaḥyā said to al-Qāsim, "Abū Muḥammad, how ugly it is for a great man like you to be asked about something in the *dīn* and then not to have any knowledge about it nor any answer!" Al-Qāsim asked him, "Why is that?" He answered, "Because you are the son of two imams of guidance: Abū Bakr and 'Umar." Al-Qāsim said to him, "More ugly than that is if, having knowledge from Allah, I should speak without knowledge or take from an untrustworthy source." He was silent and did not answer.' Mālik ibn Anas said, 'I heard Ibn Hurmuz say, "A scholar must bequeath 'I do not know' to his companions after him so that it is a fundamental principle in their hands."' Al-Haytham ibn Jamīl said, 'I saw Mālik ibn Anas asked about forty-eight questions and say, "I do not know" about thirty-two of them.'

There are many of examples of this that are transmitted from the Companions, Tābi'ūn and Muslim *fuqahā'*. That leads to attacking leadership and lack of balance in knowledge. Ibn 'Abd al-Barr said, 'Part of the blessing of knowledge and proper manners in knowledge is balance in it. If someone is not balanced in it, he does not understand or make others understand.' Yūnus ibn 'Abd al-A'lā said that he heard Ibn Wahb say that he heard Mālik ibn Anas say, 'There is nothing more lacking in our time than balance.'

If this was the case in Mālik's time, then what is it like in our time when corruption is widespread and there are many common people and people seek leadership in it for the sake of leadership, not study. Instead it is for reputation in this world and for overpowering contemporaries through debate and argument which hardens the hearts and results in spite. That is part of what cones from lack of *taqwā* and lack of fear of Allah Almighty. Where is this in respect of what is related about what happened when 'Umar talked about not making the dower of women more than forty *ūqiyyah*s, even if for a woman of lineage. A tall woman stood up and said, 'You cannot say that!' He said, 'Why?' She said, 'Because Allah Almighty says: *"If you have given your wife a large amount, do not take any of it."* (4:20)' 'Umar said, 'The woman is correct and the man is wrong!'

Wakī' related from Abū Mash'ar that Muḥammad ibn Ka'b al-Qurṭubī said, 'A man asked 'Alī about something and he spoke about it. The man said, "It is not like that, Amīr al-Mu'minīn! It is like this." 'Alī said, "You are correct and I erred. Above everyone with knowledge is a Knower."' Abū Muḥammad Qāsim ibn Aṣbagh said, 'When I travelled to the east, I stayed in Qayrawān. I took the hadith of Musaddad from Bakr ibn Ḥammād. Then I travelled to Baghdad and met people. When I finished, I returned to him to complete the hadith of Musaddad. One day I read to him the hadith of the Prophet ﷺ: "Some people of Muḍar came in striped shirts (*mujtābi-n-nimār*) …" and he said that it was "*ath-thimār*". I said, "'*Mujtābi-n-nimār*' is how I read it to all of those to whom I read it in Andalusia and Iraq." He said, "By going to Iraq, you have contradicted us and become arrogant towards us! Let us go to that Shaykh (who was in the mosque). He has knowledge of such things." We went to him and questioned him about that and he said that it was as I had said. Bakr ibn Ḥammād said, taking hold of his nose, "My nose is forced to the truth. My nose is forced to the truth." He left.'

'All-Knowing' (*al-'Alīm*) is a form used for emphasis. He is the One with great est knowledge of His creation. *'Al-Ḥakīm'* is the Judge. It is again used for emphasis.

قَالَ يَٰٓـَٔادَمُ أَنۢبِئْهُم بِأَسْمَآئِهِمْ ۖ فَلَمَّآ أَنۢبَأَهُم بِأَسْمَآئِهِمْ قَالَ أَلَمْ أَقُل لَّكُمْ إِنِّىٓ
أَعْلَمُ غَيْبَ ٱلسَّمَٰوَٰتِ وَٱلْأَرْضِ وَأَعْلَمُ مَا تُبْدُونَ وَمَا كُنتُمْ تَكْتُمُونَ ﴿٣٣﴾

33 He said, 'Ādam, tell them their names.' When he had told them their names, He said, 'Did I not tell you that I know the Unseen of the heavens and the earth, and I know what you make known and what you hide?'

He said, 'Ādam, tell them their names.'

Allah commanded him to tell the angels their names after they were arrayed before them so that they would know that He knows best what He asked them about. This was in order to demonstrate Ādam's excellence and high position. He was better than them since he had greater knowledge than them and they were made to prostrate before him and become his students and ordered to learn from him. This demonstrated that he had the rank of majesty and greatness.

Some scholars use this as evidence for the Prophethood of Ādam before he was in the Garden since Allah says: *'Tell them their names,'* and so Allah commanded him to inform the angels of that which they had no knowledge.

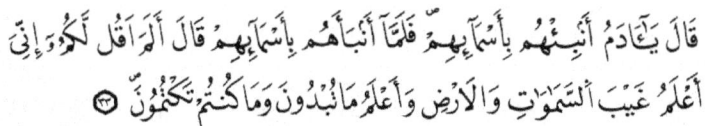

This *āyah* contains evidence for the excellence of knowledge and its possessors. In a hadith we find: 'The angels lower their wings to anyone who seeks knowledge for the pure pleasure of seeking it.' They do that for scholars alone because that is what Allah obliged them to do in the case of Ādam and so they continue to behave in the same way. When knowledge appears in a person, they are humble to him out of respect for knowledge and its possessors and pleasure at his seeking it and being involved with it. This is merely for the seekers of knowledge; how much more must that be so in the case of its masters!

Scholars disagree about who is better: the angels or the children of Ādam. Some people say that the Messengers among human beings are better than the Messengers from the angels and that human *awliyā'* are better than the *awliyā'* of the angels. Some people say that the Highest Assembly is better. Their argument is that they are *'honoured slaves, who do not precede Him in speech'* (21:26-27), and other similar *āyahs*. There is also the *ḥadīth qudsī* in which Allah says, 'If he mentions Me in an assembly, I mention him in an assembly better than them.'

Those who seek evidence for the superiority of the children of Ādam quote the *āyah*: *'Those who believe and do right actions, they are the best of creatures'* (98:7) and the words of the Prophet ﷺ: 'The angels lower their wings to anyone who seeks knowledge for the pure pleasure of seeking it.' There are other hadiths in which Allah boasts of mankind to the angels and He only boasts of the best. Allah knows best.

Some scholars have said that there is no way of concluding that the Prophets are better than the angels or that the angels are better than them, because the only way of doing so would be if there was a definitive report from Allah or from His Messenger or the consensus of the Community and nothing of that sort exists. This differs from the Qadariyyah and Qāḍī Abū Bakr who said that the angels are better. As for the statement of our people and the Shī'ah that the Prophets are better because Allah Almighty commanded the angels to prostrate to Ādam, they are told that the person to whom someone prostrates is not necessarily better than the one who prostrates. Do you not see that the Prophets and creation prostrate towards the Ka'bah when it is agreed that the Prophets are better than the Ka'bah? There is no disagreement that true prostration is only to Allah Almighty because prostration is worship and worship is only for Allah. This is clear.

He said, 'Did I not tell you that I know the Unseen of the heavens and the earth,

This is proof that no one knows anything of the Unseen except what Allah informs Him of, like the Prophets or those whom Allah teaches. Astrologers, soothsayers and such people are all liars. This will be discussed in *Sūrat al-An'ām*.

and I know what you make known

This refers to their words about Allah putting someone on the earth who would cause corruption there.

and what you hide?'

Ibn 'Abbās, Ibn Mas'ūd and Sa'īd ibn Jubayr said that what is being referred to here is the pride and rebellion which Iblīs concealed in himself. Ibn 'Aṭiyyah said that 'hide' is in the plural when only one person is meant. This is a common Arabic usage. One group said that making known and hiding has an undefined meaning about their secret and public aspects. Mahdī ibn Maymūn said, 'We were with al-Ḥasan when al-Ḥasan ibn Dīnār asked him, "What did the angels hide?" He replied, "When Allah created Ādam, the angels saw an extraordinary creature. It was as if something about that worried them. Then they turned confidentially to one another and said, 'Why are we concerned about this creature! Allah has not created anything but that we are more honoured than it in His sight.'"'

وَإِذْ قُلْنَا لِلْمَلَـٰٓئِكَةِ ٱسْجُدُوا۟ لِـَٔادَمَ فَسَجَدُوٓا۟ إِلَّآ إِبْلِيسَ أَبَىٰ وَٱسْتَكْبَرَ
وَكَانَ مِنَ ٱلْكَـٰفِرِينَ ﴿٣٤﴾

34 We said to the angels, 'Prostrate to Ādam!' and they prostrated, with the exception of Iblīs. He refused and was arrogant and was one of the unbelievers.

We said to the angels, 'Prostrate to Ādam!' and they prostrated,

'Prostrate' here means to be humble and submit. Those who say that Ādam and his sons are better than the angels find evidence in Allah's words to the angels here: *'Prostrate to Ādam!'* They say that this indicates that he was better than them. The answer to that is that the meaning of this 'prostrate' simply means to be humble in front of Ādam. An eye which 'prostrates' drops its gaze. The furthest extent of that is to put one's face on the ground. Ibn Fāris said, 'Someone prostrates when he goes low. All that prostrates is humbled.' It also means to bow the head.

If someone were to ask, 'If he was not better than them, what was the point of telling them to prostrate to him?' the answer is that, when the angels exulted in their glorification and praise, Allah commanded them to prostrate to something other than Him in order to show them that He had no need of them and their worship. Some say that they criticised and belittled Ādam and did not recognise the special nature of what Allah had created and so they were commanded to prostrate. It could be that it was a punishment for them because of what they said.

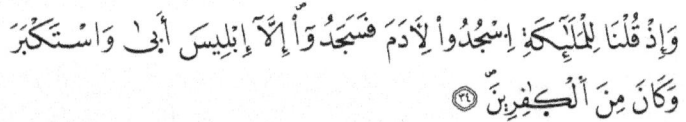

It is said that Ibn 'Abbās found evidence for the supreme excellence of human beings in the fact that Allah swore by the life of the Messenger ﷺ and said: *'By your life! They were wandering blindly in their drunkenness'* (15:72) and granted him security from punishment in His words: *'So that Allah may forgive you your earlier errors and any later ones.'* (48:2) He said to the angels: *'Were any of them to say, "I am a god apart from Him," We would repay him with Hell.'* (21:29) The answer to this is that He did not swear by the life of the angels as He did not swear by His life. He swore by heaven and earth and that did not indicate that they were worth more than the Throne and the seven Gardens. He also swore by the fig and the olive. There is no proof in what he said.

People disagree about how the angels prostrated to Ādam, although they agree that the prostration was not worship. Most say that this command to the angels was for them to place their foreheads on the ground as is done in the prayer because the form of prostration is clear in both custom and the Sharī'ah. Thus the prostration was to honour him because of his excellence and to obey Allah's command to them. Ādam acted as their *qiblah.* Some people say that it was not the '*sajdah*' (act of prostration) that is known today but rather refers to the basic linguistic meaning of the word, which is abasement and obedience. So the meaning is that humbled themselves before Ādam and acknowledged his virtue. So 'prostrated' simply means 'did what they were commanded.'

There is also disagreement about whether the prostration was exclusively to Ādam, so that it is not permitted to prostrate to anyone else in existence except Allah, or whether such prostration was permitted until the time of Ya'qūb, based on the words of Allah: *'He raised his parents up onto the throne. The others fell prostrate in front of him.'* (12:100). Most, however, say that this kind of prostration was permitted right up until the time of the Messenger of Allah ﷺ. When the trees and camels prostrated before him, the Companions said to him, 'We are more entitled to prostrate to you than trees and stray camels.' He told them, 'It is not permitted to prostrate to anyone except the Lord of the worlds.' Ibn Mājah related this in his *Sunan* and al-Bustī in his *Ṣaḥīḥ.* When Mu'ādh came from Syria, he prostrated to the Messenger of Allah ﷺ who said, 'What is this?' He said, 'Messenger of Allah, I went to Syria and saw them prostrate before their patriarchs and bishops. So I wanted to do that with you.' He stated, 'No one should do that. If I had commanded anyone to prostrate to something, I would have commanded a wife to prostrate to her husband.'

with the exception of Iblīs.

The exception is connected to what was just mentioned before (i.e. the angels), as is generally stated. Ibn 'Abbās, Ibn Mas'ūd and Ibn Jurayj and others said that Iblīs was one of the angels. Ibn 'Abbās said, 'His name was 'Azāzīl and he was one of the noblest of the angels. He had four wings and then was deprived of his angelic status. When he disobeyed Allah, Allah cursed him and he became Shayṭān.' Sa'īd ibn Jubayr said, 'The jinn were a tribe of the angels, created from fire and Iblīs was one of them. The rest of the angels were created from light.' Ibn Zayd, al-Ḥasan and Qatādah said, 'Iblīs was the father of the jinn in the same way that Ādam was the father of human beings. He was not an angel.' A similar statement is also related from Ibn 'Abbās. He said that his name was al-Ḥārith in Arabic. Sahr ibn Ḥawshab and others say, 'He was one of the jinn who were on earth. The angels fought them and captured him as a child and he worshipped with the angels.' Aṭ-Ṭabarī related that from Ibn Mas'ūd.

Others find their evidence in Allah's description of the angels: *'They do not disobey Allah in respect of any order He gives them and carry out what they are ordered to do'* (66:6), and in the *āyah*: *'Iblīs was one of the jinn.'* (18:50) The jinn are not angels. The proponents of the first position answer that nothing prevents Iblīs from issuing from the angels as a whole, since Allah knew that he would be wretched and He is not asked about what He does. There is nothing in the fact that he was created from fire nor in the development of his appetites, demonstrated by his becoming angry, that precludes him from being one of the angels. As for those who say that he was one of the jinn of the earth who was captured, to counter that it is related that Iblīs, accompanied by an army of angels, was the one who fought the jinn on earth. Al-Mahdawī and others related that.

Ath-Tha'labī related that Ibn 'Abbās said that Iblīs was from one of the clans of the angels who were called 'jinn' and who were created from smokeless fire. The angels were created from light. His name in Syriac was 'Azāzīl and in Arabic al-Ḥārith. He was one of the guardians of the Garden and chief of the angels of the lowest heaven. He had authority over it and over the earth. He was one of the angels with the greatest striving and most knowledge. He used to manage what was between heaven and earth. Because of that he saw himself as great and noble. That is what led him to unbelief and to disobey Allah. Then he was transformed into the accursed Shayṭān. Sometimes the angels are referred to as 'jinn' because of their being hidden from sight in the same way. We find in Revelation: *'They claim there is a blood-tie between Him and the jinn.'* (37:158)

He refused and was arrogant

There is a sound hadith from Abū Hurayrah in which the Prophet ﷺ said, 'When the son of Ādam recites a verse of prostration and prostrates, Shayṭān withdraws, weeping, saying, "O woe to me! Ādam was commanded to prostrate and prostrated, so he has the Garden. I was commanded to prostrate and refused, so I have the Fire." Muslim transmitted it.

He refused to prostrate because he thought he was better than Ādam, which indicates that he considered the command and wisdom of Allah to be foolish. This is the arrogance about which the Prophet ﷺ said, 'Anyone who has an atom's weight of pride in his heart will not enter the Garden!' When a man said to the Prophet ﷺ that a man likes his clothing and appearance to be good, he said ﷺ, 'Allah is beautiful and loves beauty. Pride is to disregard the truth and to despise people.' Muslim transmitted it. The accursed one clearly expressed this when he said: *'I am better than him. You created me from fire and You created him from clay.'* (38:76) Because of that, Allah made him an unbeliever. So anyone who considers any of the commands of Allah Almighty or His Messenger to be foolish is subject to the same ruling as him. There is no dispute about this.

Ibn al-Qāsim said, 'I heard that the first act of disobedience was envy and pride when Iblīs envied Ādam and Ādam desired to eat from the tree.' Qatādah said, 'Iblīs envied Ādam for the honour he had been given. He complained. "I am made of fire and this one is only made of clay."' So the first wrong action was pride, then greed which caused Ādam to eat from the tree, and then envy when the son of Ādam envied his brother.

and was one of the unbelievers.

This 'was' here means 'became'. Most interpreters say that the meaning is: Allah knew that he would become an unbeliever because an unbeliever has one reality and a believer another and Allah knows them both. This is sound because of what the Prophet ﷺ said, recorded in al-Bukhārī, 'Actions are by their seals.' It is said that Iblīs worshipped Allah for eighty thousand years and had leadership and was a guardian of the Garden, during all of which time he was gradually being drawn on, in the same way that hypocrites say the *shahādah* with their tongues and that Bal'am had the greatest Name on his tongue. He had leadership but pride was firmly rooted in him. Ibn 'Abbās said, 'He thought that he had greater excellence than the angels, which is why he said, "*I am better than him.*"' This is why Allah said: *'What prevented you from prostrating to what I created with My own Hands? Were you overcome by arrogance or are you one of the exalted?'* (38:75) The basis of his creation was the fire of Might, which is shown by the fact that He swore by it when he said: *'By Your Might, I will mislead all of them.'* (38:82). Might brings about pride so that he thought that he was better than Ādam. Abū Ṣāliḥ said, 'The angels were created from the lights of Might and Iblīs from the fire of Might.'

Our scholars say that, if someone is not a Prophet and Allah displays miracles and the breaking of normal patterns at his hand, it does not necessarily indicate that he is saint. This is opposed to what the Sufis and Shi'ites say about this matter, indicating that if he had not been a *walī*, Allah would not have made appear at his hands what He did. Our proof is that the knowledge that one of us is a *walī* of Allah can only be validated after it is clear that he has died a believer. If it is not known that someone died a believer, it cannot be unequivocally stated that he is a *walī* of Allah. That is only proven by faith. When we agree that we cannot unequivocally state that someone is true to faith and that a man cannot unequivocally state that about himself, it is known that that does not indicate someone is a *walī* of Allah. They said, 'We cannot deny that some of His *awliyā'* are known by their good outcome, the final seal on their actions, and other such things.' Shaykh Abu-l-Ḥasan al-Ash'arī and others said that. Aṭ-Ṭabarī believed that Allah intended the story of Iblīs to be a deterrent to those human beings who resemble him.

There is disagreement about whether there was any unbeliever before Iblīs or not. Some say that Iblīs was the first to disbelieve and it is also said that there were unbelievers of the jinn before him, who were on the earth. There is also disagreement about whether his *kufr* was out of ignorance or obstinacy, both things being said by the people of the *Sunnah*. There is no disagreement that he knew Allah before his disbelief. Those who say that he disbelieved out of ignorance say that knowledge was stripped from him when he disbelieved. Those who say that he disbelieved out of obstinacy say that he disbelieved in spite of his knowledge, Ibn 'Aṭiyyah said, 'Unbelief with continuing knowledge is unlikely, but still possible. Allah can disappoint whomever He wills.'

وَقُلْنَا يَٰٓـَٔادَمُ ٱسْكُنْ أَنتَ وَزَوْجُكَ ٱلْجَنَّةَ وَكُلَا مِنْهَا رَغَدًا حَيْثُ شِئْتُمَا
وَلَا تَقْرَبَا هَٰذِهِ ٱلشَّجَرَةَ فَتَكُونَا مِنَ ٱلظَّٰلِمِينَ ﴿٣٥﴾

35 We said, 'Ādam, live in the Garden, you and your wife, and eat freely from it wherever you will. But do not approach this tree and so become wrongdoers.'

We said, 'Ādam, live in the Garden, you and your wife

There is no disagreement that Allah expelled Iblīs when he became an unbeliever and put him far from the Garden and that afterwards He commanded Ādam 'to live' (*uskun*) in the Garden, in other words, to abide there and take up residence there. *Sakan*, from the same root, means any place that one feels at home in, *sikkīn* is a knife, which is so called because it stills the movement of the slaughtered animal; *miskīn* (indigent) is derived from the same root since a poor person cannot move about through lack of means; *sukkan* is the rudder of the ship because it keeps it steady.

The *āyah* shows that living in a place does not necessarily constitute ownership of it. One of the gnostics said that the use of the word '*uskun*' (live in the imperative) shows that it was for a time that would come an end. So the original entry of Ādam and Ḥawwā' into the Garden was one of a temporary and not a permanent nature. If this understanding is correct there is evidence in it for what most scholars say: that if someone gives a man a place to live, the man does not own it by living there and the owner can evict him when the tenant's term of residency ends. Ash-Sha'bī said, 'If a man says, "My house is a residence (*suknā*) for you until you die," it is his for his life and death. But if he says, "Live (*uskun*) in this house of mine until you die," it reverts to the owner when he dies."' *Suknā* and *'umrā* are similar although there is greater disagreement about the *'umrā* which will be discussed in *Hūd*. Al-Ḥarbī said that he heard Ibn al-A'rābī say, 'The Arabs did not disagree that these things are based on the property of the owners and its uses that can be assigned in the form of *'umrā*, *ruqbā*, *ifqār*, *ikhbāl*, *minḥah*, *'ariyyah*, *suknā* and *iṭrāq* (see definitions below). This is the argument of Mālik and his people for the fact that a person only owns the use of gifts except in the case of slaves. This is the view of al-Layth ibn Sa'd, al-Qāsim ibn Muḥammad and Yazīd ibn Qusayṭ.'

An *'umrā* is letting a man live in your house for the period of your life or his life. It is the same as a *ruqbā*. It is when you say, 'If you die before me, it returns to me. If I die before you, it is yours.' It comes from the term *murāqabah* which is that each of them watches (*rāqaba*) for the death of the other. That is why there is disagreement about whether it is forbidden or permitted. Abū Yūsuf and ash-Shāfi'ī permitted it. They consider it to be like a bequest. Mālik and the Kufans forbade it because each of them aims for recompense and does not know whether he will obtain it or not. There are also two hadiths on the topic forbidding it and permitting it that Ibn Mājah mentioned in his *Sunan*. The first was related by Jābir ibn 'Abdullāh: the Messenger of Allah ﷺ said, 'An *'umrā* is permitted for someone who makes it. A *ruqbā* is permitted for the one who makes it.' This hadith considers *'umrā* and *ruqbā* to be the same. The second is that Ibn 'Umar related that the Messenger of Allah ﷺ said, 'There is no *ruqbā*. If someone watches for something, it is his in his life and death.' He said that a *ruqbā* is that he says to someone else, 'It is death from me and from you.' The words 'There is no *ruqbā*' imply a prohibition while the words in the first hadith indicate permission. An-Naṣā'ī transmitted both of them. It is related from Ibn 'Abbās that *'umrā* and *ruqbā* are the same. Ibn al-Mundhir said that it is confirmed that the Messenger of Allah ﷺ said, 'An *'umrā* is permitted for someone who makes it. A *ruqbā* is permitted for someone who makes it.' He said that the hadith is sound and it provides a proof for those who say that *'umrā* and *ruqbā* are the same. It is related from 'Alī and that is the position of ath-Thawrī and Aḥmad. That is what Isḥāq said. Ṭāwus said, 'If someone makes a *ruqbā*, it is like inheritance.'

Ifqār is taken from the word for the spine and the verb is used for letting someone have an animal to ride or letting someone have game. It is the same as *ikhbāl*. *Minḥah* is a gift of milk. *Manīḥah* is a she-camel or ewe that a man gives to another to milk and then it is returned. The Messenger of Allah ﷺ said, 'An *'āriyyah* is carried out and a *minḥah* is returned. A debt is settled and a claimant is a creditor.' Abū Umāmah related it and at-Tirmidhī, ad-Dāraquṭnī and others transmitted it. It is sound. *Iṭrāq* is lending a stud to a person when he asks for it to use in his camels.

The word *zawj* (wife) in the language of the Qur'an has no *tā'* while it does have one in hadith. Ādam's wife was Ḥawwā' (Eve). She was the first to be called that when she was created from his rib without Ādam being aware of it. If pain had been involved in that process, men would not have affection for their wives. When he woke up, he was asked, 'Who is this?' 'A woman,' he answered. He was asked, 'What is her name?' 'Ḥawwā',' he replied. He was asked, 'Why is she called "*imra'ah*" (woman)?' He said, 'Because she was taken from man (*mar'*).' He was asked, 'Why did you call her Ḥawwā'?' He answered, 'Because she was created from something living (*ḥayy*).' It is related that the angels asked this to test his knowledge. They asked him, 'Do you love her, Ādam?' 'Yes,' he answered. They asked Ḥawwā', 'Do you love him, Ḥawwā'?' 'No,' she replied while in her heart her love for him was many times more than his love. They said, 'If any woman were to speak the truth about her love for her husband, Ḥawwā' would have spoken the truth.'

Ibn Mas'ūd and Ibn 'Abbās said, 'When Ādam was settled in the Garden, he walked in feeling lonely. While he slept, Ḥawwā' was created from his shortest rib on the left side so that he might find repose with her and have companionship with her. When he woke up, he saw her and asked, "Who are you?" She answered, "A woman! I was created from your rib so that you might find repose with me." That is the meaning of His words: *"It is He Who created you from a single self and made from him his spouse so that he might find repose in her."* (7:189)' Scholars say that this is why woman was created crooked because she was created from a curved rib. In the *Ṣaḥīḥ Muslim*, Abū Hurayrah said that the Messenger of Allah ﷺ said,

'Woman was created from a rib and the top of the rib is the most curved part of it. She will not be straightened. Enjoy her as she is. If you try to straighten her, you will break her, and the breaking is divorce.' A poet said:

She is the crooked rib that you will not straighten.
If you straighten the rib, you break it.
Are weakness and strength combined in a lad?
Is it not a wonder how she is both weak and powerful?

It is from this that scholars derive the inheritance of a hermaphrodite when the signs of masculinity and femininity are the same in them. If one of the ribs is missing, then they receive the portion of a man. That is related from 'Alī.

We ignore what the Mu'tazilites claimed about the Garden here not being the Garden of Eternity, but a garden on the earth. That is because Allah uses the definite article for it and the fact that when someone asks Allah for the Garden, using the definite article, He only means the Garden of Eternity. According to their innovation, if it had been the Garden of Eternity, Iblīs could not have entered it since Allah says: *'no foolish talk and no wrong action in it'* (52:23) and similar *āyah*s. It is not logically impossible for Iblīs to have entered the Garden to tempt Ādam.

Mūsā met Ādam and Mūsā said to him, 'You made your descendants wretched and expelled them from the Garden.' He used the definite article to indicate that it was the Garden of Eternity. Ādam did not deny that. If it had been other than that, Ādam would have refuted it. As Ādam was silent in the face of what Mūsā said, it was clear that the abode from which Allah expelled him was not the abode to which they were expelled. As for the *āyah*s they cite as evidence, Allah made those words about it refer to after its people enter it on the Day of Rising. That does not prevent the Abode of Eternity being eternal for those for whom Allah wills it while those for whom annihilation is decreed leave it. It is agreed that the angels enter and leave the Garden. Its keys were in the possession of Iblīs and then they were taken from him after he disobeyed. During the Night Journey, the Prophet ﷺ entered it and left it. He reported what it contains and that it is truly the Garden of Eternity.

If someone claims that what is meant is the Holy Land, which Allah purified of sins, that is ignorance on their part, because Allah commanded the tribe of Israel to enter the Holy Land, which was Greater Syria. The people who follow the Sharī'ah agree that Allah purified the Holy Land, but nevertheless acts of rebellion, disbelief and lying occurred in it. These things were not prevented by its being sanctified. Abu-l-Ḥasan ibn Baṭṭāl said that some shaykhs related that the people of the Sunnah agree that the Garden of Eternity is the one from which Ādam descended. There is no sense in the position of those who disagree with that. They ask how it is possible that with his perfect knowledge, Ādam sought the Tree of Immortality in the Abode of Eternity, the question is reversed to them and they are asked how would it be possible for Ādam to seek the Tree of Immortality in the abode of annihilation! This is not permitted by anyone who has the smallest amount of intelligence.

The majority recite *'raghad'* (freely) while an-Nakha'ī and Ibn Waththāb recite *'raghd'*.

but do not approach this tree

Do not go near it to eat from it. It is said that it means 'do not touch it' or 'do not go close to it'. Ibn 'Aṭiyyah said that this is a clear example of *sadd 'dh-dharā'i'* (the legal principle of barring the means to wrong action). Some of those who have a fine grasp of the use of language say that the instruction not to approach, in itself indicates that they were, in fact, going to fall into error and leave the Garden and not dwell in it forever, because someone who is eternal is not commanded or forbidden anything. The evidence of this is in the words of Allah: *'I am putting a caliph on the earth'* (2:30), showing that Ādam was definitely going to leave the Garden.

A tree is a plant with a trunk. Interpreters disagree about what type of tree this was. Ibn Mas'ūd, Ibn 'Abbās, Sa'id ibn Jubayr and others say that it was a grapevine and that is why wine was forbidden us. Ibn 'Abbās, Abū Malik and Qatādah say that it was wheat. Wahb ibn Munabbih said that when Allah relented towards Ādam, he made it the food of his descendants. Ibn Jurayj said that some of the Companions said that it was a fig tree as is reported from Qatādah. Ibn 'Aṭiyyah said that there is no specification of what it was which can be reliably relied upon. What is correct is to believe that Allah forbade Ādam a particular tree and then he went to it and disobeyed Him by eating from it. The tree was a test.

They also disagree about how he could eat from it in the light of the threat which follows it, *'and so become wrongdoers.'* Some people said that they ate from other than the tree which was indicated and did not interpret the prohibition as applying to the entire species, which suggests that Iblīs deluded them into taking an over-literal understanding of Allah's instruction to them. Ibn al-'Arabī said, 'It was the first act of disobedience according to this view.' It is also said that Ādam ate out of forgetfulness, forgetting the threat. The soundness of that view is indicated by what Allah says about it in His Book: *'We made a contract with Ādam before, but he forgot. We did not find that he had a firm resolve.'* (20:117) Since the Prophets are obliged to be cautious and aware because of their great knowledge and position, their obligation is greater than that of others and so by being distracted from a prohibition one becomes disobedient or in opposition.

Abū Umāmah said, 'If the forbearance of the sons of Ādam since the time Allah created creation until the Day of Rising been placed in one pan of the balance and that of Ādam had been placed in the other, it would have outweighed it and Allah says: "*We did not find that he had a firm resolve.*"' This view can be general to all the sons of Ādam and particularly about Muḥammad ﷺ who had the greatest forbearance. It can also mean the forbearance of the sons of Ādam is not that of the Prophets. Allah knows best. The first view is good.

It is said that the first of the two to eat from it was Ḥawwā' because Iblīs misled her and that the first of his words were to her because she could whisper to her husband and that it was the first trial for men from women. When she mentioned it to Ādam, he rejected it and mentioned the contract. Iblīs persisted with Ḥawwā' who, in turn, persisted with Ādam until she said, 'I will eat before you. If anything happens to me, you will be safe.' She ate and was not harmed and went to Ādam and said, 'I ate and it did not harm me.' So he ate and then their private parts became clear to them and they fell into wrong action. This is because the command to them was in the dual. So there was no punishment until they had both done it. It is sound that there was no full disobedience until they had both done it. Ādam did not see this fact and so he forgot the ruling.

That is why some scholars say that if someone says to his two wives or two slave-girls, 'If you enter the house, you are divorced, or free,' the divorce or emancipation does not occur if only one of them enters. Scholars disagree about that, taking three different positions. Ibn al-Qāsim said that divorce or emancipation only takes place when they both enter, based on the basic principle and taking the general meaning of the word. Saḥnūn also said that. Ibn al-Qāsim said another time that they are both divorced and both freed when one of them enters because part of breaking an oath is breaking all of it. So if someone swears that he will not eat these two loaves, he breaks it by eating one of them, even one bite of them. Ashhab said that only the one who enters is divorced or freed because the entry of each of them is a precondition for divorce or emancipation. Ibn al-'Arabī said that this is unlikely because part of a precondition is not a precondition by consensus.

What is sound is the first view. If the prohibition is connected to two acts, it is not broken except by both of them. If you tell two people not to enter a house and then one of them enters it, both have not differed from what was prohibited. So Allah's words: '*Do not approach this tree*' is a prohibition directed to the two of them. '*So become wrongdoers*' is its apodosis. They are not wrongdoers until they both do it. Therefore when she ate from it, she did not incur anything because what was forbidden did not fully exist. This meaning was hidden from Ādam and he wanted to eat and forgot this ruling. This is the sense of Allah's words: '*We made a contract with Ādam before, but he forgot.*' (20:115) It is said that he forgot His words: '*This is an enemy for you and your wife, so do not let him expel you from the Garden and thus make you miserable.*' (20:117)

Scholars disagree about whether the Prophets can commit minor wrong actions, for which they are punished, or not, although there is a consensus that they are protected from major wrong actions and every vice in which there is disgrace or imperfection. Aṭ-Ṭabarī and other *fuqahā'*, *mutakallimūn* and hadith scholars say that minor wrong actions are possible for them, while the Shi'ites maintain that they are protected from all of that. Some of the *fuqahā'* of Mālik, Abū Ḥanīfah and ash-Shāfi'ī say that they are protected from all minor wrong actions as they are protected from all major wrong actions because we are commanded to follow them in their actions and conduct completely without attention to context. If they were allowed minor wrong actions, it would not be possible to follow them since it would not be possible to judge which of their actions were right and which were wrong.

Some later scholars took the former position, saying that Allah would report about any wrong actions that occurred and rebuke them for them so we would know which they were. They also reported this about themselves, were frightened by it and repented of it. That is found in many cases, so that all of them cannot be argued away. This does not detract from their position. Those instances were rare and due to forgetfulness or a mistake, or an interpretation that led to that. They are good actions in respect of others and bad actions in respect of them because of their station and great worth. They are afraid about that in the Standing in the Rising even though they know that they are safe and secure. This is the truth. As al-Junayd said, 'The good actions of the pious are the evil actions of those brought near.' Even if that is reported from them in texts, that does not diminish their rank. Allah chose and purified them.

and so become wrongdoers.'

The root of the word for wrongdoers, *ẓulm*, means to put something in other than its proper place. Land which is 'wronged' (*maẓlūmah*) is land which had no well and then a well was dug. It is also called *ẓalīm*. *Ẓālim* is also used for milk which is drunk before becoming thick. A man who is *ẓālim* inflicts great injustice. *Ẓulm* is *shirk* as Allah says: '*Associating others with Him is a terrible wrong* (ẓulm).' (31:13)

فَأَزَلَّهُمَا ٱلشَّيْطَٰنُ عَنْهَا فَأَخْرَجَهُمَا مِمَّا كَانَا فِيهِ ۖ وَقُلْنَا ٱهْبِطُوا۟
بَعْضُكُمْ لِبَعْضٍ عَدُوٌّ ۖ وَلَكُمْ فِى ٱلْأَرْضِ مُسْتَقَرٌّ وَمَتَٰعٌ إِلَىٰ حِينٍ ﴿٣٦﴾

36 But Shayṭān made them slip up by means of it, expelling them from where they were. We said, 'Go down from here as enemies to each other! You will have residence on the earth and enjoyment for a time.'

but Shayṭān made them slip up by means of it,

The word for 'slip up' comes from the root *zillah* which mean error, so he made them fall into error. Allah says elsewhere: *'Shayṭān made them slip for what they had done.'* (3:155) Ḥamzah recited *'azāllahumā'* with an *alif*, meaning he pushed them away. Ibn Kaysān said that he made them move from the obedience they had to disobedience. According to this, both readings have the same idea although the reading of the majority has a stronger meaning from *'zalla'* as in His words: *'It was Shayṭān who made them slip for what they had done.'* (3:155)

This took place by means of whispering, which caused them to enter into error through their own disobedience. Shayṭān has no power to physically make a person do anything. His only power is to persuade people to commit an error on their own account. Thus the reason for Ādam's moving from one place to the other was his own wrong action. It is said that the meaning is their actual slipping down from the Garden when Allah expelled them from it. That idea is found in the reading of Ḥamzah.

expelling them from where they were.

Their expulsion from the Garden to the earth was because they were created from it and so that Ādam could be a caliph on the earth. Iblīs did not intend to expel him from the Garden but simply wanted to make him fall from his rank and to put him far from Allah in the position he enjoyed. So Iblīs did not obtain his goal and, for this reason, his rancour, resentment and bad opinion increased even more. In fact the opposite took place. Allah says: *'Then his Lord chose him and turned to him and guided him.'* (20:122) So Ādam became the caliph of Allah on the earth after he had been near Him in His abode. Ādam's high rank can be said to be Iblīs's doing because he was the reason for it and for the error which brought it about.

The commentators do not disagree that Iblīs undertook to make Ādam err but they disagree about how he did it. Ibn Mas'ūd, Ibn 'Abbās and the majority say that he did it as himself, and the evidence for that is the words of Allah: *'He swore to them, "I am one of those who give you good advice."'* (7:21) That entails speaking directly. Others, including 'Abd ar-Razzāq from Ibn Wahb, say that he entered the Garden in the mouth of a snake. It had four legs like the best Bactrian camel created by Allah. He had presented himself to many animals but only the snake entered the Garden. When the snake brought him into the Garden, Iblīs emerged from its belly and took something from the Tree that Allah had forbidden to Ādam and Ḥawwā'. He took it to Ḥawwā' and said, 'Look at this tree! How good it smells! How delicious it tastes! What a splendid colour!' He kept tempting her until Ḥawwā' took it and ate it.

Then he tempted Ādam. Ḥawwā' told him, 'Eat! I have eaten and it did not harm me!' He ate some of it and then their private parts became visible to them and they incurred a wrong action. Ādam went inside the Tree and his Lord called out to him, 'Where are you.' 'I am here Lord,' he answered. He said, 'Why do you not come out?' He replied, 'I am ashamed before you, Lord.' He said, 'Go down to the earth from which you were created.' The snake was cursed and its legs went inside of it and enmity was engendered between it and the sons of Ādam. That is why we are commanded to kill it as will be explained. Ḥawwā' was told, 'Because you made the Tree bleed, so you will suffer bleeding every month and will be made to conceive and bear children multiple times, being close to death.' Aṭ-Ṭabarī and an-Naqqāsh added, 'You will be foolish when you were wise.'

One group said that Iblīs did not enter the Garden to Ādam after he was expelled from it. He was tempted by his internal shayṭān, and the power and whispering that Allah gave him, as the Prophet ﷺ said, 'Shayṭān flows through the son of Ādam like blood.' Allah knows best. The wisdom is that Ādam's expulsion from the Garden was in order that this world should be inhabited.

It is said that the snake was a servant of Ādam in the Garden and it betrayed him by giving the enemy of Allah power over itself and showed enmity to him there. When they descended, that enmity was reinforced and the earth was made its provision. It was told, 'You are an enemy to the sons of Ādam and they are your enemy. When one of them meets you, he will crush your head.' Ibn 'Umar related that the Messenger of Allah ﷺ said, 'There are five that can be killed while in *iḥrām*.' Snakes were among them. It is related that Iblīs said to it, 'Take me into the Garden and you will be my responsibility.' Sākinah bint al-Ja'd related that Sarrā' bint Nabhān al-Ghanawiyya said that she heard the Messenger of Allah ﷺ say, '(Kill) snakes, small and large, black and white. Whoever kills them has a ransom from the Fire and whoever is killed by one is a martyr.' Scholars say that there is ransom from the Fire because of their participation with Iblīs and helping him to harm Ādam and his children. Therefore if someone kills a snake, he has killed an unbeliever. The Messenger of Allah ﷺ said, 'An unbeliever and his killer are not ever joined in the Fire.' Muslim and others transmitted it.

Ibn Jurayj related from 'Amr ibn Dīnār from Abū 'Ubaydah that Ibn Mas'ūd said, 'We were with the Prophet ﷺ at Minā when a snake passed by. The Messenger of Allah ﷺ said, "Kill it." It raced ahead of us to a rock and entered it. The Messenger of Allah ﷺ said, "Bring a palm leaf and ignite a fire on it."' Our scholars said that this hadith qualifies the prohibition of mutilation by the Prophet ﷺ and of anyone punishing someone with Allah's punishment.

Muslim related from 'Abdullāh ibn Mas'ūd: 'We were with the Prophet ﷺ in a cave when *al-Mursalāt* was revealed. We were taking it fresh from his mouth when a snake came out to us. He said, "Kill it." We hastened to kill it but it got away from us. The Messenger of Allah ﷺ said, "Allah protected it from your evil and protected you from its evil."' He did not light a fire nor use any device to kill it. It is said that perhaps there was no fire available and so that was abandoned or fire would not help with the stone and the smoke would be harmful. Allah knows best.

The command to kill snakes is part of guidance towards repelling the evil feared from snakes. When it is known that they are harmful, then it is mandatory to go quickly to kill them since he ﷺ said, 'Kill snakes with white lines on their backs and the short tailed. They cause loss of sight and miscarriage.' So he singled them out although they are included in the general command and called attention to the reason for that, which is due to the immense harm they cause. Those whose harmful nature is not verified and which are outside of houses are killed because of the general command and the fact that most snakes are harmful. Ibn Mas'ūd transmitted that he said, 'Kill all snakes. Whoever fears their revenge is not connected to me.'

As for snakes inside houses, they are not killed until they have been warned for three days since the Prophet ﷺ said, 'There are jinn in Madīnah that have become Muslim. If you see any of them, warn them for three days.' Some scholars take this hadith to only apply to Madīnah because of the jinn becoming Muslim. They said, 'We do not know whether any of the jinn outside of those in Madīnah became Muslim.' Ibn Nāfi' said that. Mālik said that it is forbidden to kill house jinn in all lands.' That is sound because Allah Almighty says: *'We diverted a group of jinn towards you to listen to the Qur'an'* (46:29) We find in *Ṣaḥīḥ Muslim* that 'Abdullāh ibn Mas'ūd said that the Prophet ﷺ said, 'A summoner from the jinn came to me and I went to them and recited the Qur'an to them.' It says in the hadith that they asked him about their provision. They were jinn from the peninsula. If this is confirmed, then none of them are killed until they are warned.

The imams related that Abu-s-Sā'ib, the freedman of Hishām ibn Zuhrah, visited Abū Sa'īd al-Khudrī in his house. He said, 'I found him praying and sat down to wait until he finished his prayer. I heard a movement in some bundles of wood in a corner of the house. I turned around and saw that it was a snake. I jumped up to kill it but he indicated to me that I should remain sitting. I did so and when he finished, he pointed to a room of the house and asked, "Do you see this room?" "Yes," I answered. He said, "Among us was a young man who had recently got married. We went with the Messenger of Allah ﷺ to the Trench and the young man would ask for permission from the Messenger of Allah ﷺ at midday to return to his wife. One day he gave him permission and told him, "Take your weapons with you. I fear that Qurayẓah may harm you." The man took his weapons and went back, He found his wife standing between the two doors. He went at her with his spear to stab her out of jealousy. She told him, "Put away your spear. Enter the house and see what has made me come out!" He went in and there was a huge snake curled up on the bed. He thrust the spear at it and pierced it and then went out having fixed it in the house. But it escaped and bit him and no one knew which of them died first, the snake or the young man. We went to the Messenger of Allah ﷺ and mentioned that to him. We said, "Pray to Allah to bring him back to life." He said, "Ask forgiveness for your brother." Then he said, "There are jinn in Madīnah that have become Muslim. If you see any of them, warn them for three days. Then if you still see it after that, kill it. It is a shayṭān."' Another transmission has that the Messenger of Allah ﷺ said, 'There are those [jinn] who live in these houses. If you see any of them, warn them to leave for three days. If it does not leave, kill it. It is an unbeliever.' The account continues: 'He told them, "Go and bury your companion."'

Our scholars say that it is not understood from this hadith that the jinn that this young man killed was a Muslim and that the jinn killed him in retaliation, because if it had been sound that retaliation had been prescribed between us and the jinn, that would only have been in the case of intentional killing. This young man did not intend to kill a Muslim soul since he had no knowledge of that. He had intended to kill something that it is legally permitted to kill. This is accidental killing in which there is no retaliation. It is more appropriate to say that unbelieving or impious jinn can be killed because of their companionship in enmity and vengeance. It killed Sa'd ibn 'Ubādah when he was found dead in his bathing area and his body had turned green. They were not aware of his death until they heard someone invisible saying:

We killed the master of Khazraj, Sa'd ibn 'Ubādah.
We shot him with an arrow that did not miss his heart!

The Prophet ﷺ said, 'There are jinn in Madīnah who have become Muslim' in order to clarify the method taken to avoid killing those of them who were Muslim and to overpower those who are unbelievers. It is related by various paths that 'A'ishah, the wife of the Prophet ﷺ, killed a snake (*jānn*) and dreamt that someone said to her, 'You killed a Muslim.' She answered, 'If it had been a Muslim, it would not have entered where the wives of the Prophet ﷺ were.' He said, 'It only entered when you were dressed.' In the morning she ordered that twelve thousand dirhams be paid in the Cause of Allah.' Ar-Rabī' ibn Badr said that the *jānn* is one of the snakes whose killing the Prophet ﷺ forbade. It walks and does not coil.

As regards the manner of warning, Mālik said, 'I prefer that it be warning for three days.' 'Īsā ibn Dīnār said that, even if it appears several times a day. He does not confine himself to three times in one day; it has to be over three days. It is also said that three times is sufficient based on the words of the Prophet ﷺ, 'Warn it three times.' 'Three' (*thalāth*) is feminine and so it means 'three times'. Mālik's view is more appropriate because the Prophet ﷺ said, 'Three days.' It is a sound text which qualifies what is unqualified. Thābit al-Bunānī mentioned that when house snakes were mentioned to 'Abd ar-Raḥmān ibn Abī Laylā, he said, 'When you see any of them in your homes, say, "I ask you by the contract which Nūḥ ﷺ made with you and the contract that Solomon ﷺ made with you." When you see any of them after that, then kill it.'

Jubayr ibn Nufayr related from Abū Tha'labah Jarthūm al-Khushanī that the Messenger of Allah ﷺ said, 'There are three sorts of jinn: a third of them fly with wings in the air, a third are snakes and dogs, and a third alight and travel on.' Abu-d-Dardā' 'Umaymir related that the Messenger of Allah ﷺ said, 'The jinn were created in three groups: one third are dogs, snakes and the vermin of the earth, a third are in the wind, and a third are like human beings with clothes and are subject to the punishment. Allah created three types of human beings. One type have hearts with which they do not understand, eyes with which they do not see, and ears which do not hear. They are like cattle, rather they are more misguided. A third have bodies like those of human beings and hearts of shayṭāns. A third will be in the shade of Allah on the Day when there is no shade but His shade.'

Animals such as snakes, scorpions, mice, geckoes and the like, which basically cause injury, are killed without disagreement because of the harm they cause. The Prophet ﷺ said, 'Five are vicious and are killed inside and outside the Ḥaram…'

The snake showed that its nature was vicious when it betrayed Ādam and let Iblīs into the Garden in its jaws. Iblīs told it that it was his responsibility and so the Messenger of Allah ﷺ commanded snakes to be killed, saying, 'Kill them, even during the prayer,' referring to snakes and scorpions. Alone among creatures, the gecko blew on the fire of Abraham and so it was cursed. This is similar to what was related about snakes. It is said that the Messenger of Allah ﷺ said, 'If someone kills a gecko, it is as if he killed an unbeliever.'

According to *Ṣaḥīḥ Muslim*, Abū Hurayrah related that the Prophet ﷺ said, 'If someone kills a gecko with the first blow, he has a hundred good deeds. There is less than that for the second and less still for the third.' The mouse showed its nature when it deliberately went to the ropes of Nūḥ's Ship and severed them. 'Abd ar-Raḥmān ibn Abī Nu'm related from Abū Sa'īd al-Khudrī that the Messenger of Allah ﷺ said, 'Someone in *iḥrām* can kill snakes, scorpions, kites, aggressive beasts, wild dogs and rats.' The Messenger of Allah ﷺ woke up and a mouse had taken the wick [of a candle] to burn down the house and so the Messenger of Allah ﷺ commanded that it be killed. The crow showed its nature when the Prophet Nūḥ sent it from the ship to bring him news of the earth and it abandoned his command and went to a carcass. All of this is similar to what the snake did.

We said, 'Go down from here'

This is addressed to Ādam, Ḥawwā', the snake and Shayṭān according to Ibn 'Abbās. Al-Ḥasan said that only Ādam, Ḥawwā' and the whisperer are intended. Mujāhid and al-Ḥasan said it was all of the descendants of Ādam and Iblīs. The word from which 'go down' is derived is *hubūṭ*, meaning 'to descend from a higher to a lower place'. Ādam landed in a place called Sarndib in India on a mountain called Būdh borne by a wind from the Garden which lingered among its trees and valleys and filled them with fragrance. Ḥawwā' landed in Jiddah, Iblīs in Ubulla, and the snake in Baysan or Sijistan. Sijistan is full of snakes.

as enemies to each other!'

'Enemy' (*'aduw*) is the opposite of friend. It comes from the verb *'adā* which means to do wrong. A wolf which is *'adawān* attacks people. *'Udwān* is pure injustice. Some scholars say that this *āyah* applies to the human body itself. This is unlikely even though the idea is sound. They find evidence in the words of the Prophet ﷺ: 'When a person's limbs say to his tongue, "Fear Allah regarding us. If you are straight, we are straight. If you are crooked, we are crooked."'

If it is asked why Allah uses the singular rather than the plural, there are two reasons. One is that 'some' and 'all' are used in the singular in word and in meaning. Both usages are found in the Qur'an. The second is that 'enemy' in the singular is used to mean the plural. Ibn Fāris said that *'aduw* is used for the singular, dual, plural and feminine.

It is important to realise that Allah Almighty did not expel Ādam from the Garden and make him go down from it as a punishment, because He only sent him down after he had repented and He had accepted his repentance. He sent him down either to discipline him or to make the test hard. The truth, however, is that his being sent down to live on the earth stemmed from a pre-eternal wisdom governing the whole matter. It was so that his descendants would spread throughout the earth and so that they could be given responsibility and tested there, and then be given their rewards and penalties in the Next World, since the Garden and the Fire are not dimensions where accountability applies. The eating of the tree was the necessary condition for Ādam's descent from the Garden and Allah does whatever He wills. He says: *'I am putting a caliph on the earth,'* and this is a great honour and noble prerogative. It was already indicated in his being created from earth.

you will have residence on the earth

This means a place of residence. As-Suddī, however, says that it refers to their graves, meaning a more permanent resting place. Allah's words: *'He made the earth a stable dwelling place'* (27:61) can bear either meaning. Allah knows best.

and enjoyment

The word used here for enjoyment (*matā'*) applies to what is enjoyed of food, clothes, life, conversation, intimacy and other such things. From it is taken the *mut'ah* (temporary) marriage since it gives a man temporary enjoyment of a woman.

for a time

Interpreters disagree about the word *'ḥīn'* (time). One group say that it means until death. This is the position of those who say that 'residence' refers to our lifetime on the earth. Some say that it means until the Last Hour, and this is the position of those who say that 'residence' refers to the grave. *Ḥīn* sometimes means a distant time and can also refer to a period of time. It can also mean a moment or a segment of time. Ibn 'Arafah said that it means a segment of time, an hour or more. Al-Azharī said that it is a noun like *'waqt'* that is used for all times, long or short. It means that he will benefit from it at every moment and its benefit is never cut off. He said that *'ḥīn'* is the Day of Rising, and it is said that it is morning and evening, as in 30:17.

Linguists disagree about the meaning of this word as do our scholars and others. Al-Farrā' stated that *'ḥīn'* can designate two types of time: a time which is undefined and a time which Allah mentions: *'It bears fruit regularly* (kulla ḥīnin) *by its Lord's permission'* (14:25) which is six months. Ibn al-'Arabī says that the meaning is unknown and no judgment is connected to it. A 'known time' is that which is connected to judgments and legal responsibility. The maximum of a known time is a year. Mālik said that it is the most general noun for time. Ash-Shāfi'ī thinks that it is less than that. Abū Ḥanīfah takes a middle position and says that it is six months.

There is no point in any of this line of thought because there is no valid analogy for its amount or any text from the Prophet ﷺ saying what its length is. One decides on the meaning after ascertaining what a statement means linguistically. If someone swears to pray for a 'a time', according to ash-Shāfi'ī that is applied to one *rak'ah* because that is the minimum supererogatory prayer, analogous to the *rak'ah* of the *witr*. Mālik and his people say that the minimum supererogatory prayer is two *rak'ahs*. Time is estimated according to the action. Ibn Khuwayzimandād said in *al-Aḥkām*: 'If someone swears not to speak to a certain person for "a time" or not to do something for "a time", then the "time" is a year.' He said that they agree in rulings that it someone swears to do something for a 'time', then more than a year is not included in the oath. This is agreed on in the School.

Mālik said, 'If someone swears not to do something for a "time", be it using the word *ḥīn*, *zamān* or *dahr*, all those terms refer to a year.' Ibn Wahb said that he was unsure about *dahr* being a year. Ibn al-Mundhir related from Ya'qūb and Ibn al-Ḥasan that *dahr* is six months. Ibn 'Abbās, the People of Opinion, 'Ikrimah, Sa'īd ibn Jubayr, 'Āmir ash-Sha'bī and 'Ubaydah said that *'It bears fruit regularly* (kulla ḥeenin)*'* (14:25) means six months. Al-Awzā'ī and Abū 'Ubayd also said that it is six months. Ash-Shāfi'ī does not have a definitive time or limit for *ḥīn*. He says that it might well mean for the duration of this world. He said that he would never break it. Scrupulousness would make it apply to a single day. Abū Thawr and others said that these terms are applied according to their normal usage in language. Aṭ-Ṭabarī and ash-Shāfi'ī said that the term is used is various ways and with different possibilities because the undefined term does not have a specific meaning in language. Some scholars said that the point of 'time' being good news to Ādam is so that he would know that he would not remain in it forever and that he would move to the Garden by the promise that he would return to it. For others, it indicates the Hereafter. Allah knows best.

فَتَلَقَّىٰٓ ءَادَمُ مِن رَّبِّهِۦ كَلِمَٰتٍ فَتَابَ عَلَيْهِ إِنَّهُۥ هُوَ ٱلتَّوَّابُ ٱلرَّحِيمُ ﴿٣٧﴾

37 Then Ādam received some words from his Lord and He turned towards him. He is the Ever-Returning, the Most Merciful.

Then Ādam received some words from his Lord

'Received' here means understood, grasped or learned. It is said that it means accept and take. He ﷺ received the Revelation. Interpreters disagree about the 'words' mentioned in this *āyah*. Al-Ḥasan, Sa'īd ibn Jubayr, aḍ-Ḍaḥḥāk and Mujāhid said that it refers Ādam's words in *Sūrat al-A'rāf*, *'Our Lord, we have wronged ourselves. If You do not forgive us and have mercy on us, we will be among the lost.'* (7:23) Mujāhid also said that the words were, 'Glory be to You, O Allah. There is no god but You. My Lord, I have wronged myself, so forgive me. You are the Ever-Forgiving, Most Merciful.' One group say that Ādam saw written on the pedestal of the Throne, 'Muḥammad is the Messenger of Allah' and sought intercession through that. Another group say that what is meant is weeping, modesty and supplication, or regret, asking for forgiveness and sorrow. Ibn 'Aṭiyyah said, 'The expression means that Ādam used nothing but the normal form of asking for forgiveness.' One of the Salaf was asked about what a sinner should say. He answered, 'He says what our father said: "*Our Lord, we have wronged ourselves...*"' (7:23) Mūsā said, *'My Lord, I have wronged myself. Forgive me.'* (28:16) Yūnus (Jonah) said, *'There is no god but You! Glory be to You! Truly I have been one of the wrongdoers.'* (21:87)

Ibn 'Abbās and Wahb ibn Munabbih said that the 'words' are 'Glory be to You, O Allah, and by Your praise. There is no god but You. I have done evil and wronged myself. Forgive me. You are the best Forgiver. Glory be to You, O Allah, and by Your praise. There is no god but You. I have done evil and wronged myself. Turn to me! You are the Ever-Relenting, the Most Merciful.' Muḥammad ibn Ka'b said that it is the words: 'There is no god but You. Glory be to You, O Allah, and by Your praise. I have done evil and wronged myself. Turn to me! You are the Ever-Relenting, the Most Merciful. There is no god but You. Glory be to You, O Allah, and by Your praise. I have done evil and wronged myself. Show mercy to me! You are the Ever-Forgiving, Most Merciful. There is no god but You. Glory be to You, O Allah, and by Your praise. I have done evil and wronged myself. Show mercy to me! You are the Most Merciful of the merciful.' It is said that the word are 'Praise be to Allah' when one sneezes. 'Words' (*kalimāt*) is the plural of *kalimah*. It is used for both a little and a lot.

and He turned towards him.

This means that Allah accepted his repentance. That occurred on the Day of 'Ashūrā' which was a Friday as has been reported. When a person repents, he returns to obedience to his Lord. The root of the word for repentance (*tawbah*) means to return.

If it is asked why the pronoun 'him' is used and not 'them' when both Ādam and Ḥawwā' participated in the wrong action, the answer is that, when Ādam was addressed at the beginning with 'live' in the masculine singular, he was singled out for receiving and the story ends with the same pronoun. It is also because a woman is respected and concealed and so Allah wished to conceal her fault. That is why He does not mention her in connection with the act of disobedience when He says: *'Ādam disobeyed his Lord and became misled.'* (20:121) It is also because the woman usually follows the man. Similarly Mūsā's servant is not mentioned with Mūsā when he is addressed in the second person singular, *'Did I not tell you?'* (18:75). It is said that His turning to him also implies His turning to her because the command was issued to both of them.

He is the Ever-Returning, the Most Merciful.

Allah describes Himself as *'at-Tawwāb'*. The verbal root is used frequently in the Qur'an in the definite and indefinite, noun and verb. The word 'Ever-returning' (*tawwāb*) can be used for both people, as in 2:222, and for Allah. Ibn al-'Arabī said that our scholars have three positions about the meaning when it is used for Allah. One is that it is permitted for the Lord and is used for Him in the Qur'an and Sunnah and it should not be interpreted. Others say that it is a real description of Allah and it is used when Allah turns towards His slave when he turns from disobedience to obedience. The third view is that when Allah turns to a person, it means that He accepts His repentance. It is possible that it refers to His words, 'I have accepted your repentance' and the fact that He makes repentance recur in the heart of the evildoer so that he performs actions in obedience to Him.

The form of the word *tā'ib*, even if it may be permissible linguistically, cannot be used for Allah because we cannot apply any names or attributes to Him except what He or His Prophet ﷺ or the community of the Muslims have used for Him even if that is possible linguistically. This is the sound position in this area, as we explained in *Kitāb al-Asmā*. Allah says: *'Allah has turned towards the Prophet, and the Muhājirūn and the Anṣār'* (9:117) and: *'Allah accepts repentance from His slaves.'* (9:104) The intensive form *tawwāb* is used of Allah to stress the action and the frequency of His acceptance of His slaves' repentance.

No one has the power to generate repentance unilaterally because Allah

Almighty alone creates all actions. This differs from the position of the Mu'tazilites and those who follow them. In the same way no one else can forgive wrong actions, and this is why our scholars say that the Jews and Christians disbelieved when they took their religious leaders as Lords by ascribing this power to them as mentioned in 9:31.

Ibn Kathīr recited '*Ādam**a***' and '*kalimāt**un***' while the rest recite '*Ādam**u***' and '*kalimāt**an***'. Both readings mean the same because Ādam received words and learned them.

Sa'īd ibn Jubayr said, 'When Ādam was sent down to earth, there was nothing there but an eagle in the air and a fish in the sea. The eagle went to the fish and spent the night with it. When the eagle saw Ādam, it said, "Fish! Today something has come down to earth that walks on two legs and strikes with its hands!" The fish said, "If you spoke the truth, then I have no escape in the sea and you have no escape on the land!"'

قُلْنَا ٱهْبِطُوا۟ مِنْهَا جَمِيعًا فَإِمَّا يَأْتِيَنَّكُم مِّنِّى هُدًى فَمَن تَبِعَ هُدَاىَ فَلَا خَوْفٌ
عَلَيْهِمْ وَلَا هُمْ يَحْزَنُونَ ٣٨

38 We said, 'Go down from it, every one of you! Then when guidance comes to you from Me, those who follow My guidance will feel no fear and will know no sorrow.'

We said, 'Go down from it,

Allah repeats the command by way of stress and harshness. It is said that the first time, it is connected to transgression and the second to bringing guidance. It is also said that the first is the descent from the Garden to heaven and the second the descent from heaven to earth. This would indicate that the Garden was in the seventh heaven as indicated by the account of the Night Journey.

every one of you!

Wahb ibn Munabbih said, 'When Ādam descended to earth, Iblīs said to the wild animals, "This is your enemy, so destroy him." They gathered and elected the dog as their leader, saying, "You are the boldest of us." When Ādam saw that, he was confused, but Jibrīl came to him and said, "Stroke the dog's head." He did so. When the animals saw that the dog was friendly to Ādam, they scattered. The dog sought security and Ādam gave it to him and he remained with him and his sons from then on.'

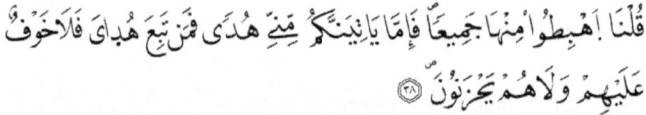

At-Tirmidhī related something similar. When Ādam descended to earth, Iblīs said to the wild animals and roused them to harm Ādam. The dog was the fiercest of them against him and then it lost heart. The report says that Jibrīl came to him and told him to put his hand on its head. He did so and it was friendly to him and calm. It became one of those who guarded him and his children and was friendly towards them. When it lost heart, it became afraid of human beings so that if one of them throws a piece of mud at it, it flees and then comes back in a friendly way. So it contains a branch of Iblīs and a branch of the stroking by Ādam. It barks, tears and attacks people by the branch of Iblīs, and by the branch of Ādam, it is calmed so that it is obedient and submits and is friendly to him and his children and guards them. Because of its loss of heart, it lolls out its tongue in all situations. That is why Allah likened evil scholars to a dog as will come in *Sūrat al-A'rāf.*

Then when guidance comes to you from Me,

There is disagreement about the meaning of '*hudā*' (guidance) here. As-Suddī said that it is the Book of Allah. It is said to be success to following Allah's guidance. One group say that it refers to the Messengers who came to Ādam from the angels and those who came to his descendants from among mankind, as in the hadith of Abū Dharr. *'From Me'* is another indication that the actions of people are created by Allah, which differs from the position of the Qadariyyah and others.

will feel no fear and will know no sorrow.'

'Khawf' (fear) is anxiety and it applies only to the future. Az-Zuhrī, al-Ḥasan, 'Īsā ibn 'Umar, Ibn Abī Isḥāq and Ya'qūb recited '*lā khawf**a***' to denote being free of it. Grammarians prefer it to be in the nominative with the *tanwīn* (*lā khawf**un***) as the beginning of a sentence because the second is definite and can only be in the nominative. *'Ḥuzn'* (sorrow) is the opposite of happiness and applies only to the past. So the meaning is that they have no fear about what lies ahead of them in the Next World nor are they sorrowful about anything that passed them by in this world. This does not deny the terrors of the Day of Rising and the fear, which the people of obedience will experience, because Allah and His Messenger have stated that the hardships of the Rising will not be lessened for those who obeyed Allah. It is when they go to the Garden that they will feel no fear, and Allah knows best.

وَالَّذِينَ كَفَرُوا وَكَذَّبُوا بِآيَاتِنَا أُولَٰئِكَ أَصْحَابُ النَّارِ هُمْ فِيهَا خَالِدُونَ ﴿٣٩﴾

39 But those who disbelieve and deny Our Signs are the Companions of the Fire, remaining in it timelessly, for ever.

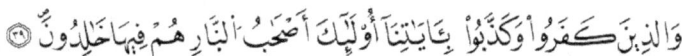

'Those who disbelieve commit *shirk*.' The word '*aṣḥāb*' (Companions) comes from the root *ṣuḥbah*, which means to be connected to a thing in any state and at any time. It entails complete adhesion to a thing and mixing with it. That is why it is used for the 'Companions of the Fire'.

يَٰبَنِيٓ إِسۡرَٰٓءِيلَ ٱذۡكُرُواْ نِعۡمَتِيَ ٱلَّتِيٓ أَنۡعَمۡتُ عَلَيۡكُمۡ وَأَوۡفُواْ بِعَهۡدِيٓ أُوفِ بِعَهۡدِكُمۡ
وَإِيَّٰيَ فَٱرۡهَبُونِ ٤٠

40 Tribe of Israel! remember the blessing I conferred on you. Honour My contract and I will honour your contract. Have dread of Me alone.

Tribe of Israel!

Isrā'īl (Israel) was Ya'qūb ibn Isḥaq ibn Ibrāhīm ﵇. Abu-l-Faraj said that he is the only Prophet to have two names except for Muḥammad ﷺ who has many names. I say, however, that it is said that the Messiah is a name of 'Īsā, and Allah also named him *Rūḥ* (Spirit) and Word. Al-Khālid ibn Aḥmad said that there were five Prophets with two names: Muḥammad was also called Aḥmad ﷺ, 'Īsā was called the Messiah, Ya'qūb was called Isrā'īl, Yūnus was called Dhū 'n-Nūn and Ilyās was called Dhū 'l-Kifl. We mentioned that 'Īsā has four names, but our Prophet ﷺ has many names as we will explain in the proper place. Isrā'īl is a non-Arabic name and so it is not declined.

Remember the blessing I conferred on you.

'*Dhikr*' (remembrance) is a word with several possibilities of meaning according to the context. When applied to the heart, it implies remembrance rather than forgetfulness. When applied to the tongue, it implies speech rather than silence. *Dhikr* also means honour as in 43:44. Ibn al-Anbārī said, 'The meaning is to remember to be grateful for Allah's blessing. There is no need to actually mention "thankfulness" when blessing is mentioned.' It is said that it means to remember with the heart, which is certainly much to be desired. In other words: 'do not forget or overlook the blessing which I bestowed on you.' '*Ni'mah*' (blessing), although singular, has a comprehensive meaning. The singular can have the meaning of the plural.

Among Allah's blessings to them were that He saved them from the people of Pharaoh, appointed Prophets from among them, sent down the Books and manna and quails to them, made fountains gush out from the rock for them, and included the mention of Muḥammad ﷺ in the Torah. Blessings to fathers are blessings to sons because they are ennobled by the nobility of their fathers.

Those with a precise grasp of the use of language say that Allah connected blessings to the tribe of Israel but did not mention that regarding the Community of Muhammad ﷺ; rather He says: *'Remember Me and I will remember you'* (2:152), so the other communities look from the blessing to the Blesser while the Community of Muḥammad look from the Blesser to the blessing.

Honour My contract and I will honour your contract.

There is disagreement about the contract referred to here. Al-Ḥasan said it is what is found in Allah's words: *'Take hold vigorously of what We have given you'* (2:63) and elsewhere as in 5:12 and 3:187. Az-Zajjāj said that what is meant are the words in the Torah about following Muḥammad ﷺ.

Allah's honouring of the contract is generally taken to mean that they will receive the reward of the Garden. It is also said that it means that if they perform their obligations with sincerity, then Allah will accept them from them. It is said that if they perform acts of worship, Allah will look after their affairs. It is said that it means that if they preserve their behaviour outwardly, Allah will adorn their hearts inwardly. It is also said that it is general to all His commands and prohibitions and what is mentioned about Muḥammad ﷺ in the Torah and elsewhere. This is the position of most scholars, and it is sound. His side of the contract is that He will admit them to the Garden. We are ordered to fulfil the contract as Allah says frequently in the Qur'an.

Have dread of Me alone.

This means 'Fear Me.' *Ruhb*, *rahb* and *rahbah* mean fear. The command is a threat. The *yā'* is omitted after the *nūn* because of the beginning of the *āyah*. Ibn Isḥāq, however, keeps the *yā'*.

وَءَامِنُوا۟ بِمَآ أَنزَلْتُ مُصَدِّقًا لِّمَا مَعَكُمْ وَلَا تَكُونُوٓا۟ أَوَّلَ كَافِرٍۭ بِهِۦ ۖ وَلَا تَشْتَرُوا۟
بِـَٔايَٰتِى ثَمَنًا قَلِيلًا وَإِيَّٰىَ فَٱتَّقُونِ ﴿٤١﴾

41 Believe what I have sent down, confirming what is with you. Do not be the first to reject it and do not sell My Signs for a paltry price. Have fear of Me alone.

Believe what I have sent down,

This means to affirm the Qur'an.

confirming what is with you.

This implies 'affirming what was sent down.' 'What is with you' is the Torah.

Do not be the first to reject it

Ibn Jurayj said that the third person pronoun translated as 'it' refers to the Qur'an but according to Abu-l-'Alīyah it refers to Muḥammad ﷺ in which case it would be 'him'.

If it is asked why '*kāfir*' (reject) is in the singular and not the plural, it is said that there is an elision which implies: 'Do not be the first group to reject it.' Al-Akhfash and al-Farrā' say that it goes back to 'the first', in other words: 'do not be the first of those who reject it.'

Do not sell My Signs for a paltry price.

This forbids them from being the first to disbelieve and taking a price for the Signs of Allah. It means: 'Do not take a bribe to change the description of Muhammad ﷺ as found in the Torah.' The rabbis used to do that when they were forbidden to do it. Some interpreters, al-Hasan and others, said that. It is said that they received food in return for knowledge as a stipend, when they were forbidden that. It is said that the rabbis used to take a wage for teaching their *dīn* when they were forbidden from doing that. Abu-l-'Āliyah said that it means: 'Do not sell My commands, prohibitions and Signs for a paltry price,' meaning do not abandon them for this world and its substance, for the sake of a livelihood which is insignificant.

Although this *āyah* addresses the tribe of Israel, it is about anyone getting something for what they did wrong. It can thus refer to anyone who takes a bribe for altering or falsifying the truth, refusing to teach what he is duty bound to teach, or refusing to convey what he knows, and which it is incumbent on him to convey, unless he is paid for it. All of that is included in the *āyah*, and Allah knows best. Abū Hurayrah reported that the Messenger of Allah ﷺ said, 'Anyone who learns knowledge which should be learned for the sake of Allah, the Mighty and Majestic, alone simply to obtain by it goods of this world will not experience the scent of the Garden on the Day of Rising.' Abū Dāwūd transmitted it.

Scholars disagree about taking a wage for teaching the Qur'an and knowledge of the *dīn* because of this *āyah* and others like it. Az-Zuhrī and the exponents of opinion (*ra'y*) forbade it, saying that it is not permitted for anyone to take a wage for teaching the Qur'an, because teaching it is one of the obligations which require sincerity and the intention of drawing near to Allah. Therefore there can be no wage for someone who does that just as there can be none for fasting or the prayer.

Ibn 'Abbās related that the Prophet ﷺ said, 'Your children's teachers are the worst of you, the least merciful to orphans and the harshest to the poor.' Abū Hurayrah said that he asked, 'Messenger of Allah, what do you say about other teachers?' He said, 'Their dirhams are unlawful, their clothes are unlawful, and their words are hypocrisy.' 'Ubādah ibn aṣ-Ṣāmit said, 'I taught the Qur'an and writing to some of the people of the Ṣuffah and one of them gave me a bow. I said, "It is not money and I can shoot it in the Way of Allah." I asked the Messenger of Allah ﷺ about it and he said, "If you are happy to wear a collar of fire, accept it."' Mālik, ash-Shāfi'ī, Aḥmad, Abū Thawr and most scholars permit accepting a wage for teaching, based on the words of the Prophet ﷺ in the hadith of Ibn 'Abbās, 'You are most entitled to take wages for the Book of Allah.' Al-Bukhārī transmitted it. This hadith is an evidentiary criterion which removes any dispute and can be relied on.

To make an analogy between such teaching and the prayer and fasting is incorrect. There is a clear difference between the two things. The prayer and fasting are individual actions of worship for a person, while teaching the Qur'an is an act of worship which can be done by other than the teacher himself. Therefore he is permitted to receive a wage for his attempting to convey the meaning of Qur'an, just as he would for teaching someone how to write the Qur'an. Ibn al-Mundhir said that Abū Ḥanīfah disliked the taking of a wage for teaching the Qur'an, but he permits hiring a man to write a tablet, poem, or known song for a known wage. So he would allow a wage for disobeying Allah but not for obeying him.

Some say that this *āyah* only applies to the tribe of Israel and there is disagreement about whether what was legislated for them applies to us. It is also said that the *āyah* is about those who should teach and refuse to do so unless they are paid. If it is not incumbent on someone, he is permitted to take a wage, based on the evidence of the *Sunnah*. It might be specifically incumbent on him except in the case of a teacher who does not have enough to support himself and his family. If that is the case, then the ruler should support him for sake of the establishment of the *dīn*. If he does not, it is up to the Muslims to do so. When Abū Bakr became caliph, he did not have enough to support his family and so he took some cloth and went to the market. He was asked about that and said, 'How else will I support my family!' They sent him back and allotted him a sufficient amount to cover his needs.

As for the hadiths about teachers mentioned above, none of them are reliable. The hadith of Ibn 'Abbās is related by Sa'īd ibn Ṭarīf from 'Ikrimah, and Sa'īd is abandoned. The hadith of Abū Hurayrah is related by 'Alī ibn 'Āṣim from Ḥammād ibn Salamah from Abū Jurham, and Abū Jurham is unknown, and Ḥammād ibn Salamah did not relate from anyone called Abū Jurham. He related it from Abu-l-Muhazzim who is abandoned. So the hadith is without foundation. The hadith of 'Ubādah was related by Abū Dāwūd from al-Mughīrah ibn Ziyād al-Mawṣulī from 'Ubādah ibn Nusayy from al-Aswad ibn Tha'labah from him. Al-Mughīrah is known by the people of knowledge, but has 'denounced' (*munkar*) hadiths. This is one of them as Abū 'Umar said. The hadith about the bow is known by the people of knowledge because it is related from 'Ubādah by two paths. It is related from Ubayy ibn Ka'b from the hadiths of Mūsā ibn 'Alī from his father from Ubayy, and it is broken.

There is no hadith about this matter which must be acted on on account of its transmission. The hadith of 'Ubādah is subject to interpretation because it is possible that he taught for the sake of Allah and then took a wage for it. It is related that the Messenger of Allah ﷺ said, 'The best of people and the best of those who walk the surface of earth are teachers. Whenever they renew the *dīn*, give to them and do not employ them and constrict them. When a teacher tells the child to say, "*In the Name of Allah, the All-Merciful, Most Merciful*," and the child says, "*In the Name of Allah, the All-Merciful, Most Merciful*," Allah writes the freeing of the child, the freeing of his teachers and the freeing of his parents from the Fire.'

Scholars disagree regarding the ruling about someone who takes a wage for leading the prayer. Ashhab related that Mālik was asked about praying behind someone who was hired to lead the people in Ramaḍān. He said, 'I hope that there will be no harm in it.' It is more strongly disliked in the obligatory prayer. Ash-Shāfi'ī and his people and Abū Thawr said, 'There is no harm in that or in praying behind him.' Al-Awzā'ī said that he cannot do that where the obligatory prayer is concerned. Abū Ḥanīfah and his people disliked it, as was already mentioned. This question is connected to the one before it and the basic principle is the same. Ibn al-Qāsim disliked taking a wage for teaching poetry and grammar while Ibn Ḥabīb said that there is nothing wrong in taking a wage for teaching poetry, letters and the battles of the Arabs. He did dislike poetry containing reference to wine, obscenity and satire. Abu-l-Ḥasan al-Lakhmī said that. According to his view, a wage is permitted for writing it and selling its books. Singing and wailing are forbidden in any case.

Another point concerning this matter is found in what is related by ad-Dārimī from Ya'qūb ibn Ibrāhīm from Muḥammad ibn 'Umar ibn al-Kumayt from 'Alī ibn Wahb al-Hamdānī that aḍ-Ḍaḥḥāk ibn Mūsā said, 'Sulaymān ibn 'Abd al-

Mālik passed through Madīnah on the way to Makka and stayed there for a few days. He inquired, "Is there anyone in Madīnah who met any of the Companions of the Prophet ﷺ?" They replied, "Abū Ḥāzim." He sent for him and when he came, he asked, "Abū Ḥāzim, what is this concealment?" Abū Ḥāzim said, "Amīr al-Mu'minīn, what concealment are you referring to?" He said, "The notable people of Madīnah came to me but you did not!" He said, "Amīr al-Mu'minīn, I ask you to seek refuge with Allah from saying what is not the case. You did not know me before today and I did not see you!"

'He turned to Muḥammad ibn Shihāb az-Zuhrī who said, "The shaykh is right and you are wrong." Sulaymān said, "Abū Ḥāzim! Why do we hate death?" He replied, "Because the Next World tests you and this world makes you prosper and so you dislike to move from prosperity to ruin." He said, "You are right, Abū Ḥāzim. What will our presentation before Allah tomorrow be like?" He said, "For the one who did good it will be like someone returning to his family after an absence. But as for the one who did evil, he will be like a runaway slave being brought back to his owner." Sulaymān wept and said, "Would that I knew what I have with Allah!" He said, "Examine your actions in the light of the Book of Allah." He asked, "Where should I look?" He said, *"The truly good will be in perfect Bliss and the dissolute will be in a Blazing Fire."* (82:13-14)

'Sulaymān asked, "Where is the mercy of Allah, Abū Ḥāzim?" Abū Ḥāzim said, "The mercy of Allah is near to those who do good." Sulaymān said, "Abū Ḥāzim, which of Allah's slaves are the noblest?" He replied, "Those with integrity and intelligence." He asked, "Which works are best?" Abū Ḥāzim said, "Performing obligations while avoiding prohibitions." Sulayman asked, "Whose supplication is heard?" He replied, "The supplication of a good-doer for a good-doer." He asked, "Which *ṣadaqah* is best?" He said, "That given to a despairing beggar and to someone who is destitute, in which there is no question of indebtedness or insult." He asked, "Which words are fairest?" He replied, "Speaking the truth in the presence of someone you fear or have hopes of." He said, "Which of the believers is the cleverest?" He replied, "A man who obeys Allah and directs other people to it." He said, "Which of the believers is the most stupid?" He replied, "A man who sinks to his brother's passion when he is a wrongdoer and sells the Next World for this one."

'Sulaymān told him, "You are right. So what do you say about us?" He asked, "Amīr al-Mu'minīn, will you let me go?" Sulaymān said, "No, rather give me advice." He said, "Amīr al-Mu'minīn, your forefathers overpowered the people with swords and took this kingdom by force without consulting the Muslims or without their pleasure until they had killed many of them. They have left us. If only you had been aware of what they said and what was said to them!" A man in the gathering said to him, "Abū Ḥāzim! What you have said is bad!" Abū Ḥāzim answered, "You lie. Allah has taken a covenant from scholars to make things clear to people and to not conceal them." Sulaymān asked him, "So how can we put things right?" He replied, "Leave aside conceit, hold to integrity and distribute equally." Sulaymān said to him, "What is our approach?" He replied, "Take from the lawful and give it to its people."

'Then Sulaymān asked him, "Abū Ḥāzim, will you keep our company so that you can take from us and we from you?" He replied, "I seek refuge with Allah!" Sulaymān asked, "Why is that?" He replied, *"I fear that I would lean towards them a little and then Allah would let me taste a double punishment in life and a double punishment in death."* (cf. 17:75) Sulaymān said, "Tell us your needs." He answered "That you save me from the Fire and make me enter the Garden." Sulaymān told him, "That is not up to me!" Abū Ḥāzim stated, "I have no need of anything else from you." He said, "Make supplication for me." Abū Ḥāzim said, "O Allah, if Sulaymān is your friend, ease him to the good of this world and the Next World. If he is Your enemy, take him by the forelock where You want and please." Sulaymān said to him, "Enough!" Abū Ḥāzim said, "I was short but it is a lot if you are one of its people. If you are not one of its people, I should not shoot from a bow with no string."

'Sulayman said, "Give me some more advice." He said, "I will advise you and be brief. Exalt your Lord and free Him from seeing you where He forbade you to be and from not seeing you where He commanded you to be."

'When Sulaymān left him, he sent him a hundred dinars and wrote to him, "Spend it and you will have the like of it many times more." He returned it to him and wrote to him, "Amīr al-Mu'minīn, I seek refuge with Allah from your asking me being a joke or my reply to you being a surrender. I am not pleased with it for you, so how could I be pleased with it for myself? When Mūsā, the son of 'Imrān, ﷺ arrived at the water of Madyan, he found shepherds drawing water there. Standing apart from them, he found two women, holding back their sheep. He questioned them and they said, 'We cannot draw water until the shepherds have driven off their sheep. You see our father is a very old man.' So he drew water for them and then withdrew into the shade and said, 'My Lord, I am truly in need of any good You have in store for me.' That was when he was hungry and fearful and without security. In spite of that he asked his Lord alone and did not ask people.

'"The shepherds did not notice but the women noticed. So when they returned to their father, they told the story to him and recounted what he had said. Their father, who was Shu'ayb, said, 'This is a hungry man.' He told one of them, 'Go and invite him.' When she came to him, she showed him respect and covered her face and said, 'My father invites you so that he can pay you your wage for drawing water for us.' It grieved Mūsā when she said, 'your wage for drawing water for us.' He, however, found that he no alternative but to follow her because he was hungry and alone in a strange place. When he followed her the wind blew her garment against her back so that the shape of her buttocks showed. Mūsā looked to the side at times and lowered his eyes at others.

'"When his patience was exhausted, he called her and said, 'Slave of Allah! Go behind me and direct me to the way by words.' When he reached Shu'ayb, supper was being prepared. He told him, 'Sit, young man and eat.' Mūsā said to him, 'I seek refuge with Allah.' Shu'ayb asked, 'Why? Aren't you hungry?' 'Yes,' he replied, 'but I fear that this may be a recompense for drawing water for them and I am from the people of a house who do not sell anything of their *dīn* even for the entire earth filled with gold.' Shu'ayb said to him, 'No, young man, but it is my custom and the custom of my fathers to give hospitality to a guest and feed him.' So Mūsā sat and ate.

'"If these hundred dinars are recompense for what I said, then carrion, blood and pig meat in a state of need are more lawful than it. If it is connected to the treasury, then there are others who deserve it as much as I do. If it is between us, then I have no need of it."'

This is how one follows the Book and the Prophets. Look at this virtuous imam and scholar and how he would not take any payment for his knowledge, his advice or his counsel. He openly made the truth clear and did not show any fear in doing so. The Messenger of Allah ﷺ said, 'Awe of someone should not prevent any of you from speaking the truth wherever he is.' In the Revelation we find: *'They strive in the Way of Allah and do not fear the blame of any censurer.'* (5:54)

Have taqwā of Me alone.

We have already mentioned the meaning of *taqwā*. It is also recited with *yā'* as we mentioned in the previous *āyah.*

وَلَا تَلْبِسُوا الْحَقَّ بِالْبَاطِلِ وَتَكْتُمُوا الْحَقَّ وَأَنتُمْ تَعْلَمُونَ ﴿٤٢﴾

42 Do not mix up truth with falsehood and knowingly hide the truth.

Do not mix up truth with falsehood

The word *labs* means mixing. That occurs when you mix the clear with the ambiguous or truth with falsehood. Allah Almighty says: *'We would have further confused* (labasnā) *for them the very thing they are confused* (yalbisūn) *about.'* (6:9) A thing is mixed up when it is mixed with something similar to it. Then it is not clear. This idea is seen in what 'Alī said to al-Ḥārith ibn Ḥawṭ: 'Ḥārith, it is muddled (*malbūs*) for you. Truth is not recognized by virtue of men. Recognise the truth and then you will recognise its people.' Sa'īd related that Qatādah said that the meaning of the phrase is 'do not mix up Judaism and Christianity with Islam. You know the *dīn* of Allah. None other is accepted; only it satisfies: that is Islam. Judaism and Christianity are innovations and are not from Allah.'

A possible meaning is *libās* (clothing) and so the *āyah* can mean: 'Do not cover'. That is as clothing covers. A man is described as the garment (*libās*) covering his wife, and his wife as covering him. *Labūs* is clothing and armour that covers. Allah says: *'We taught him the art of making garments* (labūs) *for you.'* (21:80) You are on intimate terms (*lābasa*) with a person when you know his inner self. That which covers the Ka'bah and a howdah is a *libs*.

The word used for 'falsehood' here is *bāṭil* which means when something becomes unsound and worthless. It can also mean 'in vain.' The False (*al-Bāṭil*) is one of the names of Shayṭān. A hero is also called *baṭl*, using the same root, because he makes the courage of his opponent 'in vain'. *Baṭāla* is unemployment.

Interpreters disagree about what is meant by 'truth with falsehood'. Ibn 'Abbās and others said that it means: 'do not mix what you have of the truth in the Book with falsehood by alteration or substitution.' Abu-l-'Āliyah said, 'The Jews said, "Muhammad ﷺ was sent, but not to us." So their affirmation of his mission was the truth but their denial that he was sent to them was falsehood.' Ibn Zayd said that what was meant by the truth was the Torah, and the falsehood was the changes they made to it. Mujāhid said, 'Do not mix Judaism and Christianity with Islam.' Qatādah also said that. Ibn 'Abbās's statement is the most correct because it is general and so includes all the other statements.

and knowingly hide the truth.

This can be joined as 'Do not mix and do not hide,' or there can be an elision, meaning, 'Let there not exist among you mixing the truth and concealing it.' Ibn 'Abbās said, 'It means their concealing the genuineness of the Prophet ﷺ in spite of the fact that they recognised him.' Muḥammad ibn Sīrīn said, 'A group of the children of Aaron settled in Yathrib when the tribe of Israel experienced what they did of being conquered by their enemies and humiliation. That group were the bearers of the Torah at that time. They established themselves in Yathrib, hoping that Muḥammad ﷺ would appear among them. They were believers, affirming his Prophethood. Their forebears, who were believers, passed, and were followed by one generation after another until they reached Muḥammad ﷺ. They rejected him in spite of their recognition of him. That is the context of the words of the Almighty: *'yet when what they recognize does come to them, they reject it.'* (2:89)

They knew the truth about Muḥammad ﷺ, so their rejection was one of obstinacy not ignorance. Allah is not attesting that they have knowledge, but is rather forbidding them to conceal what they know to be true. This shows that a wrong action is made all the more serious when it is done in spite of knowledge rather than in ignorance. This will be explained in 2:44.

وَأَقِيمُواْ ٱلصَّلَوٰةَ وَءَاتُواْ ٱلزَّكَوٰةَ وَٱرْكَعُواْ مَعَ ٱلرَّٰكِعِينَ ۝٤٣

43 Establish the prayer and pay *zakāt* and bow with those who bow.

Establish the prayer and pay *zakāt*

This is a command which entails a definite, undisputed obligation.

The root meaning of '*zakāt*' is grow and increase. To 'pay' is to give. It is used for crops and wealth when they increase. A man who is *zakī* is someone with increased wealth. Paying this tax out from wealth is called *zakāt*, even though doing it seems to produce the opposite of increase, since it involves reducing that wealth. The reason is because it increases the wealth in *barakah* or with the reward for paying it. It is also said that its root meaning is approbation, from which is taken the attestation of a witness's character by the *qāḍī*. So whoever pays *zakāt* obtains approbation for himself. It is further said that the root meaning of *zakāt* is purification. It is as if the one who pays it has purified himself of the liability of the right to which the poor are entitled and which Allah has imposed on him. Do you not see that the Prophet ﷺ called what was paid as *zakāt* the 'filth of people'. Allah says: *'Take zakāt from their property to purify and cleanse them''* (9:103)

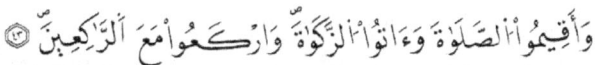

There is disagreement about what is meant by *zakāt* here. It is said that it is referring to the obligatory *zakāt* since it is connected to the prayer. It is also said to be the *zakāt al-fiṭr*. Mālik stated that according to Ibn al-Qāsim. The first is the position of the majority of scholars. According to them, the *zakāt* mentioned in the Book is general and was then clarified by the Prophet ﷺ. The imams related from Abū Sa'īd al-Khudrī that the Prophet ﷺ said, 'There is no *zakāt*

due on grain or dates until they reach five *wasqs*, nor on less than five camels nor less than five *ūqiyyahs*.' Al-Bukhārī said that it is five *ūqiyyahs* of silver. Al-Bukhārī related from Ibn 'Umar that the Prophet ﷺ said, 'There is a tenth due on land watered by rain, springs or running springs. There is half of an *'ushr* (a twentieth) on land watered by wells.' This will be further explained elsewhere. There is no text on *zakāt al-fiṭr* in the Book except the interpretation given by Mālik here and in *Surah al-A'lā*.

and bow

Linguistically the root of the word 'bow' – *raka'a* – means to bend the body. It is used metaphorically for descending in station. People disagree about why this act is specifically mentioned here. Some people say that, as bowing (*rukū'*) is one of the pillars of the prayer, it is used here to designate the prayer as a whole. This is not particular to the word 'bowing' alone since the word 'recitation' and the word 'prostration' are also used to designate the whole prayer as well. Allah says: '*The recitation of fajr* (dawn)' (17:78), meaning the *Fajr* prayer, and the Messenger of Allah ﷺ said, 'Whoever catches a prostration of the prayer has caught the whole prayer.' The people of the Hijaz use the term '*sajdah*' for a *rak'ah*.

It is said that bowing was singled out because the tribe of Israel did not have that in their prayer. It is said that it was more onerous for the people in the Jāhiliyyah so that one of those who became Muslim – I think it was 'Imrān ibn Ḥuṣayn – told the Prophet ﷺ, 'Provided that I do not have to prostrate except standing,' meaning 'not bow'. When Islam was firm in him and he was at peace with it, he performed *rukū'* in the way he was commanded to.

The legal *rukū'* is that a person bends his back from the waist and makes his back and neck level, with his fingers clasping his knees, and remains bowing, saying, 'Glory be to My Lord, the Immense' three times. That is the minimum. Muslim related that 'Ā'ishah said, 'The Messenger of Allah ﷺ used to begin the prayer with the *takbīr* and recitation with "*Praise be to Allah, the Lord of all the worlds.*"' *Rukū'* is an obligation and the Qur'an is a sunnah. The same is true of prostration as mentioned at the end of *al-Ḥajj* (22:77). The sunnah of being still is added as well as the separation between them as has already been discussed. Prostration is made clear in the hadith of Abū Ḥumayd as-Sā'idī: 'When the Prophet ﷺ prostrated, he put his forehead and nose firmly on the ground, kept his arms far from his sides, placing his hands opposite his shoulders.' At-Tirmidhī transmitted it and said that it is a sound *ḥasan* hadith. Muslim related from Anas that the Messenger of Allah ﷺ said, 'Be straight in prostration and none of you should stretch out his arms like a dog does.' Al-Barā' said that the Messenger of Allah ﷺ said, 'When you prostrate, put your palms down and raise your elbows.' Maymūnah, the wife of the Prophet ﷺ, said, 'When the Messenger of Allah ﷺ prostrated, he had his arms out in such a way that the whiteness of his armpits could be seen from behind. When he sat, he was still on his left thigh.'

Scholars disagree about someone who puts his forehead but not his nose down in prostration, or his nose but not his forehead. Mālik says that he should prostrate on both his forehead and nose. Ath-Thawrī and Aḥmad also said that. It is the view of an-Nakha'ī as well. Aḥmad said, 'It is not enough to prostrate only on one of them without the other.' Abū Khaythamah and Ibn Abī Shaybah said that. Isḥāq said, 'If he prostrates on one but not the other, his prayer is invalid.' Al-Awzā'ī and Sa'īd ibn 'Abd al-'Azīz said that what is related from Ibn 'Abbās, Sa'īd ibn Jubayr, 'Ikrimah, and 'Abd ar-Raḥmān ibn Abī Laylā is that one is commanded to prostrate on the nose. One group said that it is permitted to prostrate on the forehead and not the nose. This is the view of 'Aṭā', Ṭāwus, 'Ikrimah, Ibn Sīrīn and al-Ḥasan al-Baṣrī. That is also the view of ash-Shāfi'ī, Abū Thawr, Ya'qūb and Muḥammad. Ibn al-Mundhir said, 'Someone said that if someone puts his forehead on the ground but not his nose or his nose and not his forehead, his prayer is completely vitiated. This is the view of an-Nu'mān.' He added, 'I do not know of anyone before him with this position or anyone who followed him.'

What is sound is that prostration is putting both the forehead and nose on the ground, based on the prior hadith of Abū Ḥumayd. Al-Bukhārī related from Ibn 'Abbās that the Messenger of Allah ﷺ said, 'I was commanded to prostrate on seven bones: the forehead (and he pointed to his nose), the hands, the knees and the toes and not to tuck up the clothes and hair.' This all qualifies what is undefined of the prayer and is a specific view. Allah knows best. It is related from Mālik that it is not enough to prostrate on the forehead without the nose, as 'Aṭā' and ash-Shāfi'ī said. We prefer the first view. The obligation is not fulfilled when he does not prostrate on his forehead.

It is disliked to prostrate on the cloth of the turban, no matter whether there are one or two turns, but there is no harm in the clothes which cover the feet and knees. What is best is to prostrate directly on the ground or on that on which one prostrates. If there is something harmful there, it should be removed before starting the prayer. If someone has not done that, he may wipe it once. Muslim related from Mu'ayqīb that the Messenger of Allah ﷺ said about a man who flattens out the earth so that he can prostrate, 'If you do it, do it once.' It is related that Anas ibn Mālik said, 'We prayed with the Messenger of Allah ﷺ in intense heat and if one of us was not able to put his forehead on the earth, he would spread his garment on the ground and prostrate on it.'

When Allah says: *'Bow and prostrate'* (22:77), some of our scholars and others said, 'What is deemed bowing and prostration is enough for us, and the same is true of standing.' They did not stipulate being still in that but took the minimum designated by the name. It is as if they had not heard the firm hadiths about the nullifying of the prayer. Ibn 'Abd al-Barr said, 'Neither *rukū'*, prostration, standing after *rukū'*, and sitting between the two prostrations is satisfied until the person is straight in bowing, standing, prostrating and sitting.' That is sound in the tradition and that is the position of the majority of scholars and people of investigation. It is transmitted by Ibn Wahb and Abū Muṣ'ab from Mālik.

Qāḍī Abū Bakr ibn al-'Arabī said, 'There are many reports from Ibn al-Qāsim and others about the obligation of separation but omitting stillness.' This is very weak indeed because the Prophet ﷺ did it, commanded it and taught it. If Ibn al-Qāsim had the excuse that he had not seen that, you do not have that excuse. There is knowledge of it and the argument is established against you regarding it. An-Nasā'ī, ad-Dāraquṭnī and 'Alī ibn 'Abd al-'Azīz related that Rifā'ah ibn Rāfi' said, 'I was sitting with the Messenger of Allah ﷺ when a man came, entered the mosque and prayed. When he finished, he came and greeted the Messenger of Allah ﷺ and the people. The Messenger of Allah ﷺ said, "Go back and pray. You have not prayed." He began to pray while we were looking at him, not knowing what was wrong with it. Then he greeted the Messenger of Allah ﷺ and the people. The Messenger of Allah ﷺ said, "Go back and pray. You have not prayed." (Hammām said, "I do not know whether that happened twice or three times.") The man asked him (what was wrong) saying, "I do not know what is wrong with my prayer." He ﷺ said, "None of you has completed the prayer until he has done *wuḍū'* fully as Allah has commanded, washing his face, his hands to the elbows, wiped his head, and washed his feet to the ankles, then has declared Allah great and praised him and recited the Umm al-Qur'an and what he knows and is easy for him, said the *takbīr*, bowed, placing his palms on his knees until his joints are at rest and relaxed, then said, 'Allah hears whoever praises Him', standing upright until his back is straight and every bone takes its portion of it, then said the *takbīr* and prostrated, putting his face firmly on the ground (Hammām said, "his forehead") until his joints are at rest and relaxed, said the *takbīr* and sat upright in his seat with his back straight," and he described the prayer in its four *rak'ahs* to the end. Then he said, "None of you has a prayer until he does that."' There is a similar hadith from Abū Hurayrah that Muslim transmitted.

This is the clarification of the undefined prayer in the Book as taught and conveyed by the Prophet ﷺ to all people. If someone does not stop at this clarification, fails to do what the All-Merciful has made obligatory on him and does not obey what has been conveyed to him from his Prophet ﷺ, he is included in those about whom Allah has said: *'An evil generation succeeded who neglected the prayer and followed their appetites.'* (19:59) Al-Bukharī related that Zayd ibn Wahb said, 'Ḥudhayfah saw a man who did not fully bow or prostrate and said, "You have not prayed. If you die, you will die on other than the form on which Allah created Muḥammad ﷺ."'

with those who bow.

The word 'with' implies both togetherness and simultaneity. That is why some of those who interpret the Qur'an say that the command to pray did not at first entail attending the group prayer, but when Allah said 'with' in this *āyah*, He was commanding people to pray as a group. Scholars have two different positions about attending the group prayer. The majority say that it is a confirmed sunnah and a penalty is mandatory for anyone who regularly fails to attend it without an excuse. Some of the people of knowledge make it mandatory for the community as a whole. Ibn 'Abd al-Barr says, 'This is a sound view because it is confirmed, by consensus that it is not permitted to agree to make all the mosques empty of group prayers. If there is a group prayer in the mosque and an individual prays in his home that is permitted because the Prophet ﷺ said, "The group prayer is twenty-seven degrees better than the prayer of the person praying alone." Muslim transmitted it in a hadith from Ibn 'Umar. It is related from Abū Hurayrah that the Messenger of Allah ﷺ said, "The group prayer is twenty-five times better than the prayer of the person praying alone."'

Dāwūd said, 'The prayer in a group is a personal obligation for everyone in the same way that *Jumu'ah* is.' He cited as proof the words of the Prophet ﷺ: 'Someone who is a neighbor to a mosque has no prayer unless it is in the mosque.' Abū Dāwūd transmitted it and Abū Muḥammad 'Abd al-Ḥaqq said that it was sound. It is the position of 'Aṭā' ibn Abī Rabāḥ, Aḥmad ibn Ḥanbal, Abū Thawr and others. Ash-Shāfi'ī said, 'Someone who is able to attend the group prayer has no allowance to abandon it unless he has a valid excuse.' Ibn al-Mundhir related that. Muslim related that Abū Hurayrah said, 'A blind man came to the Prophet ﷺ and said, "Messenger of Allah, I have no guide to take me to the mosque." He asked the Messenger of Allah ﷺ to make an allowance for him to pray in his house He gave him an allowance and then he called him back and asked, "Do you hear the call to prayer?" "Yes," he answered. He said, "Then respond to it."' Abū Dāwūd has in this hadith: 'I do not find any allowance for you.' He transmitted it from the hadith of Ibn Umm Maktūm, and he mentioned that he was the one who asked.

It is related from Ibn 'Abbās that the Messenger of Allah ﷺ said, 'If someone hears the call to prayer and no excuse prevents him from coming to it, then the prayer that he prays is not accepted from him.' They asked, 'What is an excuse?' He answered, 'Fear or illness.' Abū Muḥammad 'Abd al-Ḥaqq said that this is related by Maghra' al-'Abdī. What is sound is to stop at Ibn 'Abbās: 'If someone hears the call and does not come, he has no prayer.' Qāsim ibn Aṣbagh mentioned it in his book and said that it is related from Qāḍī Ismā'īl ibn Isḥāq from Sulaymān ibn Ḥarb from Shu'bah from Ḥabīb ibn Abī Thābit from Sa'īd ibn Jubayr from Ibn 'Abbās that the Messenger of Allah ﷺ said, 'If someone hears the call and does not respond, he has no prayer unless he has a [valid] excuse.' The soundness of this *isnād* should be enough for you. Abū Isḥāq related from Maghra' al-'Abdī. Ibn Mas'ūd said, 'I remember us when only a known hypocrite failed to attend it.' The Prophet ﷺ said, 'Between us and the hypocrites is attending *'Ishā'* and *Ṣubḥ* which they are unable to attend.' Ibn al-Mundhir said, 'We related that more than one of the Companions of the Prophet ﷺ said, "If someone hears the call and does not respond, he has no prayer unless he has an excuse." They included Ibn Mas'ūd and Abū Mūsā al-Ash'arī.'

Abū Hurayrah related that the Messenger of Allah ﷺ said, 'I thought about ordering my lads to collect some firewood and then go to some people who were praying in their houses but were not ill and burning them down on them.' This is used as an argument by those who made the group prayer obligatory. It is clear with respect to the obligation. The majority take it to mean stressing the command to attend the group prayers as indicated by the hadith of Ibn 'Umar and Abū Hurayrah. They take the statement of the Companions and what is in the hadith about having no prayer to mean with regard to perfection and excellence. The same applies to what the Prophet ﷺ said to Ibn Umm Maktūm, 'respond': it is a recommendation. His words, 'I thought about' do not indicate absolute obligation because he thought about it but did not do it. It is like a threat directed at the hypocrites who failed to come to the Group Prayer and to Jumu'ah.

This idea is made clear in Muslim, when he relates that 'Abdullāh said, 'Whoever is happy to meet Allah in the morning as a Muslim should guard these prayers when they are called. Allah prescribed the *sunnah*s of guidance to your Prophet ﷺ. They are part of the *sunnah*s of guidance. If you pray in your houses as this one who failed to attend prayed in his house, then you have abandoned the *sunnah*s of your Prophet ﷺ. If you abandon the *sunnah*s of your Prophet ﷺ, then you are misguided. No man purifies himself and does it correctly and then goes to one of the mosques without Allah recording a good deed for every step he takes, raising him a degree and removing an evil deed from him. I remember us when only a known hypocrite failed to attend it. A man would come, being guided between two men, until he stood in the row.' So he made it clear that the group prayer is one of the *sunnah*s of guidance and abandoning it is misguidance. That is why Qāḍī Abu-l-Faḍl 'Iyāḍ said that there is disagreement about people who play a part in abandoning the clear *sunnah*s and whether they should be fought. What is sound is that they should be fought because this could lead to doing away with the group prayer.

According to this, as long as the Sunnah is established and clearly evident, the prayer at home is permitted and sound. Muslim related from Abū Hurayrah that the Messenger of Allah ﷺ said, 'A man's prayer in a group is about twenty degrees better than his prayer in his house and his prayer in the market. When one of you does *wuḍū'* well and then goes to mosque for no other purpose than the prayer and seeking nothing but the prayer, he does not take a step without being elevated one degree by it and one of his errors being removed until he enters the mosque. When he enters the mosque, he is in the prayer as long as he is waiting for the prayer. The angels pray for one of you as long as he is sitting in the place where he will pray. They say, "O Allah, show mercy to him! O Allah, forgive him! O Allah, turn to him!" as long as he does not disturb anyone or break *wuḍū'*.' He was asking what breaking *wuḍū'* entails and said that it is breaking wind.

Scholars disagree about the excellence connected to the group and whether it is for a group no matter where it is or whether it is only for a group in the mosque, since that is necessarily one of the actions connected to mosques as stated in the hadith. The first view is more evident because the group is what the judgment is connected to, and Allah knows best. What was mentioned of the steps to the mosque, intending to go it and remaining it have a further reward beyond the group. Allah knows best.

There is also disagreement as to whether one group is better than another based on the larger number and on the excellence of the imām. Mālik said no. Ibn Ḥabīb said that it is, because the Prophet ﷺ said, 'The prayer of a man with someone else is purer than his prayer on his own. His prayer with two men is purer than his prayer with one man. Allah loves more that which is more.' Ubayy ibn Ka'b related it and Abū Dāwūd transmitted it. Its *isnād* is soft.

They also disagree about whether someone who has prayed in a group can repeat the prayer with another group. Mālik, Abū Ḥanīfah, ash-Shāfiʿī and their people say that someone who has prayed alone in his house and his family or outside of his house can repeat the prayer in a group with the imam. If he has prayed in a group, however small, he should not repeat it in a group either smaller or larger. Aḥmad ibn Ḥanbal, Isḥāq ibn Rāhawayh and Dāwūd ibn ʿAlī said that if someone has prayed in a group and then finds another group performing that prayer, he is permitted to repeat it with them because it is supererogatory and sunnah. That is related from Ḥudhayfah, Abū Mūsā al-Ashʿarī, Anas ibn Mālik, Ṣilah ibn Zafar, ash-Shaʿbī and an-Nakhaʿī. Ḥammād ibn Ziyād and Sulaymān ibn Ḥarb also said that.

Mālik's evidence is the words of the Prophet ﷺ: 'A prayer is not prayed twice in a day.' Some of them said that they do not pray it [again]. Sulaymān ibn Yasār related that from Ibn ʿUmar. Aḥmad and Isḥāq agree that this hadith means that a person does not pray an obligatory prayer and then get up and pray it again, intending the obligation a second time. If he prays it behind an imam as a sunnah or supererogatory prayer, that is not repeating the prayer. The Prophet ﷺ said to those he commanded to repeat the prayer in a group: 'It is supererogatory for you.' It comes from the hadith of Abū Dharr and others.

Muslim related from Ibn Masʿūd that the Prophet ﷺ said, 'The one who knows the greatest amount of the Book of Allah should act as the imam of a people. If they are equal in their knowledge of recitation, then it should be the one with the best knowledge of the Sunnah. If they are equal in the Sunnah, then it should be the oldest of them in terms of Hijrah. If they are equal in the Hijrah, then it should be the one oldest in years. A man should not lead another man when the second man is in authority. No one should sit in the place of honour in a house except with the owner's permission.' Abū Dāwūd transmitted it. Shuʿbah said, 'I asked Ismāʿīl what the place of honour is, and replied that it was his rug.' At-Tirmidhī transmitted it and said that the hadith of Ibn Masʿūd is sound *ḥasan*. One acts on it according to the people of knowledge.

They said that the person most entitled to act as imam is the one with the most recitation of the Book of Allah and the one with the most knowledge of the Sunnah. They said that the owner of a house is most entitled to act as imam. Some said that when the owner of a house gives permission to someone else, there is nothing wrong with that person leading them in the prayer. Some of them disliked that and said that the Sunnah is that the owner of the house leads the prayer. Ibn al-Mundhir said, 'We related that al-Ashʿath ibn Qays put a boy forward to lead the prayer, saying that he had the most Qur'an.' Among those who said that the one who knows the most Qur'an leads the prayer were Ibn Sīrīn, ath-Thawrī, Isḥāq and the people of opinion. Ibn al-Mundhir said, 'That is what we say because it conforms to the Sunnah.' Mālik said that the one with the most knowledge leads when his state is good even though age has a right. Al-Awzā'ī said, 'The one with the most *fiqh* leads them.' That is what ash-Shāfi'ī and Abū Thawr said, with the condition that he can recite Qur'an. That is because the *faqīh* has the best knowledge of what is intended by the actions of the prayer.

They interpret the hadith to mean that the one with the most Qur'an is the one with the most *fiqh* because they learned *fiqh* from the Qur'an. Part of their custom was to call the *fuqahā'* '*qurrā'*' (reciters). They cite as evidence the fact that, in his final illness, the Prophet ﷺ advanced Abū Bakr because of his excellence and knowledge. Isḥāq said, 'The Prophet ﷺ put him forward to indicate that he was his successor after him.' Abū 'Umar mentioned that in *at-Tamhīd*. Abū Bakr al-Bazzār related with a good *isnād* from Abū Hurayrah that the Prophet ﷺ said, 'When you travel, then the one with the most Qur'an recitation should lead you in the prayer, even if he is the youngest of you. When he leads you, he is your amīr.' He said, 'We only know that it is related from the Prophet ﷺ from Abū Hurayrah by this *isnād*.'

It is permitted for a child to act as imam if he can recite the Qur'an. It is confirmed in *Ṣaḥīḥ al-Bukhārī* that 'Amr ibn Salimah said, 'We were at a watering place much-frequented by people. The caravans would pass by us and we would ask the people, "What is wrong with the people? Who is this man?" They would say, "He claims that Allah has sent him and has revealed to him such-and-such and such-and-such." I used to memorise those words and it was as if that was fixed in my heart. The Arabs waited until the Conquest to become Muslim. They used to say, "Leave him and his people be. If he overcomes them, then he is a truthful Prophet." When the Conquest took place, every tribe rushed to become Muslim, and my father rushed to become Muslim before his people. When he arrived back, he said, "By Allah, I have truly come to you from the Prophet ﷺ. He said, "Pray such-and-such a prayer at such-and-such a time, and pray such-and-such a prayer at such-and-such a time. When the time of the prayer comes, then let one of you announce it, and let the one of you who has the most Qur'an lead you." They looked and there was no one who had more Qur'an than me since I used to learn it from the caravans. They put me in front of them when I was only about six or seven years old, wearing a cloak. When I prostrated, I was exposed. A woman of the tribe said, "Will you not cover the bottom of your reciter!" So they bought and made a shirt for me. I have never been so happy to have anything as I was to have that shirt.'

Al-Ḥasan al-Baṣrī and Isḥāq ibn Rāhawayh were among those who permitted a minor child to act as imam. Ibn al-Mundhir preferred to say that it is only appropriate when the child understands the prayer and can establish it, as that is part of what the Prophet ﷺ said: 'The one with the most Qur'an recitation should lead you in the prayer' and that follows the hadith of 'Amr ibn Salimah. One of the two positions of ash-Shāfi'ī is that he can lead all the daily prayers but should not lead the *Jumu'ah* prayer. Before that he used to say that someone who is allowed to act as imam in prescribed prayers can act as imam at the *'Īds*. He said, 'But I dislike anyone but the governor acting as imam in them.' Al-Awzā'ī said, 'A boy should not act as imam in the prescribed prayer until he has reached puberty, unless it is a people who do not have anyone else who knows any of the Qur'an. Then an adolescent can act as imam.' Az-Zuhrī said that he may do that if he is needed. Mālik, ath-Thawrī and the People of Opinion forbid it altogether.

The imam [in the prayer] can be any free, adult, Muslim male who is upright, and there is no disagreement about that so long as he knows the limits of the prayer and does not use such bad Arabic in the Umm al-Qur'ān as would unsettle the meaning, such as putting a *kasrah* on the *kāf* of *'iyyāka na'budu'* (1:4) [which would make it a feminine 'you'] or a *ḍammah* on the *tā'* of *'an'amta'* [which would make it 'I bless']. Some of them say that he must observe the distinction between *ṭā'* and *ḍād* and if he does not, then he cannot act as imam, because there is a difference in meaning. Some people allow all of that if he is ignorant of recitation and those who follow him are equally ignorant.

It is not permitted for the imam to be a woman, a hermaphrodite, an unbeliever, a mad person or someone illiterate. None of these can be an imam in any case according to most scholars as will be discussed, with the exception of someone illiterate leading those who are also illiterate. Our scholars said that it is not permitted for someone illiterate who cannot recite well to act as imam when there is someone who can recite properly. That is the same as ash-Shāfi'ī said. If he leads someone who is illiterate like him, then both we and ash-Shāfi'ī believe his prayer to be valid. Abū Ḥanīfah said that if someone illiterate leads a group which includes those who can read and those who are illiterate, then the prayer of all of them is unsound. Abū Yūsuf disagreed with him and said that the prayer of the imam and those who cannot recite is valid. One group, holding a contrary position, said that the prayer of all of them is allowed because each of them has fulfilled his obligation and that is like someone doing *tayammum* leading those who have purified themselves with water, and someone sitting leading those who are standing, because each performs his obligation. The evidence for this view is found in the words of the Prophet ﷺ, 'Why does the person praying not look to see how he prays? He is only praying for himself.' Muslim transmitted it. The prayer of the follower is not tied to that of the imam. Allah knows best.

There is nothing wrong in the imamate of a man who is blind or lame, who has a palsied hand, an amputee, eunuch or slave when any of them has proper knowledge of the prayer. Ibn Wahb said, 'I do not think that someone with palsy or an amputee should lead the prayer because he has less than the rank of perfection. It is disliked for him to be imam because of that imperfection.' He is opposed by most of his companions and that is correct because the loss of a limb does not prevent any of the obligations of the prayer. A person is permitted to be a regular imam when he lacks an eye. Anas related that the Prophet ﷺ appointed Ibn Umm Maktūm to lead the people in prayer even though he was blind. By analogy and logic, the same holds true for someone lame, an amputee, someone with palsy or a eunuch. Allah knows best. It is related that Anas said about a blind man, 'What is your problem about him? Ibn 'Abbās and 'Itbān ibn Mālik led the prayer and they were blind.' That is the view of most scholars.

There is disagreement about a bastard acting as imam. Mālik said, 'I dislike him being the regular imam.' 'Umar ibn 'Abd al-'Azīz disliked it. 'Aṭā' ibn Abī Rabāḥ said that he may lead the prayer if he is approved of. That is the view of al-Ḥasan al-Baṣrī, az-Zuhrī, an-Nakha'ī, Sufyān ath-Thawrī, al-Awzā'ī, Aḥmad and Isḥāq. According to the people of opinion, the prayer behind him is valid, although they prefer others. Ash-Shāfi'ī said that he disliked someone with an unknown father being appointed a regular imam but the prayer behind him is valid. 'Īsā ibn Dīnār said, 'I do not take Mālik's position about the imamate of a bastard. Nothing of the sin of his parents adheres to him.' Ibn 'Abd al-Ḥakam said the same when he himself is worthy of acting as imam. Ibn al-Mundhir said, 'He can lead it because he is included in the words of the Messenger of Allah ﷺ: "The one who knows the most recitation leads them."' Abū 'Umar said, 'There is nothing in the traditions reported about preconditions for being imam that indicates taking account of lineage. Rather it indicates *fiqh*, recitation and righteousness in the *dīn*.'

As for slaves, Al-Bukhārī related that Ibn 'Umar said, 'When the first Muhājirūn came to al-'Aṣabah, a place at Qubā', before the arrival of the Messenger of Allah ﷺ, they were led in the prayer by Sālim, the freedman of Abū Ḥudhayfah. He knew the most Qur'an.' He said, 'Sālim, the freedman of Abū Ḥudhayfah, led the first Muhājirūn and the Companions of the Prophet ﷺ in the prayer at Qubā'. They included Abū Bakr, 'Umar, Zayd, and 'Āmir ibn Rabī'ah. 'Ā'ishah was led in the prayer by her slave Dhakwān from a copy of the Qur'an.' Ibn al-Mundhir said, 'While he was still a slave, Abū Sa'īd, the freedman of Abū Asyad, led a group of the Companions of the Messenger of Allah ﷺ that included Ḥudhayfah and Ibn Mas'ūd in the prayer.' An-Nakha'ī, ash-Sha'bī, al-Ḥasan al-Baṣrī, al-Ḥakam, ath-Thawrī, ash-Shāfi'ī, Aḥmad, Isḥāq and the people of opinion make an allowance for a slave leading the prayer. Abū Miljaz disliked it. Mālik said, 'A slave should only lead the prayer if he can recite and the free men with him cannot recite, but a slave may not lead the prayer in an *'Īd* or *Jumu'ah*."' Al-Awzā'ī allows the prayer if people pray behind him. Ibn al-Mundhir said that slaves are included in the words of the Messenger of Allah ﷺ: 'The one who knows the most recitation leads them.'

As for women leading the prayer, al-Bukhārī related that Abū Bakrah said, 'When the Messenger of Allah ﷺ heard that the people of Persia had made the daughter of Khusrau their ruler, he said, "A people will not prosper who appoint a woman over their business."' Abū Dāwūd mentioned it from 'Abd ar-Raḥmān ibn Khallād from Umm Waraqah bint 'Abdullāh. He said, 'The Messenger of Allah ﷺ used to visit her in her house and assigned her a mu'adhdhin to call the prayer for her and told her to lead the people of her house in the prayer.' 'Abd ar-Raḥmān said, 'I saw the mu'adhdhin and he was a very old man.' Ibn al-Mundhir said, 'Ash-Shāfi'ī says that any men who pray behind a woman must repeat the prayer.' Abū Thawr said that they do not have to repeat it. This is similar to the view of al-Muzanī.

Our scholars have said that it is not valid for a woman to be an imam either for men or women. Ibn Ayman related that it is permissible for her to act as an imam for other women. Ash-Shāfi'ī says that a hermaphrodite cannot be an imam for men or women. Mālik said that he may not be an imam in any case, and that is what most *fuqahā'* say.

If an unbeliever who opposes the Sharī'ah, such as a Jew or a Christian, leads the Muslims in the prayer when they do not know that he is an unbeliever, ash-Shāfi'ī and Aḥmad said that the prayer is not fulfilled and they must repeat it. Mālik and his people said that because he is not one of the people of nearness. Al-Awzā'ī said that he should be punished. Abū Thawr and al-Muzanī said that someone who prays behind him does not have to repeat it.

As for the people of innovations among the sects like the Mu'tazilites, Jahmites and others, al-Bukhārī mentioned that Ḥasan said, 'Pray, and he has his innovation.' Aḥmad said, 'Do not pray behind any of the people of sects since he invites to his sect.' Mālik said, 'One can pray behind imams of injustice, but not behind the people of sects, the Qadariyyah and others.' Ibn al-Mundhir said, 'It is not permitted to pray behind anyone whose innovation removes him to unbelief. If someone does not go that far, then the prayer behind him is valid. It is not permitted to put someone like this forward to lead the prayer.'

As for someone impious (*fāsiq*) through his actions, such as a fornicator, drinker or the like, the School disagrees about him. Ibn Ḥabīb said, 'If someone prays behind a drinker, he should always repeat it unless it is the governor to whom he owes obedience. The one who prays behind him does not have to repeat it unless he was actually drunk. This is the position of the people of Mālik that I have met.' It is related from the hadith of Jābir ibn 'Abdullāh that the Messenger of Allah ﷺ said on the minbar, 'A woman does not lead a man in the prayer. A desert Arab does not lead a Muhājir. Someone deviant does not lead someone pious unless he is someone in authority.' Abū Muḥammad 'Abd al-Ḥaqq said, "Alī ibn Zayd ibn Jud'ān related it from Sa'īd ibn al-Musayyab. Most think that 'Alī ibn Zayd is weak.

Ad-Dāraquṭnī related from Abū Hurayrah that the Messenger of Allah ﷺ said, 'If you are happy for your prayer to be pure, put forward the best of you.' Abu-l-Walīd Khālid ibn Ismā'īl al-Makhzūmī, who is weak, is in the *isnād*. Ad-Dāraquṭnī said that. Abū Aḥmad ibn 'Adī said about him, 'He used to impute hadith to trustworthy Muslims, and he related this hadith from Ibn Jurayj from 'Aṭā' from Abū Hurayrah.' Ad-Dāraquṭnī mentioned from Salām ibn Sulaymān from 'Umar from Muḥammad ibn Wāsi' from Sa'īd ibn Jubayr from Ibn 'Umar that the Messenger of Allah ﷺ said, 'Make your imams the best of you. They form a delegation between you and Allah.' Ad-Dāraquṭnī said, 'I think that this 'Umar is 'Umar ibn Yazīd, the Qāḍī of Madā'in. Salām ibn Sulaymān was also from Madā'in and is not strong. 'Abd al-Ḥaqq said that.'

The imams related that the Messenger of Allah ﷺ said, 'The imam is appointed to lead, so do not differ from him. Say the *takbīr* when he says the *takbīr*. Bow when he bows. When he says, "Allah hears whoever praises Him," say, "O Allah, our Lord, praise is Yours." Prostrate when he prostrates. When he prays sitting, all pray sitting.' Scholars disagree about someone who bows or goes down before the imam deliberately. One view is that his prayer is invalid if he does that in all or most of the prayer. That is the view of the literalists. It is related from Ibn 'Umar. Sunayd related from Ibn 'Ulayyah from Ayyūb from Abū Qilābah that Abu-l-Ward al-Anṣarī said, 'I prayed beside Ibn 'Umar and began to come up before the imam and go down before him. When the imam said the *salām*, Ibn 'Umar took my hand and pulled me to him. I exclaimed, "What is wrong with you?"

He asked, "Who are you?" I said, "So-and-so the son of so-and-so." He said, "You are from the people of a truthful house! What prevents you from praying?" I retorted, "Did you not see me beside you?" He replied, "I saw you rise before the imam and go down before him. The one who differs from the imam has no prayer.'"

Al-Ḥasan ibn Ḥayy said about someone who bows before the imam and then comes up from his bowing or prostration before the imam does that he does not count that and the prayer is not satisfied. Most *fuqahā'* say that someone who does that has acted badly but his prayer is not invalid because the basis in the group prayer and having an imam is a good sunnah. If someone differs from that after having performed his obligatory prayer with purity, bowing, prostration and all its obligatory elements, he does not have to repeat it, even if he has omitted one of its sunnahs, because, if he had wished, he could have prayed the prayer alone before the imam and it would have satisfied the requirement, although he acted badly in abandoning the group prayer. They said that if someone joins a prayer with an imam, and bows when he bows and prostrates when he prostrates, and is not in the same *rak'ah* as the imam, he has satisfied it, even if he comes up and goes down before him because he bowed with his bowing, prostrated with his prostration, and rose while following him, but he has acted badly because he has not followed the agreed upon sunnah in following an imam.

What Ibn 'Abd al-Barr related from the majority is based on the prayer of the follower not being connected to that of the imam because it lacks physical and legal following. That is not the position that most of them hold. The first view is the sound one in tradition and logic. The imam is appointed to be followed in his actions. Part of that is the words of the Almighty: *'I will make you a model* (imām) *for mankind.'* (2:124) This is the reality of 'imām' linguistically and in the Sharī'ah. Whoever differs from his imam has not followed him. Then the Prophet ﷺ clarified that: 'Say the *takbīr* when he says the *takbīr*.' He used '*fā*'' which denotes consequential order. He explained what Allah meant. Then he strongly threatened someone who gets ahead of the imam in rising or bowing: 'Does someone who lifts his head before the imam not fear that Allah will transform his head into that of a donkey or that He will give him the form of a donkey?' It is transmitted by the *Muwaṭṭā'*, al-Bukhārī, Muslim, Abū Dāwūd and others. Abū Hurayrah said that his forelock is in the hand of Shayṭān. The Messenger of Allah ﷺ said, 'Every action we have not commanded is rejected.' If someone deliberately acts differently to his imam, knowing full well that he is commanded to follow him and forbidden to differ from him, he has made light of his prayer and opposed what he has been commanded to do. Therefore the requirement of the prayer is not satisfied. Allah knows best.

If he raises his head out of forgetfulness before the imam, Mālik says, 'The Sunnah about someone who forgets and does that in bowing or prostration is that he goes back, bowing or prostrating, and waits for the imam. This is an error on the part of one who does it because the Prophet ﷺ said, "The imam is appointed to lead, so do not differ from him."' Ibn 'Abd al-Barr said, 'The apparent meaning of what Mālik said is that this does not oblige the one who did it deliberately to go back because he said, "This is an error on the part of one who does it."'

This disagreement applies to other than the *takbīr al-iḥrām* and *salām*. The *salām* has already been discussed. As for the *takbīr al-iḥrām*, the majority believe that that of the follower may be said only after that of the imam with the exception of one of two views related from ash-Shāfi'ī: if the follower says the *takbīr al-iḥrām* before that of the imam, that is allowed for him based on the hadith of Abū Hurayrah that the Messenger of Allah ﷺ went to the prayer and when he had said the *takbīr*, he left indicating that they should remain as they were. He went out and then came back, his head dripping water, and led them in the prayer. When he finished he said, 'I was in *janābah* but forgot to have a *ghusl*.' There was also the hadith of Anas: 'He said the *takbīr* and I said it with him.'

Muslim related that Abū Mas'ūd said, 'The Messenger of Allah ﷺ used to brush our shoulders in the prayer, saying, "Straighten your rows and do not differ lest your hearts differ. Those of understanding and intelligence should be closest to me, then those after them and then those after them."' Abū Mas'ūd said, 'Today you are in the greatest disagreement.' The hadith of 'Abdullāh adds, 'Beware of the tumults of the market.' The words 'Straighten your rows' is a command to make the rows straight, especially the first row which is right behind the imam as will be explained in *Ṣūrat al-Ḥijr*, Allah willing.

Scholars disagree about how to sit in the prayer because of the different traditions that have come regarding that. Mālik and his people said that the person praying has his buttocks on the ground with his right foot upright and left foot folded under as is related in the *Muwaṭṭā'* from Yaḥyā ibn Sa'īd: 'Al-Qāsim ibn Muḥammad showed them how to sit in the *tashahhud*, and he kept his right foot vertical and laid his left foot down, and sat on his left haunch, not on his foot. Then he said, "Abdullāh ibn 'Abdullāh ibn 'Umar saw me doing this and related to me that his father used to do the same thing.'

This idea comes in *Ṣaḥīḥ Muslim* where 'Ā'ishah said, 'The Messenger of Allah ﷺ used to begin the prayer with the *takbīr* and recitation of the *Fātiḥah*. When he bowed, he did not raise or lower his head, but in between that. When he raised his head from bowing, he did not prostrate until he was standing upright. When he raised his head from prostration, he did not prostrate until he was sitting up straight. He used to say the greeting after every two *rak'ah*s. He would lay his left foot down and have his right foot vertical. He forbade sitting on the heels like Shayṭān and he forbade that a man rest on his arms like an animal. He would end the prayer with the *taslīm*.'

Allah knows best, but according to this hadith, Ibn 'Umar said that the sunnah of the prayer is to have the right foot vertical and the left foot folded under. Ath-Thawrī, Abū Ḥanīfah and his people, and al-Ḥasan ibn Ṣāliḥ ibn Ḥayy say that he has his right foot vertical and sits on the left foot, based on the hadith of Wā'il ibn Ḥujr. That is what is stated by ash-Shāfi'ī, Aḥmad, and Isḥāq for the middle sitting. They have the same position as Mālik about the final one in *Ẓuhr*, *'Aṣr*, *Maghrib* and *'Ishā'* based on the hadith of Abū Ḥumayd as-Sā'idī that al-Bukhārī related. He said: 'I saw that when the Prophet ﷺ said the *takbīr*, he placed his hands opposite his shoulders. When he bowed in *rukū'*, he placed his hands on his knees and then bent his back straight. When he raised his head, he stood up straight until each vertebra had returned to its place. When he went into prostration, he placed his arms so that they were neither stretched out nor held close. The toes of his feet pointed towards the qiblah. When he sat after the first two *rak'ah*s, he sat on his left foot and kept his right foot upright. When he sat after the last *rak'ah,* he extended his left foot across, keeping the other upright, and sat on his buttocks.' Aṭ-Ṭabarī said that it is good to do this. All of that is confirmed from the Prophet ﷺ.

Mālik related from Muslim ibn Abī Maryam that 'Alī ibn 'Abd ar-Raḥmān al-Mu'āwī said, "Abdullāh ibn 'Umar saw me playing with some pebbles in the prayer. When it finished, he forbade me to do that, saying, "Do as the Messenger of Allah ﷺ did." I asked, "What did the Messenger of Allah ﷺ do?" He said, "When he sat in the prayer, he placed his right hand on his right thigh and he closed his fist and pointed his index finger, and he placed his left hand on his left thigh. That is what he used to do."' Ibn 'Abd al-Barr said, 'What Ibn 'Umar described about placing the right hand on the right thigh and closing all the fingers of his hand except for the index finger with which he pointed, and placing the left hand on the left thigh, opened with the fingers spread is all the agreed sunnah of sitting in the prayer. I do not know of any disagreement between scholars regarding it. It is enough for you. They do, however, disagree about moving the index finger. Some of them think that you move it and some think that you do not. All of that is related in sound traditions from the Prophet ﷺ. All of it is permitted. Praise be to Allah.' Sufyān ibn 'Uyaynah related this hadith from Muslim ibn Abī Maryam with the same idea, but he adds to it. Sufyān said, 'Yaḥyā ibn Sa'īd related to us from Muslim and then I met him and listened to him. He added in it: "It is a whisk against Shayṭān. No one forgets as long as he points with his finger and says this."'

Abū Dāwūd related in the hadith of Ibn az-Zubayr that the Prophet ﷺ used to point with his index finger when he made supplication, but did not move it. That is what is believed by some Iraqis. Some of them forbade moving it. Some of our scholars think that extending it is indicating constant *tawḥīd*. Most of the scholars of the people of Mālik and others believe that it is moved although they have two different views about continuing to move it. Those who believe that it is continuous say that it is to remind one of continuing presence in the prayer and is a hammer with which to repel Shayṭān as Sufyān mentioned. Those who think that it is not continuous think that it is moved in the articulation of the words of the *shahādah*. The interpretation is that it is as if he were articulating *tawḥīd* with that limb. Allah knows best.

They disagree about how a woman should sit in the prayer. Mālik said that it is the same as a man and that there is no difference after the *takbīr al-iḥrām* except in dress and loudness. Ath-Thawrī said that a woman is covered in her gown from one side. That is related from Ibrāhīm an-Nakha'ī. Abū Ḥanīfah and his people said that a woman sits in the manner easiest for her. That is the view of ash-Sha'bī: she sits in whatever way is easy for her. Ash-Shāfi'ī said that she should sit in the manner that will most cover her.

Muslim related that Ṭāwus said, 'We asked Ibn 'Abbās about *iq'ā'* – sitting on the feet [with the feet facing outwards). He answered, "It is the Sunnah." We said to him, "We think that it is coarseness on the part of a man." He replied, "It is the Sunnah of your Prophet ﷺ."' Scholars disagree about the description of *iq'ā'*. Abū 'Ubayd said, '*Iq'ā'* is that a man sits on his buttocks with his thighs raised as dogs and beasts do.' Ibn 'Abd al-Barr said, 'This is the form of *iq'ā'* that is agreed upon and the scholars do not disagree about it.' This is the explanation of linguists and a group of the people of *fiqh*. Abū 'Ubayd said, 'As for the people of hadith, they consider *iq'ā'* to be to put the buttocks on the heels between the two *sajdah*s.' Qāḍī 'Iyāḍ said, 'What seems most likely to me in respect of the interpretation of the *iq'ā'* which Ibn 'Abbās said is the sunnah, is that which the *fuqahā'* say is about putting the buttocks on the heels between the two *sajdah*s. That is how it is explained by Ibn 'Abbās that part of the sunnah is to have the buttocks touch the heels.' Ibrāhīm ibn Maysarah related it from Ṭāwus. Abū 'Umar mentioned it. The Qāḍī said, 'It is related that a group of the Salaf and Companions used to do that. The *fuqahā'* of the cities in general do not espouse it, calling it *iq'ā'*.' 'Abd ar-Razzāq mentioned from Ma'mar from Ibn Ṭāwus that his father saw Ibn 'Umar, Ibn 'Abbās and Ibn az-Zubayr sitting in *iq'ā'* between the two *sajdahs*.

There is no disagreement among scholars who say that the *taslīm* is obligatory and those who say that say that the second *taslīm* is not obligatory except for what is related from al-Ḥasan ibn Ḥayy who stated that two *taslīms* are mandatory. Abū Ja'far aṭ-Ṭaḥāwī said, 'We did not find any of the people of knowledge besides him who believe that there are two *taslīms* who say that the second one is one of the obligations.' Ibn 'Abd al-Barr said, 'Part of the argument of al-Ḥasan ibn Ṣāliḥ about both being obligatory is the words: "If someone breaks *wuḍū'* after the first but before the second, his prayer is invalid," and the words of the Prophet ﷺ, "The *taslīm* brings one out of the prayer." Then he made clear how the *taslīm* is: to the right and to the left. Part of the argument of those who say that only the first *taslīm* rather than the second is mandatory is the words of the Prophet ﷺ, "The *taslīm* brings one out of the prayer." That is a single *taslīm*.'

This question is based on taking the minimum implication of the word (*taslīm*) or the last of it. Since one enters the prayer by one *takbīr* by consensus, then leaving it is also by one *taslīm*, except for the firm sunnahs which have come. There is the hadith of Ibn Mas'ūd, which has the greatest multiple transmission, that of Wā'il ibn Ḥujr al-Ḥaḍramī, that of 'Ammār, that of al-Barā' ibn 'Āzib, that of Ibn 'Umar and that of Sa'd ibn Abī Waqqāṣ that the Prophet ﷺ said two *taslīms*. Ibn Jurayj, Sulaymān ibn Bilāl, and 'Abd al-'Azīz ibn Muḥammad ad-Darāwardī all related from 'Amr ibn Yaḥyā al-Māzinī from Muḥammad ibn Yaḥyā ibn Ḥabbān that his uncle, Wāsi' ibn Ḥabbān, said, 'I said to Ibn 'Umar, "Tell me what the prayer of the Messenger of Allah ﷺ was like." He mentioned the *takbīr* whenever he raised his head and went down. He mentioned, "Peace be upon you and the mercy of Allah" to his right and "Peace be upon you and the mercy of Allah" to his left.' Ibn 'Abd al-Barr said, 'This has a sound Madinan *isnād* while the famous normative practice in Madīnah is one *taslīm*. That is a practice transmitted by the people of Madīnah by multiple transmissions from old to old. The like of that is a sound argument for the normative practice in every land because it is not hidden that it happens several times every day. The same is true of the normative practice in Kufa and elsewhere of two *taslīms* which has extensive multiple transmissions from them. Everything like this is a disagreement about what is permissible, as is the case with the adhan. Similarly an objection to a single *taslīm* or two *taslīms* has not been related from any scholar in the Hijaz, Iraq, Syria or Egypt. Instead that is well known among them. The hadith about a single *taslīm* has been related by

Sa'd ibn Abī Waqqāṣ, 'Ā'ishah and Anas although it is defective and not considered to be sound by the people who know the science of hadith.'

Ad-Dāraquṭnī related that Ibn Mas'ūd said, 'It is part of the Sunnah to say the *tashahhud* silently.' Mālik preferred the *tashahhud* of 'Umar ibn al-Khaṭṭāb which is: 'Greetings belong to Allah. Pure actions belong to Allah. Good words and prayers belong to Allah. Peace be upon you, Prophet, and the mercy of Allah and His blessings. Peace be upon us and on the slaves of Allah who are right-acting. I testify that there is no god but Allah and I testify that Muḥammad is His slave and His Messenger.' Ash-Shāfi'ī and his people and al-Layth use the *tashahhud* of Ibn 'Abbās who said, 'The Messenger of Allah ﷺ used to teach us the *tashahhud* in the same way he taught us a *sūrah* of the Qur'an. It is: "Blessed greetings, prayers, good words belong to Allah. Peace be upon you, Prophet, and the mercy of Allah and His blessings. Peace be upon us and on the slaves of Allah who are right-acting. I testify that there is no god but Allah and I testify that Muḥammad is His slave and His Messenger."'

Ath-Thawrī, the Kufans and most of the people of hadith use used the *tashahhud* of Ibn Mas'ūd which Muslim also related. He said, 'We used to say in the prayer behind the Messenger of Allah ﷺ: "Peace be upon Allah. Peace be upon so-and-so." One day the Messenger of Allah ﷺ said, "Allah is Peace. When one of you sits in the prayer, he should say, "Greetings, prayers and good words belong to Allah. Peace be upon you, Prophet, and the mercy of Allah and His blessings. Peace be upon us and on the slaves of Allah who are right-acting." (When you say that, it applies to every righteous slave of Allah in the heaven and the earth.) "I testify that there is no god but Allah and I testify that Muḥammad is His slave and His Messenger." Then you can choose whatever supplication you wish.' That is the position of Aḥmad, Isḥāq and Dāwūd. Aḥmad ibn Khālid in Andalusia preferred and inclined to it. A similar *tashahhud* to that of Ibn Mas'ūd is related both *marfū'* and *mawqūf* from Abū Mūsā al-Ash'arī. All of this is disagreement about something permissible and there is nothing of an obligatory nature in it. Praise be to Allah alone.

This is a summary of the rulings on the imam and the one following him contained in His words, '*bow with those who bow*'. The position about standing in the prayer will be discussed in 2:238. The ruling about a sick imam and other rulings of the prayer will also be discussed there. The ruling of someone who is sick but not the imam will be discussed in *Āl 'Imrān*. The ruling of someone performing the obligatory prayer behind someone performing a supererogatory prayer will be discussed under the Fear Prayer in *an-Nisā'*. The ruling about the imam praying while higher than the follower will be discussed in *Maryam* as well as matters about the times, the adhan and mosques. All of this explains His words: *'establish the prayer'*. Some of its rulings were mentioned at the beginning of the *sūrah*. Praise be to Allah.

أَتَأْمُرُونَ ٱلنَّاسَ بِٱلْبِرِّ وَتَنسَوْنَ أَنفُسَكُمْ وَأَنتُمْ تَتْلُونَ ٱلْكِتَٰبَ أَفَلَا تَعْقِلُونَ ﴿٤٤﴾

44 Do you order people to piety and forget yourselves, when you recite the Book? Will you not use your intellect?

Do you order people to piety

This is a question implying a rebuke. What is meant, according to the people of interpretation, are Jewish scholars. Ibn 'Abbās said, 'A man of the Jews of Madīnah said to his son-in-law, his kin, and those who had a milk relationship with the Muslims, "Be firm in holding to what you have and on what this man (meaning Muḥammad ﷺ) orders you to do. His business is true." So they ordered their people to do that, but they did not do it.' Ibn 'Abbās said, 'The Jews used to command their followers to follow the Torah but they contradicted it by their denial of the description of Muḥammad ﷺ in it.' Ibn Jurayj said, 'The rabbis encouraged people to obey Allah while they committed acts of disobedience themselves.' One group said, 'They encouraged others to give *ṣadaqah* but were themselves miserly.' All these ideas are similar. The people who deal in indications (*ishārāt*) say that the meaning is: 'Do you ask people for the realities of meanings when you disobey their outward meaning?'

There will be a severe punishment for someone who is like this. Ḥammād ibn Salamah related from 'Alī ibn Zayd that Anas reported that the Messenger of Allah ﷺ said, 'On my Night Journey I passed by some people who were cutting of their lips with scissors of fire. I asked, "Jibrīl, who are they?" He said, "Those are the speakers of the people of this world who commanded people to devoutness and forgot themselves. They used to recite the Book but did not understand."' Abū Umāmah related that the Messenger of Allah ﷺ said, 'Those who commanded people to piety and forgot themselves will drag their intestines into the Fire of Hell. They will be asked, "Who are you?" and will answer, "We are those who commanded people to do good but forgot ourselves."'

This indicates that the punishment of someone who knows what is right and wrong and that it is obligatory to perform the requirements of both is worse than that of someone who does not know. That is because it is as if he were making light of the prohibitions and rulings of Allah. He does not benefit from his knowledge.

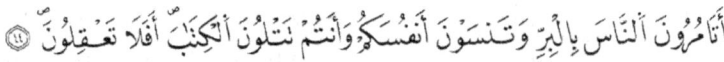

The Messenger of Allah ﷺ said, 'The worst of people on the Day of Rising will be a scholar whom Allah does not make benefit from his knowledge.'

Know that the rebuke in the *āyah* is for abandoning acts of piety, not for ordering them. This is why in His Book Allah censures those who command acts of piety but do not perform them themselves. He censured them with a rebuke which will last until the Day of Rising. Manṣūr the Faqīh said:

People who command us to do what they do not do
    are mad even if they do not bring us down.

Abu-l-'Atāhiyyah said:

You described the godfearing as if you possessed that quality,
    yet the smell of sins issues from your garment.

Abu-l-Aswad ad-Du'alī said:

Do not forbid something when you do the same.
    It is a terrible sin if you do that.
Begin with your own self and forbid it its errors.
    If you stop committing them, you are wise.
Then if you admonish, it will be accepted,
    and what you say will be followed and instruction will be of use.

Abū 'Amr ibn Maṭar said, 'I was present in the gathering of the ascetic, Abū 'Uthmān al-Ḥīrī, and he came out and sat in the place where he normally sat to remind people. He was silent for a long time. Then a man called Abu-l-'Abbās called out, "Do you think you are saying something by your silence?" He recited:

"Only a godfearing person commands people to be godfearing.
    A doctor is the one who treats the sick."'

Ibrāhīm an-Nakha'ī said, 'I dislike attributing a specific cause to three *āyahs*: *"Do you order people to piety..."* (2:44), *"Why do you say what you do not do?"* (61:2) and *"I would clearly not want to go behind your backs and do something I have forbidden you to do."* (11:88)' Salm ibn 'Amr said:

'How ugly is someone who admonishes people to be ascetic
    when he is not ascetic.
If he had been true in his asceticism,
    the mosque would have been his house, morning and evening.
Dismissing this world is of no consequence
    when one asks people for gifts and presents.

Provision is allotted to those you see.
All people, no matter their colour, obtain it.'

Al-Ḥasan told Muṭarrif ibn 'Abdullāh, 'Warn your companions!' He answered, 'I fear that I will say what I do not do.' He said, 'May Allah have mercy on you! Which of us does what he says! Shayṭān wants to be victorious by this. Then no one would command the correct or forbid the bad.' Mālik said that Rabī'ah ibn Abī 'Abd ar-Raḥmān heard Sa'īd ibn Jubayr say, 'If a person did not command the correct or forbid the bad unless there was nothing of it in himself, no one would command the correct or forbid the bad.' Mālik said, 'He spoke the truth. Who is there who has nothing of it in himself?'

The word for 'piety' – *birr* – means obedience and righteous action. It also means truthfulness. It also means a fox cub and the bleating of sheep when they are herded. So it is a word with multiple meanings. *Burr* is wheat and *barr* is respectfulness and esteem, such as that which should be shown to one's parents.

and forget yourselves

This means 'fail to do them yourselves' which is a common usage of the word '*nasā*' (forget) as it is used frequently in the Qur'an and in hadith. The root can also designate the opposite of remembrance and memory. A man who is described as '*nasyān*' is very forgetful.

'Selves' (*anfūs*) is the plural of '*nafs*' which is the soul. Part of the evidence for the fact that the '*nafs*' is also the soul (*rūḥ*) is the words of the Almighty: *'Allah takes back people's souls* (anfus) *when death arrives.*' (39:42) That is made clear in the words of the Prophet ﷺ in the words that Bilāl said to the Prophet ﷺ in the hadith of Ibn Shihāb, 'Messenger of Allah, He Who detained my soul (*nafsī*) detained your soul,' and the words of the Prophet ﷺ in the hadith of Zayd ibn Aslam: 'Allah takes our souls (*arwāḥ*). If He wishes, He returns them to us.' Mālik related it. *Nafs* also means 'blood'.

when you recite the Book?

This is a great rebuke to the one who understands. '*Tatlūna*' means 'to recite'. The Book is the Torah and it also applied to anyone who does the same as they did. The root of '*tilāwah*' (recitation) means 'to follow', which is why it is used for recitation because words follow one another so that they form a sequence.

Will you not use your intellect?

Will you not prevent yourselves from being in this state? The word *'aql* (intellect) implies restraint, from which comes the hobble *('iqāl)* of the camel because it prevents it from moving. The word is also sometimes used for blood money because it restrains the relative of the victim from killing the perpetrator. *I'tiqāl* is a spasm of the stomach or restraining of the tongue. A fortress is called *'ma'qil'*. *'Aql* is the opposite of ignorance. *'Aql* is also a red cloth that Arab women use to cover howdahs. Az-Zajjāj says, 'Someone described as *'āqil* is someone who does what Allah has obliged him to do. If does not do it, then he is ignorant.'

The people who follow the truth agree that the intellect is an existent thing which is neither timeless nor non-existent because, if it had been non-existent, it would describe some essences and not others. Since it exists, it is impossible to say it is timeless since there is nothing timeless except Allah. Philosophers have stated that the intellect is timeless. Some of them believe that it is a subtle essence in the body from which rays spread, like a lamp in a house, and by it one distinguishes between the realities of known things. Some of them say that it is a simple uncompounded essence. Then they disagree about its location. One group say that it is located in the brain because the brain is the locus of sensation. Another group say that it is located in the heart because the heart is the lode of life and the core of the senses.

The statement that the intellect is an essence is false since essences are similar. If the intellect had been an essence, then every essence would be an intellect. It is said that the intellect is that by which things are perceived in respect of the realities of ideas. Even if this statement is closer to the one before it, it is far from being correct since perception is one of the attributes of the living, and the intellect is something contingent. That is impossible for it as it is impossible for it to experience pleasure and appetite.

Shaykh Abu-l-Ḥasan al-Ash'arī, Abū Isḥāq al-Isfarāyanī and others who possess full understanding said that the intellect is knowledge as is indicated by the fact that one does not say, 'I grasped but did not know.' Qāḍī Abū Bakr said, 'The intellect consists of requisite knowledge of the necessary nature of necessary things, permissibility of permissible things, and impossibility of impossible things.' That is what is preferred by Abu-l-Ma'ālī in *al-Irshād*. His preference in *al-Burhān* is that it is an attribute by which knowledge is grasped. He opposes the school of the Qāḍī and deduced that his school is unsound. He related in *al-Burhān* that al-Muḥāsibī said that the intellect is an instinct. Abū Bakr related that ash-Shāfi'ī and Abū 'Abdullāh ibn Mujāhid said that the intellect is the tool of discrimination. It is related that Abu-l-'Abbās al-Qalānisī said that the intellect is the faculty of discrimination. It is related that al-Muḥāsibī said that the intellect consists of lights and insights. Then he put these views in order and said, 'The first does not have a sound transmission from ash-Shāfi'ī and Ibn Mujāhid.' The word 'tool' is used for an actual tool and its usage here is metaphorical. The same is true of those who say that it is a faculty. Only power is understood from a faculty. Al-Qalānisī used the widest of the expressions as is the case with that of al-Muḥāsibī. The intellect is neither a form or a light, but lights and insight use it. This will be explained in the *Āyat* of *Tawḥīd*.

وَاسْتَعِينُوا۟ بِالصَّبْرِ وَالصَّلَوٰةِ ۚ وَإِنَّهَا لَكَبِيرَةٌ إِلَّا عَلَى ٱلْخَٰشِعِينَ

45 Seek help in steadfastness and the prayer. But that is a very hard thing, except for the humble:

Seek help in steadfastness and the prayer.

The meaning of the word used for steadfastness – *ṣabr* – is restraint and it is used for binding a person; and it also means endurance. Allah has commanded us in His Book to persist in obedience to Him and to restrain ourselves from committing acts of disobedience by telling us to be steadfast. It is said that a person first refrains (*ṣabara*) from acts of disobedience, and once he has done so he becomes steadfast (*ṣābara*) in obedience. This is the soundest of what is said.

Ṣalāh (the prayer) is mentioned rather than other acts of worship. When something happened to the Prophet ﷺ, he sought refuge in the prayer. Ibn 'Abbās was once told about the death of his brother – or, it is said, a daughter of his – when he was on a journey and he said, 'A weak spot Allah has protected, a burden Allah has spared us, and a reward which Allah will bring.' Then he went off the road and prayed and went back to his camel, reciting, *'Seek help in steadfastness and the prayer.'*

Some people say that what is meant, according to linguistic usage, is supplication. This is like the *āyah* of Allah: *'When you meet a troop, then stand firm and remember Allah'* (8:45) because firmness is *ṣabr* and *dhikr* is supplication. A third position was espoused by Mujāhid who said that, in this *āyah*, *ṣabr* referred to fasting. The month of Ramadan is called 'The Month of *Ṣabr*'. The reason for this is that fasting curbs appetites and makes one ascetic in this world and the prayer keeps one from lewd action and what is disliked. Allah knows best.

Steadfastness in the face of injury and in performing acts of obedience is part of striving against the self and curbing it from its appetites and preventing it from becoming proud. It is one of the qualities of the Prophets and righteous. Yaḥyā ibn al-Yamān said, 'Steadfastness is to not desire any state except that which Allah has placed you in and to find pleasure in whatever He has decreed for you in this world and the Next.' 'Alī said, 'Steadfastness in relation to faith is like the head in relation to the body.' Aṭ-Ṭabarī agreed with 'Alī and said, 'That is because faith is recognition by the heart, affirmation with the tongue and action with the limbs. If someone is not steadfast in acting with his limbs, he does not truly have faith.' Steadfastness in carrying out the Sharī'ah is comparable to the head of a person's body: it is not complete without it.

Allah describes the reward for various actions and puts a limit on it. He says: *'Those who produce a good action will receive ten like it.'* (6:160) But He makes the reward of the steadfast limitless and praises the people who have it: *'The steadfast will be paid their wages in full without any reckoning.'* (39:10) and: *'But if someone is steadfast and forgives, that is the most resolute course to follow.* (42:43) It is also said that *'The steadfast will be paid their wages in full without any reckoning'* (39:10) means those who fast because of the words of the Almighty in the sound report from the Prophet ﷺ: 'Fasting is Mine and I repay it.' He did not mention any exact reward as He did not mention one for steadfastness. Allah knows best.

One of the virtues of *ṣabr* is that Allah describes Himself as having it, as in the hadith of Abū Mūsā when the Prophet ﷺ said, 'There is no one or nothing with more patience in the face of an insult which he hears than Allah Almighty is. They claim that He has a son and yet He still gives them health and provides for them.' Al-Bukhārī transmitted it. Our scholars say that, in the case of Allah, *ṣabr* has the meaning of forbearance, in that He defers the punishment from those who deserve it. The description of Him as having *ṣabr* does not come in the Revelation, but in this hadith where it is interpreted by scholars to mean forbearance, and so one of His Names is *aṣ-Ṣabūr*, because of His great forbearance towards those who disobey Him.

But that is a very hard thing,

Interpreters disagree about what the word 'that' refers to here. It is said to refer to the prayer alone because it is harder for people than fasting, given that steadfastness here refers to fasting. The prayer is the prison of the lower self while fasting is just denial of its appetites. Someone who denies one or two appetites is not the same as someone who denies all his appetites. Fasting denies the appetite for women, food and drink but one is able to enjoy other appetites like talking, walking and looking and other such things. So there is consolation for the denied appetites. The one who prays, however, is denied all those things and all his limbs are restrained in the prayer from all appetites. That is why the prayer is harder for the self and a greater burden on it. It is said to refer to both of them but usually it is taken to mean the prayer.

This is the same as when Allah says: *'those who hoard up gold and silver and do not spend it in the Way of Allah'* (9:34) when the primary reference is to silver because it was the predominant currency used for trade. And: *'When they see a chance of trade or entertainment they scatter off to it.'* (62:11) It is said that since steadfastness is included in the prayer, it refers to it. It is also said to refer to worship as a whole which entails both fasting and the prayer. It is said to be a use of the verbal noun here, in which case it would mean that 'seeking help' is what is difficult. It is said to refer to responding to Muḥammad ﷺ because *ṣabr* and prayer are part of what he called to. It is said that it refers to the Ka'bah because one is commanded to pray towards it. '*Kabīrah*' means burdensome and difficult. It is hard for all except the humble, for whom it is easy. The people of meanings say that they are those who are supported from pre-eternity by the qualities of being chosen and guided.

except for the humble:

'Khāshi'īn' is the plural of *khāshi'*, someone who is humble. Humility is a quality in the soul which shows itself in stillness and humbleness. Qatādah said, *'Khushū''* (humility) is in the heart where it takes the form of fear and appears outwardly as the lowering of the eye in the prayer.' Az-Zajjāj said, 'A humble person is one in whom the effect of abasement can be seen.' The word is used of a house which has fallen down. This is the root meaning. A 'humble' place is one which has nothing to indicate where it is. The verb is used for lowering the voice and lowering the eyes. *Khush'ah,* which comes from the same root, means a low hill. A land which is *khāshi'* is a place covered in dust with no place where one can alight.

Al-A'mash said that he asked Ibrāhīm an-Nakha'ī about humility and he said, 'A'mash! You want to be an imam for the people and do not know what humility is! Humility does not consist of eating coarse food and wearing coarse clothes and bowing the head. Humility is to see the noble and lowly as having the same right and to be humble towards Allah in every obligation He has imposed on you.' 'Umar ibn al-Khaṭṭāb looked at a young man with a bowed head and said, 'You! Lift your head up! Humility is not more than what is in the heart!' 'Alī ibn Abī Ṭālib said, 'Humility is in the heart, in your hands being gentle with the Muslims, and in not looking about during the prayer.' This will be discussed in 23:2. So someone who makes a display of humility, beyond what is in his heart, displays hypocrisy on top of hypocrisy. Sahl ibn 'Abdullāh said, 'A person is not humble until every hair in his body manifests humility by the words of Allah, *"The skins of those who fear their Lord tremble."* (39:23)'

This is praiseworthy humility because when the heart is still, the outward must also be humble, and the person who has it will inevitably display it; so you will see him with his head bowed, courteous and submissive. The Salaf used to strive to be like that. The blameworthy form is artificial, pretending to weep with a bowed head as the ignorant do in order to be viewed with respect. That is deceit from Shayṭān and part of human ego. Al-Ḥasan related that a man sighed in the presence of 'Umar ibn al-Khaṭṭāb as if he was in sorrow. 'Umar clouted him. When 'Umar spoke, he was heard. When he walked, he went quickly. When he struck, he caused pain. He was a truthful worshipper and truly humble. Ibn Abī Najīḥ related that Mujāhid said, 'The humble are truly the believers.'

ٱلَّذِينَ يَظُنُّونَ أَنَّهُم مُّلَٰقُواْ رَبِّهِمْ وَأَنَّهُمْ إِلَيْهِ رَٰجِعُونَ ﴿٤٦﴾

46 those who are aware that they will meet their Lord and that they will return to Him.

This describes the humble. The word for being aware, *ẓann*, means certainty in this context according to the majority of scholars. The normal meaning of *ẓann* entails some doubt but it can be used to mean certainty as in this *āyah* and elsewhere.

يَٰبَنِيٓ إِسْرَٰٓءِيلَ ٱذْكُرُواْ نِعْمَتِيَ ٱلَّتِيٓ أَنْعَمْتُ عَلَيْكُمْ وَأَنِّي فَضَّلْتُكُمْ
عَلَى ٱلْعَٰلَمِينَ ﴿٤٧﴾

47 Tribe of Israel! remember the blessing I conferred on you and that I preferred you over all other beings.

He means the beings of their time. The people of every time are considered a 'world'. It is said that the preference was because they had a lot of Prophets and other advantages.

وَٱتَّقُواْ يَوْمًا لَّا تَجْزِي نَفْسٌ عَن نَّفْسٍ شَيْـًٔا وَلَا يُقْبَلُ مِنْهَا شَفَٰعَةٌ
وَلَا يُؤْخَذُ مِنْهَا عَدْلٌ وَلَا هُمْ يُنصَرُونَ ﴿٤٨﴾

48 Have fear of a Day when no self will be able to compensate for another in any way. No intercession will be accepted from at, no ransom taken from it, and they will not be helped.

Have fear of a Day

This is a command which is also a threat, and '*yawm*' (Day) here refers to the punishment and terror of the Last Day.

When no self will be able to compensate for another in any way

This means that no one will be punished for the sin of anyone else nor can he avert it from him. We find in the *Ṣaḥīḥ* that Abū Burdah ibn Niyār said about sacrifices, 'It will not satisfy [the requirement] for anyone after you.' '*Lā tajzī*' means: it does not settle, suffice nor satisfy if there is nothing against it, but it does if there is without any choice involved in respect to rights. Abū Hurayrah reported that the Messenger of Allah ﷺ said, 'Anyone who has done an injustice to his brother with regard to his honour or anything else should seek to be absolved by him before the Day when there will be neither dinar nor dirham. If he has some right actions, they will be taken from him to counterbalance any injustice he did and if he does not have any good actions, some of the bad actions of his friend will be taken and he will be made to carry them.' Al-Bukhārī transmitted it.

No intercession will be accepted from it,

The word for intercession is derived from the root '*shaf'ah*' (even) which means one of a pair and to make an odd number even. *Shuf'ah* (pre-emption) is called that because it is used when someone adds the property of his partner to his own. *Shafī'* is someone with pre-emption or intercession. A camel which is *shāfi'* is one which is pregnant when there is a young foal still with it.

The position of the people who hold to the truth is that intercession is a reality, while the Mu'tazilites deny it and believe that sinful believers who enter the Fire will remain in it forever. There are mutually supporting reports that sinful rebellious people from the nations of the Prophets, who affirm the Unity of Allah, will be interceded for by the angels, Prophets, martyrs and righteous. There are two firm grounds for refuting the Mu'tazilites. The first is the numerous hadiths with multiple transmissions which affirm intercession, and the second is the consensus of the Salaf in their acceptance of these reports. No one denies them and everyone agrees that they are sound and accepts them as decisive evidence for the soundness of the creed of the people who hold to the truth and the falseness of the claims of the Mu'tazilites.

The Mu'tazilites claim that there are *āyahs* in the Book which refute these traditions, like, *'The wrongdoers will have no close friend or any intercessor who might be heard'* (40:18) and *'Anyone who does evil will be repaid for it'* (4:123) and here *'no intercession will be accepted from it.'* We reply that these *āyah*s are general to every wrongdoer and the general has no definite application, so these *āyah*s do not apply to everyone who does evil and to every soul. What is meant by them is the unbelievers rather than the believers which is supported by the evidence of the traditions reported about that.

Allah established intercession for some people and denied it to others. He says about the unbelievers: *'The intercession of the interceders will not help them'* (74:48), *'They only intercede on behalf of those with whom He is pleased'* (21:28), and *'Intercession with Him will be of no benefit except from someone who has His permission.'* (34:23) By this we know that intercession will help the believers but not the unbelievers. Commentators agree that what is meant by this *āyah* is the unbelievers, not every self. If you say that there is punishment for every rebellious wrongdoer, we do not say that they will be for ever in the Fire, by the evidence of the hadiths we related and by the words of Allah: *'He forgives whomever He wishes for other than that'* (4:48) and *'No one despairs of solace from Allah except for people who are unbelievers.'* (12:87)

With regard to *'those with whom He is pleased'* (21:28), if they point out that the deviant is not pleasing, we reply that He did not say, 'those who are not pleasing.' Allah is pleased to grant intercession to the unifiers since He says: *'They have no right of intercession. None do but those who have a contract with the All-Merciful.'* (19:87) The Prophet ﷺ was asked, 'What is the contract which Allah has made with His creation?' He replied. 'That they believe in Him and not associate anything with Him.'

If they say that those who are pleasing are those who repent and have made a contract with Allah by repenting to Him, since the angels ask forgiveness for them and Allah says: *'Forgive those who turn to you and who follow Your Way'* (40:7), and thus that the intercession of the Prophets is only for the people of repentance and not people of wrong actions, our reply is as follows: What you maintain obliges Allah to accept repentance. If Allah accepts the repentance of the wrongdoer, there is no need for intercession or asking forgiveness. The commentators agree that what is meant by 'forgive those who turn,' refers to turning away from *shirk* and 'follow Your Way,' means the Path of the believers. They asked Allah to forgive them for their wrong actions other than *shirk* as He says: *'He forgives whomever He wishes for other than that'* (4:48).

If they say, 'All the Community hope for the intercession of the Prophet ﷺ and if it was particularly for the people of wrong actions, their request would be invalid,' our reply is that every Muslim seeks the intercession of the Messenger ﷺ and desires Allah to accept it, since no one believes himself to be entirely free of wrong actions and to have performed everything Allah has required of him. Everyone acknowledges that they have shortcomings and so they fear the punishment and hope for salvation. The Prophet ﷺ said, 'None of you will be saved by his actions.' They said, 'Not even you, Messenger of Allah?' He said, 'Not even me unless Allah covers me with His mercy.'

Ibn Kathīr and Abū 'Amr recite '***t**uqbalu*' because *shafā'ah* is feminine. The rest have it in the masculine as '***y**uqbalu*', taking it as referring to 'intercessor'.

no ransom will be accepted from it, and none will be helped.

'Adl means 'ransom' whereas *'idl* means 'like'. The *'adl* of a thing is that which is equal to a thing, of the same dimension in size. *'Naṣr'* is 'help' and *anṣār* are helpers as in 3:52.

The reason for the revelation of this *āyah* is that the tribe of Israel said, 'We are the sons of Allah, beloved of Him and the sons of His Prophets, and our forebears will intercede for us.' So Allah informed them about the Day of Rising on which day such intercession will not be accepted and no ransom will be taken. He mentioned intercession, ransom and help because they are the things on which human beings rely in this world. Someone who falls into hardship is only rescued by intercession, help or ransom.

وَإِذْ نَجَّيْنَٰكُم مِّنْ ءَالِ فِرْعَوْنَ يَسُومُونَكُمْ سُوٓءَ ٱلْعَذَابِ يُذَبِّحُونَ
أَبْنَآءَكُمْ وَيَسْتَحْيُونَ نِسَآءَكُمْ ۚ وَفِى ذَٰلِكُم بَلَآءٌ مِّن رَّبِّكُمْ عَظِيمٌ ۝٤٩

49 Remember when We rescued you from the people of Pharaoh. They were inflicting an evil punishment on you, slaughtering your sons and letting your women live. In that there was a terrible trial for you from your Lord.

Remember when We rescued you from the people of Pharaoh.

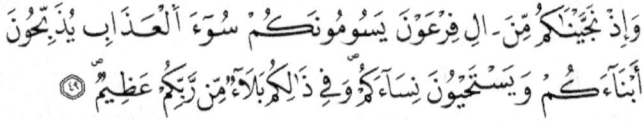

The word '*idh*' ('when', translated here by 'Remember when') means 'Remember My blessing when...' and the following *āyahs* mention some of the blessings which the tribe of Israel enjoyed: being rescued from their enemies and Prophets being placed among them. It is addressed to those present but refers to their ancestors. Allah says *'We rescued you'* because the rescue of their forefathers was a reason for the existence of those present. The word '*najā*' (rescue) comes from the root *najwah* which is a raised place on the earth. So a rescued person is someone who emerges out of constriction into expansion. The '*āl*' of Pharaoh means his family, followers and all who follow his *dīn*. Similarly, the *āl* of the Prophet ﷺ refers to those who follow his *dīn* in his time and at all times, whether related to him or not. Whoever does not follow his *dīn* is not one of his family or his people, even if he is related to him. Evidence for this is in the words of Allah: *'We drowned the people of Pharaoh'* (2:50) and elsewhere. This is why it is said that Abū Lahab and Abū Jahl were not part of the people or family of the Prophet ﷺ even if they had actual kinship with him. That is why Allah Almighty said of Nūḥ's son: *'He is definitely not one of your family. He is someone whose action was not righteous.'* (11:46) We find in *Ṣaḥīḥ Muslim* that 'Amr ibn al-'Āṣ said, 'I heard the Messenger of Allah ﷺ say aloud and not secretly, "The family of my father (meaning so-and-so) are not my friends. But my friends are Allah and the righteous believers."'

One group said that the *āl* of Muḥammad ﷺ consists only of his wives and children based on the hadith of Abū Ḥumayd as-Sā'idī: 'They said, "Messenger of Allah, how should we pray for blessing on you?" He replied, "Say: 'O Allah, bless Muḥammad, his wives and children as You blessed the family of Ibrāhīm. Give blessing to Muḥammad, his wives and children as You gave blessing to Ibrāhīm. You are Praiseworthy, Glorious.'"' Muslim related it. One group of the people of knowledge said that *ahl* (family) is known and *āl* are the followers. The first view is sounder based on what we have mentioned and on the hadith of 'Abdullāh ibn Abī Awfā in which it is reported that when people brought their *ṣadaqah* to the Messenger of Allah ﷺ, he would say, 'O Allah, bless them.' 'Abdullāh said, 'My father brought his *ṣadaqah* and he said, "O Allah, bless the family (*āl*) of Abū Awfā."'

Pharaoh may have been the name of the king himself but it is more probable that it was the title of the rulers of Egypt, like Caesar and Khusrau were titles of the emperors of Rome and Persia, and Negus the title of the ruler of Abyssinia. It is said, according to the People of the Book, that this Pharaoh's actual name was Qābūs. Wahb said that it was al-Walīd ibn Muṣ'ab ibn ar-Riyyān. His *kunyah* was Abū Murrah. He was from the Banū 'Amlīq ibn Lāwidh ibn Iram ibn Sām ibn Nūḥ. As-Suhaylī said, 'Every ruler of the Copts and Egypt is called Pharaoh.' Al-Mas'ūdī said that the Arabic translation of 'Pharaoh' is not known.

They were inflicting an evil punishment on you, slaughtering your sons

The word used for inflicting (*yasūmūna*) indicates a constant punishment because *sawm* means constancy. *Sā'imah* describes sheep because they are always grazing. 'Evil punishment' means the worst kind of punishment. It can mean 'constant punishment'. The evil punishment consisted of making them slaves and chattels. They had to build, till the land, harvest and serve, and anyone who did not work had to pay a poll tax.

'Slaughtering' is in Form II, indicating frequency. *Dhabḥ* is slitting and *dhibḥ* is something slaughtered. *Dhubāḥ* is the split at the base of the fingers. Pharaoh was slaughtering male children and letting the women live. One group said that 'sons' means 'men' and they were called that because they had been sons. The first view is sounder because it is more evident. Allah ascribes the action to the people of Pharaoh even though they were acting on his command since it was they who imposed the punishment. This informs us that someone who does something is punished for his action even if he is just following orders. Aṭ-Ṭabarī says that when a tyrant orders someone to kill someone, the one who does the killing is criminally responsible.

Scholars have three different views regarding this legal question. One is that they are both killed: the one who commanded it and the one who actually carried it out. This is the view of an-Nakha'ī. Ash-Shāfi'ī and Mālik also said that, giving some additional details. Ash-Shāfi'ī said that when the ruler commands a man to kill another man and the one who is commanded knows that that it is unjust to kill him, then both he and the ruler are subject to retaliation, just as is the case with two joint killers. If the ruler forces him to do it while the one commanded knows that the command to kill is unjust, the ruler is subject to retaliation and there are two views about the one he commanded. One is that he is subject to retaliation and the other is that he is not, but that he owes half the blood money. Ibn al-Mundhir related that.

Our scholars say that the one commanded must be one of those who must obey the one who gave the command, who is at the same time someone whose power to harm is feared, as is the case with the sultan and the master of a slave. In that case retaliation is obliged against both. If he is one of those who are not forced to obey, then the actual killer is killed alone and not the one who issued the command. That is like when a father orders a son, a teacher one of his students, or an artisan one of his apprentices, provided the person ordered is of age. If he is not of age, then the killing is of the one who ordered it and the *'āqilah* relatives of the boy pay half of the blood money.

Ibn Nāfi' said that a master is not killed when he orders his slave, even if he does not speak Arabic, to kill a man. Ibn Ḥabīb takes the position of Ibn al-Qāsim, that they are both killed. If the command is issued by someone the person commanded does not fear to disobey, and there is no compulsion, then only the one commanded is killed, not the one who gave the command. He is, instead, beaten and imprisoned. Aḥmad said that if a master orders his slave to kill a man, the master is killed. This position is related from 'Alī ibn Abī Ṭālib and Abū Hurayah. 'Alī said that the slave is imprisoned. Aḥmad said that the slave is imprisoned and beaten. Ath-Thawrī said that the slave is disciplined. Al-Ḥakam and Ḥammād said that the slave is killed. Qatādah said that they are both killed. Ash-Shāfi'ī said that if the slave is fluent and understands, then the slave is killed and the master punished, but if the slave does not speak the language, then retaliation is taken from the master. Sulaymān ibn Mūsā said, 'The one who gives the command is not killed, but his hands are amputated and then he is punished and imprisoned.' That is like what is stated by 'Aṭā', al-Ḥakam, Ḥammād, ash-Shāfi'ī, Aḥmad and Isḥāq about a man who orders a man to kill another man. Ibn al-Mundhir mentioned it. Zafar said that neither is killed, and that is the third position. It is related by Abū al-Ma'alī in *al-Burhān*. He thought that neither of them is separate in respect to retaliation and therefore he thinks that neither of them is killed. Allah knows best.

In that was a terrible trial for you from your Lord.

The words 'in that' indicate everything that went on. The word here for trial (*balā'*) can also be a blessing as Allah says elsewhere using the same root: '*...test the believers with this excellent trial.*' (8:17). Abū al-Haytham said that *balā'* can be good or bad and its root means testing. Allah tests His slave with good actions to test his gratitude, and tests him with affliction, which he dislikes, to test his steadfastness. Therefore both are called *balā'*. The majority say that, in this instance, it refers to the slaughtering of the male children and so here it is an evil test. There was a test and affliction in the slaughter.

وَإِذْ فَرَقْنَا بِكُمُ ٱلْبَحْرَ فَأَنجَيْنَٰكُمْ وَأَغْرَقْنَآ ءَالَ فِرْعَوْنَ وَأَنتُمْ تَنظُرُونَ ﴿٥٠﴾

50 And when We parted the sea for you and rescued you, and drowned the people of Pharaoh while you watched.

When Allah parted the sea, each side was like a great mountain. The image comes from parting the hair and '*furqān*' from the same root is used for separating the truth from falsehood. '*Bikum*' here means 'for you' because the preposition 'bi' can also mean 'li'. It is also said that 'bi' has its normal meaning and so it means 'We parted the sea by your entering it.' They travelled between the two bodies of water which were parted. The word *baḥr* (sea) indicates a large expanse of water, usually salty. A horse is described as *baḥr* when it has a long stride. 'We rescued you' means that 'We brought you out of it.'

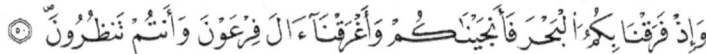

and drowned the people of Pharaoh

There are varying views on the part of scholars about how the tribe of Israel was saved. Aṭ-Ṭabarī mentioned that Allah revealed to Mūsā to travel from Egypt with the tribe of Israel. Mūsā ordered them to borrow jewellery and goods from the Copts. Allah had made that lawful for the tribe of Israel. Mūsā set out with them at the beginning of the night. Pharaoh was informed and said, 'Do not follow them until the cock crows.' That night not a single cock in Egypt crowed. On that night Allah made many of the sons of the Copts die and so they were busy burying them. They set out to pursue them early in the morning as Allah says in 26:60, and Mūsā went to the edge of the sea. The tribe of Israel numbered about 600,000. Pharaoh's numbers were a million and two hundred thousand. It is said that Pharaoh pursued Mūsā with a million steeds, not counting the mares. It is said that Israel, who is Ya'qūb, entered Egypt with seventy-six of his descendants and Allah made their numbers grow and blessed his offspring until they were 600,000 men of fighting age when they went to the sea on that day, not counting old men, children and women.

Abū Bakr 'Abdullāh ibn Muḥammad ibn Abī Shaybah mentioned from Shabābah ibn Sawwār from Yūnus ibn Abī Isḥāq from Abū Isḥāq from 'Amr ibn Maymūn from 'Abdullāh ibn Mas'ūd that when Mūsā set out at night with the tribe of Israel, the news reached Pharaoh and he commanded that a sheep be slaughtered and then said, 'By Allah, I will not finish skinning it before six hundred thousand Copts have gathered to me.'

He said that Mūsā went on until he reached the sea and told it to part. The sea replied to him, 'You are arrogant, Mūsā! Have I parted for any of the children of Ādam so that I should part for you?' There was a man with Mūsā on a steed of his and that man said, 'Where do you command us to go, Prophet of Allah?' He replied, 'I have only been commanded to go in this direction.' He charged in with his horse and it swam and he came out and repeated, 'Where do you command us to go, Prophet of Allah?' He replied, 'I have only been commanded to go in this direction.' He said, 'By Allah, you did not lie and are not accused of lying!' He plunged in and it swam with him until he once more emerged. He asked again, 'Where do you command us to go, Prophet of Allah?' He replied, 'I have only been commanded to go in this direction.' He said, 'By Allah, you did not lie and are not accused of lying!' So Allah revealed to him: *'Strike the sea with your staff.'* (26:63) So Mūsā struck it with his staff and *'it split in two, each part like a towering cliff.'* (26:63) There were twelve paths through it for the twelve tribes. Each tribe had a path that they could see. The cliffs of water became arches and windows so that they could see one another.

When Mūsā's people emerged and only the people of Pharaoh remained, the sea collapsed in on them and drowned them. He mentioned that it was the Red Sea and that the man who was on the horse with Mūsā was his lad, Yūsha', son of Nūn. Allah revealed to the sea, 'Part for Mūsā when he strikes you.' The sea spent the night trembling. He struck the sea in the morning. Its *kunyah* was Abū Khālid. Ibn Abī Shaybah mentioned that. Most commentators narrate this regarding the story. What we have mentioned is sufficient and it will be further explained in the relevant *sūrah*s.

Allah Almighty mentioned the deliverance and the drowning, but did not mention the day when that occurred. Muslim related from Ibn 'Abbās that the Messenger of Allah ﷺ came to Madīnah and found the Jews fasting on the day of 'Āshūrā'. The Messenger of Allah ﷺ asked them, 'What is this day you are fasting?' They replied, 'This is a great day in which Allah delivered Mūsā and his people and drowned Pharaoh and his people. Mūsā fasted it out of thankfulness and we also fast it.' The Messenger of Allah ﷺ said, 'We are more entitled to Mūsā than you are.' So the Messenger of Allah ﷺ fasted it and commanded that it be fasted. Al-Bukhārī also transmitted that from Ibn 'Abbās and the fact that the Prophet ﷺ told his Companions, 'You are more entitled to Mūsā than they are, so fast it.'

The apparent meaning of these hadiths is that the Prophet ﷺ fasted 'Āshūrā' and commanded that it be fasted to imitate Mūsā, according to what the Jews had told him. That is not the case. When 'Ā'ishah related it, she said that Quraysh had fasted the day of 'Āshūrā' in the Jāhiliyyah. Then when he came to Madīnah, he fasted it and commanded that it be fasted. When Ramadan was prescribed, then he abandoned fasting 'Āshūrā'. Whoever wished could fast it and whoever wished did not. Al-Bukhārī and Muslim transmitted this.

It might be said that it is probable that Quraysh fasted it in imitation of the Jews because they heard about it from them as they considered them to be people of knowledge and therefore the Prophet ﷺ fasted it during the Jāhiliyyah in Makkah. Then when he came to Madīnah he found the Jews fasting it and said, 'We are closer and more entitled to Mūsā than you,' and so he fasted it to follow Mūsā. He made it obligatory and stressed the command to fast it to the extent that even children fasted it. This is taken as evidence by those who speciously claim that the Prophet ﷺ may have worshipped according to the religion of Mūsā. This is not the case as will be explained in *al-An'ām* (6:90).

There is some disagreement about whether the day of 'Āshūrā' is the ninth or the tenth of Muḥarram. Ash-Shāfi'ī believed that it is the ninth based on the hadith of al-Ḥakam ibn al-A'raj who said, 'I went to Ibn 'Abbās and found him using his cloak as a pillow at Zamzam. I said, "Tell me about the fast of 'Āshūrā'." He said, "When you see the new moon of Muḥarram, count the days and begin the fast on the ninth." I asked, "Is that how Muḥammad ﷺ fasted it?" "Yes," he answered.' Muslim transmitted it. Sa'īd ibn al-Musayyab, al-Ḥasan al-Baṣrī, Mālik and a group of the Salaf believed that it is the tenth. At-Tirmidhī mentioned the hadith of al-Ḥakam and did not describe it as sound or good. Then he added after it from Qutaybah from 'Abd al-Wahhāb from Yūnus from al-Ḥasan that Ibn 'Abbās said, 'The Messenger of Allah ﷺ commanded that 'Āshūrā' be fasted on the tenth.' Abū 'Īsā said that the hadith of Ibn 'Abbās is a sound ḥasan hadith.

At-Tirmidhī related that Ibn 'Abbās said, 'Fast the ninth and the tenth and be different to the Jews.' This hadith is taken by ash-Shāfi'ī, Aḥmad ibn Ḥanbal and Isḥāq. Others have said that his words, 'count the days and begin the fast on the ninth' do not contain a proof about not fasting the tenth. Rather it means to fast the ninth alongside the tenth. They said that fasting the two days combines the hadiths. His words to al-Ḥakam about that being how the Prophet ﷺ fasted it means 'if he had lived'. He did not fast the ninth on its own. That is made clear by what Ibn Mājah in the *Sunan* and Muslim in the *Ṣaḥīḥ* transmitted from Ibn 'Abbās that the Messenger of Allah ﷺ said: 'If I live until next year, I will fast today and the ninth.'

Abū Qatādah related that the Prophet ﷺ said, 'As for fasting the day of 'Āshūrā.' I hope that Allah will expiate the year before it.' Muslim and at-Tirmidhī transmitted it.

while you watched.

'While you looked on with your own eyes.' They saw the drowning of the people of Pharaoh when they had been saved and that was the greatest favour to them. It is said that they were brought out to them so that they could see them. This is one blessing after another. It is also said to mean reflecting with the inner eye because they were too busy to actually stop and watch. It is said that it means that you were in the state that someone would be if they looked. This is something that you would do. The first is more likely because they were in no state to reflect when they emerged from the sea. That is because when Allah had saved them and drowned their enemy, they said, 'Mūsā! Our hearts are not at peace as to whether Pharaoh has truly drowned!' Then Allah commanded the sea so that they could look at him.

Abū Bakr ibn Abī Shaybah mentioned from Qays ibn 'Ubbād that the tribe of Israel said, 'Pharaoh has not died and he will never die!' When Allah heard their denial of their Prophet, He cast him up on the shore like a red ox so that the tribe of Israel could see him. When they were at peace about it and were sent on the road to the cities of Pharaoh to reach his treasures and be immersed in blessing, they saw a people devoting themselves to some idols of theirs. They said, 'Mūsā, give us a god as they have gods.' Mūsā rebuked them and said, 'Do you desire other than Allah as a god when He has preferred you over all the worlds (meaning those of his time)?' Then he commanded them to go to the Holy Land, which had been the home of their forefathers, and to purify themselves of the land Pharaoh. The Holy Land was in the possession of tyrants who had conquered it. So they needed to fight to remove them. They said, 'Do you want to us make us meat for the tyrants? If would have been better for us if you had left us in Pharaoh's power!' Allah says about this: *'My people! Enter the Holy Land which Allah has ordained for you!'* to *'We will stay sitting here.'* (5:21-24) He prayed and against them and called them deviants.

Therefore they remained wandering in the wilderness for forty years as a punishment. Then He showed mercy to them and gave them manna and quail as will be mentioned. Then Mūsā went to Mount Sinai to bring them the Torah and they adopted the Calf. Then they were told, 'You have reached Jerusalem, so enter the door in prostration and say, "*Ḥiṭṭah.*"' These other stories will be dealt with in the appropriate places.

وَإِذْ وَٰعَدْنَا مُوسَىٰٓ أَرْبَعِينَ لَيْلَةً ثُمَّ ٱتَّخَذْتُمُ ٱلْعِجْلَ مِنۢ بَعْدِهِۦ وَأَنتُمْ
ظَٰلِمُونَ ﴿٥١﴾

51 And when We allotted to Mūsā forty nights. Then you adopted the Calf when he had gone and you were wrongdoers.

And when We allotted to Mūsā forty nights.

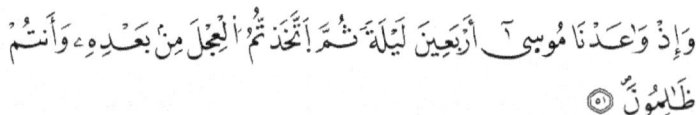

Abū 'Amr recited *'w**a**'adnā'* without an *alif*, and Abū 'Ubayd preferred it and did not acknowledge *'w**ā**'adnā'* because Form III can be attributed to human beings, whereas Allah alone has the true threat and promise as we find elsewhere in the Qur'an. Makkī said that the literal meaning of the word is a promise from Allah Almighty to Mūsā and so it is necessary to apply it to that by the literal meaning of the text, which is that the action is attributed to Allah alone. That is the reading of al-Ḥasan, Abū Rajā', Abū Ja'far, Shaybah and 'Īsā ibn 'Amr. It is the reading of Qatādah and Abū Isḥāq. Abū Ḥātim said that the common reading is without *alif* because Form III is mutual between two creatures, each of whom makes a promise. Al-Jawharī said that *mī'ād* is an appointment in time and place. It can, however, be used of a single person in Arabic and so has the same meaning as Form I. An-Naḥḥās said that Form III is better, and it is the reading of Mujāhid, al-A'raj, Ibn Kathīr, Nāfi', al-A'mash, Ḥamzah and al-Kisā'ī.

Mūsā is a foreign name and so it is not declined. Copts call water '*mū*' and tree '*shā*'. Mūsā was found in the basket in the water by a tree and so he was called Mūsā because of that. As-Suddī said, 'When his mother feared for him, she put him in a box and threw it into the river as Allah had inspired her to do. She put him in the water between the trees at the house of Pharaoh. The maids of Āsiyah, the wife of the Pharaoh, came out to do washing and found him and so he was named from the place.' Ibn Isḥāq said that he was Mūsā ibn 'Imrān ibn Yashar ibn Qāhit ibn Lāwī ibn Ya'qūb Isrā'īl ibn Isḥāq ibn Ibrāhīm.

The majority say that the forty nights referred to were the whole of Dhū 'l-Qa'dah and the first ten days of Dhū 'l-Ḥijjah. That was after they had crossed the sea and his people asked him to give them a Book from Allah. Mūsā went to Sinai with seventy of the best of the tribe of Israel and climbed the mountain and Allah allotted them forty nights.

Then you adopted the Calf when he had gone and you were the wrongdoers

Some commentators say that the tribe of Israel waited twenty days and twenty nights and then said, 'He has broken His promise,' and they adopted the Calf. The Sāmirī told them, 'This is your god and the god of Mūsā,' and they accepted what he said. Hārūn forbade them to do that, saying, *'My people! It is just a trial for you. Your Lord is the All-Merciful, so follow me and obey my command!'* (20:90) but they did not obey him and they all, except for 12,000 of them as is reported, insisted on worshipping the Calf. When Mūsā returned, he found them doing that and threw down the Tablets. He recovered six pieces from the broken Tablets. The surviving pieces contained the lawful and unlawful and other things they needed. He destroyed the Calf with fire and threw the ashes into the sea. They drank love of the Calf from its water. Yellowness appeared on their lips and their bellies were swollen. They repented, but their repentance was not accepted unless they killed one another, as we find in Allah's earlier words in *āyah* 54. They stood face to face wielding knives and swords from sunrise until full daylight arrived and then killed one another indiscriminately without any consideration of family ties until Mūsā called to Allah, 'Lord! The tribe of Israel is annihilated!' Allah had mercy on them and poured out His bounty on them and accepted the repentance of those who remained and made the rest martyrs.

If it is asked why nights rather than days are mentioned, the answer is that it is because the night precedes the day and so it comes first. That is how it is in dating: the months begin with the first nights and the days follow them.

An-Naqqāsh said that this *āyah* provides evidence for continuous fasting. If Allah had mentioned the days, it would be possible to believe that Mūsā broke the fast during the night. So the text demands that he fasted night and day for forty days. The Sufis use this as evidence for continuous fasting and that the best of it is forty days. This will be discussed in the proper place.

'Then you adopted the Calf when he had gone' means 'you took it as a god after Mūsā left.'

ثُمَّ عَفَوْنَا عَنكُم مِّنۢ بَعْدِ ذَٰلِكَ لَعَلَّكُمْ تَشْكُرُونَ ﴿٥٢﴾

52 Then We pardoned you after that so that perhaps you would show thanks.

Then We pardoned you after that

Allah is able to pardon His creation and this can take place before or after punishment. This differs from forgiveness when there is no punishment at all. When someone deserves punishment and it is abandoned, then that is pardon. Pardon (*'afw*) is the effacement of the wrong action. It means, 'We effaced your wrong actions and excused you.' It is derived from the wind effacing tracks. The words *'after that'* refer to the worship of the Calf. The word *'ijl* (Calf) comes from their haste (*isti'jāl*) to worship it. Allah knows best. *'Ijl* and *'ijjawl* mean 'calf' and the plural is *'ajājīl*.

so that perhaps you would show thanks.

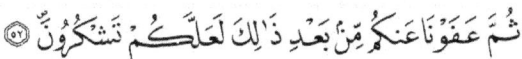

This means 'Be grateful for Allah's pardoning you'. *Shakr* is to show, and an animal that is *shakūr* has fat showing on it more that would be provided by its fodder. Its reality is to praise a person for kindness shown to you as mentioned in our commentary on the *Fātiḥah*. Al-Jawharī said that it is praising a good-doer for kindness he has shown you. *Shukrān* (thankfulness) is the opposite of *kufrān* (ingratitude). At-Tirmidhī and Abū Dāwūd report from Abū Hurayrah from the Prophet ﷺ: 'A person who does not thank people does not thank Allah.' Al-Khaṭṭābī notes that this has two meanings. One is that the one whose nature is to be ungrateful for what he receives from people and does not thank them for their kindness will also inevitably be ungrateful for Allah's blessings and fail to thank Him. The other is that Allah does not accept the thanks of a slave for His goodness to him when that person does not thank people for their goodness to him and is ungrateful for their kindness since the two are connected.

Scholars have said many things about gratitude to Allah. Sahl ibn 'Abdullāh said, 'Thankfulness is striving to obey, together with avoiding disobedience secretly and openly.' Another group said, 'Thankfulness is acknowledgement of your inability to thank the Blesser. That is why Allah says: *"Work, family of Dāwūd in thankfulness."* (34:13) Dāwūd asked, "How can I be thankful, O Lord? Thankfulness is a blessing from you!" He said, "By acknowledging Me and thanking Me even though you recognise that thankfulness is a blessing from Me." He said, "O Lord, show me Your most hidden blessing to me!" He said. "Breathe, Dāwūd." Dāwūd took a breath. Allah said, "Who counts this blessing night and day?"' Mūsā asked, 'How can I thank You when my actions cannot repay even the smallest blessing which You have given me?' So Allah revealed to Him, 'Mūsā, now you have truly thanked Me.'

Al-Junayd said, 'The reality of thankfulness is the ability to be thankful.' He also said, 'Once, when I was a boy of seven, I was playing in front of as-Sarī as-Saqaṭī while a group of people with him were discussing thankfulness. He asked me, "Boy, what is thankfulness?" I replied, "Not to disobey Allah in respect of His blessings." He told me, "I fear that your portion from Allah lies in your tongue."' Al-Junayd said, 'I still weep on account of what as-Sarī said to me.' Ash-Shiblī said, 'Thankfulness is humility and continuing to do good actions, opposing appetites, doing acts of obedience, and being always on the watch for the Compeller of the heavens and the earth.' Dhū 'n-Nūn al-Miṣrī said, 'Thankfulness to the one above you is by obedience, to your equal by equivalence, and to those below you by charity and beneficence.'

وَإِذْ ءَاتَيْنَا مُوسَى ٱلْكِتَٰبَ وَٱلْفُرْقَانَ لَعَلَّكُمْ تَهْتَدُونَ ۝٥٣

53 Remember when We gave Mūsā the Book and discrimination so that perhaps you would be guided.

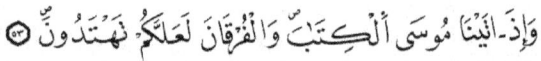

'*Idh*' is used for the past and '*idhā*' for the future. It is generally agreed that the Book mentioned here is the Torah, but there is disagreement about the meaning of the word '*furqān*' (discrimination). Al-Farrā' and Quṭrub said that the meaning is: 'We gave Mūsā the Torah and Muḥammad the *Furqān*.' An-Naḥḥās said that that is grammatically wrong. Az-Zajjāj said that the *Furqān* is the Book and it has two names here. Al-Farrā' related it. The best of what is said about the matter is what Mujāhid said: 'It means discrimination between the truth and falsehood, meaning, in other words, what Allah taught him.' Zayd said that it refers to the splitting of the sea so that they could cross. It is said to be separation from grief, because they were enslaved under the Egyptians, as is the meaning in 8:29. It is said to be the argument and proof as Ibn Baḥr said. It is said that the *wāw* (and) is connective and the phrase means: 'We gave Mūsā the discriminating Book'. The evidence for this interpretation is found in: *'We gave Mūsā the Book, complete and perfect for him who does good, elucidating everything'* (6:154): the lawful and unlawful, disbelief and belief, promise and threat, and other things. It is also said to refer to their separation from the people of Pharaoh, who were drowned while they were saved. It is said that it means "the Day of Discrimination" which was the day of the Battle of Badr when Allah helped Muḥammad ﷺ and his Companions and destroyed Abū Jahl and his people. *'Perhaps you will be guided'* from misguidance.

وَإِذْ قَالَ مُوسَىٰ لِقَوْمِهِۦ يَٰقَوْمِ إِنَّكُمْ ظَلَمْتُمْ أَنفُسَكُم بِٱتِّخَاذِكُمُ
ٱلْعِجْلَ فَتُوبُوٓا۟ إِلَىٰ بَارِئِكُمْ فَٱقْتُلُوٓا۟ أَنفُسَكُمْ ذَٰلِكُمْ خَيْرٌ لَّكُمْ عِندَ بَارِئِكُمْ
فَتَابَ عَلَيْكُمْ ۚ إِنَّهُۥ هُوَ ٱلتَّوَّابُ ٱلرَّحِيمُ ﴿٥٤﴾

54 And when Mūsā said to his people, 'My people, You wronged yourselves by adopting the Calf so turn towards your Maker and kill yourselves. That is the best thing for you in your Maker's sight. And He turned towards you. He is the Ever-Returning, the Most Merciful.

And when Mūsā said to his people, 'My people, You wronged yourselves by adopting the Calf

'Qawm' (people) is a group of men rather than women as seen in 49:11. Those with knowledge of the precise use of language say that the Calf represents a person's lower self and whoever abases it and opposes its desires is freed from its tyranny. However, it clearly refers to the actual Calf, which the tribe of Israel worshipped, as is stated in the Revelation.

so turn towards your Maker and kill yourselves.

When Allah told them to turn towards Him, they asked how to do that and He told them to kill themselves. Some interpreters who seek out the motivation for actions have said that the meaning of this was that they abased their lower selves by acts of obedience and thus expiated their excesses, but the sound view is that they actually killed one another in the way we saw above in the commentary on *āyah* 51. 'Killing' is ending movement, and when the term is applied to wine, it is diluting its strength with water. Sufyān ibn 'Uyaynah said, 'Accepted repentance is a blessing from Allah which He has bestowed on this Community and not on others. The repentance of the tribe of Israel entailed killing.'

It is agreed that Allah did not command everyone who worshipped the Calf to kill himself. Az-Zuhrī said that when they were ordered to do this, they formed two rows and killed one another until they were told, 'Enough!' That was martyrdom for those killed and repentance for the living, as we already mentioned. Some commentators say that He sent tyrants to them who did the killing. It is said that those who worshipped the Calf stood in a row and those who had not worshipped it attacked them with weapons and killed them. It is said that the seventy who had been with Mūsā and did not worship the Calf killed those who had worshipped it. Other things are said about the method involved.

One point taken from this is that if a community does not actively combat wrongdoing when it occurs among them, they all become liable to punishment. Jābir said that the Messenger of Allah ﷺ said, 'If, among a people, disobedience is committed, and there are those there stronger and more powerful than those committing it who do not change it, Allah will envelop them all with a punishment.' Ibn Mājah transmitted it in the *Sunan*. When the killing reached seventy thousand, Allah pardoned them as Ibn 'Abbās and 'Alī said. Allah removed killing from them because they had exerted themselves in it. Allah has not bestowed on this community any blessing greater than repentance.

The Divine Name *al-Bāri'*, 'Maker', is different from *al-Khāliq*, 'Creator'. *Al-Bāri'* is the innovator who makes something new which never existed before whereas *al-Khāliq* is the one who decrees and moves things from one state to another. *Bariyyah* is creation.

and He turned towards you.

This refers to those who remained after the slaughter. He pardoned those who remained.

وَإِذْ قُلْتُمْ يَٰمُوسَىٰ لَن نُّؤْمِنَ لَكَ حَتَّىٰ نَرَى ٱللَّهَ جَهْرَةً فَأَخَذَتْكُمُ
ٱلصَّٰعِقَةُ وَأَنتُمْ تَنظُرُونَ ٥٥

55 And when you said, 'Mūsā, we will not believe in you until we see Allah with our own eyes.' So the thunderbolt struck you dead while you were looking.

ثُمَّ بَعَثْنَٰكُم مِّنۢ بَعْدِ مَوْتِكُمْ لَعَلَّكُمْ تَشْكُرُونَ ۝٥٦

56 Then We brought you back to life after your death, so that perhaps you would show thanks.

When you said, 'Mūsā, we will not believe in you until we see Allah with our own eyes.'

It is said that this refers to the seventy men picked out by Mūsā. That is because when they heard what Allah had said, they said: *'We will not believe in you...'* But belief in the Prophets is mandatory after they have displayed their miracles so Allah sent down lightning from heaven which struck them dead. Then Mūsā prayed to his Lord and He brought them back to life. The full story of this incident will be found later in *Sūrat al-A'rāf.* Ibn Fūrak said that it is possible that their punishment was for asking to see Allah openly which was beyond the power of Mūsā to grant.

There is disagreement about the possibility of seeing Allah. Most innovators deny its possibility in either this world or the Next. Those who follow the *Sunnah* and the Salaf say it is possible in both worlds, and say that it will certainly happen in the Next World. This means that what they asked Mūsā for was not an impossibility. This will be discussed in *Sūrat al-An'ām* and *Sūrat al-A'rāf.*

The root of *'with our own eyes'* (*jahr*) means publicly or with one's own eyes. Ibn 'Abbās said that. The root means appearing. It is used for reciting with the voice audibly and *mujāharah* is acting in disobedience openly. When you see something unconcealed, you see it 'openly' (*jihār, jahr*). There are two possible meanings for the expression here. One is that it is connected to their speech, meaning 'they openly said to Mūsā'. The other is that it describes the way they desired to see Allah, meaning with their own eyes, openly and directly. The use of the word also stresses the difference between seeing in a dream and seeing while awake.

So the thunderbolt struck you dead while you were looking

If it is asked how they could die while they were looking, the reply is that the Arabs use this expression when something is very close at hand. It is also said that it refers to what they were doing when the thunderbolt struck.

Then We brought you back to life after your death, so that perhaps you would show thanks.

Qatādah said that they died and their spirits left them and then were returned to their bodies so that their natural lifespans could be fulfilled. An-Naḥḥās said that it is evidence against those of Quraysh who did not believe in the resurrection and also evidence against the People of the Book. 'Perhaps you will be grateful for being resurrected after death.' Some people say that it means, 'We gave you knowledge after your ignorance.'

Al-Māwardī said, 'There are two different positions about the continuance of responsibility of those brought back after death. One is that it continues and the other is that it is removed.' The first view is the soundest because, when the tribe of Israel saw the mountain in the air about to fall to them and the fire surrounding them, that was part of what forced them to believe and their legal responsibility continued and so they were like the people of Yūnus. It is impossible that they should cease to be responsible. Allah knows best.

وَظَلَّلْنَا عَلَيْكُمُ الْغَمَامَ وَأَنزَلْنَا عَلَيْكُمُ الْمَنَّ وَالسَّلْوَىٰ ۖ كُلُوا مِن طَيِّبَاتِ
مَا رَزَقْنَاكُمْ ۖ وَمَا ظَلَمُونَا وَلَٰكِن كَانُوا أَنفُسَهُمْ يَظْلِمُونَ ﴿٥٧﴾

57 And We shaded you with clouds and sent down manna and quails to you: 'Eat of the good things We have provided for you.' They did not wrong Us; rather it was themselves they were wronging.

And We shaded you with clouds

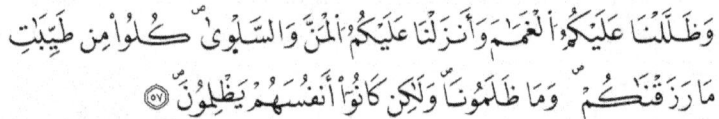

Allah caused the clouds to act as an awning above them. *Ghamām* (clouds) is the plural of *ghamāmah*. Al-Farrā' said that it can mean the same as *saḥāb* because they both cover the sky. The verb is also used for covering the heart. As-Suddī said that they are white clouds. That was to protect them from the heat of the sun of the sun in the day and they dispersed at the end of the day so that they would have the light of the moon at night. Commentators say this was when they were in the desert between Egypt and Palestine after they refused to enter the city of the tyrants and fight them and said to Mūsā, *'You and your Lord go and fight.'* (5:24) For that they were punished by having to wander for forty years in a small area of desert. It is related that they walked for the entire day and stopped at night and in the morning they were once more where they had been the previous morning. In the desert, they asked Mūsā, 'Who will provide us with food?' and Allah sent down manna and quails for them. They asked, 'Who will protect us from the heat of the sun?' and the clouds shaded them. They asked, 'What will we have to give us light?' So there was a pillar of light for them wherever they went. Makkī said it was a pillar of fire. They asked, 'Where will we find water!' And Mūsā was ordered to strike the stone. They asked, 'Who will provide us with clothes!' So their garments did not wear out or become ragged and the children's clothes grew as they grew. Allah knows best.

and sent down manna and quails to you:

There is disagreement about the word '*mann*'. It is said to be simply manna which is what most commentators say. It is also said to be sweet gum or honey or a sweet drink. Wahb ibn Munabbih said it was flat bread. It is said that it is a verbal noun for all that Allah gives as a blessing (*manna*) to His slaves without effort or cultivation on their part. We also have the words of the Messenger of Allah ﷺ in the hadith of Sa'īd ibn Zayd ibn 'Amr ibn Nufayl: 'Truffles are the manna which Allah sent down for the tribe of Israel and their juice contains healing for the eye.' One variant has: '...the manna which Allah sent down for Mūsā.' Muslim transmitted it. Our scholars say that this hadith indicates that truffles are part of what Allah sent down to the tribe of Israel, which He created for them in the desert. Abū 'Ubayd said, 'It is likened to manna because there is no toil in it of sowing, irrigation or treatment. So it is part of that, i.e. part of the blessing to the tribe of Israel, since it is obtained without effort.' It is related that it used to rain down on them from dawn to sunset, like snow, and a man would take enough for the day. If anyone stored any of it, it went bad except on Friday, when they stored it for the Sabbath and it did not go bad because Saturday was their day of worship and nothing came down to them on the Sabbath.

Since the Prophet ﷺ stated that truffles are a cure for the eyes, some of those with expertise in medicine say that either it cools the eye of some heat in it and so it is used on its own, or it is compounded with other things. Abū Hurayrah believed that may be used undiluted in all eye illnesses. This is as Abū Wajzah used honey in all illnesses, even in kohl as will explained in *an-Naḥl*.

There is also disagreement about the quails, *salwā* in Arabic. It is said to be actual quails as aḍ-Ḍaḥḥāk said. Ibn 'Aṭiyyah said that there is consensus that it is birds of some kind. In fact, there is no consensus, because some commentators claim that it is honey.

'Eat of the good things We have provided for you.'

An elision is implied, namely: 'We said, "Eat..."' The words 'good things' entail both lawfulness and deliciousness.

They did not wrong Us; rather it was themselves they were wronging

This means that they were not thankful for the blessings they received but responded with acts of disobedience to Allah.

وَإِذْ قُلْنَا ٱدْخُلُوا۟ هَٰذِهِ ٱلْقَرْيَةَ فَكُلُوا۟ مِنْهَا حَيْثُ شِئْتُمْ
رَغَدًا وَٱدْخُلُوا۟ ٱلْبَابَ سُجَّدًا وَقُولُوا۟ حِطَّةٌ نَّغْفِرْ لَكُمْ خَطَٰيَٰكُمْ
وَسَنَزِيدُ ٱلْمُحْسِنِينَ ﴿٥٨﴾

58 Remember when We said, 'Go into this town. And eat from it wherever you like, freely. Enter the gate prostrating and say, "Relieve us of our burdens!" Your mistakes will be forgiven. We will grant increase to all good-doers.'

Remember when We said, 'Go into this town and eat from it wherever you like, freely.

A town in Arabic is called a *qaryah* because there is a concentration of people in it. The root of the verb from which it is derived describes the act of water collecting in a tank. Another meaning is hospitality (*qirā*) for the guest. *Miqrah*, from the same root, means a tank. *Qarī* is a water course. *Maqāri* is a large bowl.

Commentators disagree about where this town was. Most say it was Jerusalem but it is also said to be Jericho. 'Umar ibn Shabbah said, 'It was the capital and the residence of the king.' Ibn Kaysān said Syria. Aḍ-Ḍaḥḥāk said Ramla, Jordan, Palestine and Tadmur. The great blessing involved was that, after their wandering, they were allowed to leave the desert and enter this town.

The instruction to eat is one of permission rather than command the adverb and '*freely*' indicates plenty and the lifting of the restrictions to which they had been subject in the desert.

Enter the gate prostrating and say, 'Relieve us of our burdens!'

The gate referred to is said by Mujāhid and others to be the gate of Jerusalem which people know as the Bāb Ḥiṭṭah. It is said to be the Qubbah Gate towards which Mūsā and the tribe of Israel prayed. The word '*sujjad*' (prostrating), according to Ibn 'Abbās, here means 'bent over bowing'. It is said to mean humbling oneself without any particular way of doing it.

There is considerable discussion about the exact significance of the word '*ḥiṭṭah*' translated as 'Relieve us of our burdens!' Al-Akhfash says it means, 'Relieve us of our wrong actions.' An-Naḥḥās said that there was a hadith from Ibn 'Abbās:

'They were told to say: "There is no god but Allah."' Another hadith says that they were told to say: 'Forgiveness!' In other words: 'Say this, and your wrong actions will be removed.' Ibn Fāris said that '*ḥiṭṭah*' was a word they were commanded to say so that their wrong actions would be removed.

It is possible that they used to use this expression in their worship, which is apparent from the hadith related by Muslim from Abū Hurayrah that the Messenger of Allah ﷺ said, 'The tribe of Israel were told, "Enter the gate prostrating and say, 'Relieve us of our burdens.' Your mistakes will be forgiven," but they altered it and entered sliding on their buttocks, saying, "That (*ḥiṭṭah*) is a grain of barley!"' Al-Bukhāri transmitted it. It is also related that they said, '*ḥinṭah*' (wheat) and '*ḥibbah*' (seed). Ibn Qutaybah said that they said '*ḥiṭṭā*' which is 'red wheat' in Hebrew. Al-Harawī related it from as-Suddī and Mujāhid. The upshot of all these various things that are said is that Allah gave them a command but they disobeyed it, were insolent and made mockery of it. So Allah punished them. Ibn Zayd said, 'The plague destroyed seventy thousand of them.' It is also related that the door was made low so that they would have to enter it bowing, but they entered it on their backsides Allah knows best.

Scholars use this *āyah* as evidence for changing the wording of expressions in the Sharī'ah as long as it does not form part of an act of worship which requires that specific wording. When it is a question of an act of worship in which a particular form of wording is specified, it is not permitted to alter it since Allah censures that in His words here. If it is just the idea which is intended, it can be changed to something else which conveys the same meaning. But not all scholars agree about this. It is related from Mālik, ash-Shāfi'ī and Abū Ḥanīfah that a scholar can express the meaning of a text, provided that he conveys the entire meaning. That is the position of the majority. A considerable number of scholars, however, forbid that, including Ibn Sīrīn, Ibn al-Qāsim ibn Muḥammad, and Rajā' ibn Ḥaywah. Mujāhid said, 'One can shorten the hadiths of the Messenger of Allah ﷺ, but not add to them.' Mālik ibn Anas was very exact where the hadiths of the Messenger of Allah ﷺ were concerned, even as to whether a verb had a *tā'* or *yā'*. Thus a group of the imams of hadith think that they must be related with exactitude. Even if they hear something incorrect grammatically, they will not alter it. Abū Miljaz related from Qays ibn 'Ubbād that 'Umar ibn al-Khaṭṭāb said, 'If someone hears a hadith, he should relate it as he heard it. Then he is safe.' The like of that is related from 'Abdullāh ibn 'Amr and Zayd ibn Arqam.

There is a similar disagreement about changing the order of words or adding to them or omitting them. Some say that it is the meaning that is important and do not consider the exact wording necessary, and some say that it must be exact. This is better in respect of cautiousness but most scholars hold a different position. The view that it is permitted is the sound one, Allah willing. It is known that the Companions related events and used different wording in their accounts of the same event. They had concern for the meanings and did not repeat or write down hadiths. It is related from Wāthilah ibn al-Asqa': 'We have not transmitted to you all that the Messenger of Allah ﷺ reported to us. The meaning is enough for you.' Qatādah said that Zurārah ibn Awfā said, 'I met a number of the Companions of the Prophet ﷺ and they used different words that had the same meaning.' An-Nakha'ī, al-Ḥasan and ash-Sha'bī did not present hadiths just by meaning. Al-Ḥasan said, 'When you get the meaning, it is acceptable.' Sufyān ath-Thawrī said, 'If I tell you, "I relate to you as I heard," do not believe me. It is the meaning.' Wakī' said, 'If the meaning did not have a wide scope, people would be destroyed.'

Scholars agree that it is permitted to transmit the Sharī'ah to non-Arabs in their language and to translate it for them. That is transmission by meaning. Allah actually does that in His Book when He recounts things that have passed and recounts stories with different wording in different places but with the same meaning, and He transmits their wording in Arabic which may have a different order, elision and addition. If it is permitted to change Arabic into another language, then it is more appropriate for that to be done in Arabic. This is sound.

Some people may remark that the Prophet ﷺ said, 'Allah makes flourish someone who hears my words and conveys them as he heard them,' and what is confirmed about the Prophet ﷺ instructing a man to say when he went to bed, 'I have believed in Your Book which You sent down and Your Prophet whom You sent.' The man said, 'Your Messenger whom You sent,' and the Prophet ﷺ insisted, 'Your Prophet whom You sent.' They observe that he did not allow the one to whom he taught that supplication to use different wording, and it said, 'He recited it as he heard it.' The answer to this is that his words, 'He recited it as he heard it,' refer to its ruling rather than the precise words.

The fact that what is meant is the ruling is indicated by his words, 'Many a person with *fiqh* is not a *faqīh* and many a person with *fiqh* goes to one with more *fiqh* than him.' The hadith itself has been transmitted with different wording while its meaning is the same. It is entirely possible that the expressions of the Prophet ﷺ used different wording at different times. The mere fact that a hadith is transmitted with different wordings indicates that that is permitted. When the Prophet ﷺ told him to use 'Prophet' rather than 'Messenger', that is because 'Prophet' is more praiseworthy and each of these two words has its proper place.

'Messenger' can be used for all people while 'Prophet' is only for the Prophets themselves. Those who are sent are better than the Prophets because they have both Prophethood and the Message. Success is by Allah.

Ibn al-'Arabī said about this: 'The disagreement concerning this matter can be conceived of as belonging to the time of the Companions and Tābi'ūn because they were equal in their knowledge of natural language. We do not doubt that it is not permitted for those after them since natures have changed and customs are different. This is the truth, and Allah knows best.'

Your mistakes will be forgiven.

There are three readings of the word "forgiven" in this *āyah*: Nāfi' recites 'they will be forgiven' (*yughfar* with *yā'*); Ibn 'Āmir recites '*tughfar*' with *tā'*; and the rest recite 'We will forgive' (*naghfir* with *nūn*). That is the clearest of them because He says before, 'We said.'

We will grant increase to all good-doers.'

This means those who did not worship the Calf. It is said that Allah will forgive the sins of those who store up, and increase His goodness to those who do not. It is said that He will forgive the errors of those who disobey and increase His goodness to those who do good. A 'good-doer' is someone whose *tawḥīd* is sound, who conducts himself well, performs his obligations and spares the Muslims his evil. We find in a hadith: '*Iḥsān* is that you worship Allah as if you were seeing Him. Even if you do not see Him, He sees you.' Jibrīl said, 'You spoke the truth.' Muslim transmitted it.

فَبَدَّلَ ٱلَّذِينَ ظَلَمُوا۟ قَوْلًا غَيْرَ ٱلَّذِى قِيلَ لَهُمْ فَأَنزَلْنَا عَلَى ٱلَّذِينَ ظَلَمُوا۟
رِجْزًا مِّنَ ٱلسَّمَآءِ بِمَا كَانُوا۟ يَفْسُقُونَ ﴿٥٩﴾

59 But those who did wrong substituted words other than those they had been given. So We sent down a plague from heaven on those who did wrong because they were deviators.

But those who did wrong substituted words other than those they had been given.

The wrongdoers changed the words they had been told to use. That was when they said '*ḥinṭah*' instead of '*ḥiṭṭah*', and they added a letter and so they were punished since adding to the *dīn* and innovating in the Sharī'ah is a terrible crime and causes great harm. This to due to their changing the word which indicated their repentance. That in itself merits punishment, so how much more must that be the case when the attributes of what is worshipped are altered! Words are less than actions, so what about changing actions! The verb '*baddala*' (substituted) means to replace a thing with something else. The *Abdāl* are a category of righteous people who always exist in the world and are so called because, when one of them dies, Allah replaces him with another.

So We sent down a plague from heaven on those who did wrong

'Those who did wrong' is repeated a second time rather than simply using the pronoun 'them' because of the gravity if what they did. Repetition is of two types. One is when it is used, as here and in 2:79, in a second phrase after the first has been completed, which intensifies the terribleness of the action done. The second is when there is repetition before the sense of the word is complete, as in *'The Undeniable. What is the Undeniable?'* (69:1) and elsewhere, in which case the result is to honour the thing mentioned. The word '*rijz*' (plague) is a Divine punishment and it also means 'filth'.

وَإِذِ ٱسْتَسْقَىٰ مُوسَىٰ لِقَوْمِهِۦ فَقُلْنَا ٱضْرِب بِّعَصَاكَ ٱلْحَجَرَ
فَٱنفَجَرَتْ مِنْهُ ٱثْنَتَا عَشْرَةَ عَيْنًا قَدْ عَلِمَ كُلُّ أُنَاسٍ مَّشْرَبَهُمْ
كُلُوا۟ وَٱشْرَبُوا۟ مِن رِّزْقِ ٱللَّهِ وَلَا تَعْثَوْا۟ فِى ٱلْأَرْضِ مُفْسِدِينَ ٦٠

60 And when Mūsā was looking for water for his people, We said, 'Strike the rock with your staff.' Then twelve fountains gushed out from it and all the people knew their drinking place. 'Eat and drink of Allah's provision and do not go about the earth corrupting it.'

And when Mūsā was looking for water for his people,

The type of *'looking for water'* referred to here is what you do when there is no water and there has been no rain for some time. Then you display true slavehood, poverty, need, abasement, repentance and integrity. Our Prophet Muḥammad ﷺ did the same when he asked for rain and went out to the place of prayer, humble, abased and making supplication. If we show no repentance and nothing but obstinacy and opposition to the Lord, how can we ask for rain? The Prophet ﷺ said in a hadith related by Ibn 'Umar: 'They do not refuse to pay the *zakāt* due on their property without being denied rain from heaven. Were it not for the animals, they would not have any rain at all.'

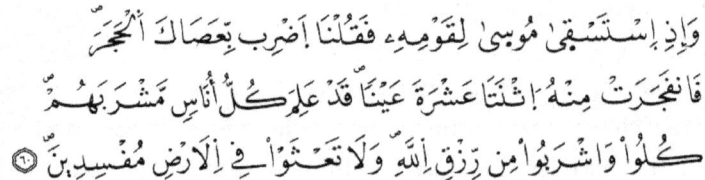

The *sunnah* of the Rain Prayer is to go out to the place of prayer, and for there to be a *khuṭbah* and the prayer. That is the position of most scholars. Abū Hanifah believes that this prayer is not *sunnah* nor is going out for it. In his view there should only be supplication. He cited the sound hadith which al-Bukhārī and Muslim transmitted, but there is no proof in it. That was a supplication whose answer was hastened and so nothing else is needed and it is not intended to clarify the Sunnah. Enough clarification for us, however is the hadith of 'Abdullāh ibn Yazīd al-Māzinī: 'The Messenger of Allah ﷺ went out to ask for rain and reversed his cloak and prayed two *rak'ahs*.' Muslim transmitted it. More about the rain prayer will come in *Sūrat Hūd*, Allah willing.

Then twelve fountains gushed out from it

Something is elided here implying he struck it and it gushed. Allah has the power to make water gush and to split the stone without the blow but He wanted to connect causes to effects. This is His wisdom for His slaves in respect of their obtaining their desires and to determine their reward and punishment according to that in the Hereafter. The meaning of the verb *infajara* is to burst out by breaking through, as dawn splits the sky. *Fujrah* designates the place where water pours out.

When Mūsā asked for water for his people, he was instructed to strike the stone with his staff at the same time as making supplication. The stone in question was cubiform and about the size of a sheep's head. They travelled with it. It is also said that they did not carry it with them, but found it at every stop. This is an even greater Sign. It is said that Mūsā could hit any stone he wished, which is a yet greater miracle. It is said that Allah commanded him to strike a particular stone. Sa'īd ibn Jubayr said that it is the stone on which Mūsā put his clothes when he washed and which ran away with his clothes. Ibn 'Aṭiyyah said, 'There is no disagreement that it was a separate cubiform stone. Three springs flowed out from each face when Mūsā struck it. When they had enough water, they set out and the water stopped.

What our Prophet Muḥammad ﷺ was given when springs of water gushed from his hand is a greater miracle. We have seen water gushing from stones at the beginning and end of the day and night, but no Prophet before our Prophet ﷺ had the miracle of water issuing from between flesh and blood. Trustworthy imams and reliable *fuqahā'* related that 'Abdullāh said, 'We were with the Prophet ﷺ but did not find water. A basin was brought and he put his hand in it and I saw the water gushing from between his fingers. He said, "Come to purification."' Al-A'mash said, 'Sālim ibn Abi-l-Ja'd said that he asked Jābir, "How many were there on the day?" He answered, "One thousand five hundred."'

and all the people knew their drinking place.

Each of the tribes knew its own spring and did not drink from any other. *Mashrab* is place where one drinks. It is also called *mashrūb*. The word for tribes in reference to the tribes of Israel is *'asbāṭ'* whereas *'qabā'il'* is used for Arab tribes. There were twelve tribes, descended from the sons of Ya'qūb. Each had their own exclusive spring. We have heard that there were fifty thousand in each tribe.

'Eat and drink of Allah's provision

The elision implies: Eat the manna and quails and drink of the water issuing from the stone.

and do not go about the earth corrupting it.'

The expression '*ta'thaw*' (go about) already implies extreme corruption which is forbidden and the word 'corrupting' (*mufsidīn*) is added for more emphasis. *'Uththah*, which is derived from the same root, is the moth that eats cloth. These words permit blessings and counting them while the earlier one forbids disobeying Allah.

وَإِذْ قُلْتُمْ يَٰمُوسَىٰ لَن نَّصْبِرَ عَلَىٰ طَعَامٍ وَٰحِدٍ فَٱدْعُ لَنَا رَبَّكَ يُخْرِجْ
لَنَا مِمَّا تُنۢبِتُ ٱلْأَرْضُ مِنۢ بَقْلِهَا وَقِثَّآئِهَا وَفُومِهَا وَعَدَسِهَا وَبَصَلِهَا ۖ قَالَ
أَتَسْتَبْدِلُونَ ٱلَّذِى هُوَ أَدْنَىٰ بِٱلَّذِى هُوَ خَيْرٌ ۚ ٱهْبِطُوا۟ مِصْرًا فَإِنَّ لَكُم مَّا
سَأَلْتُمْ ۗ وَضُرِبَتْ عَلَيْهِمُ ٱلذِّلَّةُ وَٱلْمَسْكَنَةُ وَبَآءُو بِغَضَبٍ مِّنَ ٱللَّهِ ۗ ذَٰلِكَ
بِأَنَّهُمْ كَانُوا۟ يَكْفُرُونَ بِـَٔايَٰتِ ٱللَّهِ وَيَقْتُلُونَ ٱلنَّبِيِّۦنَ بِغَيْرِ ٱلْحَقِّ ۗ ذَٰلِكَ
بِمَا عَصَوا۟ وَّكَانُوا۟ يَعْتَدُونَ ﴿٦١﴾

61 And when you said, 'Mūsā, we will not put up with just one kind of food so ask your Lord to supply to us some of what the earth produces – its green vegetables, cucumbers, grains, lentils and onions,' he said, 'Do you want to replace what is better with what is inferior? Go back to Egypt, then you will have what you are asking for.' Abasement and destitution were stamped upon them. They brought down anger from Allah upon themselves. That was because they rejected Allah's Signs and killed the Prophets without any right to do so. That was because they rebelled and went beyond the limits.

And when you said, 'Mūsā, we will not put up with just one kind of food

They said this when they were in the desert and became bored with a diet of manna and quails and remembered their previous life in Egypt. Al-Ḥasan said, 'Some people brought with them vegetables and onions and they inclined to their bad old ways. Their natures yearned for their old habits and they spoke these words. They refer to manna and quails as one food because they ate them together or because it was always the same thing.' It is said that it is 'one food because they ate them together, or had them all the time, morning and evening.

The word *ṭa'ām* (food) can refer both to what is eaten and what is drunk. This usage is also found in other *āyahs*. Allah says: *'Anyone who does not taste it* (yaṭ'amhu) *is with me.'* (2:249) and *'When you have eaten* (ṭa'imtum) *disperse.'* (33:53) The Messenger of Allah ﷺ said of the water of Zamzam, 'It is a food to eat and a healing for illness.' If *salwā* is honey, then it was drunk as well. Perhaps what is meant is wheat, as we find the same word used in hadiths for what can be used for *zakāt al-fiṭr*.

so ask your Lord to supply to us some of what the earth produces – its green vegetables, cucumbers, grains, lentils and onions,'

What is implied here are all those things produced by the earth which are edible. *Baql* are plants without trunks while *shajar* have trunks. There is disagreement about what *fūm*, translated here as grains, means. It is said to mean garlic, like *thūm* because it is like green vegetables as Juwaybir related from aḍ-Ḍaḥḥāk. It is also said that it means 'grains' and that is what is related from Ibn 'Abbās and most commentators. An-Naḥḥās preferred it and that it is more appropriate. Those who say that have sound *isnāds* and Juwaybir does not reach their level even though al-Farrā' and al-Kisā'ī prefer the first view. Abū Isḥāq az-Zajjāj said, 'How can people ask for food without wheat in it when wheat is the basis of nourishment?' Abū Naṣr al-Jawharī said that *fūm* is wheat. Some said that it is chick-peas in the Syrian dialect. Al-Farrā' said that it is an ancient dialect. 'Aṭā' and Qatādah said that it is every grain used for bread.

Scholars disagree about eating onions and garlic with their unpleasant smell. The majority of scholars agree that it is permitted because of firm hadiths on the subject. One group of literalists, who say that the prayer must be performed in a group, forbid it because eating them would prevent people going to the prayer. They said that if something prevents the performance of an obligation, then it is unlawful to use it, and they cite as evidence the fact that the Messenger of Allah ﷺ called it 'foul'. Allah described His Prophet ﷺ as forbidding foul things. The proof of the majority is what is confirmed from Jābir that the Prophet ﷺ was brought a kettle containing vegetables and he caught an unpleasant smell from it. He was told what vegetables it contained and said, 'Take it to them,' referring to some of his Companions who were with him. When he saw that they were reluctant to eat it, he said, 'Eat. I converse with one you do not converse with.' Muslim and Abū Dāwūd transmitted that. This makes it clear that it is particular to him while permitted for others.

We find in *Ṣaḥīḥ Muslim* from Abū Ayyūb that the Prophet ﷺ was staying with him and he prepared some food for the Prophet ﷺ which contained garlic. When it was returned, he asked about the place of the fingers of the Prophet ﷺ and was told, 'He did not eat.' He was alarmed and went up and asked, 'Is it unlawful?' he replied, 'No, but I dislike it.' He said, 'I dislike what you dislike.' This is a text showing that it is not unlawful. That is like what Abū Sa'īd al-Khudrī related from the Prophet ﷺ when they ate garlic at the time the conquest of Khaybar: 'People, it is not for me to make unlawful what Allah has made lawful, but it is a plant whose smell I dislike.'

These hadiths show that the ruling is particular to him since he alone conversed with the angel even though the hadith of Jābir makes the ruling the same for him and others when he said: 'Whoever eats this garlic plant (or 'onions and garlic') should not come near our mosques. The angels are harmed by the what harms of the sons of Ādam.' 'Umar ibn al-Khaṭṭāb said, 'People, you eat two plants which I only think are foul: onion and garlic. I saw when the Messenger of Allah ﷺ noticed their scent from a man in the mosque, he ordered that he be taken out to al-Baqī'. Whoever eats them should kill them by cooking.' Muslim transmitted it.

lentils and onions

It is related from the Prophet ﷺ through 'Alī: 'You must have lentils. They are blessed and pure. They make the heart tender and increase tears. Seventy Prophets were blessed with them, the last of whom was 'Īsā ibn Maryam.' Ath-Tha'labī and others mentioned it. One day 'Umar ibn 'Abd al-'Azīz would eat bread with oil, one day with meat and one day with lentils. Al-Ḥalīmī said that lentils and oil are the food of the righteous. If its only virtue had been that it was what Ibrāhīm gave as hospitality in his city, that would have been enough. They lighten the body so that it is light for worship and do not provoke the appetites as meat does. Wheat, among all the grains, is *fūm* in the sound position. Barley, which was the food of the people of Madīnah, was the food of the people of Madīnah as lentils were the food of the town of Ibrāhīm. Each of the two grains enjoys a position of excellence with a Prophet.

he said, 'Do you want to replace what is better with what is inferior?

'Replacing' is putting one thing is place of another. *Adnā* (inferior), according to az-Zajjāj, is derived from *danūw*, meaning 'of mediocre worth'. 'Alī ibn Sulaymān said that it comes from *danā'a*, meaning 'lower', and the *hamza* has been removed. It is also said that it is derived from *dūn*, meaning 'base', and the original form would be *adwan*.

They disagree about what makes manna and quail better than what they asked for. There are five reasons given. One is that vegetables are relatively unimportant compared to manna and quail which are of higher quality. The second is that it is since manna and quail were Allah's gift to them and He had commanded them to eat them, by eating them, they were following a divine command, which would ensure them a reward in the Next World. The same did not apply to what they were asking for which was, therefore, inferior. The third reason is that what Allah gave them is in fact better and more delicious than what they were asking for. The fourth is that what they were given entailed no work or fatigue on their part and what they were asking for could only be obtained by tillage, harvesting and hard work. The fifth is that there was no doubt about the lawfulness and purity of what came to them there since it came directly from Allah whereas the produce of the earth can be impaired by unlawful transactions and other corrupt practices.

This *āyah* contains evidence that it is permitted to eat good things and delicious foods. The Prophet ﷺ loved sweets and honey, and drank delicious cold water as will be mentioned in *al-Mā'idah* and *an-Naḥl*.

Go back to Egypt, then you will have what you are asking

This command was an impossibility for them so it was a challenge they could not rise to because they were in the desert and this was their punishment. It is said that they were given what they asked for. It is also said that *miṣr* means any city as 'Ikrimah related from Ibn 'Abbās. One group said that it means the city where Pharaoh lived. Those with the first view deduce that the literal meaning of the Qur'an is the command to enter the city and that is supported by the transmission that they live in Syria after the wilderness. The other group deduce from what is in the Qur'an that Allah made the tribe of Israel inherit the houses of the family of Pharaoh.

Abasement and destitution were stamped upon them. They brought down anger from Allah on them.

These qualities stayed with them and were decreed for them. The verb *ḍaraba* (stamp) is used for 'striking a tent. *Dhillah* is abasement and belittling. *Maskanah* is poverty. There is no Jew, even if he wealthy, who does not have an air of poverty about him. It is said that the abasement referred to was the obligation of *jizyah*. Al-Ḥasan and Qatādah said that their 'destitution' (*maskanah*) implied humiliation, as taken from *sukūn*. It means that poverty makes them move little as az-Zajjāj said Abū 'Ubaydah said that *dhillah* is belittlement and *maskanah* is the verbal noun from *miskīn* (very poor).

The fact that they denied Allah's Book and the miracles of His Prophets such as 'Īsā, Yaḥyā, Zakariyyā and Muḥammad ﷺ is why that was obliged for them.

That was because they rejected Allah's Signs

They denied His Book and the miracles of His Prophets such as 'Īsā, Yaḥyā, Zakariyyā and Muḥammad ﷺ.

and killed the Prophets without any right to do so.

The root of Prophet (*nabī'*) is *nabā*, which means to appear. It comes from *nabwah* meaning something high. The position of a Prophet is high. Nāfi' recites 'Prophets' (*nabī'īn*) with a *hamzah* throughout the Qur'an except in two places in *Sūrat al-Aḥzāb* in which he recites it without *maddah* or *hamzah*. The *hamzah* is omitted in these two places because of the conjunction of two *hamzah*s with a *kasrah*. The rest omit the *hamzah* in all of that. Those who read it with *hamzah* do so because it comes from the verb *anba'a*, to report and its active participle is *munbi'* and the plural of *nabi'* is *anbiyā'*. It is also said that the plural is *nubā'*. Al-'Abbās ibn Mirdās as-Sulamī says in praise of the Prophet ﷺ:

> O Seal of the Prophet (*nubā'*), you are sent
> With the truth. The guidance in every path is your guidance.

This is why it is recited with *hamzah*.

In the case of those who disagree and omit the *hamzah*, some of them say that it is derived from a verb with a *hamzah*, but then smooth out the *hamzah*. Some of them say it is derived from *nabā, yanbū*, meaning to be visible. So *nabiyy* comes from *nubūwah* which is elevation. So the rank of the Prophet is high. Nabiyy without a *hamzah* is also the path and so the Messenger is called *nabiyy* because people are guided by him like the path. A poet said:

> The place of the Prophet (*nabiyy*) on (Mt) Ka'ib
> has become broken crumbled pebbles.

So the Prophets are like paths for us in the land. It is related that a man said to the Prophet ﷺ, 'Peace be upon you, Prophet (*nabi'*) of Allah,' using the *hamzah* and the Prophet ﷺ replied, 'I am not the *Nabi'* of Allah (with *hamzah*), but I am the *Nabiyy* of Allah (without *hamzah*).' Abū Alī said that the *isnād* of this hadith is weak. Part of what reinforces its weakness is that words of the eulogy, 'O Seal of the Prophet (*nubā'*),' were recited to him and it is not reported that he objected.

The words 'without any right to do so' emphasise the atrocity and the wrong action that they committed. If it is observed that this is evidence that there might be an occasion on which it might be right to kill a Prophet, even though it is known that the Prophets are protected from those who attack them, we reply that that is not the case. When they are killed, it must be wrongly. No Prophet can be killed by right; if they are killed it is in defence of the truth. If it is asked how could it be permitted for the unbelievers to have power over the Prophets, the answer is that it was a mark of honour for them and increased their stations, like those of the believers who are killed in the Way of Allah. Ibn 'Abbās and al-Ḥasan said, 'No Prophet was ever killed except for those of them who had been commanded to fight, and everyone commanded to fight is helped.'

إِنَّ ٱلَّذِينَ ءَامَنُوا۟ وَٱلَّذِينَ هَادُوا۟ وَٱلنَّصَٰرَىٰ وَٱلصَّٰبِـِٔينَ مَنْ ءَامَنَ بِٱللَّهِ وَٱلْيَوْمِ
ٱلْءَاخِرِ وَعَمِلَ صَٰلِحًا فَلَهُمْ أَجْرُهُمْ عِندَ رَبِّهِمْ وَلَا خَوْفٌ عَلَيْهِمْ
وَلَا هُمْ يَحْزَنُونَ ﴿٦٢﴾

62 Those who believe, those who are Jews, and the Christians and Sabaeans, all who believe in Allah and the Last Day and act rightly, will have their reward with their Lord. They will feel no fear and will know no sorrow.

Those who believe,

This refers to those who believe in Muḥammad ﷺ. Sufyān said that what is meant are the hypocrites, so it is as if He were saying, 'Those who outwardly believe.' That is why they are joined with the Jews, Christians and Sabaeans. Then He clarified the judgment by mentioning Allah and the Last Day.

those who are Jews,

The verb *hādū* means 'to be Jews', and it is ascribed to Yahūdhā (Judah), who was the oldest son of Ya'qūb. It is said that they were called that because of their turning away from worshipping the Calf and repenting, and so it means repentance. We find in the Revelation: '*We have truly turned to You*' (7:156) where the verb is *hudnā*. Ibn 'Arafah said that it means: 'have faith in Your command'.

and the Christians

The word for Christians, *naṣārā*, is the plural of *naṣrānī*. It is said that the name is derived from Nazareth where 'Īsā lived. 'Īsā was called a Nazarene and so that was applied to his followers, as Ibn 'Abbās and Qatādah said. Al-Jawharī also said that. It is also said that it comes from the word *anṣār* which means 'helpers'.

and Sabaeans

The singular is either *ṣābi'ī* or *ṣāb* which is why there is a disagreement about whether it has a *hamzah*. All, except for Nāfi', have it with a *hamzah*. Linguistically, the Arabic word (*ṣābi'*) means one who inclines from one *dīn* to another *dīn*. The Arabs used it to describe someone who became Muslim. So the Sabaeans separated from the religion of the People of the Book.

There is no disagreement that the Jews and Christians are People of the Book and so it is permitted to marry their women and eat their food. *Jizyah* is imposed on them. There is disagreement about the Sabaeans. As-Suddī said that they are a sub-group of the People of the Book, as Isḥāq ibn Rāhawayh states. Ibn al-Mundhir and Isḥāq say that there is nothing wrong in eating the animals they slaughter because they are People of the Book. Abū Ḥanīfah says the same. Ibn 'Abbās, however, says that one should not marry their women. Other things are said about them.

It is reported from Ibn 'Abbās that this *āyah* is abrogated by *"If anyone desires anything other than Islam as a* dīn, *it will not be accepted from him."* (3:85) Others said that it is not abrogated and that it is about those who believe in the Prophet ﷺ and who are firm in their belief.

وَإِذْ أَخَذْنَا مِيثَٰقَكُمْ وَرَفَعْنَا فَوْقَكُمُ ٱلطُّورَ خُذُوا۟ مَآ ءَاتَيْنَٰكُم بِقُوَّةٍ
وَٱذْكُرُوا۟ مَا فِيهِ لَعَلَّكُمْ تَتَّقُونَ ﴿٦٣﴾ ثُمَّ تَوَلَّيْتُم مِّنۢ بَعْدِ ذَٰلِكَ
فَلَوْلَا فَضْلُ ٱللَّهِ عَلَيْكُمْ وَرَحْمَتُهُۥ لَكُنتُم مِّنَ ٱلْخَٰسِرِينَ ﴿٦٤﴾

63 Remember when We made the covenant with you and lifted up the Mount above your heads: 'Take hold vigorously of what We have given you and pay heed to what is in it, so that hopefully you will be godfearing.' 64 Then after that you turned away, and were it not for Allah's favour to you and His mercy, you would have been among the lost.

Remember when We made the covenant with you and lifted up the Mount above your heads:

This *āyah* explains the meaning of: *'When We uprooted the mountain, lifting it above them like a canopy.'* (7:171) Abū 'Ubaydah said that it means that it was removed from its place and raised above the surface of the earth. There is disagreement about what 'the Mount' (*aṭ-ṭūr*) is. It is said to be the name of the mountain where Allah spoke to Mūsā and where the Torah was revealed to him (Sinai), and this was what Ibn Jurayj said that Ibn 'Abbās said. Aḍ-Ḍaḥḥāk said that it is a mountain on which plants grow, unlike most others on which they do not grow. Mujāhid and Qatādah said it could be any mountain and Mujāhid said that *aṭ-ṭūr* is simply the Syriac word for mountain.

The Mount was lifted in this way because, when Mūsā brought the Tablets from Allah, which contained the Torah to the tribe of Israel, he told them, 'Take them and hold fast to them.' But they replied, 'No! Not unless Allah tells us to do the same as you tell us!' So they were struck dead and then brought back to life. Mūsā again told them to take them and again they refused. So Allah commanded the angels to uproot one of the mountains of Palestine and it was held over them like a cloud. The sea was behind them and a fire in front of them and they were told to take on the covenant otherwise the mountain would fall on top of them. They prostrated in repentance and accepted the Torah and the covenant. Aṭ-Ṭabarī said that one of the scholars said, 'If they had taken it the first time, there would have been no need for a covenant.' So their prostration was done reluctantly because they were looking at the mountain in fear. When Allah showed mercy to them, they said, 'There is no prostration better than one that Allah accepts and by which He shows mercy to Him slaves.' They continue to prostrate reluctantly. Ibn 'Aṭiyyah said, 'The only thing that can be sound is that Allah Almighty created faith in their hearts at the moment of their prostration. It is not that they believed unwillingly and that their hearts were not at peace with that.'

Take hold vigorously of what We have given you

'We said" is elided before 'Take.' *'Bi-quwwah'* (vigorously, lit. with strength) means with gravity and striving, as Ibn 'Abbās, Qatādah and as-Suddī stated. It is said that it means with sincerity. Mujāhid said, '"With strength" means "putting it into action".' It is also said to mean 'with a lot of study'.

and pay heed to what is in it,

This means 'reflect and observe Allah's commands and warnings in it and do not neglect that and waste it'. It is the same with all the Divine Books: you must act according to them and not just recite them on the tongue. To do otherwise is to waste them. This is what is stated by ash-Sha'bī and Ibn 'Uyaynah as will be discussed later. (2:101) An-Nasā'ī related from Abū Sa'īd al-Khudrī that the Messenger of Allah ﷺ said, 'The worst of people is an impious man who recites the Qur'an and pays no heed to any of it.' So he explained that the goal is to put it into action. Mālik said, 'The Qur'an can be recited by someone who has no good in him. This was an obligation for those before us just as it is obliged for us.'

Allah says: *'Follow the best that has been sent down to you from your Lord.'* (39:55) So He commanded us to follow His Book and act by it, but we have abandoned it just as the Jews and Christians did. There remain people with many books and copies of the Qur'an who do not benefit from that at all because they are dominated by ignorance, desire for power, and the following of appetites. We find in at-Tirmidhī that Abu-d-Dardā' said, 'We were with the Prophet ﷺ and he looked towards heaven and said, "This is a time in which knowledge will be snatched away from its people until they have none left." Ziyād ibn Labīd al-Anṣārī asked, "How can it be snatched away from us when we recite the Qur'an! By Allah, we recite it and our women and children recite it." He replied, "May your mother be bereft, Ziyād! I consider you to be like those in who know the Torah and Gospel which the Jews and Christians have. What help was it to them?"' An-Nasā'ī transmitted it from Jubayr ibn Nufayr from 'Awf ibn Mālik al-Ashja'ī by a sound path.

In the *Muwaṭṭā'* we read that 'Abdullāh ibn Mas'ūd remarked to someone, 'You are in a time when men of understanding (*fuqahā'*) are many and Qur'an reciters are few, when the *ḥudūd* defined in the Qur'an are protected and its letters are neglected, when few people ask and many give, when they make the prayer long and the *khuṭbah* short, and put their actions before their desires. A time will come for people when their *fuqahā'* are few but their Qur'an reciters are many, when the letters of the Qur'an are guarded carefully but its *ḥudūd* are neglected, when many ask but few give, when they make the *khuṭbahs* long but the prayer short, and they put their desires before their actions.' (*Muwaṭṭā'* 9.24.91) Yaḥyā said, 'I asked Ibn Nāfi' about what is meant by "put their desires before their actions," and he replied, "They follow their desires and abandon the actions prescribed for them."'

Then after that you turned away

This is a physical term which is used metaphorically for turning away from commands, religion and faith. 'After that' means after the evidence you have seen and after your taking of the covenant and the raising of the mountain.

وَلَقَدْ عَلِمْتُمُ ٱلَّذِينَ ٱعْتَدَوْا۟ مِنكُمْ فِى ٱلسَّبْتِ فَقُلْنَا لَهُمْ كُونُوا۟ قِرَدَةً خَٰسِـِٔينَ ﴿٦٥﴾

65 You are well aware of those of you who broke the Sabbath. We said to them, 'Be apes, despised, cast out.'

You are well aware of those of you who broke the Sabbath

The word '*sabt*' (sabbath) is derived from *sabat* which means 'cutting off'. That is because it was a day of rest, cut off from the rest of the week.

'You are well aware' means you recognise them individually and you know the ruling against them. The difference between the terms is that recognition (*ma'rifah*) is directed at the essence of what is named and knowledge (*'ilm*) is directed at the states of the named. If you say, 'I recognise Zayd,' it means him himself, and if you say, 'I know Zayd,' it means his states in respect of excellence or imperfection.

An-Nasā'ī related that Ṣafwān ibn 'Assāl reported that a Jew said to his friend, 'Let us go to this Prophet.' His friend said, 'Do not say "Prophet"! He might hear you. He has four eyes!' They went to the Messenger of Allah ﷺ and asked him for seven clear commandments and he told them: 'Do not associate anything with Allah; do not steal; do not fornicate; do not kill anyone Allah has made inviolate, unless with a legal right; do not slander an innocent person to a ruler; do not use magic; do not consume usury; do not slander chaste women; and do not turn your backs in retreat when the fighting is fierce; and, as Jews, you have one specially for you: that you do not profane the Sabbath.' They kissed his hands and feet and said, 'We testify that you are a Prophet!' He asked, 'What prevents you from following me, then?' They replied. 'Dāwūd prayed that the line of Prophets would continue to be from his descendants and we fear that if we follow you, the other Jews will kill us.' At-Tirmidhī transmitted it and said that it is a sound good hadith.

It is possible that the *āyah* refers to rulings about the Sabbath in general, or it may just refer to the Sabbath on which they caught the fish. The first view is that of al-Ḥasan. Ashhab related that Mālik said, 'Ibn Rūmān related that a man would take a string and make a loop and throw it down after the fish. One end of the string was tied to a peg. Then he would leave it until Sunday. People were silent at what was done until a lot of fish were caught and they were taken to the markets. The deviants were public about their catch. One group openly forbade them to do that and withdrew, saying, 'We will not live with you.' The town was divided by a wall. One morning those who had forbidden them to do what they were doing were sitting in their gatherings and none of the transgressors came out. They said, 'Something has happened to the people.' They climbed up the wall to look and there were apes. They opened the gate and went in and the apes went to their kin and smelled their garments and wept. They were told, 'Did we not forbid you?' They nodded their heads in agreement. Qatādah said that the children became apes and the old men pigs. Only those who had forbidden them were saved; the rest were destroyed. This will be further discussed in *al-A'rāf*.

There are two different positions about whether those transformed had offspring. Az-Zajjāj said that some people say that it is possible that apes are descended from them. Qāḍī Abū Bakr ibn al-'Arabī preferred that. The majority say that they did not reproduce, and the apes, pigs and other things already existed before that. Those who were transmogrified were destroyed and nothing of them remains because wrath and the punishment smote them. They only lasted three days. Ibn 'Abbās said that none of them survived more than three days: they did not eat or drink or reproduce. Ibn 'Aṭiyyah said that it is related and confirmed from the Prophet ﷺ that those transmogrified did not reproduce, eat or drink, and did not live more than three days.

This is what is sound of both views. Ibn al-'Arabī and others cite as evidence for the first position the words of the Prophet ﷺ: 'A group of the tribe of Israel were lost. It is not known what happened them. I only think that they were turned into mice. Do you not see that they do not drink if camel milk is put in front of them but do drink if sheep's milk is put in front of them?' Abū Hurayrah related it in Muslim. There is also the hadith about the lizard which Muslim related from Abū Sa'īd and Jābir. Jābir said, 'The Prophet ﷺ was brought a lizard and refused to eat it, saying, "I do not know. Perhaps it is from one of the generations that were transmogrified."' Ibn al-'Arabī said, 'We find in al-Bukhārī that 'Amr ibn Maymūn said, "In the Jāhiliyyah I saw a monkey that fornicated. They stoned it and I stoned it with them."' The term 'fornicated' is omitted from some variants. Ibn al-'Arabī said, 'If it is asked whether animals have knowledge of laws which they inherited from past generations until the time of 'Amr, we say that that is the case because the Jews altered stoning and Allah wanted it to be carried out on those transmogrified to be a stronger proof against those who denied that and altered it, so that their books, their rabbis and those who had been transmogrified would all bear witness against them and they would know that Allah knows what they conceal and what they make public and that He takes account what they change and alter. The proof will be established against them while they are unaware of that. He will help His Prophet and not help them.'

This is what he says in *al-Aḥkām*, and there is no proof for any of it. The story of 'Amr was mentioned by al-Ḥumaydī in *Jam' bayna-ṣ-Ṣaḥīḥayn*: 'Abū Mas'ūd ad-Dimishqī recounted that in the two *Ṣaḥīḥayn* collections 'Amr ibn Maymūn al-Awdī has a story which Ḥuṣayn related from him. He said, 'In the Jāhiliyyah I saw a monkey that fornicated. The monkeys gathered around it and stoned it and I stoned it with them.' That is how Abū Mas'ūd related it. He did not mention in any place that al-Bukhārī transmitted it in his book. We investigated that and found it in some copies, but not all of them. It is mentioned in the Book of the Jāhiliyyah. The transmission of an-Nu'aymī from al-Farabrī has nothing about this report about monkeys. It may be one of the insertions into al-Bukhārī. That which al-Bukhārī says in the *Tārīkh al-kabīr* is: "Nu'aym ibn Ḥammād told me that Hushaym reported from Abū Balj and Ḥuṣayn that 'Amr ibn Maymūn said, 'In the Jāhiliyyah I saw monkeys gathered around a female monkey and they stoned it and I stoned it with them.'" The word "fornicated" does not appear in it. If this transmission is sound, al-Bukhārī transmitted it as evidence that 'Amr ibn Maymūn was alive in the Jāhiliyyah. His opinion in the Jāhiliyyah is of no importance.'

Abū 'Umar mentioned 'Amr ibn Maymūn in *al-Istī'āb* and the fact that his *kunyah* was Abū 'Abdullāh. He said that he was considered to be one of the great Tābi'ūn of the Kufans. He said, 'He is the one who saw the monkey stoning in the Jāhiliyyah if that is sound, because its transmitters are unknown. Al-Bukhārī mentioned it from Nu'aym from Hushaym from Ḥuṣayn from 'Amr ibn Maymūn. 'Abbād ibn al-'Awwām narrated it from Ḥuṣayn as Hushaym related it. The long story depends on 'Abd al-Malik ibn Muslim from 'Īsā ibn Ḥiṭṭān who are not authoritative. A group of the people of knowledge object to relating fornication to those who are not legally responsible and for *ḥadd* punishments to be carried out on animals. If it were sound, it would apply to men and jinn because both acts of worship are for both of them alone. As for the words of the Prophet ﷺ, 'I only think that they were turned into mice' and 'Perhaps it is from one of the generations that were transmogrified,' and the like, this is only suspicion and fear of mice, lizards and other things being transmogrified. This was conjecture on his part before the revelation that Allah did not allow them to reproduce. When this was revealed, he was no longer afraid of that. He knew that lizards and mice were not transmogrified. Then, when someone asked him whether or not apes and pigs were transmogrified, he ﷺ said, 'Allah does not destroy a people or punish a people and then give them offspring. Apes and pigs existed before that.' This is a clear sound text that 'Abdullāh ibn Mas'ūd related and Muslim transmitted in the

Book of the Decree. Texts confirm that lizard was eaten in his presence and on his table without him objecting to it. It is related from Mujāhid in the commentary on this that only their hearts were transformed and their mouths were like those of apes. As far as I know, no one else has said this.

فَجَعَلْنَٰهَا نَكَٰلًا لِّمَا بَيْنَ يَدَيْهَا وَمَا خَلْفَهَا وَمَوْعِظَةً لِّلْمُتَّقِينَ ٦٦

66 We made it an exemplary punishment for those there then, and those coming afterwards, and a warning to those who are godfearing.

We made it an exemplary punishment

Various things are said about the word 'it' here. It is said to refer to the punishment and it is said to refer to the town. It is said to be the whole nation which was transformed. It is said to be snakes, but this is unlikely. The word *nakāl* (exemplary punishment) applies to restraint and punishment. *Ankāl* are fetters because they restrain. *Nikl* is used for a heavy bit in a bridle which restrains the animal. *Nakila* is to refrain from a matter. *Tankīl* is to inflict a penalty on enemies which acts as a deterrent to others. Ibn 'Abbās and as-Suddī said 'those there then' refers to those among the transmogrified at the time who did not accept their wrong actions and 'those coming afterwards' are those who did not commit that sort of wrong action. Al-Farrā' said that those who were transmogrified were made an exemplary punishment for past wrong actions and those who came after them should fear transmogrification for their wrong actions. Ibn 'Aṭiyyah said that this is a good view and both pronouns refer to the punishment. Al-Ḥakam related from Mujāhid from Ibn 'Abbās is that it is for those with them and those who will come after them. An-Naḥḥās preferred that and said that it is closer to the meaning. Allah knows best. Ibn 'Abbās said that it is for towns with them and after them.

and a warning to those who are godfearing.

Al-Khalīl said that 'warning' is reminding about good which will make the heart tender. It was a warning to everyone with *taqwā* separate from the obdurate unbelievers. Ibn 'Aṭiyyah says that this includes every godfearing person of every nation. Az-Zajjāj says that it is an admonishment only for the godfearing of the community of Muḥammad ﷺ to refrain from what Allah has forbidden lest they experience a punishment like that of the people who profaned the Sabbath.

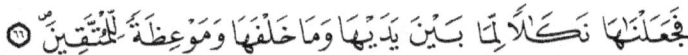

وَإِذْ قَالَ مُوسَىٰ لِقَوْمِهِۦٓ إِنَّ ٱللَّهَ يَأْمُرُكُمْ أَن تَذْبَحُوا۟ بَقَرَةً ۖ قَالُوٓا۟ أَتَتَّخِذُنَا هُزُوًا ۖ قَالَ أَعُوذُ بِٱللَّهِ أَنْ أَكُونَ مِنَ ٱلْجَٰهِلِينَ ﴿٦٧﴾

67 And when Mūsā said to his people, 'Allah commands you to sacrifice a cow,' they said, 'What! Are you making a mockery of us?' He said, 'I seek refuge with Allah from being one of the ignorant!'

And when Mūsā said to his people, 'Allah commands you to sacrifice a cow,'

'Commands you' is read by Abū 'Amr as *'ya'murkum'* with *sukūn* and elision of the *ḍammah* because it is heavy [instead of *'ya'murukum'*]. This comes first in terms of recitation while *'you killed someone'* (2:72) comes first in terms of meaning, before the episode of the cow. It is possible that 'killed someone' was revealed first and then the command to sacrifice afterwards. It is also possible that the order of revelation is as it is. It is also possible that the command to sacrifice was given and then the killing occurred and they were commanded to strike the deceased with part of it. 'And' does not necessarily convey sequence as we see in other *āyahs*.

There is no disagreement that the *dhabḥ* method (cutting the throat and carotid arteries) is used for slaughtering sheep and the *naḥr* method (stabbing through the throat) for camels, and that one can choose either of them for cattle. It is said that *dhabḥ* is more fitting because Allah mentioned it. Ibn al-Mundhir said, 'I do not know of anyone who made the meat unlawful when the wrong form of slaughter had been used.' Mālik disliked it but something can be disliked but not unlawful. The rulings regarding sacrifices will be discussed in *Sūrat al-Mā'idah.* Al-Māwardī said that they were commanded to sacrifice one particular cow because it was the same species that they had worshipped, so that what they had esteemed would be demeaned in their eyes and they would know the answer to worshipping it in themselves. This idea is a reason for slaughtering the cow but not a reason for the answer to a request. What was meant by it was to revive the one who was killed by killing that which is alive so as to show Allah's power in originating things from their opposites.

The word '*baqarah*' (cow) refers to the female while *thawr* is the word for a bull, like *nāqah* and *jamal* in the case of camels. It is said that *baqarah* is a single cow. The root means 'to split open', since cattle split the earth open when they plough it. From this comes the term *'al-Bāqir'* used for Abū Ja'far ibn 'Alī Zayn 'l-'Ābidīn because he split open (*baqara*) knowledge and recognized its root. *Baqīrah* is a bodice without sleeves.

They said, 'What! Are you making a mockery of us?' He said, 'I seek refuge with Allah from being one of the ignorant!'

They said that to Mūsā when they replied to him. That was because they found someone murdered among them and were uncertain about who the killer was. They disagreed and exclaimed, 'Murder takes place while the Messenger of Allahgis among us!' They came to him and asked him for clarification. That was before *qasāmah* [a collective oath taken by the people about a murder victim] was revealed in the Torah. They asked Mūsā to pray to his Lord and He commanded them to sacrifice a cow. When they heard that from Mūsā, which was not a clear answer to their question, they asked him about it and asked for a decision. They asked if he was mocking them. *Haz'* is playing and mockery. He sought refuge with Allah because leaving someone who asks for guidance unanswered and mocking him is ignorance and not one of the qualities of the Prophets. Ignorance is the opposite of knowledge. He sought refuge from ignorance as they were ignorant in asking this question of someone who reported to them from Allah.

The form of words indicates the unsound faith of those who said that. It is not possible to believe that of a Prophet who has displayed miracles. He said, 'Allah commands you to do that.' If today anyone had said that about any of the words of the Prophet ﷺ, it would be necessary to call that person an unbeliever. Some people believed that that came from their coarse nature and disobedience, as was the case in the division of the spoils of Ḥunayn when someone said, 'This is a division which is not for the sake of Allah' and as another said, 'Be fair, Muḥammad!' This is the clearest evidence that ignorance is ugly and corrupts the *dīn*.

This *āyah* indicates the prohibition against mocking the *dīn* of Allah and the *dīn* of the Muslims and those who must be esteemed, and that to do so is ignorance. The person who does that merits punishment. Joking, however, is not part of mockery. Indeed, the Prophet ﷺ and the imams after him used to make jokes. Ibn Khuwayzimdād said, 'We heard that a man went to the Qāḍī of Kufa, 'Ubaydullāh ibn al-Ḥasan, and 'Ubaydullāh joked with him, asking, "Is this cloak of yours from the wool of a ewe or that of a ram?" The man exclaimed, "Don't be ignorant, Qāḍī!" 'Ubaydullāh said to him, "Where do you find that joking is ignorance?" The man recited this *āyah* to him, and 'Ubaydullāh turned away from him because he saw that the man was ignorant and could not distinguish joking from mockery when they are not the same.'

قَالُوا ادْعُ لَنَا رَبَّكَ يُبَيِّن لَّنَا مَا هِيَ ۚ قَالَ إِنَّهُ يَقُولُ إِنَّهَا بَقَرَةٌ لَّا فَارِضٌ
وَلَا بِكْرٌ عَوَانٌ بَيْنَ ذَٰلِكَ ۖ فَافْعَلُوا مَا تُؤْمَرُونَ ﴿٦٨﴾

68 They said, 'Ask your Lord to make it clear to us what it should be like.' He said, 'He says it should be a cow, not old or virgin, but somewhere between the two, so do as you have been told.'

They said, 'Ask your Lord to make it clear to us what it should be like.'

This shows how prone they were to disobedience. If they had obeyed the command and slaughtered any cow, the goal would have been achieved, but they made things difficult for themselves so Allah made things difficult for them. Ibn 'Abbās, Abu-l-'Āliyah and others said that. Something similar is related from al-Ḥasan al-Baṣrī from the Prophet ﷺ.

He said, 'He says it should be a cow, not old or virgin, but somewhere between the two.

This indicates the permission for abrogation before an act takes place because the command to slaughter a cow meant any cow. When they wanted further description, He superseded the first ruling with another one. *'Fāriḍ'* (old) means one which has had many calves and 'virgin' means one which has had none.

So do as you have been told.'

This repeats the command and reinforces it. It indicates that a command of this type is mandatory (*wujūb*) in the language of the *fuqahā'*. This is sound as it is mentioned in the fundamentals of *fiqh*, and the command is immediate. That is also the position of most of the *fuqahā'*. Proof of that is found in the fact that when they did not hasten to do what they were commanded, Allah found them lacking. It is also said that it does not indicate immediacy because he did not reprimand them for the delay. Ibn Khuwayzimandād said that.

قَالُوا ادْعُ لَنَا رَبَّكَ يُبَيِّن لَّنَا مَا لَوْنُهَا ۚ قَالَ إِنَّهُ يَقُولُ إِنَّهَا
بَقَرَةٌ صَفْرَاءُ فَاقِعٌ لَّوْنُهَا تَسُرُّ النَّاظِرِينَ ﴿٦٩﴾

69 They said, 'Ask your Lord to make it clear to us what colour it should be.' He said, 'He says it should be a yellow cow, the colour of sorrel, a pleasure to all who look.'

They said, ‘Ask your Lord to make it clear to us what colour it should be.’

In other words, they were asking, “Should it be black, white or red?” ‘*Lawn*’ (colour) is also a category.

He said, ‘He says it should be a yellow cow, the colour of sorrel,

Most commentators say that the word *ṣafrā’* has its normal meaning here of yellow. Makkī said that even the horns and hooves were the same colour. Al-Ḥasan and Ibn Jubayr said that only the horns and hooves were yellow. Al-Ḥasan said that it means black but this is unlikely, because the word only means black when referring to camels as in 77:33. This is because the black colour in camels has a yellowish tinge. If actual black had been meant, He would not have stressed the word used with being ‘*fāqi‘*’ which means that it is pure yellow, not black. There are various adjectives which the Arabs add to colours, and ‘*fāqi‘*’ is used for yellow. ‘*Fāqi‘*’ means ‘pure’ with no other colour in its hide.

a pleasure to all who look.’

Wahb said that the sunlight danced off its hide. Ibn ‘Abbās said that yellow is cheering. It is encouraged to have yellow sandals, as an-Naqqāsh related from him. ‘Alī ibn Abī Ṭālib said that someone who wears yellow sandals has less cares. Ath-Tha‘labī related this from him.

قَالُوا ادْعُ لَنَا رَبَّكَ يُبَيِّن لَّنَا مَا هِيَ إِنَّ الْبَقَرَ تَشَٰبَهَ عَلَيْنَا وَإِنَّا إِن شَاءَ
اللَّهُ لَمُهْتَدُونَ ﴿٧٠﴾

70 They said, ‘Ask your Lord to make it clear to us what it should be like. Cows are all much the same to us. Then, if Allah wills, we will be guided.’

They said, ‘Ask your Lord to make it clear to us what it should be like. Cows are all much the same to us.

This was their fourth question so they still did not obey the command even when it had been made abundantly clear to them. *Baqar* is used because it is the plural, which is meant here.

Then, if Allah wills, we will be guided.’

The use of ‘if Allah wills’ in this sentence shows their eventual repentance and obedience. It is an indication that they regretted their lack of acceptance of what they had been commanded to do. It is related that the Prophet ﷺ said, 'If they had not said "if Allah wills" they would never have been guided to it at all.' Mentioning 'guidance' indicates concern for it.

قَالَ إِنَّهُۥ يَقُولُ إِنَّهَا بَقَرَةٌ لَّا ذَلُولٌ تُثِيرُ ٱلْأَرْضَ وَلَا تَسْقِي ٱلْحَرْثَ مُسَلَّمَةٌ
لَّا شِيَةَ فِيهَا ۚ قَالُوا۟ ٱلْـَٔـٰنَ جِئْتَ بِٱلْحَقِّ ۚ فَذَبَحُوهَا وَمَا كَادُوا۟ يَفْعَلُونَ ﴿٧١﴾

71 He said, 'He says it should be a cow not trained to plough or irrigate the fields – completely sound, without a blemish on it.' They said, 'Now you have brought the truth.' So they sacrificed it – but they almost did not do it.

He said, 'He says it should be a cow not trained to plough or irrigate the fields –

Al-Ḥasan said that the cow was undomesticated and hence untrained for ploughing or irrigating. This *āyah* provides evidence for singling out animals by their description. If they are definitely known in that way, then an advance sale is permitted. That is the position of Mālik and his people, al-Awzā'ī, al-Layth and ash-Shāfi'ī. The same applies to everything which has a clearly defined description since here Allah gives a description that takes the place of specification. The Messenger of Allah ﷺ said, 'A woman should not describe another women to her husband so that it is as if he could see her.' Muslim transmitted it. So here description takes the place of seeing.

completely sound, without a blemish on it.'

Musallama (sound) means that the cow must not be lame or have any other impairments as Qatādah and Abu-l-'Āliyah said. It is not said that it is free of work because it was already made clear that it did no work. Al-Ḥasan said that it means free of any trace of trace of work. *'Without a blemish on it'* means that nothing mars its colour at all, there being no hint of any other colour. The root of *'shīyah'* (blemish) is *'washyi'* and the *wāw* has been elided.

These specific qualities of the cow were imposed because the tribe of Israel were difficult and so Allah made the matter difficult for them. The *dīn* of Allah is ease. It is blameworthy to go deep into asking the Prophets and others about matters of detail in this way. We ask Allah for well-being.

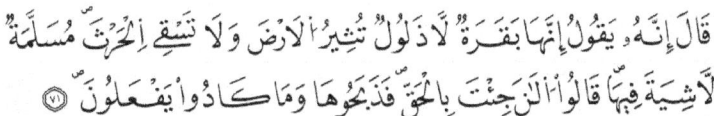

There are various stories related about this cow. The gist of them is that a man of the tribe of Israel had a son and he had a calf which he released in the woods, saying, 'O Allah, I entrust this calf to You for this boy.' The man died and when the child was grown, his mother told him, 'Your father entrusted a calf to Allah for you, so go and fetch it.' He went, and when the cow saw him, it came to him and he took it by the horn, even though it was wild, and he led it to his mother. The people met him and found that he had the cow that they were commanded to sacrifice. They haggled with him for it. Its price was said to be thirty dinars or its weight in gold. Allah knows best.

They said, 'Now you have brought the truth.'

Meaning 'made the truth clear'. Qatādah said that that is what it means.

So they sacrificed it – but they almost did not do it.

Because of their rebellion and excessive questioning or because of the high price of the cow. It is said that it was out of fear of being disgraced in the eyes of those who spoke about them, as Wahb ibn Munabbih said.

وَإِذْ قَتَلْتُمْ نَفْسًا فَادَّارَأْتُمْ فِيهَا وَاللَّهُ مُخْرِجٌ مَا كُنْتُمْ تَكْتُمُونَ ٧٢

72 Remember when you killed someone and violently accused each other of it, and Allah brought out what you were hiding.

Remember when you killed someone and violently accused each other of it.

This was discussed at the beginning of the story. There are two positions about the motive for the murder. One is that a man wanted to marry a beautiful daughter of his to his uncle's son but the uncle refused, so he killed him and took him to another village and dumped his body there. It is also said that he dumped his body between two villages.

The second view is that the man murdered the other out of desire for the inheritance he would receive. He claimed that some tribes had killed him. 'Ikrimah said that they had a temple with twelve doors, one for each tribe, and they found the dead man in the doorway of one of the tribes and each accused the other. They then went to Mūsā n with their quarrel and he told them to sacrifice a cow. Mujāhid said that 'violently accuse' is to disagree and quarrel.

If he was killed for his inheritance, a murderer does not inherit. That was stated by 'Abīdah as-Salmānī. Ibn 'Abbās said that this man killed his uncle in order to inherit from him. Ibn 'Aṭiyyah said that our sharī'ah has a similar ruling. In the *Muwaṭṭā'* Mālik related the story of Uḥayḥah ibn al-Julāḥ and his uncle and it is the reason for a killer not inheriting. Then Islam confirmed that just as many things from the Jāhiliyyah were confirmed. There is no disagreement between scholars that a murderer does not inherit from the blood money or the property of his victim except for an aberrant group, all of whom are people of innovation.

Someone who kills by accident does inherit from the property, but not the blood money according to Mālik, al-Awzāʿī, Abū Thawr and ash-Shāfiʿī because he is not suspected of killing in order to inherit and take his property. That is not the position of ath-Thawri, Abu Hanifa or ash-Shāfi'ī. According to another position: neither the murderer nor the accidental killer inherit any of the property or the blood money. That is also the view of Shurayḥ, Ṭāwus, ash-Shaʿbī and an-Nakhaʿī. Ash-Shaʿbī related that ʿUmar, ʿAlī and Zayd said that neither the murderer nor the accidental killer inherit anything. Both views are related from Mujāhid.

فَقُلْنَا ٱضْرِبُوهُ بِبَعْضِهَا كَذَٰلِكَ يُحْيِ ٱللَّهُ ٱلْمَوْتَىٰ وَيُرِيكُمْ ءَايَٰتِهِۦ لَعَلَّكُمْ تَعْقِلُونَ ﴿٧٣﴾

73 We said, 'Hit him with part of it!' In that way Allah gives life to the dead and He shows you His Signs so that hopefully you will understand.

We said, 'Hit him with part of it!'

The part referred to is said to have been the tongue because that is the organ of speech, and it is said to have been with the rump end of the tail. It is also said to have been the leg or another of the bones. In any case, the corpse was struck with it. Then the dead man identified his killer and reverted back to being a lifeless corpse.

Mālik used this episode as evidence for the validity of applying the *qasāmah* oath on the basis of the last words of the dying victim of a homicidal attack when he says, 'So-and-so killed me.' Ash-Shāfiʿī and most scholars forbid this, claiming that it is contrary to the principle that a suspect is innocent, except when there is absolute certainty of his guilt, and in that case there is only probability because the words of the victim may be true or false. They say that the case of the man of the tribe of Israel was a miraculous one and so it does not apply in normal circumstances. Ibn al-ʿArabī replies that the miracle consisted of the bringing back to life and that, therefore, what the man said has the same ruling as the words of any person who is alive. This is a fine area of knowledge which only Mālik grasped. It does not say in the Qur'an that when he said it was obligatory to believe what he said. Rather the *qasāmah* was commanded. Al-Bukhārī, ash-Shāfiʿī and a group of scholars found that unlikely and said, 'How can what he says about blood be accepted when what he says about dirhams is not accepted?'

Scholars disagree about the ruling of the *qasāmah*. It is related that Sālim, Abū Qilābah, 'Umar ibn 'Abd al-'Azīz and al-Ḥakam ibn 'Uyaynah hesitated about giving judgment on it. Al-Bukhārī inclined to that because the hadith of the *qasāmah* comes in a different place. Most say that the ruling of the *qasāmah* is confirmed from the Prophet ﷺ, but then there is disagreement about how it is carried out. One group said that the claimants first give their oaths and, when they have sworn, they are entitled. If they refrain, then the defendants swear fifty oaths and are free. This is the view of the people of Madīnah, al-Layth, ash-Shāfi'ī, Aḥmad and Abū Thawr. It is what is demanded by the hadith of Ḥuwayyiṣah and Muḥayyiṣah that the imams related.

Another group believed that one begins with the oaths of the defendants who swear and then are free. That is related from 'Umar ibn al-Khaṭṭāb, ash-Sha'bī and an-Nakha'ī. Ath-Thawrī and the Kufans take that view. They cite as evidence the hadith of Sa'īd ibn 'Ubayd from Bushayr ibn Yasār. In it they began with the oaths of the defendants who were Jews. Abū Dāwūd related from az-Zuhrī from Abū Salamah ibn 'Abd ar-Raḥmān from some of the Anṣār that the Prophet ﷺ said to the Jews, beginning with them, 'Will fifty of your men swear?' They said to the Anṣār, 'Seek entitlement.' They said, 'Then we swear to what we did not see, Messenger of Allah!' So the Messenger of Allah ﷺ assigned the blood money against the Jews since the victim had been found among them. He ﷺ also said, 'The defendant gives the oath.' They said that this is a definite principle in claims. The Sharī'ah calls attention to its wisdom when the Prophet ﷺ says, 'If people were to be given what they claim, then people would have laid claim to the blood and property of people. The oath is offered to the defendant.'

Those who take the first view say that the hadith of Sa'īd ibn 'Ubayd about starting with the Jews is considered by the people of hadith to be weak. An-Nasā'ī transmitted it and said, 'As far as I know, Sa'īd ibn 'Ubayd is not corroborated in this transmission.' The hadith of Bushayr comes from Sahl about the Prophet ﷺ beginning with the claimants according to Yaḥyā ibn Sa'īd, Ibn 'Uyaynah, Ḥammād ibn Zayd, 'Abd al-Wahhāb ath-Thaqafī, 'Īsā ibn Ḥammād and Bishr ibn al-Mufaḍḍal. These are seven. Even if Mālik has it *mursal*, a group have it connected. It is sounder than the hadith of Sa'īd ibn 'Ubayd. Abū Muḥammad al-Aṣīlī said, 'It is not permitted for a single hadith to contradict one of a group, although Sa'īd ibn 'Ubayd said in his hadith that the Messenger of Allah ﷺ gave him blood money consisting of a hundred of the *zakāt* camels, but *zakāt* is not used for blood money and not given to other than the people entitled to it.' The hadith in Abū Dāwūd is *mursal* and does not counter sound connected hadiths. They answer about holding to the fundamental principle by the fact that this ruling is a fundamental principle itself for the sanctity of human life.

Ibn al-Mundhir said, 'It is established that the Messenger of Allah ﷺ made the claimant provide the evidence and the defendant has to take an oath. It is necessary to judge by the apparent meaning of that, unless Allah makes it specific in His Book or on the tongue of His Prophet ﷺ that the ruling is only about one particular thing and is excluded from the general ruling. One thing specified by the Book is the necessity of imposing the *ḥadd* punishment on a slanderer if he does not have two witnesses who testify to the truth of his accusation. A special case is someone who accuses his wife: the *ḥadd* punishment is removed from him when he testifies four times. One thing specified by the Sunnah is the ruling that the Prophet ﷺ gave for the *qasāmah*. Ibn Jurayj related from 'Aṭā' from Abū Hurayrah that the Prophet ﷺ said, "The claimant must provide evidence and the one who denies it swears an oath," except in the case of the *qasāmah*. Ad-Dāraquṭnī transmitted it. What Mālik said about this in the *Muwaṭṭā'* is sufficient.'

They also disagree about the necessity of imposing retaliation by the *qasāmah*. One group oblige retaliation based on it, and that is the view of Mālik, al-Layth, Aḥmad and Abū Thawr, because of what the Prophet ﷺ said to Ḥuwayyiṣah, Muḥayyiṣah and 'Abd ar-Raḥmān, 'Will you swear and thereby be entitled to the blood of your companion?' Abū Dāwūd related from 'Amr ibn Shu'ayb from his father from his grandfather that the Prophet ﷺ killed a man from the Banū Naḍr ibn Mālik on the basis of the *qasāmah*. Ad-Dāraquṭnī said that text of 'Amr ibn Shu'ayb from his father from his grandfather is sound. Similarly Abū 'Umar ibn 'Abd al-Barr considers the hadith of 'Amr ibn Shu'ayb to be sound and authoritative. Al-Bukhārī said, 'I saw 'Alī ibn al-Madīnī, Aḥmad ibn Ḥanbal, al-Ḥumaydī and Isḥāq ibn Rāhawayh using him as an authority.' Ad-Dāraquṭnī said that in the *Sunan*.

Another group said that there is no retaliation on the basis of the *qasāmah*, but it obliges blood money. This is related from 'Umar and Ibn 'Abbās and it is the view of an-Nakha'ī and al-Ḥasan. It was believed by ath-Thawrī and the Kufans, ash-Shāfi'ī and Isḥāq. They cite as evidence what Mālik related from Ibn Abī Laylā ibn 'Abdullāh ibn Sahl ibn Abī Ḥathmah that the Prophet ﷺ said to the Anṣār: 'Either they will pay blood money for your companion or war will be declared on them.' They said that this indicates that it is a question of blood money rather than retaliation. They said that his words about being entitled to the blood of 'your companion' means the blood money for the life of the man killed because the Jews were not their companions. Whoever is entitled to the blood money of a person is entitled to his blood because blood money may be taken in case of deliberate killing and that would make one entitled to blood.

Justified suspicion (*lawth*) requires the *qasāmah*. *Lawth* means that it is probable that the one who claimed that there was murder is speaking the truth, such as when there is testimony of a single upright witness to seeing the killing or seeing the victim shouting covered in blood, or when the suspect is found close to him with blood on himself. There is disagreement about *lawth* and what it is. Mālik said, 'It is the words of the victim, "So-and-so killed me." The testimony of an upright witness also furnishes justified suspicion.' That is found in what Ibn al-Qāsim related from him. Ashhab related that Mālik implemented the *qasāmah* when the witness is not upright or is a woman. Ibn Wahb related that the testimony of women furnishes justified suspicion. Muḥammad related from Ibn al-Qāsim that the testimony of two women constitutes justified suspicion, but not that of only one.

Qāḍī Abū Bakr ibn al-'Arabī said, 'There is great disagreement about *lawth*. The well known position of the School is that it is when there is a single upright witness.' Muḥammad said, 'I prefer that and that view was taken by Ibn al-Qāsim and Ibn 'Abd al-Ḥakam.' It is related from 'Abd al-Malik ibn Marwān that when someone who is wounded or struck down says, 'So-and-so killed me' and then dies, there is a *qasāmah*. That is the position of Mālik and al-Layth ibn Sa'd. Mālik cited as evidence the victim of the tribe of Israel who said, 'So-and-so killed me.'

Ash-Shāfi'ī said, 'Justified suspicion is on the evidence of a single upright witness or producing evidence, even from someone who is not considered upright.' Ath-Thawrī and Kufans obliged a *qasāmah* on the mere discovery of a murdered victim. They said there is no need to take account of the words of the victim or a witness. They said, 'If a victim is found where a people are located and there are indications of violence on the body, then the people of that location are required to swear that they have not killed him and they pay the blood money. If there is no trace of violence on him, then they do not owe anything unless there is evidence against one of them.' Sufyān said, 'This is something about which there is consensus with us.' That is a weak position about which the people of knowledge disagree and there is no precedent for it. That is because it is contrary to the Qur'an and the Sunnah and because that is obliging the males of the clan to pay money without any evidence being established against them and no admission on their part.

Mālik and ash-Shāfi'ī believed that when a victim is found where a group of people are located, his blood is not demanded and the people of the nearest house are not seized for his death, because it is possible that he was killed and then dumped at someone's door in order to throw suspicion on them. Therefore no one is seized for something like this until the reasons that are stipulated for the obligation of the *qasāmah* are shown to exist. 'Umar ibn 'Abd al-'Azīz said, 'This is is one of the things about which judgment is delayed until Allah judges it at the Rising.'

Al-Qāsim ibn Mas'adah said, 'I asked an-Nasā'ī, "Mālik said that there is no *qasāmah* except when there is justified suspicion. Why, then, is the hadith of the *qasāmah* reported with no element of suspicion in it?" An-Nasā'ī replied, "Mālik put the enmity that existed between them and the Jews in the place of suspicion, and he put suspicion, or the words of the victim, in the place of enmity."' Ibn Zayd said, 'The basis for this is found in the story of the tribe of Israel when Allah brought to life the murder victim when he was struck with part of the cow. He then said, "So-and-so killed me," and enmity is tantamount to suspicion.' Ash-Shāfi'ī said, 'We do not consider the words of the victim to constitute justified suspicion.' Ash-Shāfi'ī said, 'When there is clear enmity between two peoples, such as that which existed between the Anṣār and the Jews, and a murder victim is found in one of the two parties and they do not mingle with other people, then the *qasāmah* is obliged for him.'

There is disagreement about a murder victim who is discovered in a place that has been rented. The People of Opinion say that action is against the people of that quarter, not the inhabitants of that property. If they sell their houses and then the victim is discovered, the blood money is owed by the seller, not the inhabitants. If the house-owners are absent and have rented out the houses, then the *qasāmah* and blood money is due from the absent owners and not the inhabitants among whom the victim was discovered.

Then among them Ya'qūb retracted this view and said, 'The *qasāmah* and blood money is on the inhabitants of the houses.' This view is related from Ibn Abī Laylā. He argued that the people of Khaybar were resident workers and a victim was found among them. Ath-Thawrī, 'We say that it is against the owners of the houses.' Aḥmad said, 'The position taken is that of Ibn Abī Laylā regarding *qasāmah* but not blood money.' Ash-Shāfi'ī said, 'It is all the same. There is no blood money nor retaliation except by established evidence or what obliges the *qasāmah* which is carried out by the guardians.' Ibn al-Mundhir said, 'This is sounder.'

There are no less than fifty oaths in the *qasāmah* because of what the Prophet ﷺ said in the hadith of Ḥuwayyiṣah and Muḥayyiṣah, 'Fifty of you will swear for one of them.' Those seeking entitlement each swear an oath. If they are less than fifty, or some of them refuse but do not permit pardon, then the oaths are divided between the others. In the case of deliberate killing an oath from less than two men is not acceptable. An oath [for *qasāmah*] may not be sworn by only one man or by women. The fifty oaths are sworn by guardians and by those of the paternal kin (*'aṣabah*) who help them. This is the position of Mālik, al-Layth, ath-Thawrī, al-Awzā'ī, Aḥmad and Dāwūd.

Muṭarrif related from Mālik that no one may swear along with the defendant. They themselves swear, whether they are one or more, fifty oaths by which they free themselves. That is the view of ash-Shāfi'ī. Ash-Shāfi'ī said, 'Only an heir swears, whether the killing is deliberate or accidental.' There is no oath sworn for property and entitlement to it except in the case of those who have personal ownership or the heirs to whom Allah has given ownership. Heirs swear oaths according to their shares of inheritance. That was stated by Abū Thawr, and Ibn al-Mundhir preferred it. It is sound because someone who has no claim against him has no reason to take an oath. The goal of these oaths is to be free of the claim. Anyone who has no claim against him is free of claims.

Mālik said that, in the case of accidental killing, a man or woman may swear the oaths, in whatever way will complete the fifty, by one or by many, and then the oath-taker is entitled to his inheritance. If someone refuses to swear, then he is not entitled to anything. If someone who was absent comes after the swearing of oaths, nothing is obliged against him in respect of what he would have had to swear if he had been present, based on his inheritance. This is the famous view of Mālik. It is also related from him that there is no *qasāmah* for accidental killing.

This concludes the issues and rulings regarding *qasāmah*. Success is by Allah.

This story of the cow contains evidence that all true aspects of any Sharī'ah which existed before ours are also binding on us, as many *mutakallimūn* and *fuqahā'* have said.

In that way Allah gives life to the dead and He shows you His Signs so that hopefully you will understand.

As He gave life to this man after his death, so Allah will revive everyone on the Last Day. He shows you His Signs and His power so that you might understand and not disobey Him.

ثُمَّ قَسَتْ قُلُوبُكُم مِّن بَعْدِ ذَٰلِكَ فَهِيَ كَالْحِجَارَةِ أَوْ أَشَدُّ قَسْوَةً ۚ وَإِنَّ مِنَ الْحِجَارَةِ
لَمَا يَتَفَجَّرُ مِنْهُ الْأَنْهَارُ ۚ وَإِنَّ مِنْهَا لَمَا يَشَّقَّقُ فَيَخْرُجُ مِنْهُ الْمَاءُ ۚ وَإِنَّ مِنْهَا لَمَا
يَهْبِطُ مِنْ خَشْيَةِ اللَّهِ ۗ وَمَا اللَّهُ بِغَافِلٍ عَمَّا تَعْمَلُونَ ﴿٧٤﴾

74 Then your hearts became hardened after that, so they were like rocks or even harder still. There are some rocks from which rivers gush out, and others which split open and water pours out, and others which crash down from fear of Allah. Allah is not unaware of what you do.

Then your hearts became hardened after that,

'Hardened' refers to hardness, severity and unbendingness. This refers to the lack of repentance on the part of the Jews and their refusal to submit to the Signs of Allah. Abu-l-'Āliyah, Qatādah and others said that what is meant here are the hearts of all the tribe of Israel. Ibn 'Abbās, however, says that what is meant are the hearts of the heirs of the victim because when he was brought to life and named his killer and then became dead again, they denied it and said, 'He lied' after seeing this great sign. So their hearts were made blind and they were the most adamant in denying their Prophet. But the judgment of Allah was carried out by their being killed.

At-Tirmidhī reported from 'Abdullāh ibn 'Umar that the Messenger of Allah ﷺ said, 'Do not speak a lot without mentioning Allah. A lot of words without mentioning Allah produces hardness of the heart. The furthest of people from Allah are the hard-hearted.' In the *Musnad* of al-Bazzār Anas reported that the Prophet ﷺ said, 'Four things are part of wretchedness: unresponsive eyes, hard hearts, far-reaching hopes and greed for this world.'

There are some rocks from which rivers gush out,

This refers to springs which become ever larger until they become rivers or rocks that simply split, even if no water comes out.

and others which crash down from fear of Allah.

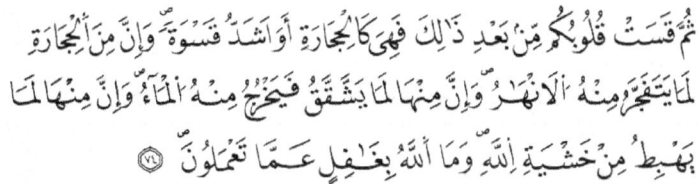

Some rocks benefit more than hearts because water emerges from them. Mujāhid said, 'No rock falls from the top of a mountain, nor river from a rock nor water emerges from it, except out of fear of Allah. Allah revealed the Qur'an about that.' Ibn Jurayj said something similar. Some *mutakallimūn* say that the rocks, in this instance, mean hail which falls from the clouds. It is said that 'crash down' is metaphorical. Ibn Baḥr said that it means, 'Some hearts fall down.' The first, however, is the soundest. It does not prevent some inanimates from having knowledge as we find in various accounts of the Prophet's miracles. An example is the palm trunk against which the Prophet ﷺ used to lean when he gave a *khuṭbah.* When he moved from it, it moaned. It is confirmed that the Prophet ﷺ said, 'There is a stone that used to greet me in the Jāhiliyyah. I still recognise it.' There are other examples.

Allah is not unaware of what you do.

He is aware of your actions so that He does not miss anything, large or small, without recording it against you. Ibn Kathīr has the reading with *yā'*: ***ya****'malūna*, 'they do'.

أَفَتَطْمَعُونَ أَن يُؤْمِنُوا لَكُمْ وَقَدْ كَانَ فَرِيقٌ مِّنْهُمْ يَسْمَعُونَ
كَلَامَ اللَّهِ ثُمَّ يُحَرِّفُونَهُ مِن بَعْدِ مَا عَقَلُوهُ وَهُمْ يَعْلَمُونَ ﴿٧٥﴾

75 Do you really hope they will follow you in faith when a group of them heard Allah's Word then, after grasping it, knowingly distorted it?

Do you really hope they will follow you in faith

This question implies a negative response as there was no hope for the faith of a group of Jews because they had already rejected. It is addressed to the Companions of the Prophet ﷺ. That is because some of the Anṣār wanted the Jews to become Muslim because of their alliance with them and proximity to them. It is said that it is addressed to the Prophet ﷺ alone. Ibn 'Abbās says that it means: 'Do not be sad about their denial of you.' He reported that they were evil people already.

When a group of them heard Allah's Word

Farīq (group) is a plural noun with no singular form. What is meant by this are the seventy men, whom Mūsā chose to hear the Speech of Allah, but who then did not obey and altered His words when they told their people. This is what ar-Rabī' and Ibn Isḥāq said. This interpretation is somewhat weak. As-Suddī and others said that they were not able to listen and they were confused and wanted Mūsā to repeat it for them. When they left a group of them then altered what they had heard of the words of Allah on the tongue of their Prophet.

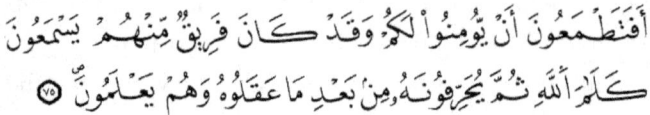

People disagree about how Mūsā recognised the Speech of Allah when he had not heard it before. Some say that he heard words without letters or voices, with no pause or breath, and knew that it could not be a human voice but must be the voice of the Lord of the worlds. Others said that he heard words which did not come from any direction and so he knew they were not of human origin. It is said that his entire body heard it and so he knew that it was the Speech of Allah. It is said that the miracle indicated that it was the Speech of Allah when he was told to cast down his staff and it became a serpent. That was proof of the truth of the matter and confirmation of His words: *'I am your Lord.'* (20:12) It is said that he concealed something inside himself which only He who knows the Unseen worlds would know and Allah informed him of that and so he knew that he was addressed by Allah.

and then, after grasping it, knowingly distorted it?

Mujāhid and as-Suddī said that they were the Jewish scholars who altered the Torah and made what was unlawful lawful and what was lawful unlawful, following their own whims and desires. This is to rebuke them because of what their fathers did. It indicates that any scholar who is opinionated regarding the truth is far from right guidance because he knows the promise and threat, and yet still follows his own opinion.

وَإِذَا لَقُوا۟ ٱلَّذِينَ ءَامَنُوا۟ قَالُوٓا۟ ءَامَنَّا وَإِذَا خَلَا بَعْضُهُمْ إِلَىٰ بَعْضٍ
قَالُوٓا۟ أَتُحَدِّثُونَهُم بِمَا فَتَحَ ٱللَّهُ عَلَيْكُمْ لِيُحَآجُّوكُم بِهِۦ عِندَ رَبِّكُمْ
أَفَلَا تَعْقِلُونَ ﴿٧٦﴾ أَوَلَا يَعْلَمُونَ أَنَّ ٱللَّهَ يَعْلَمُ مَا يُسِرُّونَ وَمَا يُعْلِنُونَ ﴿٧٧﴾

76 When they meet those who believe, they say, 'We believe.' But when they go apart with one another, they say, 'Why do you speak to them about what Allah has decided about you, so they can use it as an argument against you before your Lord? Will you not use your intellect?' 77 Do they not know that Allah knows what they keep secret and what they make public?

When they meet those who believe, they say, 'We believe.'

This is about the hypocrites.

But when they go apart with one another,

This refers to the Jews because some of them outwardly become Muslim but were actually hypocrites. They would talk to the believers about how their ancestors were being tormented. So the Jews said to them:

Why do you speak to them about what Allah has decided about you,

'When you speak regarding the punishment which Allah has ordained for you, so that they can say, "We are more honoured with Allah than you are."' This is the meaning according to Ibn 'Abbās and as-Suddī. It is said that when 'Alī came near Qurayẓah on the day of Khaybar, he heard them insulting the Messenger of Allah ﷺ. He went to him and said, 'Messenger of Allah, do not go to them,' and he tried to stop him. He said, 'I think that you heard them insulting me. If they had seen me, they would have refrained.' He went up to them. When they saw him, they refrained. He told them, 'You have broken the treaty, brothers of apes and pigs. May Allah disgrace you and send His vengeance on you!' They replied, 'You are not ignorant, Muḥammad. Do not be rash towards us! Who has told you this! This report can only have come from us!' The root of the word used for '*fataḥa*' (decided) means to give a judgment or decision but the word can also indicate help and assistance as well as judgment.

So they can use it as an argument against you before your Lord?

That is generally taken as referring to the Next World but it is also said that it means 'when your Lord is mentioned'. Al-Ḥasan said that *ḥujjah* means straight words in general. Part of that is *maḥajjah*, the road.

Will you not use your intellect?'

This is generally taken to be the words of the rabbis to their followers but it is also possible that it is addressed by Allah to the believers, meaning. 'Do you not know that the tribe of Israel do not believe and therefore this is the way they behave?' Then Allah follows that with another rebuke.

وَمِنْهُمْ أُمِّيُّونَ لَا يَعْلَمُونَ ٱلْكِتَـٰبَ إِلَّآ أَمَانِىَّ وَإِنْ هُمْ إِلَّا
يَظُنُّونَ ﴿٧٨﴾

78 Some of them are illiterate, knowing nothing of the Book but wishful thinking. They only speculate.

Some of them are illiterate,

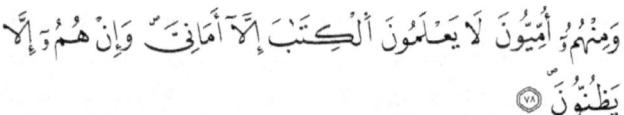

'Them' may refer to the Jews alone or to both the Jews and the hypocrites. The word '*ummiyyūn*' (illiterate) means that they can neither read nor write. It is derived from *ummiyyah*, meaning 'to be still in the state in which your mother bore you, without having learned to read or write'. An aspect of that is the words of the Prophet ﷺ: 'We are an unlettered nation. We do not write or reckon.' Ibn 'Abbās said that they are illiterate because they do not affirm of the Mother of the Book. Abū 'Ubaydah said, 'They are called "illiterate" since the Book was sent down on them, as if they were ascribed to the Mother of the Book, so it is as he were saying that among them are People of the Book who do not know the Book.' 'Ikrimah and aḍ-Ḍaḥḥāk said that it refers to the Christian Arabs. It is said that they are some of the People of the Book whose Book was removed because of the wrong actions they committed, and so they became illiterate. 'Alī said that they are the Magians. The first explanation is more likely, and Allah knows best.

knowing nothing of the Book but wishful thinking.

Abū Ja'far, Shaybah and al-A'raj recited '*amānī*' rather than '*amāniyy*'. '*Amāniyy*' (wishful thinking) is the plural of *umniyah* (recitation) from *amnuyah* as we see in '*without Shayṭān insinuating something into his recitation while he was reciting* (tamannā).' (22:52) *Amāniyy* also means 'lies'. That is how Ibn 'Abbās and Mujāhid explain it here. It is also what a person wishes for and desires, and so Qatādah said that the meaning is that they desire what they in reality do not have. It is also said that it means 'to value'.

They only speculate.

This means that they lie and come up with new things because they have no knowledge about whether what they recite is true or not. They merely imitate what their rabbis recite. Abū Bakr al-Anbārī said, 'The grammarian, Aḥmad ibn Yaḥyā, told me that the Arabs use *ẓann* (speculation) for knowledge, doubt and lies. When the evidence for knowledge is established and is greater than the evidence for doubt, then *ẓann* becomes knowledge. When the proofs for knowledge and those for doubt are equal, then *ẓann* is doubt. When the proofs for doubt are more than the proofs for knowledge, then *ẓann* is lies.' Here Allah means that they are lying.

Our scholars say that Allah describes the rabbis as changing and altering their Book and Allah says in the next *āyah*: '*Woe to them for what their hands have written!*' (2:79) That is because they studied the matter, but their scholars were bad shepherds, greedy for worldly things, and so they looked for things to draw people's attention towards themselves. Therefore they made up new things in their Law and altered it. They added these inventions to the Torah and told their foolish followers, 'This is from Allah' so that it would be accepted from them and would establish their power. By so doing they obtained nothing but the rubble and filth of this world.

They said various things. One is, *'We are under no obligation where the Gentiles* (lit. illiterate) *are concerned'* (3:75), referring to the Arabs, meaning that whatever property of theirs they usurped was lawful for them. Another thing they said was that no sins they committed would harm them because they were beloved by Allah and His sons. (cf. 5:18) Allah is exalted above that! The Torah has: 'My rabbis and sons of My Messengers!' They changed it to 'My loved ones and My sons.' Allah said that they were lying in 5:18. They also said, 'Allah will not punish us. If He does punish us, it will only be for forty days,' (cf. 2:80), that being the number of days they were worshipping the Calf. Allah made it clear that eternity in the Fire and the Garden is the result of unbelief and faith. It is not what they say.

فَوَيْلٌ لِّلَّذِينَ يَكْتُبُونَ ٱلْكِتَٰبَ بِأَيْدِيهِمْ ثُمَّ يَقُولُونَ هَٰذَا مِنْ
عِندِ ٱللَّهِ لِيَشْتَرُوا۟ بِهِۦ ثَمَنًا قَلِيلًا فَوَيْلٌ لَّهُم مِّمَّا كَتَبَتْ
أَيْدِيهِمْ وَوَيْلٌ لَّهُم مِّمَّا يَكْسِبُونَ ٧٩

79 Woe to those who write the Book with their own hands and then say 'This is from Allah' to sell it for a paltry price. Woe to them for what their hands have written! Woe to them for what they earn!

Woe

There is disagreement about what *'wayl'* (woe) means. 'Uthmān ibn 'Affān related from the Prophet ﷺ that it is a mountain of fire. Abū Sa'īd al-Khudrī said that Wayl is a valley in Hell situated between two mountains whose depth is a fall of forty years. Sufyān and 'Aṭā' ibn Yasār said that Wayl is a valley in Hellfire through which flows the pus of the people of the Fire. It is said to be a cistern in the Fire. Az-Zahrāwī said that others said that it is a gate of Hell. Ibn 'Abbās said that it is harsh punishment. Al-Khalīl says that it is intense evil. Al-Aṣma'ī said that it is being in distress and seeking mercy. Sībuwayh said that *'wayl'* is used for someone who has fallen into destruction and *'wayḥ'* seeks to restrain someone on the verge of destruction. Ibn 'Arafah said that *'wayl'* is sorrow. It is also said to be extreme sorrow and the expression is used in times of great sorrow and distress. Its root is said to be that destruction which invites woe. Al-Farrā' said that its root is *'way'*, meaning sorrow.

to those who write the Book

The first to write with the pen was the Prophet Idrīs, as we read in the hadith of

Abū Dharr, transmitted by al-Ājurrī. It is said that Ādam was given writing and his descendants inherited it.

with their own hands.

This is for emphasis because it is well known that writing is done with the hands. This kind of linguistic usage is often used for stress in the Qur'an. The fact that they wrote it also indicates that it was not revealed to them, but they are the ones who fabricated it. It came from them, even if they did not physically write it.

This *āyah* and the one before it warn against making any alterations or changes or additions to the Sharī'ah. Anyone who alters, changes or innovates something in the *dīn* of Allah, which is not in it and not permitted in it, is subject to this terrible threat and painful punishment. The Messenger of Allah ﷺ cautioned his community about what he knew would occur at the end of time. He said, 'Those of the People of the Book before you divided into seventy-two sects and this community will divide into seventy-three, all of whom will be in the Fire except for one.' He cautioned them against originating something from themselves in the *dīn* which is contrary to the Book of Allah, the Sunnah or the sunnah of the Companions by which they misguide people. What he cautioned about has, in fact, occurred and become widespread. We belong to Allah and to Him we return.

to sell it for a paltry price.

It is paltry because it will inevitably disappear and have no permanence, or because it is unlawful as there is no blessing in anything unlawful and it does not grow in the sight of Allah.

وَقَالُوا۟ لَن تَمَسَّنَا ٱلنَّارُ إِلَّآ أَيَّامًا مَّعْدُودَةً ۚ قُلْ أَتَّخَذْتُمْ عِندَ ٱللَّهِ
عَهْدًا فَلَن يُخْلِفَ ٱللَّهُ عَهْدَهُۥٓ ۖ أَمْ تَقُولُونَ عَلَى ٱللَّهِ مَا لَا تَعْلَمُونَ ﴿٨٠﴾

80 They say, 'The Fire will only touch us for a number of days.' Say, 'Have you made a contract with Allah — then Allah will not break His contract — or are you rather saying about Allah what you do not know?'

They say, 'The Fire will only touch us for a number of days,'

As was mentioned above 'They' in this *āyah* refers to the Jews. There is disagreement about the reason for its revelation. It is said that the Prophet ﷺ asked the Jews, 'Who are the people of the Fire?' They replied, 'We are. Then you will follow us.' He said, 'You lie. You know that we will not follow you,' and this was revealed. Ibn Zayd said that. 'Ikrimah said that Ibn 'Abbās said, 'When the Messenger of Allah ﷺ came to Madīnah, the Jews were saying, "The duration of this world is seven thousand [years]. People will be punished in the Fire for one day of the days of the Next World for each thousand years of the days of this world. That is seven days." Then Allah revealed this *āyah*.' This is what Mujāhid said. Others said that the Jews said that the Torah says that Hellfire is a distance of forty years across. They will cross a year's length every day until they have gone right across and then leave Hellfire. Aḍ Ḍaḥḥāk related that from Ibn 'Abbās. Ibn 'Abbās said that the Jews claim that they found written in the Torah that there is a length of forty years between the sides of Hell until they reach the tree of Zaqqūm. They said, 'We will be punished until we reach the Tree of Zaqqūm and then Hell will depart and be destroyed.' Ibn 'Abbās and Qatādah said, 'The Jews said, "Allah swore that they would only enter the Fire for forty days, the number of days that the Calf was worshipped." Allah said that they were lying.'

This *āyah* refutes Abū Hanīfah and his people in their conclusion that the words of the Prophet ﷺ, 'Leave the prayer during the days of your menstruation' is evidence that the period of menstruation is what can be called 'the days of menstruation'. For this reason they say that the minimum time for a menstrual period is three days and its maximum ten days because, for any period less than three days, the singular or dual is used and for numbers more than ten the singular is also used and not the plural. The reply to this is that Allah uses the plural 'days' in other ways than this way, as when He says about fasting that is for *'known days'* (2:184) and in that case it is known to mean the entire month of Ramadan and here *'The Fire will only touch us for a number of days'* (3:24) means forty days.

Have you made a contract with Allah?

Have you sent ahead good deeds, in that you believed and obeyed Allah, so that it would be obliged for you to come out of the Fire? Or do you know that by His Revelation which He entrusted to you? He ends by rebuking them.

بَلَىٰ مَن كَسَبَ سَيِّئَةً وَأَحَاطَتْ بِهِۦ خَطِيٓـَٔاتُهُۥ فَأُوْلَٰٓئِكَ
أَصْحَٰبُ ٱلنَّارِ هُمْ فِيهَا خَٰلِدُونَ ۝٨١ وَٱلَّذِينَ ءَامَنُواْ وَعَمِلُواْ ٱلصَّٰلِحَٰتِ
أُوْلَٰٓئِكَ أَصْحَٰبُ ٱلْجَنَّةِ هُمْ فِيهَا خَٰلِدُونَ ۝٨٢

81 No indeed! Those who accumulate bad actions and are surrounded by their mistakes, such people are the Companions of the Fire, remaining in it timelessly, for ever; 82 whereas those who believe and do right actions, such people are the Companions of the Garden, remaining in it timelessly, for ever.

The matter is not as they claim. This *āyah* is a clear refutation of the claim the Jews make. The bad actions referred to are said to be *shirk*. Ibn Jurayj said, 'I asked 'Aṭā' about the expression "accumulate bad actions" and he said, "It means *shirk*," and recited *"Those who perform bad actions will be flung head-first into the Fire."* (27:90)' Al-Ḥasan and Qatādah said that it means all major wrong actions.

This *āyah* is also important because it indicates that there are two preconditions for salvation and that both are necessary: faith and right action. It is similar to what Allah says: *'Those who say, 'Our Lord is Allah,' and then go straight.'* (41:30) When Sufyān ibn 'Abdullāh ath-Thaqafī asked the Prophet ﷺ, 'Messenger of Allah, tell me something about Islam which will preclude my having to ask anyone after you,' the Prophet ﷺ said, 'Say, "I have believed in Allah," and go straight.' Muslim transmitted it. This was discussed in *āyah* 35. Nāfi' recited 'mistakes' in the plural while the rest have it in the singular.

وَإِذْ أَخَذْنَا مِيثَٰقَ بَنِيٓ إِسْرَٰٓءِيلَ لَا تَعْبُدُونَ إِلَّا ٱللَّهَ وَبِٱلْوَٰلِدَيْنِ
إِحْسَانًا وَذِي ٱلْقُرْبَىٰ وَٱلْيَتَٰمَىٰ وَٱلْمَسَٰكِينِ وَقُولُواْ لِلنَّاسِ حُسْنًا
وَأَقِيمُواْ ٱلصَّلَوٰةَ وَءَاتُواْ ٱلزَّكَوٰةَ ثُمَّ تَوَلَّيْتُمْ إِلَّا قَلِيلًا
مِّنكُمْ وَأَنتُم مُّعْرِضُونَ ۝٨٣

83 Remember when We made a covenant with the tribe of Israel: 'Worship none but Allah and be good to your parents and to relatives and orphans and the very poor. And speak good words to people. And establish the prayer and pay *zakāt*.' But then you turned away – except a few of you – you turned aside.

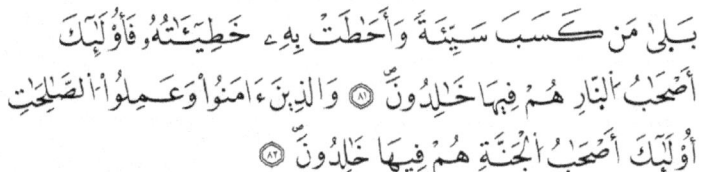

Remember when We made a covenant with the tribe of Israel: 'Worship none but Allah

There is disagreement about the covenant referred to here. Makkī said that it is the covenant which they made when they were brought out from the loins of Ādam (cf. 7:172), and it is also said that it was the covenant on the tongues of their Prophet, while they were rational and alive, that they would worship none but Allah. Worship entails affirming the Unity of Allah, confirming His Messenger and implementing what is revealed in His Books.

'Worship' was recited in the imperative by Ubayy and Ibn Mas'ūd. The reading of Ibn Kathīr, Ḥamzah and al-Kisā'ī recited it with *yā'*: 'they worship'. Al-Farrā', az-Zajjāj and a group said, 'It means that Allah's contract with them was conditional on their not worshipping anything other than Allah, being good to their parents, and not shedding blood.'

and be good to your parents

Allah connects being good to one's parents with *tawḥīd* because the first development in the womb comes from Allah, and the second, which involves upbringing and teaching, is in the hands of one's parents. That is why Allah Almighty enjoined thankfulness to them, as in His words: *'Give thanks to Me and to your parents.'* (31:14) Being good to parents implies keeping their company correctly and courteously, being humble to them, obeying them, praying for forgiveness for them, and maintaining ties with the people they love.

and to relatives

They are commanded to be good to their relatives by maintaining ties with them and giving them gifts.

and orphans

Yatāmā (orphans) is the plural of *yatīm*. An orphan is a child without a father. In animals, an orphan is one without a mother. Al-Māwardī said that the term 'orphan' can be used of a human child without a mother, but the first is what is well known. The root meaning is to be alone. An orphan child is without his father. An 'orphan' in poetry is a verse which has no line before or after it. An 'orphan pearl' is a peerless one. This *āyah* commands people to be kind to orphans and encourages caring for them and protecting their property, which will be explained in *an-Nisā'*. The Messenger of Allah ﷺ said, 'I and an orphan's guardian, whether he is a relative or a non-relative, will be like these two in the Garden,' and the transmitter, Mālik ibn Anas, indicated his index and middle fingers. Abū Hurayrah related it and Muslim transmitted it. Abū Muḥammad 'Abd al-Ghanī ibn Sa'īd transmitted from al-Ḥasan ibn Dīnār from Abū Sa'īd al-Baṣrī, who is al-Ḥasan ibn Wāṣil, from al-Aswad ibn 'Abd ar-Raḥmān from Hiṣṣān that Abū Mūsā al-Ash'arī reported that the Prophet ﷺ said, 'When an orphan sits with some people at their table, Shayṭān does not come near it.' He also transmitted from Ḥusayn ibn Qays, who is Abū 'Alī ar-Raḥabī, from 'Ikrimah that Ibn 'Abbās reported that the Prophet ﷺ said, 'If someone includes a Muslim orphan at his table until Allah enriches him, he will be forgiven his wrong actions entirely unless he does something which is unforgivable. And if Allah takes away the two things a person loves most and he remains steadfast and in expectation of the reward, he will be forgiven his wrong actions entirely.' They asked, 'What are the two things he loves most?' He replied, 'His two eyes,' and then continued, 'and whoever has three daughters or three sisters and supports them and is good to them until they marry or die all his wrong actions will be forgiven unless he does something which is unforgivable.' A bedouin man who had emigrated called out, 'Messenger of Allah, or two?' The Messenger of Allah ﷺ said, 'Or two.' Ibn Abbās said that it is a *gharīb* hadith.

The index finger (*sabbābah*) is the one that is next to the thumb. It was called '*sabbābah*' in the Jāhiliyyah they used it when insulting someone. When Allah brought Islam, they disliked this name and called it '*mushīrah*' (indicator) because they used it to indicate Allah in *tawḥīd*. It is also called '*sabbāḥah*' (swimmer) in some hadiths. Eventually the Jāhiliyyah term dominated. It is related that the index finger of the Messenger of Allah ﷺ was longer than his middle finger and the ring finger was shorter than the middle finger. Yazīd ibn Hārūn related from 'Abdullāh ibn Miqsam aṭ-Ṭā'ifī that his aunt, Sārah bint Miqsam, heard Maymūnah bint Kardam say, 'I went out on the ḥajj that the Messenger of Allah ﷺ performed and I saw the Messenger of Allah ﷺ on his camel and my father asked him some questions. He saw me and I, a young girl, was surprised at how much longer his finger next to the thumb was than the rest of his fingers.' He ﷺ said, 'He and I will be like these two in the Garden.' Hegalso said, 'I, Abū Bakr and 'Umar will be gathered on the Day of Rising like this,' and he pointed with three fingers.

and the very poor

It means: 'We commanded them to be good to the very poor.' They are those who are in need and those who are destitute. This contains encouragement to give *ṣadaqah* and solace to people in need, and to keep an eye on the conditions of the poor and weak. Muslim reported from Abū Hurayrah that the Prophet ﷺ said,

'Someone who strives on behalf of widows and the poor is like someone who fights in the way of Allah and like someone who continually stands at night in prayer and like someone who continually fasts.' Ibn al-Mundhir said, 'Ṭāwus thought that looking after sisters was better than doing jihād in the Cause of Allah.'

and speak good words to people.

The sentence implies: 'Speak words which contain good for people' since *ḥusn* (good) is a verbal noun. Ḥamzah and al-Kisā'ī recited *ḥasan*. Al-Akhfash said that they mean the same. Ibn 'Abbās said that it means, 'Say to them: "There is no god but Allah" and instruct them to say it.' Ibn Jurayj said: 'Speak the truth to people about Muḥammad ﷺ and do not alter his description.' Sufyān ath-Thawrī said: 'Command them to what is known to be right and forbid them what is recognised as wrong.' Abu-l-'Āliyah said that it means: 'Speak good words to them and excuse them as you yourself would want to be excused.'

All of this encourages noble character. A person should be gentle when he speaks to people and maintain a cheerful face with both the pious and the impious, the one who holds to the *Sunnah* and even to the innovator, provided you do not flatter him or say anything which might appear to approve of his position. Allah Almighty said to Mūsā and Hārūn, *'Speak to him with gentle words.'* (20:44) No speakers could be better than Mūsā and Hārūn and no one impious could be worse than Pharaoh, and yet Allah commanded them to be gentle with him. Ṭalḥah ibn 'Umar said, 'I said to 'Aṭā', "You are a man with whom people from different sects meet and I am a man who tends to be sharp. I tell them some harsh home truths." He replied, "Do not do that! Allah says: *'Speak good words to people.'* The Jews and Christians are included in this *āyah*, so what about others?"' It is related that the Prophet ﷺ told 'Ā'ishah, 'Do not use obscenities. If obscenity had been a man, it would have been a bad man.'

It is said that *an-nās* (people) in this *āyah* refers to Muḥammad ﷺ as Allah says: *'Or do they in fact envy people for the bounty Allah has granted them.'"* (4:54) So it would mean: 'Speak good words to the Prophet.'

Al-Mahdawī related that Qatādah said that this verse was abrogated by the *Āyah* of the Sword. Ibn 'Abbās is reported as saying, 'This *āyah* was revealed at the beginning and then abrogated by the *Āyah* of the Sword.' Ibn 'Aṭiyyah said, 'This indicates that our Community was instructed to act like this at the beginning of Islam, but abrogated in respect of the tribe of Israel. Allah knows best.'

and establish the prayer and pay *zakāt*

This is directed to the tribe of Israel. Ibn 'Aṭiyyah said, 'Their *zakāt* used to be burned: a fire would descend and burn what was accepted and leave what was not accepted. So it was not like the *zakāt* of the nation of Muḥammad ﷺ.'

But then you turned away – except a few of you – you turned aside.

This is addressed to the Jews who were the contemporaries of Muḥammad ﷺ. The turning away done by their ancestors is ascribed to them since they also continued to do the same thing. The few who did not were men like 'Abdullāh ibn Sallām, who became Muslim. It is said that *tawallaytum* (turning away) is with the body and *mu'riḍūn* (turning aside) is with the heart.

وَإِذْ أَخَذْنَا مِيثَٰقَكُمْ لَا تَسْفِكُونَ دِمَآءَكُمْ وَلَا تُخْرِجُونَ أَنفُسَكُم مِّن
دِيَٰرِكُمْ ثُمَّ أَقْرَرْتُمْ وَأَنتُمْ تَشْهَدُونَ ۝٨٤

84 And when We made a covenant with you not to shed your own blood and not to expel yourselves from your homes, you agreed and were all witnesses.

It is the tribe of Israel which is being addressed here, but the meaning includes those after them. *Safk* (shedding) is pouring out. The word for self (*nafs*) is derived from *nafāsah* (preciousness), so the self of a person is the dearest thing he has. They agreed to this covenant which was made with them and their ancestors. Their hearts were witnesses to this covenant. Witnessing can also mean being present, so they witnessed the bloodshed and expulsion.

The Jews were a single religious community and so their affairs were unified and they were like a single individual. Therefore one of them killing another was like him killing himself. It is said that retaliation is meant here, commanding them not to kill someone so that they are killed in retaliation, so that it is as if they were shedding their own blood. The same applies to committing fornication or apostasy which would also entail their own deaths. Allah made a covenant with the tribe of Israel in the Torah not to kill each other or expel anyone or enslave him or let him be robbed and other such things. This was all forbidden to us as well but all those things occur in the trials we are experiencing. 'We belong to Allah and to Him we return!' The Revelation says: *'Or to confuse you into sects and make you taste one another's violence.'* (6:65).

Ibn Khuwayzimdād said that the meaning may be literal, commanding them not to commit suicide nor to be expelled from their houses through their own foolishness, nor for a man to kill himself through overwork or self-imposed affliction, nor to wander in the desert without seeking shelter in people's houses out of ignorance of religion and foolishness. It can be taken to apply to all those things. It is reported that 'Uthmān ibn Maz'ūn gave his allegiance along with ten others of the Prophet's Companions. They decided to wear ragged garments, wander in the desert, not take refuge in houses, or eat meat or go near women. The Prophet ﷺ heard about that and went to 'Uthmān's house but did not find him there. He asked his wife, 'What is this that we have heard about 'Uthmān?' She disliked to disclose her husband's secrets or to lie to the Prophet ﷺ, so she said, 'Messenger of Allah, if you have heard something, it is as you have heard it.' He said, 'Say to 'Uthmān from me: "Are you opposed to my *Sunnah* or following a religion other than mine? I pray and sleep, fast and break the fast, have intercourse with women, resort to houses and eat meat. Anyone who dislikes my *Sunnah* is not with me."' So 'Uthmān and his companions stopped doing what they were doing.

ثُمَّ أَنتُمْ هَٰؤُلَآءِ تَقْتُلُونَ أَنفُسَكُمْ وَتُخْرِجُونَ فَرِيقًا مِّنكُم مِّن
دِيَٰرِهِمْ تَظَّٰهَرُونَ عَلَيْهِم بِالْإِثْمِ وَالْعُدْوَٰنِ ۝ وَإِن يَأْتُوكُمْ أُسَٰرَىٰ
تَفْدُوهُمْ وَهُوَ مُحَرَّمٌ عَلَيْكُمْ إِخْرَاجُهُمْ أَفَتُؤْمِنُونَ بِبَعْضِ
الْكِتَٰبِ وَتَكْفُرُونَ بِبَعْضٍ فَمَا جَزَآءُ مَن يَفْعَلُ ذَٰلِكَ مِنكُمْ إِلَّا
خِزْيٌ فِي الْحَيَوٰةِ الدُّنْيَا وَيَوْمَ الْقِيَٰمَةِ يُرَدُّونَ إِلَىٰ أَشَدِّ الْعَذَابِ
وَمَا اللَّهُ بِغَٰفِلٍ عَمَّا يَعْمَلُونَ ۝٨٥

85 Then you are the people who are killing yourselves and expelling a group of you from their homes, ganging up against them in wrongdoing and enmity. Yet if they are brought to you as captives, you ransom them, when it was forbidden for you to expel them in the first place! Do you then, believe in one part of the Book and reject another? What repayment will there be for any of you who do that except disgrace in this world and on the Day of Rising, they will be returned to the harshest of punishments. Allah is not unaware of what they do.

أُولَٰئِكَ الَّذِينَ اشْتَرَوُا الْحَيَوٰةَ الدُّنْيَا بِالْآخِرَةِ فَلَا يُخَفَّفُ عَنْهُمُ
الْعَذَابُ وَلَا هُمْ يُنصَرُونَ ﴿٨٦﴾

86 Those are the people who trade the Next World for this world. The punishment will not be lightened for them. They will not be helped.

This *āyah* is addressed to some of the Jews who had attacked other Jews. It was revealed about the Jewish tribes of Qaynuqā' and an-Naḍīr. Qaynuqā' were the enemies of the Jewish tribe of Qurayẓah, and the Arab tribe of Aws were the allies of Qaynuqā' and the Arab tribe of Khazraj were the allies of Qurayẓah. So an-Naḍīr, Aws and Khazraj formed a brotherhood and Qurayẓah and an-Naḍīr also formed a brotherhood. Then they split up and fought. When the war ended, they ransomed their captives and that is what Allah is censuring here.

ganging up against them in wrongdoing and enmity.

Taẓẓāharūna (ganging up) means helping each other in wrongdoing. It is derived from the word *ẓahr* (back) because they strengthened one another like the back strengthens a person. *Ithm* (wrongdoing) is an action for which the one who does it deserves to be blamed. 'Enmity' (*'udwān*) is excess in injustice and overstepping the limits in it. The Madinans and Makkans read 'ganging up' as '*ta**ẓẓ**āharūna*', from *tataẓāhrūna* and the *tā'* is elided into the *ẓā'*, doubling it, while the Kufans read it as *'ta**ẓ**āharūna'* without the *shaddah.*

Yet if they are brought to you as captives, you ransom them, when it was forbidden for you to expel them in the first place!

The word for 'captive' (*asīr*) is derived from *isār* which is the leather thong by which a litter is secured and held in place. It is used for someone who is captured, whether or not he is physically bound. The majority recite *usārā* in the plural except for Ḥamzah who recites *asrā*. In the case of 'ransom', Nāfi', Ḥamzah and al-Kisā'ī recite *tu**fād**ūhum* while the rest recite *ta**fd**ūhu'*. It is derived from *fidyah,* which is demanding a ransom for captives.

Our scholars say that there are four clauses in the covenant: not to kill, not to expel, not to gang up against people, and the command to ransom captives. They turned away from all that they agreed to except for ransoming and so Allah rebuked them for that. That is why He asks: *'Do you, then, believe in one part of the Book,'* referring to the Torah, *'and reject another?'* (2:85)

By Allah, we ourselves, the Muslims, have turned from all good in the course of the troubles that have beset us and we too gang up against one another. Would that it was with other Muslims but in many cases it is with unbelievers! We leave our brothers in abasement and degradation under the rule of the idolaters when it is an obligation for all Muslims to fight to free them. There is no power or strength except by Allah, the Immense!

Our scholars say that it is obligatory to ransom captives even if not a single dirham is left. Ibn Khuwayzimandād said, 'This *āyah* contains the obligation to ransom captives. Confirming that are reports that the Prophet ﷺ ransomed captives and commanded that they be ransomed. That was what the Muslims did and there is a consensus regarding it.' It is obliged to ransom captives using money from the Treasury. If that is not possible, then it is a general obligation for the Muslims. When one of them does it, the obligation is cancelled for the rest.

وَلَقَدْ ءَاتَيْنَا مُوسَى ٱلْكِتَٰبَ وَقَفَّيْنَا مِنۢ بَعْدِهِۦ بِٱلرُّسُلِ وَءَاتَيْنَا
عِيسَى ٱبْنَ مَرْيَمَ ٱلْبَيِّنَٰتِ وَأَيَّدْنَٰهُ بِرُوحِ ٱلْقُدُسِ أَفَكُلَّمَا جَآءَكُمْ رَسُولٌۢ
بِمَا لَا تَهْوَىٰٓ أَنفُسُكُمُ ٱسْتَكْبَرْتُمْ فَفَرِيقًا كَذَّبْتُمْ وَفَرِيقًا تَقْتُلُونَ ﴿٨٧﴾

87 We gave Mūsā the Book and sent a succession of Messengers after him. We gave 'Īsā, son of Maryam, the Clear Signs and reinforced him with the Purest Rūḥ. Why then, whenever a Messenger came to you with something your lower selves did not desire, did you grow arrogant, and deny some of them and murder others?

We gave Mūsā the Book and sent a succession of Messengers after him.

The Book here is the Torah. The word used for '*sent a succession*' is derived from *qafā*, which means to come second, following in the tracks of the one that comes first, and, in this way, comes to mean following after. Every Messenger who came after Mūsā came affirming the Torah and the binding command up until 'Īsā.

We gave 'Īsā, son of Maryam, the Clear Signs and reinforced him with the Purest Rūḥ.

'The Clear Signs' are proofs and evidence. 'Reinforce' is to strengthen. The 'Purest *Rūḥ*' is said by Ibn 'Abbās and Qatādah to be Jibrīl. Ḥassān said:

Jibrīl is Allah's Messenger to us
and the Purest *Rūḥ*. It is not concealed.

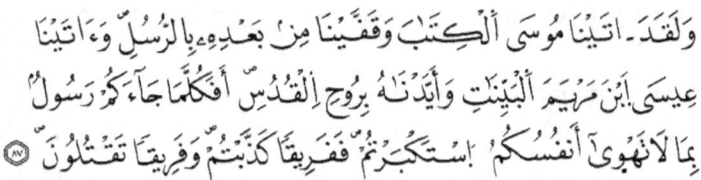

An-Naḥḥās said that Jibrīl is called a *rūḥ*, and purity is attributed to him, because Allah formed him as a *rūḥ* without any parent, which is why 'Īsā is also called a *rūḥ*. Ghālib ibn 'Abdullāh related that Mujāhid said, 'The Pure is Allah Almighty, as al-Ḥasan said, and the *Rūḥ* is Jibrīl.' Abū Rawq related from aḍ-Ḍaḥḥāk that Ibn 'Abbās said, 'The Purest *Rūḥ* is the name by which 'Īsā brought the dead to life.' Sa'īd ibn Jubayr and 'Ubayd ibn 'Umayr said that. It is the Greatest Name of Allah. It is said that what is meant is the Gospel which is here called *rūḥ* in the same way that Allah calls the Qur'an a *rūḥ* in His words: *'We have revealed to you a* Rūḥ *by Our command.'* (42:52) The first is more likely, and Allah knows best.

Why then, whenever a Messenger came to you with something your lower selves did not desire, did you grow arrogant!

'Why did you refuse to respond out of disdain for the Messengers and thinking the Message unlikely?' The root of *hawā* (desire) means 'to incline to something'. The plural is *ahwiyah*. Al-Jawharī said that it is called that because of the fact that it makes a person incline to the Fire and therefore it is only used for what is not true and has no good in it. This *āyah* shows that aspect of it but it can, in fact, also be used in a good sense, as we find in various hadiths.

deny some of them and murder others?

Among those they denied were 'Īsā and Muḥammad and among those they killed were Yaḥyā and Zakariyā.

وَقَالُوا۟ قُلُوبُنَا غُلْفٌۢ ۚ بَل لَّعَنَهُمُ ٱللَّهُ بِكُفْرِهِمْ فَقَلِيلًا مَّا يُؤْمِنُونَ ﴿٨٨﴾

88 They say, 'Our hearts are uncircumcised.' Rather, Allah has cursed them for their disbelief. What little belief they have!

They say, 'Our hearts are uncircumcised.'

'They' are the Jews again. 'Uncircumcised' means that they have a covering over them. It is similar to Allah's words: *'Our hearts are covered up against what you call us to.'* (41:5) 'Ikrimah said that there was a stamp on them. Linguists use this term for the sheathing of a sword. It means that their hearts are veiled from understanding and discrimination. Ibn 'Abbās said that the meaning is: 'Our hearts are filled with knowledge and we have no need of the knowledge of Muḥammad ﷺ or anyone else.' It is said that '*ghulf*' is the plural of *ghilāf*.

Rather, Allah has cursed them for their disbelief.

Allah refutes them. Allah makes it clear that the reason for their aversion to faith is that they have been cursed for their disbelief and defiance in earlier times. This is repaying wrong action with something worse than it. The root of '*la'n*' (curse) has the meaning of 'driving away and putting far away'. '*La'īn*' is used for a man who is an outcast and is also used for a wolf. This means that Allah has put them far from His mercy, or from His success and guidance, or from every good.

What little belief they have!

It is said that this can also mean, 'They believe only a little of what they have and reject most of it.' Al-Wāqidī said, 'They do not believe, whether a little or a lot.'

وَلَمَّا جَآءَهُمْ كِتَٰبٌ مِّنْ عِندِ ٱللَّهِ مُصَدِّقٌ لِّمَا مَعَهُمْ وَكَانُوا۟ مِن قَبْلُ
يَسْتَفْتِحُونَ عَلَى ٱلَّذِينَ كَفَرُوا۟ فَلَمَّا جَآءَهُم مَّا عَرَفُوا۟ كَفَرُوا۟ بِهِۦ
فَلَعْنَةُ ٱللَّهِ عَلَى ٱلْكَٰفِرِينَ ﴿٨٩﴾

89 When a Book does come to them from Allah, confirming what is with them – even though before that they were praying for victory over the unbelievers – yet when what they recognise does come to them, they reject it. Allah's curse is on the unbelievers.

'Them' means the Jews, and the 'Book' here is the Qur'an, while 'what is with them' refers to the Torah and Gospel. The word for 'praying for victory' here (*yastaftiḥūn*) comes from the root *fataḥa* and implies the opening of something which is locked, and is used, for instance, for the opening of a door. An-Nasā'ī reports that Abū Sa'īd al-Khudrī said that the Prophet ﷺ said, 'Allah gave victory to the community because of its weak members by means of their supplication, prayer and sincerity.' An-Nasā'ī also reports from Abu-d-Dardā' that the Messenger of Allah ﷺ said, 'Help me in seeking out the weak. They are supported. You are provided for on account of the weak among you.' Ibn 'Abbās reported that the Jews of Khaybar fought the tribe of Ghaṭafān and were defeated and so the Jews used this supplication, saying, 'We ask You by the right of the unlettered Prophet whom You promised to send us at the end of time to make us victorious against them.' They then defeated the tribe of Ghaṭafān. But when the Prophet was indeed sent, they rejected him and so Allah revealed this.

بِئْسَمَا اشْتَرَوْا بِهِۦٓ أَنفُسَهُمْ أَن يَكْفُرُوا بِمَآ أَنزَلَ اللَّهُ
بَغْيًا أَن يُنَزِّلَ اللَّهُ مِن فَضْلِهِۦ عَلَىٰ مَن يَشَآءُ مِنْ عِبَادِهِۦ فَبَآءُو بِغَضَبٍ
عَلَىٰ غَضَبٍ وَلِلْكَٰفِرِينَ عَذَابٌ مُّهِينٌ ﴿٩٠﴾

90 What an evil thing they have sold themselves for in rejecting what Allah has sent down, outraged that Allah should send down His favour on whichever of His slaves He wills. They have brought down anger upon anger on themselves. The unbelievers will have a humiliating punishment.

Outraged that Allah should send down His favour

The word '*bi's*' in Arabic conveys full censure as '*ni'm*' conveys full praise. The word '*baghyan*' (outraged) refers to their envy according to Qatādah and as-Suddī. Al-Asmā'ī said the same verb is used when a wound putrefies. It is said that its root meaning is connected with selling something, which is why a prostitute is called *baghī*. They were outraged that Allah sent down His favour on His Prophet ﷺ. Instead of *'yu**nazz**ilu'* (send down), Ibn Kathīr, Abū 'Amr, Ya'qūb and Ibn Muḥayṣin recite *'yu**nz**ilu'* (send down).

They have brought down anger upon anger on themselves.

The 'anger' referred to here is Divine punishment. It is said that the first anger is on account of their worship of the Calf and the second on account of their rejection of Muḥammad ﷺ. Ibn 'Abbās said that. 'Ikrimah said that it is because the Jews first rejected 'Īsā and then rejected Muḥammad. Qatādah also said that their first disbelief was by rejecting the Gospel and the second was by rejecting the Qur'an. Some people said that the word is repeated twice to stress the severity of what will happen to them.

The unbelievers will have a humiliating punishment.

The word *muhīn* (humiliating) is only used when referring to the punishment of unbelievers. The punishments which befall rebellious Muslims in this world and the Next are a purification for them.

وَإِذَا قِيلَ لَهُمْ ءَامِنُواْ بِمَآ أَنزَلَ اللَّهُ قَالُواْ نُومِنُ بِمَآ أُنزِلَ عَلَيْنَا
وَيَكْفُرُونَ بِمَا وَرَآءَهُۥ وَهُوَ الْحَقُّ مُصَدِّقًا لِّمَا مَعَهُمْ قُلْ فَلِمَ تَقْتُلُونَ
أَنۢبِئَآءَ اللَّهِ مِن قَبْلُ إِن كُنتُم مُّومِنِينَ ﴿٩١﴾

91 When they are told, 'Believe in what Allah has sent down,' they say, 'We believe in what was sent down to us,' and they reject anything beyond that, even though it is the truth, confirming what they have. Say, 'Why then, if you are believers, did you previously kill the Prophets of Allah?'

When they are told, 'Believe in what Allah has sent down,' they say, 'We believe in what was sent down to us,'

'What Allah has sent down' refers here to the Qur'an. What was sent down to them was the Torah. Al-Farrā' said that they reject anything other than it. Qatādah said that they reject anything after it as Abū 'Ubayd said. The meaning is the same. Al-Jawharī said that *warā* means 'after'. The word can also mean 'before', being one of the words that can have opposite meanings.

Why then, if you are believers, did you previously kill the Prophets of Allah?

Allah refutes their claim that they believe in what was revealed to them. He says that they are lying and rebukes them by asking them why, in that case, did they kill the Prophets when that was forbidden in their Book? It is addressed to those Jews who were present with Muḥammad ﷺ while their ancestors are meant. It is said to their descendants because they have continued on the same path.

وَلَقَدْ جَآءَكُم مُّوسيٰ بِالْبَيِّنَٰتِ ثُمَّ اتَّخَذتُّمُ الْعِجْلَ مِنۢ بَعْدِهِۦ
وَأَنتُمْ ظَٰلِمُونَ ﴿٩٢﴾

92 Mūsā brought you the Clear Signs; then, after he left, you adopted the Calf and were wrongdoers.

Reference to 'the Clear Signs' of Mūsā can be found in Allah's words: *'We gave Mūsā seven clear signs.'* (17:101) They were: the staff, the drought, the white hand, the blood, the plague, the locusts, the lice, the frogs and the splitting of the sea. It is said that the expression 'Clear Signs' refers to the Torah and the evidence it contains. The use of the word 'then' indicates that they did this after receiving the Signs, which makes their wrong action all the worse.

وَإِذْ أَخَذْنَا مِيثَٰقَكُمْ وَرَفَعْنَا فَوْقَكُمُ ٱلطُّورَ خُذُوا۟ مَآ ءَاتَيْنَٰكُم
بِقُوَّةٍ وَٱسْمَعُوا۟ ۖ قَالُوا۟ سَمِعْنَا وَعَصَيْنَا وَأُشْرِبُوا۟ فِى قُلُوبِهِمُ ٱلْعِجْلَ
بِكُفْرِهِمْ ۚ قُلْ بِئْسَمَا يَأْمُرُكُم بِهِۦٓ إِيمَٰنُكُمْ إِن كُنتُم
مُّؤْمِنِينَ ﴿٩٣﴾

93 Remember when We made a covenant with you and lifted up the Mount above your heads: 'Take hold vigorously of what We have given you and listen.' They said, 'We hear and disobey.' They were made to drink the Calf into their hearts because of their disbelief. Say, 'If you are believers, what an evil thing your faith has made you do.'

The first part of this *āyah* has been discussed previously in the commentary on 2:63 above.

They said, 'We hear and disobey.'

There is disagreement about whether this was the actual words they used or whether they did an action which took the place of the words, and so it was metaphorical.

They were made to drink the Calf into their hearts because of their disbelief.

In other words love of the Golden Calf penetrated them. It means that their hearts imbibed it. It is a metaphor because the whole matter of the Calf had become firm in their hearts. We read in a hadith, 'Seditions will be presented to the hearts like a mat, reed by reed. A black spot is formed in the heart of anyone who is made to drink them.' Muslim transmitted it. Their love of the Calf is referred to as drinking rather than eating because drinking something makes it penetrate right through the whole of the body.

As-Suddī and Ibn Jurayj said that Mūsā filed down the Calf and put it in water and told the tribe of Israel to drink that water. They all drank it and those who loved the Calf had gold filings on their lips. His scattering into the sea is indicated by His words: *'Then we will scatter it as dust into the sea.'* (20:97) Their drinking it and its showing on their lips is refuted by His words: *'They were made to drink the Calf into their hearts.'*

Say, 'If you are believers, what an evil thing your faith has made you do.'

The faith referred to is that which they claimed by their words, 'We believe in what was sent down to us.' It is said that these words were addressed to the Prophet ﷺ and he was commanded to rebuke them. So it means, 'Muḥammad, tell them that what they were doing is evil.'

قُلْ إِن كَانَتْ لَكُمُ الدَّارُ الْآخِرَةُ عِندَ اللَّهِ خَالِصَةً مِّن دُونِ
النَّاسِ فَتَمَنَّوُا الْمَوْتَ إِن كُنتُمْ صَادِقِينَ ﴿٩٤﴾

94 Say, 'If the abode of the Next World with Allah is for you alone, to the exclusion of all others, then long for death if you are telling the truth.

وَلَن يَتَمَنَّوْهُ أَبَدًا بِمَا قَدَّمَتْ أَيْدِيهِمْ وَاللَّهُ عَلِيمٌ بِالظَّالِمِينَ ﴿٩٥﴾

95 But they will never ever long for it because of what they have done. Allah knows the wrongdoers.

When the Jews made their various false claims, as Allah reports from them in His Book, such as: *'The Fire will only touch us for a number of days'* (2:80), and *'No one will enter the Garden except for Jews and Christians'* (2:111), Allah told His Prophet ﷺ what to say to them. They were told to wish for death, because if someone really believes that he is one of the people of the Garden he will prefer death to life in this world, since he will obtain the bliss of the Garden and the difficulties of this world will be removed from him by it. But they shrank from doing that, out of fear of Allah, because of the terrible things they had done, thus demonstrating that they did not really believe what they said and indicating their greed for this world. If they had truly longed for death they would have died, as is related from the Prophet ﷺ when he said, 'If the Jews had really longed for death, they would have died and seen their place in the Fire.' It is said that Allah kept them from longing for it so as to make that a Sign for His Prophet ﷺ. These are all aspects of the fact that they did not long for death as they claimed. It is related by 'Ikrimah from Ibn 'Abbās that what is meant is: 'Wish for death for the party which is lying: you or us.' They did not do so because they knew that they were lying.

The observation may be made that longing can be expressed with the tongue or with the heart, and so how is it known that they did not wish for it in their hearts? The reply to that is that the Qur'an stated that when Allah says: *'they will never ever long for it.'* If they had wished for it in their hearts, it would have appeared on their tongues so that they could refute the Prophet ﷺ and invalidate his argument. This is clear.

وَلَتَجِدَنَّهُمْ أَحْرَصَ ٱلنَّاسِ عَلَىٰ حَيَوٰةٍ وَمِنَ ٱلَّذِينَ أَشْرَكُوا۟ يَوَدُّ أَحَدُهُمْ لَوْ يُعَمَّرُ أَلْفَ سَنَةٍ وَمَا هُوَ بِمُزَحْزِحِهِۦ مِنَ ٱلْعَذَابِ أَن يُعَمَّرَ وَٱللَّهُ بَصِيرٌۢ بِمَا يَعْمَلُونَ ﴿٩٦﴾

96 Rather you will find them the people greediest for life, along with the idolaters. One of them would love to be allowed to live a thousand years. But being allowed to live would not save him from the punishment. Allah sees what they do.

It is said that this refers to the Jews and it is said that the words about them stop at 'life'. The Arab idolaters only knew this life and had no knowledge of the Hereafter. So then what is referred to is another group of idolaters, namely the Magians. That is clear in that they say to someone who sneezes, 'Live a thousand years!' They believed that to be the extent that their reckoning would last. Al-Ḥasan believes that it refers to the Arab idolaters because they did not believe in the resurrection after death and hoped for a long life.

Allah sees what they do.

Allah sees those who wish to live a thousand years. '***Ya***'*malūn*' (they do) is also read '***ta***'*malūn*' (you do). Those who recite the second say that it implies: 'Tell them, Muḥammad, that Allah sees what they do.' Scholars say that Allah describes Himself as knowing hidden matters. The word '*baṣīr*' (see) in Arabic also means 'to know something' and be aware of it. You could use it for someone who has knowledge of medicine (*baṣīr bi 't-ṭibb*) or *fiqh*. Al-Khaṭṭābī said that Allah knows and sees. It is also said that the phrase means that Allah makes the things we do visible by creating the faculty of seeing and perception, so Allah gives His servant sight.

قُلْ مَن كَانَ عَدُوًّا لِّجِبْرِيلَ فَإِنَّهُۥ نَزَّلَهُۥ عَلَىٰ قَلْبِكَ بِإِذْنِ ٱللَّهِ مُصَدِّقًا لِّمَا بَيْنَ يَدَيْهِ وَهُدًى وَبُشْرَىٰ لِلْمُؤْمِنِينَ ﴿٩٧﴾

97 Say, 'Anyone who is the enemy of Jibrīl should know that it was he who brought it down upon your heart, by Allah's authority, confirming what came before, and as guidance and good news for the believers.

The reason for the revelation of this *āyah* is that the Jews said to the Prophet ﷺ, 'Every Prophet has one of the angels bring him the Message and Revelation from His Lord. Who is your companion so that we might follow you?' 'Jibrīl,' he replied. They said. 'That is the one who brings war and fighting. He is our enemy! If you had said Mīkā'īl, who brings down the rain and mercy, we would have followed you.' So Allah revealed this. At-Tirmidhī transmitted it. There are two possibilities for the second pronoun 'it' which might also be read as 'he'. It might possibly mean: 'Allah sent down Jibrīl to your heart' or, more likely, 'Jibrīl brought down the Qur'an to your heart.' The heart is mentioned because it is the locus of the intellect and knowledge and accepts gnosis. The *āyah* indicates the nobility of Jibrīl and censures his enemies. 'Allah's authority' is His will and knowledge. 'What came before' is the Torah.

مَن كَانَ عَدُوًّا لِّلَّهِ وَمَلَٰٓئِكَتِهِۦ وَرُسُلِهِۦ وَجِبْرِيلَ وَمِيكَىٰلَ
فَإِنَّ ٱللَّهَ عَدُوٌّ لِّلْكَٰفِرِينَ ۝٩٨

98 Anyone who is the enemy of Allah and of His angels, and of His Messengers and of Jibrīl and Mīkā'īl, should know that Allah is the enemy of the unbelievers.'

This is a threat and rebuke to the enemies of Jibrīl and is an announcement that enmity towards some results in Allah's enmity towards those who show it. The enmity of the slave of Allah is shown by his disobedience to Allah, his failure to obey Him, and enmity towards His friends. Allah's enmity to the slave is shown by punishing him and by the effects of enmity on him.

If it is asked why Allah singled out Jibrīl and Mīkā'īl for mention when they have already been included under the general category of 'angels', the reply is that they are singled out for mention in order to honour them. It is also said that they are singled out because the Jews had mentioned the two of them and they were the cause of the *āyah* being revealed.

Various things are said by linguists about these two names. The forms given for Jibrīl's name are: Jibrīl, which is the Ḥijāzī form, Jabrā'īl, Jabra'il, Jibriyil, Jabr'īn, Jibrīn. The forms for Mīkā'il are: Mīkā'il (as Nāfi' has it), Mīkā'īl, Mīkāl (Ḥijāzī), Mīk'īl, Mīkāyil, and Mīkā'al.

Ibn 'Abbās says that *jabr* means 'slave' and *mīkā* means 'owned'. *Īl* is the Name of Allah, thus both names mean 'slave of Allah'.

وَلَقَدْ أَنزَلْنَآ إِلَيْكَ ءَايَٰتٍۭ بَيِّنَٰتٍ وَمَا يَكْفُرُ بِهَآ إِلَّا ٱلْفَٰسِقُونَ ﴿٩٩﴾

99 We have sent down Clear Signs to you and no one rejects them except the deviators.

Ibn 'Abbās said that this is the reply to Ibn Ṣūriyā when he said to the Prophet ﷺ, 'Muhammad, you have not brought us anything which accords with our knowledge and no clear sign has been sent down to you for us to follow.' Then this *āyah* was revealed.

أَوَكُلَّمَا عَٰهَدُوا۟ عَهْدًا نَّبَذَهُۥ فَرِيقٌ مِّنْهُم بَلْ أَكْثَرُهُمْ لَا يُؤْمِنُونَ ﴿١٠٠﴾

100 Why is it that, whenever they make a contract, a group of them disdainfully tosses it aside? No indeed! Most of them do not believe.

The Jews had made a contract that they would believe in Muḥammad when he was sent and would side with him against the Arab idolaters. Then when he was sent, they rejected him. 'Aṭā' says that the *āyah* refers to the agreements which the Prophet ﷺ made with the Jews which they subsequently broke.

وَلَمَّا جَآءَهُمْ رَسُولٌ مِّنْ عِندِ ٱللَّهِ مُصَدِّقٌ لِّمَا مَعَهُمْ نَبَذَ فَرِيقٌ
مِّنَ ٱلَّذِينَ أُوتُوا۟ ٱلْكِتَٰبَ كِتَٰبَ ٱللَّهِ وَرَآءَ ظُهُورِهِمْ كَأَنَّهُمْ
لَا يَعْلَمُونَ ﴿١٠١﴾

101 When a Messenger comes to them from Allah confirming what is with them, a group of those who have been given the Book disdainfully toss the Book of Allah behind their backs, just as if they did not know.

They tossed it behind them by rejecting the Messenger. As-Suddī said, 'They cast aside the Torah and adopted the book of Āṣaf and the magic of Hārūt and Mārūt.' It is said that it can refer to the Qur'an. Ash-Sha'bī said that they used to read it but rejected acting by it. Sufyān ibn 'Uyaynah said, 'They covered the Book in silk and brocade and adorned it with gold and silver but did not make lawful what it made lawful or unlawful what it made unlawful.'

وَٱتَّبَعُوا۟ مَا تَتْلُوا۟ ٱلشَّيَـٰطِينُ عَلَىٰ مُلْكِ سُلَيْمَـٰنَ ۖ وَمَا كَفَرَ سُلَيْمَـٰنُ
وَلَـٰكِنَّ ٱلشَّيَـٰطِينَ كَفَرُوا۟ يُعَلِّمُونَ ٱلنَّاسَ ٱلسِّحْرَ وَمَآ أُنزِلَ
عَلَى ٱلْمَلَكَيْنِ بِبَابِلَ هَـٰرُوتَ وَمَـٰرُوتَ ۚ وَمَا يُعَلِّمَانِ مِنْ أَحَدٍ
حَتَّىٰ يَقُولَآ إِنَّمَا نَحْنُ فِتْنَةٌ فَلَا تَكْفُرْ ۖ فَيَتَعَلَّمُونَ مِنْهُمَا مَا يُفَرِّقُونَ
بِهِۦ بَيْنَ ٱلْمَرْءِ وَزَوْجِهِۦ ۚ وَمَا هُم بِضَآرِّينَ بِهِۦ مِنْ أَحَدٍ إِلَّا بِإِذْنِ ٱللَّهِ ۚ
وَيَتَعَلَّمُونَ مَا يَضُرُّهُمْ وَلَا يَنفَعُهُمْ ۚ وَلَقَدْ عَلِمُوا۟ لَمَنِ ٱشْتَرَىٰهُ
مَا لَهُۥ فِى ٱلْـَٔاخِرَةِ مِنْ خَلَـٰقٍ ۚ وَلَبِئْسَ مَا شَرَوْا۟ بِهِۦٓ أَنفُسَهُمْ ۚ
لَوْ كَانُوا۟ يَعْلَمُونَ ﴿١٠٢﴾

102 They follow what the shayṭāns recited in the reign of Sulaymān. Sulaymān did not disbelieve, but the shayṭāns did, teaching people sorcery and what had been sent down to Hārūt and Mārūt, the two angels in Babylon, who taught no one without first saying to him, 'We are merely a trial and temptation, so do not disbelieve.' People learned from them how to separate a man and his wife but they cannot harm anyone by it, except with Allah's permission. They have learned what will harm them and will not benefit them. They know that any who deal in it will have no share in the Next World. What an evil thing they have sold themselves for if they only knew!

They follow what the shayṭāns recited in the reign of Sulaymān.

Allah here reports about the group who discarded the Book by pursuing magic. They were the Jews. As-Suddī said, 'The Jews opposed Muhammad ﷺ but the Torah and the Qur'an spoke in one voice, so they discarded the Torah and adopted the book of Āsaf and the magic of Hārūt and Mārūt.'

Muḥammad ibn Isḥāq said, 'When the Messenger of Allah ﷺ mentioned Sulaymān as one of the Messengers, some of the rabbis said, "Muḥammad claims that the son of Dāwūd was a Prophet! By Allah, he was nothing but a sorcerer!" Then Allah revealed: *"Sulaymān did not disbelieve, but the shayṭāns did."* This means that the rabbis told people that what Sulaymān did with respect to riding the seas and subjugating the birds and jinn was magic.'

Al-Kalbī said, 'The shayṭāns wrote magic and necromancy as dictated by Āsaf, the scribe of Sulaymān during the time when Allah had removed his kingdom from him, and they buried what they wrote in the place where Sulaymān prayed. Sulaymān was not aware of this. When Sulaymān died, they unearthed the books and told people, "He ruled you by this, so learn it." The scholars of the tribe of Israel said, "We seek refuge with Allah from this being the knowledge of Sulaymān!" whereas the fools accepted that it was and learned it and discarded the books of their Prophets until Muḥammad ﷺ was sent. Then Allah revealed Sulaymān's innocence of the accusation they made.'

'Aṭā' said that '*ittaba'ū*' (follow) in this *āyah* means 'read' while Ibn 'Abbās says that it actually means 'follow'. Aṭ-Ṭabarī said that it means 'prefer' since they preferred it to other things.

'In the reign' (*mulk*) means during the time of his Sharī'ah and Prophethood. Az-Zajjāj said that al-Farrā' said that it means during the time of his reign. It is said that it means during his kingship and so it is about his stories, qualities and reports. The shayṭāns here are said to be shayṭāns of the jinn. When shayṭān is used for a human being, it refers to someone who is obdurate in misguidance.

Sulaymān did not disbelieve but the shayṭāns did,

This declares his innocence. Although they did not explicitly accuse him of disbelief, the Jews accused him of magic and, since magic entails disbelief, they were, in fact, ascribing disbelief to him. The disbelief of the shayṭāns is established because they taught magic.

teaching people sorcery

The root meaning of '*siḥr*' (sorcery) is distortion and producing illusions. It happens when a sorcerer does something and the person under the spell imagines something to be different from what it is. This resembles a mirage which someone sees and imagines to be water or someone on a ship who imagines that the trees and mountains are travelling with him. It is said to be derived from diverting a child when he is tricked. Allah says: *'You are merely someone bewitched* (musaḥḥarīn)' (26:153), i.e. shaped with magic. It is said that the root of *siḥr* is 'concealment', because a sorcerer does it in concealment. It is also said that its root is 'diversion', since it diverts a person from what is really happening. Its root is also said to be 'enticement' and all that entices and bewitches you. Al-Jawharī said that spells and charms and anything whose means are subtle in that way can be called sorcery.

There is disagreement about whether it is real or not. The Mu'tazilites say that it is simply deceit and has no basis in reality. Ash-Shāfi'ī says that it is whispering and illness. He said, 'We think that its function is talismanic and is based on the effect of the particular qualities of the stars or by the shayṭāns making things easy which were difficult.'

We believe that it is true and that it has a reality and that Allah creates through it whatever He wishes, as will be explained. There is also a kind of magic which is merely sleight of hand and legerdemain. Another aspect is spells. Another aspect is words which are memorised and talismans which use the Names of Allah. That may also be part of the work of shayṭāns, or medicines and fumes and other things.

The Messenger of Allah ﷺ called eloquence in speech sorcery. He said, 'Some kinds of eloquence are sorcery.' Mālik and others transmitted it. That is because they make the false seem credible so that the listener imagines it to be true. That statement is said, by some, to imply censure and by and by others to imply praise. Censure is more likely, because a person may obtain something which is not rightfully his by means of it.

Another kind of sorcery is the sort whose perpetration makes the one who does it an unbeliever. This includes such claims as changing the forms of people and transforming them into animals, going on a month's journey in a single night, flying through the air and other such things. If anyone does that so that people will imagine that it is true, that turns him into an unbeliever. Abū 'Amr said, 'If anyone claims to be a sorcerer who can change animals from one form to another, or turn a person into a donkey and the like, and to have the power to transform bodies and destroy and alter them, this is someone who should be killed because he rejects the Prophets, laying claim to Prophethood himself, since he tries, by the use of trickery, to perform the same feats as them. As for the one who admits that his magic is simply deceit, distortion and illusions, he is not killed unless he does something else for which the punishment is death.'

Sunnīs believe that sorcery is real. Most Mu'tazilites and some Shāfi'īs believe that it is baseless and is only distortion and illusion so that a thing is made to appear other than what it is. They say that it is a sort of legerdemain, as Allah says: *'they appeared to him, by their magic, to be slithering around.'* (20:66) He did not say that it was real, but that it appeared so. This is not evidence because we do not deny that illusion-making is part of magic but other matters are confirmed which defy explanation. If magic did not have a reality, it would not be possible to teach it and the fact that Allah mentioned them teaching it indicates that it is real.

Allah says that the sorcerers *'produced an extremely powerful magic'* (7:116) and scholars agree that *Sūrat al-Falaq* was revealed because of the magic of Labīd ibn al-Aṣamm. That is reported in al-Bukhārī and Muslim. When the spell was removed, the Prophet ﷺ said, 'Allah healed me.' Healing only occurs by removing an illness. So both Allah and the Prophet have reported that it is real. We find no denial of its existence among the Companions or the Tābi'ūn. There is a consensus regarding it. Sufyān related from Abu-l-A'war from 'Ikrimah that Ibn 'Abbās said, 'Magic was taught in one of the towns of Egypt called Farama.' Anyone who denies it is unbeliever who denies Allah and His Messenger.

Our scholars say that it is not denied that breaking of normal patterns occurs through sorcerers and that, although it is not in the normal power of a human being to cause illness, separation, madness, paralysis of a limb and other things, it is, nevertheless, a human possibility. It is, however, Allah who creates these things when the magic takes place, just as He creates fullness after eating and quenching of thirst through drinking.

Muslims agree that there was no magic involved in what Allah did in relation to the locusts, lice, frogs, splitting the sea, the transformation of the staff, bringing the dead to life and other such signs of the Prophets. Our scholars said that the difference between magic and a Prophetic miracle is that magic can exist with a sorcerer or someone else and a group of people can know it and can do it at the same time, whereas Allah does not give anyone but His Prophet the power to perform a miracle. A sorcerer cannot claim to be a Prophet and what he does is not a miracle. A miracle must be accompanied by a true claim to Prophethood and the challenge to imitate it.

Fuqahā' differ about the ruling of a Muslim and *dhimmī* sorcerer. Mālik believed that when a Muslim does magic with words which constitute disbelief, he should be killed and not asked to repent. Even if he were asked to repent, his repentance would not be accepted because he would conceal his sorcery like a heretic or fornicator, and because Allah Himself called sorcery disbelief. Ibn Ḥanbal, Abū Thawr, Isḥāq, ash-Shāfi'ī and Abū Ḥanīfah also said that. The execution of sorcerers is reported from 'Umar, 'Uthmān, Ibn 'Umar, Hafsah, Abū Mūsā, Qays ibn Sa'd and seven Tābi'ūn. It is related that the Prophet ﷺ said, 'The *ḥadd* punishment for a sorcerer is to be struck with the sword.' At-Tirmidhī transmitted it, but it is not strong. Only Ismā'īl ibn Muslim has it and they consider him to be weak. Ibn al-Mundhir related that. It is related that 'Ā'ishah sold a witch who had used magic on her and used the price to free slaves.

Ibn al-Mundhir said, 'When a man admits that he did magic with words which constitute disbelief, then he must be killed, even if he repents. The same applies if there is clear evidence against him. If the words that he used in his magic are not tantamount to disbelief, it is not permitted to kill him. If he deliberately inflicts an injury on the person who has been subjected to his sorcery, retaliation is obliged. If there is no retaliation for it, there is blood money.'

Ibn al-Mundhir also said, 'When the Companions of the Messenger of Allah ﷺ disagree about something, we are obliged to follow the view which is closest to the Book and the Sunnah. It is possible that the magic for which some of them commanded the sorcerer to be executed did indeed constitute disbelief and this corresponds to the Sunnah of the Messenger of Allah ﷺ. It is also possible that the magic of the witch whom 'Ā'ishah sold did not actually constitute disbelief. If the hadith about killing sorcerers is sound, then it is only possible when the magic of the sorcerer amounts to disbelief, and so that is in keeping with what is reported from the Prophet ﷺ: "A Muslim's blood is only lawful by one of three things…"'

This is true. The blood of Muslims is protected and only allowed when there is certainty, and when there is disagreement there is no certainty, Allah knows best. Some scholars say that magic can only be performed through disbelief and arrogance or by esteeming Shayṭān and thus sorcery is evidence of disbelief. Allah knows best. It is related that ash-Shāfi'ī said, 'A sorcerer is not killed unless he kills by his magic and says that it was deliberate. If he does not say it was deliberate, he is not killed but pays blood money for accidental homicide. If he causes harm, he is punished according to the extent of harm he caused.' Ibn al-'Arabī said that this is false for two reasons. One is that he does not know the reality of magic which, in fact, consists of formulae which revere things other than Allah to which powers and entities are ascribed. The second is that Allah clearly states in His book that the shayṭāns disbelieved.

The Mālikīs argue that a sorcerer's repentance is not accepted because sorcery is something hidden and not shown and so his repentance cannot be relied on. The person who is asked to repent is someone who openly apostatises. Mālik said that if a sorcerer or heretic repents before there is testimony against him, his repentance is accepted. His proof is the words of Allah: *'But when they saw Our violent force, their faith was of no use to them.'* (40:85) This indicates that their faith is of use to them before the punishment arrives. This is the same.

It is said that a *dhimmī* sorcerer is killed, but Mālik said that he is not killed unless he kills and that he is liable for injuries caused. He is killed if he does something not part of his *dhimmah* treaty. Ibn Khuzayimandād said, 'There are differing transmissions from Mālik about a *dhimmī*. Sometimes he said that he is asked to repent and his repentance consists of becoming Muslim. Sometimes he said that he is killed even if he becomes Muslim. Someone from the Abode of War is not killed when he repents. That is also what Mālik said about a *dhimmī* who insults the Prophet ﷺ: he is asked to repent and his repentance consists of becoming Muslim. Sometimes he said that he is killed and not asked to repent, as is the case with a Muslim. Mālik also said that a *dhimmī* who does sorcery is punished unless he kills someone with his sorcery or causes some event and he is punished accordingly for it. Others said that he is killed because he has broken the treaty.' The heirs of a sorcerer do not inherit from him because he is an unbeliever unless his sorcery is not called disbelief. Mālik said that a woman who makes her husband impotent with respect to herself or another by the magical use of knots is punished and not killed.

They disagree about whether a sorcerer is asked to undo his magic from the person bewitched. Sa'īd ibn al-Musayyab permitted it, according to what al-Bukhārī mentioned. Al-Muzanī inclined to that, but al-Ḥasan al-Baṣrī disliked it. Ash-Sha'bī said that there is no harm in amulet charms. Ibn Baṭṭāl said, 'We find in the letter of Wahb ibn Munabbih that one should take seven leaves from a lote-tree, crush them between two stones, mix them with water and then over that recite the Throne Verse. Then take three sips from it and wash the body with it. It will remove what he is afflicted by, Allah willing. It is good for a man prevented from having sex with his wife [because of magic].'

Most Mu'tazilites deny the existence of shayṭāns and the jinn. This indicates their weakness because not only is it not logically impossible to affirm their existence but also the texts of the Book and the *Sunnah* indicate their existence. An intelligent person who clings to the rope of Allah must accept things which are beyond normal experience when there is a text stating that they exist. Allah says: '*the shayṭāns disbelieved*' and He also mentions them elsewhere and the Prophet ﷺ mentioned them and therefore they must exist.

and what (*mā*) had been sent down to Hārūt and Mārūt, the two angels in Babylon,

'*Mā*' means negation [i.e. '*and it was not sent down to the two angels*'] and that is conjoined to '*Sulaymān did not (*mā*) disbelieve.*' That is mentioned because the Jews said the two angels (*malakayn*) that Allah sent with magic were Jibrīl and Mīkā'īl. Allah denies that. 'Hārūt and Mārūt' are an appositive for the earlier 'shayṭāns'. This is the most fitting interpretation of the *āyah*. It is the soundest of what is said about them and one pays no attention to another interpretation. Sorcery comes from the shayṭāns because of the subtleness of their essence and their trivial understanding. It is mostly women who practise it. Allah refers to them when He says: '*women who blow on knots.*' (113:4)

And it also said that '*mā*' is conjoined to the magic [i.e. '*teaching people magic and what had been sent down to Hārūt and Mārūt, the two angels in Babylon*']. Anyway it is clear that Allah sent down magic to the angels as a test for people. Allah tests His slaves in whatever way He wishes. This is why the angels said, 'We are merely a trial. We inform you that the act of sorcery is disbelief. If you obey us, you will be saved. If you disobey, you will be destroyed.'

It is related from 'Alī, Ibn Mas'ūd, Ibn 'Abbās, Ibn 'Umar, Ka'b al-Aḥbār, as-Suddī and al-Kalbī that when there was a lot of corruption among the descendants of Ādam in the time of Idrīs, the angels condemned them. Allah Almighty said, 'If you had been in their position and been formed as they are formed, you would have acted as they have acted.' They answered, 'Glory be to You! It is not fitting for us to do that!' He said, 'Then choose two angels from the best of you.' They chose Hārūt and Mārūt. He sent them down to earth and inserted lust in them. Not a month had passed before they were tempted by a woman called 'Bīdakht' in Nabatean, 'Nāhīl' in Persian and 'az-Zuhrah' in Arabic. They argued about her and tried to seduce her. She refused unless they entered her religion, drank wine, and killed a soul whom Allah had made inviolable. They agreed to what she wanted and drank wine and had sex with her. A man saw them and they killed him. She asked them about the Name by which they ascended to heaven and they taught it to her. She spoke it, ascended and was transformed into a star.

Sālim reported from his father from 'Abdullāh that Ka'b related that the day had not ended before they had committed what Allah had forbidden them. According to another hadith, they were given a choice between the punishment of this world and the punishment of the Next World and they chose the punishment of this world. So they are punished at Bablyon in an underground passage. It is said that it is the Babylon in Iraq and it is also said that it is the one at Nihawand. 'Aṭā' related from Ibn 'Umar that when he saw Venus (Zuhrah) and Suhayl, he cursed and reviled them and said, 'Suhayl was a tax-collector in Yemen who wronged people and az-Zuhrah was the woman of Hārūt and Mārūt.'

All of this is weak and nothing to do with Ibn 'Umar and others. None of it is sound. It is a view refuted by the basic principles of the angels who are the guardians Allah assigned over His Revelation and His emissaries to His Messengers: *'They do not disobey Allah in respect of any order He gives them and carry out what they are ordered to do.'* (66:6) *'They do not precede Him in speech and they act on His command.'* (21:27) *'They glorify Him by night and day, without ever flagging.'* (21:20) Logically, it is not denied that disobedience could occur from the angels, the opposite of what they are obliged exist in them, and lust created in them, since everything imaginable is within Allah's power. This is the source of the fear of the Prophets, *awliyā'*, and excellent scholars. But the occurrence of this permissible matter is only perceived by report, and it is not sound.

Part of what indicates the fact that it is not sound is that Allah created the stars and the planets when He created the heavens. We read in a report: 'When heaven was created, He created in it seven orbits: Saturn, Jupiter, Mars, Mercury, Venus, the sun and the moon.' This is the meaning of His words: *'each one swimming in a sphere'*. (21:33) This confirms that Venus and Suhayl existed before the creation of Ādam. The words of the angels, 'It is not fitting for us to do that!' would mean: 'You are not able to tempt us.' This is unbelief. We seek refuge with Allah from it and from ascribing it to the noble angels, may Allah bless them all! We declare them free from that and they are free from what the commentators mentioned. Glory be to Allah, your Lord, the Lord of Might, from what they describe!

Ibn 'Abbās, Ibn Abzā, aḍ-Ḍaḥḥāk and al-Ḥasan read the word as *malikayn*, which means two kings, and take it as referring to Dāwūd and Sulaymān. This is weak as Ibn al-'Arabī stated. Al-Ḥasan said that they were two louts at Babylon who were kings. Bābil (Babylon) is a region in the earth. It is said to be Iraq and the surrounding area. Ibn Mas'ūd said to the people of Kufa, 'You are between Hira and Babylon.' Qatādah said, 'It extends from Nineveh to Ra's al-'Ayn.' Some people said that it is in Morocco, which Ibn 'Aṭiyyah says is weak. Some people said that it is the mountain of Nineveh. Allah knows best.

There is disagreement about why it is called 'Bābil'. It is said that 'Babel' is called that because of the 'babble' of languages when the tower of Nimrod fell. It is said that it is called that because when Allah Almighty wanted to make the sons of Ādam have different languages, he sent a wind that gathered them from the far corners of the earth to Babel and then Allah confounded their language there and then that wind separated them into lands. *Balbalah* is separation. Al-Khalīl said something to that effect. Abū 'Umar ibn 'Abd al-Barr said, 'One of the most concise and best things said about *balbalah* is what Abū Dāwūd ibn Abī Hind related from 'Ilbā' ibn Aḥmar from 'Ikrimah from Ibn 'Abbās that when Nūḥ descended from al-Jūdī, he built a city called Thamānīn ('Eighty') and on the day when tongues were confounded, there were eighty languages, one of which was Arabic. The people did not understand one another.'

'Abdullāh ibn Bishr al-Mazinī related that the Messenger of Allah ﷺ said, 'Fear this world. By the One who has my soul in His hand, it has more sorcery in it than Hārūt and Mārūt.' Our scholars say that this world has more sorcery than both of them because it bewitches you by deceiving you. Its temptation is concealed and it leads you to compete in greed for it, to amass it and deny it to others until it comes between you and obedience to Allah and comes between you and seeing the truth and observing it. Therefore this world is more enthralling than them. It takes your heart away from Allah, from establishing His right and from the promise and the threat. The sorcery of this world is love of it, enjoying its appetites and being deluded by its false hopes until it takes hold of your heart. That is why the Messenger of Allah ﷺ said, 'Love of a thing makes one blind and deaf.'

who taught no one without first saying to him, 'We are merely a trial and temptation, so do not disbelieve.'

'Alī is reported as saying that the angels taught people by warning them against magic, but that does not mean that they were inviting them to it. Az-Zajjāj says, 'This is the position held by most of the people with expertise in language and investigation. It means that they taught people the prohibition and said to them, "Do not do this. Do not use that to come between a man and his wife."' Although this world is a greater temptation because its temptation is hidden, they said, *'We are merely a trial and temptation, so do not disbelieve.'* One group said that that is by learning sorcery, and another group said that it is by using it. Al-Mahdawī said, 'It is mockery because they said that to those whom they were certain were misguided.'

People learned from them how to separate a man and his wife

As-Suddī said, 'They used to say to those who came to them, "*We are merely a trial and temptation, so do not disbelieve.*" If the person refused to go back, they would say, "Go to this pile of ashes and urinate on it." When he urinated on it, a light would leave him, shining, on the way to heaven. It was his faith. Then a black smoke would emerge from it and enter his ears. It is disbelief. When he told them what he had seen, then they would teach him how to separate a man and his wife.' One group believe that a sorcerer cannot do more than cause separation, as Allah mentions here, because Allah mentioned that when He criticised sorcery and the aim of learning it. If they had been able to do more than that, they say, Allah would have mentioned that. Another group say that separating a man and his wife is the most common application of magic and does not preclude magic of other kinds, like causing love and hatred, causing evil to part a man from his wife, and to come between a man and his heart. That includes pains and illnesses. All of that can be witnessed, and denying it is pure obstinacy.

But they cannot harm anyone by it, except with Allah's permission

It is said that this refers to the Jews and it is said that it is refers to the shayṭāns. 'It' refers to sorcery. 'Allah's permission' here means His will and decree, not His command, because Allah does not command the reprehensible and then judge people according to it. Az-Zajjāj said, 'It means "only by the knowledge of Allah."' An-Naḥḥās said that this is incorrect.

They have learned what will harm them and will not benefit them.

Meaning in the Next World even if they obtain some benefit from it in this world. It is said that it will also harm them in this world because the harm which results from magic and causing disunion rebounds on the sorcerer in this world if he is discovered because he will be disciplined and punished and the ill fame of sorcery is attached to him.

وَلَوْ أَنَّهُمْ ءَامَنُوا۟ وَٱتَّقَوْا۟ لَمَثُوبَةٌ مِّنْ عِندِ ٱللَّهِ خَيْرٌ ۖ لَّوْ كَانُوا۟
يَعْلَمُونَ ﴿١٠٣﴾

103 If only they had believed and been godfearing! A reward from Allah is better, if they only knew.

'They' here refers to the sorcerers.

يَـٰٓأَيُّهَا ٱلَّذِينَ ءَامَنُوا۟ لَا تَقُولُوا۟ رَٰعِنَا وَقُولُوا۟ ٱنظُرْنَا وَٱسْمَعُوا۟ ۗ
وَلِلْكَـٰفِرِينَ عَذَابٌ أَلِيمٌ ﴿١٠٤﴾

104 You who have faith! do not say, '*Rā'inā*,' say, '*Unẓurnā*,' and listen well. The unbelievers will have a painful punishment.

This is talking about another act of ignorance on the part of the Jews and the purpose is to forbid Muslims from doing the same thing. The meaning of *rā'inā* is 'look at us and we will look at you' because the form of the verb dictates that. It further signifies 'protect us and we will protect you; watch us and we will watch you.' Using this word, however, entails coarseness and the believers were commanded to choose a better word with a finer meaning.

Ibn 'Abbās said, 'The Muslims used to say to the Prophet ﷺ, "*Rā'inā!*" by way of asking and desire, from *murā'āh* (supervision, respect). In Hebrew it was a curse, meaning "Listen, you do not hear." So the Jews took advantage of that and said, "We curse him secretly. Now we will curse him openly!" and they used to use the word to address the Prophet ﷺ and then laugh about it. Sa'd ibn Mu'ādh overheard them because he knew their language. He told them, "The curse of Allah be on you! If I hear a single man of you say it to the Prophet ﷺ, I will lop his head off!" They replied, "But you say it!" Then the *āyah* was revealed and they were forbidden to do it so that the Jews would not imitate them and intend a bad meaning by it.'

This *āyah* contains evidence for two rulings. One is that you should avoid ambiguous expressions which could be disparaging or allude to faults. A corollary of this is that slander can be by allusion and we say that doing this obliges the *ḥadd* punishment whereas Abū Ḥanīfah and ash-Shāfi'ī said that the aspect of doubt involved removes the *ḥadd*. This will be discussed in *an-Nūr*.

The second ruling to be gained from the *āyah* is that *sadd adh-dharā'i'* (the blocking of the means), and the protection it gives, constitutes a valid legal principle, which is the position of Mālik and also of Aḥmad ibn Ḥanbal in one transmission from him. The Book and Sunnah provide evidence for this principle. *Dharī'ah* (means) is something which is not prohibited in itself but it is feared that someone who does it will fall into the prohibited. In the Qur'an this *āyah* demonstrates the principle. The way the principle is applied here is that the Jews used to say this phrase, which was a curse in their language. Then Allah informed the Muslims about it and issued the prohibition of the use of this phrase because, although it is all right in itself, it is the means to the evil result.

There are also Allah's words: *'Do not curse those they call upon besides Allah, in case that makes them curse Allah in animosity without knowledge.'* (6:108) So Allah forbids cursing their gods – something that is not wrong in itself – out of the fear that they would retaliate. Allah says: *'Ask them about the town that was by the sea.'* (7:163) Allah forbade them to fish on the Sabbath when the fish came to them near the surface on the Sabbath. They blocked them off on the Sabbath and then took them on Sunday. That blockage was the means to catching. So Allah transmogrified them into apes and pigs. Allah also mentioned to us the idea of being on guard about that. He told Ādam and Ḥawwā': *'Do not approach this tree'* (2:35).

As for the Sunnah, there are many firm, sound hadiths, including the hadith of 'Ā'ishah that Umm Habibah and Umm Salamah mentioned to the Messenger of Allah ﷺ a church they had seen in Abyssinia with images, and the Messenger of Allah ﷺ said, 'Among those people, when a righteous man died, they built a place of prayer over his grave and adorned it with those images. Those are the worst of creatures in the sight of Allah.' Al-Bukhārī and Muslim transmitted it. Our scholars have said that those earlier people did that to console themselves by seeing those images and remembering the righteous behaviour of the people buried there and they strove as they had striven and worshipped Allah at their graves. Then time passed and those after them were ignorant of their aims and Shayṭān whispered to them that their fathers and forefathers had worshipped those images and so they started to worship them. The Prophet ﷺ warned against the same thing happening and strongly objected to people doing that. He blocked the means to that and said, 'The anger of Allah is terrible against people who take graves of their Prophets and righteous men as mosques,' and 'O Allah, do not make my grave an idol which is worshipped.'

Muslim related that an-Nu'mān ibn Bashīr say that he heard the Messenger of Allah ﷺ say, 'The *ḥalāl* is clear and the *ḥarām* is clear. But between the two there are doubtful things about which most people have no knowledge. Whoever exercises caution with regard to what is doubtful, shows prudence in respect of *dīn* and his honour. Whoever involves himself in doubtful things is like a herdsman who grazes his animals near a private preserve *(ḥimā)*. He is bound to enter it.' So the Prophet ﷺ forbade doing doubtful things out of the fear of falling into the forbidden. That is *sadd adh-dharā'i* '.

The Prophet ﷺ said, 'A person will not achieve the status of being one of the godfearing until he leaves what does not concern him out of consideration for what does concern him.' He also said, 'One of the major wrong actions is for a man to abuse his parents.' They said, 'O Messenger of Allah, is it possible for a man to abuse his parents?' He answered, 'Yes. He may curse another man's father who in turn curses his father, or curse his mother and he in turn curses his mother.' So he made provoking abuse of fathers the same as actual cursing fathers.

The Prophet ﷺ said, 'When you transact using the sale-and-buy transaction (*'īnah*), follow the tails of cattle, are satisfied with farming, and abandon jihad, then Allah will impose abasement on you that He will not remove from you until you return to the *dīn*.' Abū 'Ubayd al-Harawī said, '*'Īnah* is when a man sells goods to another man at a known price until a set term and then buys them back from him at a lower price than that for which he sold them.' He said, 'If, in the presence of someone who wants an *'īnah*, someone buys goods from another man at a known price and takes possession of them, and then buys them from the one who wants an *'īnah* for a greater price than that which he bought them for until a fixed term, and then the buyer buys them from the first seller for cash and a lower price, this is also *'īnah*, but a lesser form than the first one. Some of them consider it to be permissible. It is called *'īnah* because the cash is obtained by the owner of the item. That is because *'ayn* is the ready cash and the buyer buys the item in order to sell it for ready cash which is immediate.'

Ibn Wahb related from Mālik that an *umm walad* belonging to Zayd ibn al-Arqam mentioned to 'Ā'ishah ؓ that she sold a slave to Zayd for 800 until the stipend arrived and she then bought the slave back from him for 600 in cash. 'Ā'ishah said, 'An evil sale and an evil purchase! Tell Zayd that his jihād with the Messenger of Allah ﷺ will be nullified if he does not repent!' Such a statement is not made based on mere opinion because nullification of action is only known through revelation. So it is confirmed that it goes back to the Prophet ﷺ. 'Umar ibn al-Khaṭṭāb said, 'Abandon usury and doubt.'

This is our evidence for *sadd adh-dharā'i'* on which the Mālikīs based the Book of ends of terms and other questions regarding sales and other things. The Shāfi'īs do not have a chapter on ends of terms because they consider that to consist of different sales transactions.

say, '*Unẓurnā*,' and listen well.

They are commanded to speak to him ﷺ with respect. It means: 'Turn to us and look at us.'

مَّا يَوَدُّ الَّذِينَ كَفَرُوا مِنْ أَهْلِ الْكِتَابِ وَلَا الْمُشْرِكِينَ أَن يُنَزَّلَ
عَلَيْكُم مِّنْ خَيْرٍ مِّن رَّبِّكُمْ ۗ وَاللَّهُ يَخْتَصُّ بِرَحْمَتِهِ مَن يَشَاءُ ۚ
وَاللَّهُ ذُو الْفَضْلِ الْعَظِيمِ ١٠٥

105 Those of the People of the Book who disbelieve and the idolaters do not like anything good to be sent down to you from your Lord. But Allah selects for His mercy whomever He will. Allah's favour is truly vast.

But Allah selects for His mercy whomever He wills.

'Alī ibn Abī Ṭālib said, that this means for His Prophethood which He singled out for Muhammad ﷺ. Some people say that the mercy of the Qur'an is what is intended and others say that the mercy mentioned here is general to all types of mercy that Allah has given to His slaves, both now and in the past. The verb *raḥima* means to have compassion. *Raḥm*, *marḥamah* and *raḥmah* mean 'mercy'. Ibn Fāris said that. Allah's mercy to His slaves is His blessing them and pardoning them.

مَا نَنسَخْ مِنْ ءَايَةٍ أَوْ نُنسِهَا نَأْتِ بِخَيْرٍ مِّنْهَآ أَوْ مِثْلِهَآ ۗ أَلَمْ تَعْلَمْ أَنَّ
ٱللَّهَ عَلَىٰ كُلِّ شَىْءٍ قَدِيرٌ ﴿١٠٦﴾

106 Whenever We abrogate an *āyah* or cause it to be forgotten, We bring one better than it or equal to it. Do you not know that Allah has power over all things?

Whenever We abrogate an *āyah* or cause it to be forgotten,

This is a very important *āyah* about judgments. Its cause was that the Jews envied the Muslims when they turned away from Jerusalem and faced the Ka'bah, and they attacked Islam for that, saying that Muḥammad commanded his Companions to do one thing and then forbade it, and maintained that the Qur'an was of his own making. They contradicted one another and so Allah revealed: *'If We replace one āyah with another one...'* (16:101) and this *āyah.*

This subject is very important and scholars must be aware of it. Only ignorant fools deny it because of the effect of events on rulings and recognition of the lawful and unlawful. Abu-l-Bakhtarī said, "Alī entered the mosque while a man was causing the people there to become frightened. He asked, "What is this?" They answered, "A man who is reminding people." He said, "He is not a man who reminds people. He says, 'I am so-and-so son of so-and-so, so acknowledge me.'" He sent for him and asked, "Do you know the abrogating from the abrogated?" "No," he replied. He said, "Then leave our mosque and do not admonish people in it.'"

There are two aspects to abrogation or supersession (*naskh*). The first is transfer, like from one Divine Book to another. According to this, all the Qur'an is 'abrogated' in the sense that was taken from the Preserved Tablet and sent down to the House of Might in the lowest heaven. This has nothing to do with this *āyah.* The second form of abrogation is invalidation and removal, which is what is meant here. This, in turn, is divided into two types.

The first is supersession, which is the invalidation of something and its removal, and then putting something else in its place. The verb, *nasakha*, is used for the sun replacing the shadow when it takes its place. That is its meaning in this *āyah.* In *Ṣaḥīḥ Muslim* we find: 'There is no Prophethood at all which is not superseded by the next (*tanāsakha*).' The community has moved from one state to another. Ibn Fāris said that *naskh* refers to the Book, and it means to remove a command before it is acted on and then supersede it with something else, like an *āyah* revealed about a matter and then superseded by another. The verb is used for the sun replacing shade, old age replacing youth and the succession of heirs by successive deaths. There is a succession of ages and generations.

The second type of abrogation is the removal of a thing without replacing it with something else, as wind obliterates (*nasakha*) a track. This meaning is seen in the words of Allah: *'Allah revokes* (yansakhu) *what Shayṭān insinuates'* (22:52), i.e. removes it and so it is not recited nor does it have a replacement elsewhere in the Qur'an.

Pertinent to this matter is what is related from Ubayy and 'Ā'ishah to the effect that *Sūrat al-Aḥzāb* (33) was originally the same length as *Sūrat al-Baqarah* as will be later clarified. Evidence for this is also found in what Abū Bakr al-Anbārī transmitted that Sahl ibn Ḥunayf said while in the assembly of Sa'īd ibn al-Musayyab. He said that a man stood up in the night to recite a *sūrah* of the Qur'an but was unable to recite any of it. Another man rose and could not recite any of it either. So in the morning they went to the Messenger of Allah ﷺ. One said, 'I stood in the night to recite a *sūrah* of the Qur'an and I could not recite any of it.' The other stood up and said, 'The same thing happened to me, Messenger of Allah!' Yet a third rose and said, 'And the same thing happened to me, Messenger of Allah.' The Messenger of Allah ﷺ said, 'It was part of what Allah abrogated yesterday.'

Some modern groups of those who are called Muslims deny that such an occurrence is possible. They are veiled from the consensus of the Salaf that it occurs in the Sharī'ah. Some Jewish groups also reject that and they are veiled from what comes in the Torah since they claim that Allah told Nūḥ when he left the Ship, 'I make every animal edible for you and your descendants. I allow all of them for you, like plants, except for blood. Do not consume it.' Then He forbade many animals to Mūsā and the tribe of Israel. There is also the fact that Ādam married a brother to a sister, and Allah forbade that to Mūsā and others. Ibrāhīm was ordered to sacrifice his son and then told not to do it. Mūsā commanded the tribe of Israel to kill those of them who worshipped the Calf and then stopped that. There are many examples of this. This is transfer from one act of worship to another and one ruling to another for the sake of best interest.

Intelligent people do not disagree that the laws of the Prophets are intended to meet the best interests of people in the *dīn* and this world. It would have been obliged in the beginning had He not known the end of matters. The One Who knows that changes things addressed according to the change in what is in their best interests, just as a doctor takes note of the changes in his patient. Allah takes note of that in His creation by His will and volition. There is no god but Him.

What He asks of them changes, but His knowledge and will do not change. That is impossible in respect of Allah.

The Jews considered supersession and initiation to be the same and therefore they did not permit it and were misled. An-Naḥḥās said, 'The difference between abrogation and initiation is that supersession is transferring an act of worship from one form to another so that something lawful becomes unlawful or something unlawful becomes lawful. As for initiation, it is leaving what was previously obliged as when you say, 'Go to so-and-so today,' and then you say, 'Do not go to him.' You decide to turn from the first statement. This is connected to people's imperfections. Know that the real Abrogator is Allah Almighty. What He says is called abrogation since abrogation occurs by it, one judgment being replaced by another. It is said that the fast of Ramaḍān superseded the fast of 'Ashūrā', replacing one form of worship with another.

The sayings of our scholars differ regarding the definition of *naskh.* That which intelligent people who follow the *Sunnah* hold is that it is the removal of an established legal ruling by a further instruction which comes later in time. That is the definition of 'Abd al-Wahhāb and Qāḍī Abū Bakr, who added, 'If it were not for that, the prior ruling would remain firmly in place.' So they retain the linguistic definition which means 'removal' while avoiding the logical consequence of taking that literally. That which was abrogated, according to our Imams, the people of the Sunnah, constitutes a firm judgment in itself.

Our scholars disagree about whether reports are subject to abrogation. Most say that abrogating is specific to commands and prohibitions and that reports cannot be affected by abrogation since it is impossible to attribute falsehood to Allah. It is said that when a report contains a legal ruling, then supersession is permitted. It might be imagined that making what is general specific is abrogation, but that is not the case because specification does not remove the general *('āmm)*. If something moves the general ruling to something else, then that is abrogation, not specification. If someone refers to it as abrogation, that is metaphorical rather than actual.

One should know that there are reports in the Sharī'ah which appear to be general and all-inclusive but are then limited later so that that their generality is removed. It is like Allah's words: *'If My slaves ask you about Me, I am near. I answer the call of the caller when He calls on Me.'* (2:186) The literal meaning of this *āyah* is that he answers everyone who calls on Him in any case, but this is limited elsewhere as when He says: *'If He wills, He will deliver you from whatever it was that made you call on Him.'* (6:41) Someone without intelligence must suppose that this is abrogation in reports, but that is not the case. It is part of restriction of the unrestricted.

Our scholars say that abrogation is permitted from what is onerous to what is easier. A case in point is the abrogation of the ruling on standing firm in jihād when the odds are ten to one by that of standing firm when they are two to one. But it is also permitted to move from the easier to the harder, as happened when the fast of 'Ashurā' and some other days were exchanged for Ramadan as will be mentioned. And like can be abrogated by like, as happened in the case of the qiblah changing from Jerusalem to the House of Allah in Makkah. Matters can also be abrogated without being replaced, like giving *ṣadaqah* before conversing with the Prophet ﷺ. The Qur'an can be abrogated by the Qur'an, the Sunnah by a *mutawātir* hadith, and a single hadith by another single hadith.

Astute Imāms also say that the Qur'an can be abrogated by the *Sunnah*. An example of that is the words of the Prophet ﷺ: 'There is no bequest to an heir.' It is acknowledged by Mālik but ash-Shāfi'ī and Abū al-Faraj al-Mālikī rejected it. The first is a sounder approach by the evidence that all is the judgment of Allah Almighty and from Him, even if the names differ. Flogging was also dropped in the *ḥadd* punishment for the adulterer who is stoned. That was only dropped by the *Sunnah* which the Prophet ﷺ made clear.

They also say that the *Sunnah* can be abrogated by the Qur'an. That happened when the qiblah was changed when the original qiblah was not mentioned in the Qur'an. The *āyah* we are looking at here is another case: it demands that women should not be returned to the unbelievers when that had been part of the treaty that the Prophet ﷺ made with Quraysh. Astute scholars agree that it is logically permitted for the Qur'an to be abrogated by a single hadith but they disagree about whether it actually occurs. Abu-l-Ma'ālī and others believe that it happened when the people of the Mosque of Qubā' changed their qiblah but others reject that. It is not proper to abrogate a text through analogy since one of the preconditions of analogy is that it does not differ from a definitive text.

All of this occurred during the lifetime of the Prophet ﷺ. The Community agree that there is no abrogation after his death, once the Sharī'ah was firmly in place. This is why there is a consensus that there is no abrogation after the end of Revelation. When we find a consensus which is apparently contrary to a text, it is known that the consensus relied on an abrogating text which we do not know about. An opposed text is not acted upon and, therefore, it must have been abrogated even though it remains a *sunnah* which is read and reported. An example of this is the *āyah* of the *'iddah* (waiting period of a widow) of a year which is recited in the Qur'an. Reflect on this. It is something important. There is abrogation of a ruling while its recitation is left, like the giving of *ṣadaqah* before conversing with the Prophet (58:12). The opposite can also occur when the recitation is abrogated but not the ruling, which happened in the case of the *āyah* of stoning. It is also possible for both recitation and ruling to be abrogated. What astute scholars believe is that if someone has not heard about the abrogation, he continues to act according to the first ruling. They also permit abrogation of a ruling before it is acted on, as in the story of Ibrāhīm sacrificing his son and the obligation of the prayer being fifty prayers before it was made five.

There are means for recognising an abrogating text. One is when the expression indicates it, like the words of the Prophet ﷺ, 'I used to forbid visiting graves. Now you may visit them. I forbade drinking except from skins, now you may drink from every container, but do not drink intoxicants.' Another indication is when the transmitter mentions the date, as when he says, 'It was the year of the Ditch,' when it is known that what was abrogated occurred before it. Another indication is when it is stated: 'Such-and-such a ruling is abrogated.' Yet another means is when the entire Community agree that the ruling is abrogated.

Most recite 'abrogate' as '*n**a**ns**a**kh*' which is the normal usage. Ibn 'Āmir recites '*n**u**ns**i**kh*' from Form IV.

or cause it to be forgotten,

It is said that this means: 'omit it'. It is removed from you so that you do not read or remember it. '*Nunsihā*' (forgotten) is also recited with a *hamzah* (*nuns**i'**hā*) meaning 'to defer', meaning 'We defer its sending down or its abrogation to a later date.'

We bring one better than it or equal to it.

This means 'more beneficial for people'. The benefit is immediate if the abrogating ruling is easier and in the Next World if it is harder. It is also said that it is superior in that it has a greater benefit and reward since there is no disparity in the worth of the Words of Allah.

أَلَمْ تَعْلَمْ أَنَّ ٱللَّهَ لَهُۥ مُلْكُ ٱلسَّمَٰوَٰتِ وَٱلْأَرْضِ وَمَا لَكُم مِّن دُونِ
ٱللَّهِ مِن وَلِيٍّ وَلَا نَصِيرٍ ١٠٧

107 Do you not know that Allah is He to Whom the kingdom of the heavens and the earth belongs and that, besides Allah, you have no protector and no helper?

This means that He brings into existence and originates and has sovereignty and authority over all things and that His will and command is carried out in every instance. The Prophet ﷺ is addressed while his entire community is intended. It is said that it means: 'Say to them, Muḥammad: "Do you not know that Allah has authority over the heavens and earth and that you have no protector apart from Allah?"'

أَمْ تُرِيدُونَ أَن تَسْـَٔلُوا رَسُولَكُمْ كَمَا سُئِلَ مُوسَىٰ مِن قَبْلُ ۗ وَمَن
يَتَبَدَّلِ الْكُفْرَ بِالْإِيمَانِ فَقَدْ ضَلَّ سَوَاءَ السَّبِيلِ ﴿١٠٨﴾

108 Or do you want to question your Messenger as Mūsā was questioned before? Anyone who exchanges faith for disbelief has definitely gone astray from the level way.

'*Am*' (or) in fact means 'indeed' you do want and it is a rebuke. This is said to refer to their demanding proofs of Prophethood, such as asking him to bring Allah and the angels. Ibn 'Abbās and Mujāhid said that they asked for Ṣafā to be turned into gold. 'Level' (*sawā'*) means the middle way of something. It is said that it means the aim, and so it would be 'astray from the goal of the Path', which is obeying Allah. Ibn 'Abbās said that the reason for this *āyah* was that Rāfi' ibn Khuzaymah and Wahb ibn Zayd said to the Prophet ﷺ, 'Bring us a Book from heaven which we can read and make rivers flow for us and we will follow you.'

وَدَّ كَثِيرٌ مِّنْ أَهْلِ الْكِتَابِ لَوْ يَرُدُّونَكُم مِّن بَعْدِ إِيمَانِكُمْ كُفَّارًا
حَسَدًا مِّنْ عِندِ أَنفُسِهِم مِّن بَعْدِ مَا تَبَيَّنَ لَهُمُ الْحَقُّ ۖ فَاعْفُوا وَاصْفَحُوا
حَتَّىٰ يَأْتِيَ اللَّهُ بِأَمْرِهِ ۗ إِنَّ اللَّهَ عَلَىٰ كُلِّ شَيْءٍ قَدِيرٌ ﴿١٠٩﴾

109 Many of the People of the Book would love it if they could make you revert to being unbelievers after you have become believers, showing their innate envy now that the truth is clear to them. But you should pardon and overlook until Allah gives His command. Truly Allah has power over all things.

وَأَقِيمُوا۟ ٱلصَّلَوٰةَ وَءَاتُوا۟ ٱلزَّكَوٰةَ ۚ وَمَا تُقَدِّمُوا۟ لِأَنفُسِكُم مِّنْ خَيْرٍ
تَجِدُوهُ عِندَ ٱللَّهِ ۗ إِنَّ ٱللَّهَ بِمَا تَعْمَلُونَ بَصِيرٌ ١١٠

110 Establish the prayer and pay *zakāt*. Any good you send ahead for yourselves, you will find with Allah. Certainly Allah sees what you do.

Many of the People of the Book would love it if they could make you revert to being unbelievers after you have become believers, showing their innate envy now that the truth is clear to them.

They do so simply out of envy without having any legitimate authorisation for it from their Book or anywhere else. The *āyah* is about the Jews.

There are two types of envy: blameworthy envy and praiseworthy envy. The blameworthy kind is when you desire Allah's blessing to be removed from your brother Muslim whether you want it to come to you or not. Allah censured this type in His Book when He says: *'Or do they in fact envy people for the bounty Allah has granted them.'* (4:54) It is blameworthy because it is tantamount to thinking that Allah is foolish and that He has blessed someone who does not deserve His blessing.

The praiseworthy type is what comes in the sound hadith in which the Prophet ﷺ said, 'You may only have envy in two cases: for a man to whom Allah has given the Qur'an and he gets up and recites it throughout the night, and for a man to whom Allah has given wealth and he spends it throughout the night and the day.' This sort of envy is called *ghibtah* rather than *ḥasad* and al-Bukhārī has a chapter on envying people for their knowledge and wisdom. Its reality is that you desire to have the good and blessing which your Muslim brother has, without any good being removed from him. It is possible to call this aspiration, as the Almighty says: *'Let people with aspiration aspire to that!'* (83:26) But you should pardon and overlook until Allah gives His command. 'The truth' is Muḥammad ﷺ and the Qur'an which he brought.

But you should pardon and overlook until Allah gives His command.

The root of the word *'afu* (pardon) means not to call to account for wrong action. The root of *safḥ* (overlook) is to remove its effect from the heart. This *āyah* is, however, abrogated by Allah's words: *'Fight those who do not believe … abasement'* (9:29) according to Ibn 'Abbās. It is said that it is abrogated by *'kill the idolaters.'* (9:5) Abū 'Ubaydah said, 'Every *āyah* which obviates fighting is Makkan and is abrogated by the command to fight. Ibn 'Aṭiyyah said about this, 'His ruling that this *āyah* is Makkan is weak because the hostilities with the Jews only occurred in Madīnah.'

Ibn 'Aṭiyyah's opinion is sound. Al-Bukhārī and Muslim related from Usāmah ibn Zayd that the Messenger of Allah ﷺ rode a donkey with a saddlecloth made in Fadak and Usāmah ibn Zayd rode behind him. He went to visit Sa'd ibn 'Ubādah in the Banū 'l-Ḥārith branch of al-Khazraj before the Battle of Badr. On the way he passed by a gathering containing 'Abdullāh ibn Ubayy ibn Salūl, and that was before 'Abdullāh ibn Ubayy became Muslim. The gathering contained a mixture of Muslims. idolaters, pagans, and Jews. 'Abdullāh ibn Rawāḥah was also in the gathering.

When the dust from the donkey reached the gathering, 'Abdullāh ibn Ubayy covered his nose with his cloak and then said, 'Don't cover us with dust!' The Messenger of Allah ﷺ greeted them and then stopped. He dismounted and invited them to Allah and recited the Qur'an to them. 'Abdullāh ibn Ubayy ibn Salūl said, 'You! There is nothing better than what you say if it is the truth. So do not annoy us with it in our gatherings. Return to your mount and only recount it to those who come to you.' 'Abdullāh ibn Rawāḥah said, 'Indeed, Messenger of Allah! Bring it to us in our gatherings. We like that!' So the Muslims, idolaters and Jews abused one another until they were practically fighting. The Prophet ﷺ kept on calming them down until they were quiet.

Then the Messenger of Allah ﷺ mounted his animal and went on to visit Sa'd ibn 'Ubādah. The Messenger of Allah ﷺ said, 'Sa'd, did you hear what Abū Ḥubāb (meaning 'Abdullāh ibn Ubayy) said? He said such-and-such.' Sa'd ibn 'Ubāda said, 'O Messenger of Allah, pardon him and overlook it. By the One who sent down the Book to you with the truth, Allah brought you with the truth which He sent down to you after the people of this little town had already agreed to crown him. When that was prevented on account the truth which Allah gave you, he was vexed because of that. That is why he did what you saw.' The Messenger of Allah ﷺ pardoned him.

The Messenger of Allah ﷺ and the Companions used to pardon the idolaters and the People of the Book as Allah commanded them to do and they endured much harm from them. Allah says: *'You will hear many abusive words from those given the Book before you and from those who are idolaters'* (3:186), and *'Many of the People of the Book would love it...'*

The Messenger of Allah ﷺ continued to pardon them as long as Allah commanded him to do so until the time when Allah gave permission to fight them. When the Messenger of Allah ﷺ went on the Badr expedition, Allah killed the nobles of Quraysh through him and Ibn Ubayy ibn Salūl and those of the idolaters and pagans with him, said, 'This is a business which has proved to be victorious,' and they gave allegiance to the Messenger of Allah in Islam, and became Muslim. The command of Allah was the killing of Qurayẓah and the exile of the Banū 'n-Naḍīr.

Any good you send ahead for yourselves, you will find with Allah.

We read in a hadith: 'When someone dies, people ask, "What did he leave behind?" while the angels ask, "What did he send ahead?"' Al-Bukhari and an-Nasā'ī transmitted that 'Abdullāh [ibn Mas'ūd] reported that the Messenger of Allah ﷺ said, 'Which of you loves the property of his heir more than his own property?' They said, 'Messenger of Allah, there is none of who does not love his own property more than that of his heir?' The Messenger of Allah ﷺ said, 'No, there is none of you who does not love the property of his heir more than his own property. Your own property is what you send ahead and the property of your heir is what you leave behind.' 'Umar ibn al-Khaṭṭāb passed by the graveyard of Baqī' al-Gharqad and said, 'Peace be upon you, people of the graves. The news with us is that your wives have married, your houses are lived in and your property has been divided up.' An invisible voice answered him, 'Ibn Khaṭṭāb! The news with us is that we have found what we sent ahead, profited from what we spent, and lost what we left behind.' A poet said:

Send ahead righteous action before you die
and work. There is no path to immortality.

Another said:

Send ahead hopeful repentance for yourself
before you die and before tongues are tied.

Yet another said:

Your mother bore you weeping
while the people around you were laughing with joy.
Work for a day when they will weep
and you will be laughing with joy on the day of your death.

وَقَالُوا لَن يَدْخُلَ ٱلْجَنَّةَ إِلَّا مَن كَانَ هُودًا أَوْ نَصَٰرَىٰ تِلْكَ أَمَانِيُّهُمْ
قُلْ هَاتُوا بُرْهَٰنَكُمْ إِن كُنتُمْ صَٰدِقِينَ ﴿١١١﴾

111 They say, 'No one will enter the Garden except for Jews and Christians.' Such is their vain hope. Say, 'Produce your evidence if you are telling the truth.'

بَلَىٰ مَنْ أَسْلَمَ وَجْهَهُۥ لِلَّهِ وَهُوَ مُحْسِنٌ فَلَهُۥٓ أَجْرُهُۥ عِندَ رَبِّهِۦ وَلَا خَوْفٌ
عَلَيْهِمْ وَلَا هُمْ يَحْزَنُونَ ﴿١١٢﴾

112 Not so! All who submit themselves completely to Allah and are good-doers will find their reward with their Lord. They will feel no fear and will know no sorrow.

They say, 'No one will enter the Garden except for Jews and Christians.'

This means that the Jews said that none but Jews would enter the Garden and the Christians said that none but Christians would enter it.

Say, 'Produce your evidence, if you are telling the truth.'

The *burhān* (evidence) referred to in this *āyah* is the kind which produces certainty. Aṭ-Ṭabarī says that the purpose of demanding evidence here is to confirm the truth and refute those who deny it. Rather than telling the truth, they are, in fact, lying about both their faith and also their statement concerning entering the Garden.

Not so! All who submit themselves completely to Allah

Aslama (submit) here means 'to be humble and submit' is said to mean to be sincere in action. The words 'themselves completely' is literally 'their faces' and is used because it is the noblest part of the human being and because it is the home of the senses and the place where might and abasement show themselves most clearly. For this reason the Arabs used the word 'face' to designate the entire person.

وَقَالَتِ اِ۬لْيَهُودُ لَيْسَتِ اِ۬لنَّصَٰرَىٰ عَلَىٰ شَےْءٍ وَقَالَتِ اِ۬لنَّصَٰرَىٰ لَيْسَتِ اِ۬لْيَهُودُ
عَلَىٰ شَےْءٍ وَهُمْ يَتْلُونَ اَ۬لْكِتَٰبَ كَذَٰلِكَ قَالَ اَ۬لذِينَ لَا يَعْلَمُونَ مِثْلَ
قَوْلِهِمْ فَاللَّهُ يَحْكُمُ بَيْنَهُمْ يَوْمَ اَ۬لْقِيَٰمَةِ فِيمَا كَانُواْ فِيهِ يَخْتَلِفُونَ ﴿١١٣﴾

113 The Jews say, 'The Christians have nothing to stand on,' and the Christians say, 'The Jews have nothing to stand on,' yet they both recite the Book. Those who do not know say the same as they say. Allah will judge between them on the Day of Rising regarding the things about which they differ.

The Jews say, 'The Christians have nothing to stand on,' and the Christians say, 'The Jews have nothing to stand on,' yet they both recite the Book.

Each of them claims that the other group have nothing and that they are more entitled to mercy than them. 'The Book' means the Torah and the Gospel.

Those who do not know say the same as they say.

'Those who do not know' are said by the majority to be the unbelieving Arabs because they had no Book. 'Aṭā' said that what is meant are the nations before the Jews and Christians. Ar-Rabī' ibn Anas said that it means: 'That is what the Jews said before the Christians.'

Ibn 'Abbās said that the reason for the revelation of this *āyah* was that some Christians of Najrān came to the Prophet ﷺ and the Jewish rabbis also came and they argued in the presence of the Prophet ﷺ each said this about the other.

وَمَنَ اَظْلَمُ مِمَّن مَّنَعَ مَسَٰجِدَ اَ۬للَّهِ أَن يُذْكَرَ فِيهَا اَ۪سْمُهُۥ وَسَعَىٰ فِے خَرَابِهَا
أُوْلَٰٓئِكَ مَا كَانَ لَهُمُۥٓ أَن يَدْخُلُوهَا إِلَّا خَآئِفِينَ لَهُمْ فِے اِ۬لدُّنْيَا خِزْيٌ وَلَهُمْ
فِے اِ۬لْءَاخِرَةِ عَذَابٌ عَظِيمٌ ﴿١١٤﴾

114 Who could do greater wrong than someone who bars access to the mosques of Allah, preventing His name from being remembered in them, and goes about destroying them? Such people will never be able to enter them – except in fear. They will have disgrace in this world and in the Next World they will have a terrible punishment.

Who could do greater wrong than someone who bars access to the mosques of Allah, preventing His Name from being remembered in them,

By 'mosques' here Allah means either Jerusalem and the area around it or the Ka'bah. The plural is used to honour the mosque because it is the qiblah for all other mosques. It is also said that what is meant are all mosques.

People disagree about what is meant by this *āyah* and about whom it was revealed. Some commentators said that it was revealed about Nebuchadnezzar because he destroyed Jerusalem. Ibn 'Abbās and others say that it was revealed about the Christians and it means, 'How, Christians, can you claim to be people of the Garden when you laid waste to Jerusalem and prevented those who pray from praying in it?' In that case the sense of the *āyah* would be astonishment at what the Christians did to Jerusalem, in spite of their esteem for it, and that they did what they did out of their animosity towards the Jews. It is related that this devastation remained until the time of 'Umar. It is said that it was revealed about the idolaters when they prevented the worshippers and the Prophet ﷺ from reaching the Sacred Mosque in the year of al-Ḥudaybīyah. It is said that what is meant is anyone who bars access to any mosque until the Day of Rising. That is sound because the expression is general, and Allah knows best.

The destruction of mosques can be actual, like the destruction wrought by Nebuchadnezzar on Jerusalem and also by the Christians when they attacked the tribe of Israel under one of their emperors (possibly Vespasian). They slaughtered the people, looted the city, burned the Torah, and put excrement in the Temple and destroyed it. But it can also have a metaphorical meaning, as the idolaters prevented the Messenger of Allah ﷺ from reaching the Sacred House. Or in general, it could mean letting mosques fall into disuse.

Our scholars said, 'This *āyah* provides the legal basis for our ruling that it is not permitted to forbid a woman from making *ḥajj* if she has not performed it, whether or not she has a *maḥram*, nor should she be prevented from praying in mosques as long as it is it is not feared that that will be a cause of immoral behaviour. The Prophet ﷺ said, "Do not bar the female slaves of Allah from the mosques of Allah."'

The *āyah* is also why it is said that it is not permitted to demolish a mosque, sell it, or to let it become unused, even if the town in which it is located falls into ruins. One should not forbid the construction of a mosque unless the aim of building it is to cause dissension, as would be the case when people build a mosque beside another mosque or close to it, and their intention is to cause dissension among the people of the first mosque and ruin it. In such a case, the second mosque should be destroyed and its construction forbidden. It is also why it is not permitted to have two Friday mosques in the same city, or two imāms in the same mosque, or two group prayers said in the same mosque. This will be explained in *Sūrat at-Tawbah*, Allah willing, and elsewhere. The *āyah* also indicates esteem for the prayer and that it is the best of actions and has the greatest reward, and that preventing it is the greatest of wrong actions.

Every place in which Allah is worshipped and prostrated to (*sajada*) is called a mosque (*masjid*). The Messenger of Allah ﷺ said, 'The whole earth was made a mosque and is pure for me (to pray in).' The Companions agreed that when an area is singled out for the prayer by a declaration, it is no longer private property and becomes public for all Muslims. If a man builds a mosque in his house and screens it off from people and singles it out for himself, it remains his property and does not become a mosque in the true sense of the word. If he opens it to everyone, its ruling is that of general mosques and it is no longer private property.

Such people will never be able to enter them – except in fear.

When the Muslims gain control of them and they are under their authority, then it will not be possible for the unbelievers to enter them, and, if they do enter them, it will be in fear that the Muslims will attack them and punish them for entering them. This is an indication that unbelievers should never be allowed to enter mosques as will come in *Sūrat at-Tawbah*, Allah willing. If the *āyah* is about the Christians, it is related that it points ahead to the time of 'Umar's reconstruction of Jerusalem after its conquest by the Muslims and his ruling that any Christian who enters the mosque of Jerusalem should be beaten, even though it had previously been their place of worship. If it is considered to be about Quraysh, it is said that it refers to the announcement made after the proclamation of the Prophet ﷺ: 'After this year, no idolater should perform the *ḥajj* nor do *ṭawāf* of the House naked.' It is said that what is meant is the command to struggle against them and eradicate them so that none of them enters Sacred Mosque except in fear. It is, in fact, a prohibition in the form of a report.

They will have disgrace in this world and in the Next World they will have a terrible punishment.

Qatādah reports that the word 'disgrace' refers to killing in the case of the *ḥarbī*, and *jizyah* in the case of the *dhimmī*. As-Suddī said that their disgrace in this world will be the coming of the Mahdī, and the conquest of 'Amuriyya, Rumiyah, Constantinople and other cities. If it refers to Quraysh, it is said to refer to their disgrace at the Conquest of Makkah and the punishment in the Next World of those of them who died unbelievers.

وَلِلَّهِ ٱلْمَشْرِقُ وَٱلْمَغْرِبُ فَأَيْنَمَا تُوَلُّوا۟ فَثَمَّ وَجْهُ ٱللَّهِ إِنَّ ٱللَّهَ وَٰسِعٌ عَلِيمٌ ﴿١١٥﴾

115 Both East and West belong to Allah, so wherever you turn, the Face of Allah is there. Allah is All-Encompassing, All-Knowing.

Both East and West belong to Allah,

East is where the sun rises and West is where it sets, so the *āyah* implies that all things are subject to Allah's sovereignty, along with all the directions and creatures contained within them. He is the One who originated them and brought them into existence. These two directions — East and West — are singled out for connection to Him as a mark of honour, like 'the House of Allah', and because the reason for the revelation of the *āyah* dictates that, as will be made clear.

So wherever you tum, the Face of Allah is there.

Scholars disagree about the reason for the revelation of this *āyah*. There are five positions. 'Āmir ibn Rabī'ah says, 'It was revealed about some people who prayed in a direction other than the *qiblah* on a dark night, as is transmitted by at-Tirmidhī: "We were with the Prophet ﷺ on a journey during a dark night and we did not know where the *qiblah* was. Each of us prayed according to his own devices. In the morning, we mentioned that to the Messenger of Allah ﷺ and this *āyah* was revealed."' Abū 'Īsā said that this hadith lacks a proper *isnād* and we only know it from the hadith of Ash'ath as-Sammān. Abū ar-Rabī' Ash'ath ibn Sa'īd is weak. But most of the people of knowledge accept the implied judgment and say that if someone prays on a cloudy day in a direction other than the qiblah and then it later becomes clear to him that he did not pray in the right direction, his prayer is allowed. That was stated by Sufyān, Ibn al-Mubārak, Aḥmad and Isḥāq. It is also the position of Abū Ḥanīfah and Mālik, although Mālik says: 'It is preferred for him to repeat (the prayer) within the time but that is not an obligation on him because he has performed his obligation as he was commanded to do. Perfection is to seek to correct it within the time and there is evidence in the *sunnah* in the case of someone who prayed alone and then caught that prayer in its time in the group. He repeated it with them. It is only recommended for someone to repeat it if he had his back to the qiblah or faced a direction very much away from the qiblah. If, by his *ijtihād,* he was only a little to the right or left, he does not need to repeat it either in the time or after the time.'

Al-Mughīrah and ash-Shāfi'ī said that such a prayer is invalid because facing the qiblah is one of the preconditions of the prayer. What Mālik said is sounder because the direction of qiblah can be abandoned out of necessity in hand-to-hand combat and is also permitted as a dispensation while travelling. Ibn 'Umar said, 'It was revealed about travellers who turn wherever their mounts turn.' Muslim transmitted it. He said, 'The Messenger of Allah ﷺ used to pray on his camel going from Makkah to Madīnah whatever the direction the camel was facing. About that was revealed: "*...so wherever you turn, the Face of Allah is there.*"' There is no disagreement between scholars that it is permitted to pray *nāfilah* prayers while mounted, going by this hadith. No one, however, is permitted to deliberately abandon qiblah in a *farḍ* prayer for any other direction, unless that is due to intense fear.

Mālik has differing opinions about someone who is ill and prays on his litter. In one opinion he says that he may not pray a *farḍ* prayer on the back of a camel, even if he is very ill. Saḥnūn said, 'If he does that, he should repeat the prayer.' He said on another occasion, 'If he is one of those who can only pray on the ground using gestures, then he can pray on the camel after it has been halted and made to face qiblah.' They agree that it is not valid for anyone who is healthy to pray a *farḍ* prayer except on the ground, unless he is in a state of fear.

Fuqahā' disagree about a traveller on a journey in which the prayer cannot be shortened. Mālik and his people and ath-Thawrī said, 'There can be no voluntary prayers on a camel except during a journey on which the prayer may be shortened, because all the journeys which are reported from the Messenger of Allah ﷺ in which he performed *nāfilah* prayers were those during which the prayer may be shortened. Ash-Shāfi'ī, Abū Ḥanīfah, al-Ḥasan ibn Ḥayy, al-Layth ibn Sa'd and Dāwūd ibn 'Alī said that it is permitted to perform *nāfilah* prayers while mounted outside a city on a journey of any length, whether or not the prayer may be shortened, because the reports do not specify one journey rather than another, so it is permitted in every journey.

Abū Yūsuf said that it is even permitted to pray mounted in a city using gestures going by a report in which Anas ibn Mālik prayed on a donkey in an alley in Madīnah using gestures. Aṭ-Ṭabarī said, 'It is permitted for every rider or walker, resident or travelling, to perform *nāfilah* prayers while mounted or on his feet using gestures.' Al-Athram said, 'Aḥmad ibn Ḥanbal was asked about praying on a mount while resident. He answered, "I have heard about doing that while on a journey. I have not heard about it while resident."' Ibn al-Qāsim said, 'Someone who performs *nāfilah* on a camel-litter performs them while seated. His standing is cross-legged. He bows, placing his hands on his knees and then lifts his head.'

Qatādah said, 'It was revealed about the Negus. When he died, the Prophet ﷺ called the Muslims to pray over him outside Madīnah. They said, "How can we pray over a man who has died? He prayed to other than our qiblah." The Negus was the King of Abyssinia. His name was Aṣḥamah which means "gift". He was praying towards Jerusalem when he died after the qiblah has been changed to the Ka'bah. So the *āyah* was revealed. Also revealed about him was: *"Among the People of the Book there are some who believe in Allah."* (3:199) So this was an excuse for the Negus.'

The prayer that the Prophet ﷺ prayed with his Companions was in 9 AH. This is used as evidence by those who permit praying over someone who is absent. That was the position of ash-Shāfi'ī. One of the stranger points about the prayer over the dead person is what ash-Shāfi'ī said: 'One prays over someone who is absent. I was in Baghdad in the gathering of Fakhr 'd-dīn [ar-Rāzī]. A man from Khorasan entered and he asked, "How is so-and-so?" He told him, "He has died." He exclaimed, "We belong to Him and to Him we return!" Then he told us, "Get up and pray for him." He got up and led us in the prayer for him. That was six months after his death, the distance it took to travel between the two lands.'

We believe that the basis for that is the prayer of the Prophet ﷺ over the Negus. Our scholars, however, say that that was especially for the Prophet ﷺ for three reasons. The first is that the earth was flattened for him, north and south, so that he could see the bier of the Negus as he was able to see the al-Aqṣā Mosque. Those who disagree say that there was no point in seeing him; the benefit is in conveying his blessing. The second is that the Negus had no relative among the Muslims to perform the prayer for him. Those who disagree about this say that it is impossible for a king following a religion not to have followers. The third reason is that the Prophet ﷺ wanted to pray over the Negus to bring him mercy and seek the friendship of the kings after him since they saw his concern for him when he was alive and after his death. Those who disagree say that the blessing of the supplication of the Prophet ﷺ and others is agreed to reach the deceased. Ibn al-'Arabī said, 'What I think about the Prophet's prayer over the Negus is because he knew that the Negus and those who believed along with him did not have any report about how the funeral prayer was performed and knew that they would bury him without it. That is why he hastened to perform the prayer for him.'

The first interpretation is better because if he actually could see him, then he was not praying over someone absent. He was praying over someone present that he could see. Someone absent is not seen. Allah knows best.

Ibn Zayd said, 'The Jews recommended to the Prophet ﷺ that he should pray facing Jerusalem. When he did, they said, "He was only guided by us." Then, when the qiblah was changed to the Ka'bah, the Jews said, "*What has turned them from their* qiblah *they used to face?*" and this *āyah* was revealed.' According to this position, there is a sequence in the events leading up to it. When the Jews objected to the qiblah changing, Allah Almighty made it clear that He makes His slaves worship however He wishes. If He wishes, He commands them to face Jerusalem, and if He wishes, He commands them to face the Ka'bah. He is not questioned about what He does, but they will be questioned.

Another view is that this *āyah* is abrogated by Allah's words: *'Wherever you come from, turn your face to the Masjid al-Ḥarām.'* (2:149) Ibn 'Abbās said that it seems that in the beginning a man prayed in whatever direction he wished to and then that was abrogated. Qatādah says that the *āyah* which abrogated it was: *'Turn your face, therefore, towards the Masjid al-Ḥarām.'* (2:144) Abū 'Īsā at-Tirmidhī related it.

Yet another view related from Mujāhid and aḍ-Ḍaḥḥāk is that it remains a firm ruling. It means: wherever you are in the east or the west, there is the face of Allah which you are commanded to face and that is the direction of the Ka'bah. Mujāhid and Ibn Jubayr said that when *'Call on Me and I will answer you'* (40:60) was revealed, people asked, 'Where?' and *'so wherever you tum, the Face of Allah is there'* was revealed. Ibn 'Umar and an-Nakha'ī said, 'Wherever you tum on your journeys and when moving about, the face of Allah is there.' It is further said that it is connected to Allah's words in the previous *āyah* (2:114) 'Who could do greater wrong?' and means: 'O believers, the lands of Allah are vast enough for you, so those who ruin the mosques of Allah cannot prevent you from turning your faces towards Allah's qiblah no matter where you are on the earth.' It is said that when the Prophet ﷺ was barred from the House in the Year of al-Ḥudaybīyah, the Muslims were saddened by that.

Those who say that it is abrogated say that there is no objection to that inasmuch as it is a report because it can convey the meaning of a command. It is possible that *'wherever you turn, the Face of Allah is there'* can mean 'towards the Face of Allah.

People disagree about the interpretation of the word *'wajh'* (Face) as ascribed to Allah Almighty in the Qur'an and the *Sunnah.* Astute scholars say that it refers to created existence and is used for it as a metaphor, since the face is the most apparent part of the body and the most sublime. Ibn Fūrak said, 'The attribute of the thing is mentioned and it is meant to designate the One described by it. The expression "having a face" means that something has existence.' Ibn 'Abbās said, 'The Face designates Allah Himself as He says: *"but the Face of your Lord will remain, Master of Majesty and Generosity"* (55:27).' Some imams say that this designation should be affirmed when it is heard, even if it contradicts what intellects demand of attributes that are appropriate for the Eternal. Ibn 'Aṭiyyah says that this is weak and what is actually meant is Allah's existence. It is also said that it means the direction which one faces, in other words, the qiblah, and it is also said that it means what you aim at.

Another opinion is that the word *'wajh'* (Face), as ascribed to Allah, means: 'Wherever the pleasure of Allah lies and His reward,' going by Allah's words: *'We feed you only out of desire for the Face of Allah.'* (76:9), meaning in order to please Him and seek His reward, and by the words of the Prophet ﷺ: 'If anyone builds a mosque by which he desires the Face of Allah, Allah will build for him its like in the Garden.' He said, 'On the Day of Rising a sealed page will be brought and set before Allah Almighty. The Almighty will say to the angels, "Take this away and bring that one." The angels will say, "By Your might, we only saw good!" He Who knows best will say, "This was for other than My Face. I only accept actions that were done for My Face,"' i.e. by those that were sincere. Ad-Dāraquṭnī transmitted it. It is said that it means: 'Allah is there' and *'wajh'* is connective. Al-Kalbī and al-Qutabī said that. It is like what the Mu'tazilites say.

Allah is All-Encompassing, All-Knowing.

He gives His slaves latitude in their *dīn* and does not oblige them to do anything which is beyond their capacity. It is said that 'All-Encompassing' means that His knowledge encompasses everything, as in Allah's words: *'He encompasses everything in knowledge.'* (20:98) Al-Farrā' said that the name All-Encompassing indicates the Generous whose giving encompasses everything as in Allah's words: *'My mercy encompasses everything.'* (7:156) It is said that His forgiveness is all-encompassing. It is said that He is gracious to His slaves and has no need of their actions.

وَقَالُوا۟ ٱتَّخَذَ ٱللَّهُ وَلَدًا ۗ سُبْحَـٰنَهُۥ ۖ بَل لَّهُۥ مَا فِى ٱلسَّمَـٰوَٰتِ وَٱلْأَرْضِ ۖ كُلٌّ لَّهُۥ
قَـٰنِتُونَ ﴿١١٦﴾

116 They say, 'Allah has a son.' Glory be to Him! No, everything in the heavens and earth belongs to Him. Everything is obedient to Him.

They say, 'Allah has a son.' Glory be to Him!

This refers to what the Christians say about the Messiah being the son of God. It is also said that it refers to the Jews' statement about 'Uzayr being the son of God. It is said that it is about the unbelieving Arabs who say that the angels are the daughters of Allah. These points will be discussed in *Sūrat Maryam* and *Sūrat al-Anbiyā'*.

Al-Bukhārī transmitted from Ibn 'Abbās that the Prophet ﷺ said, 'Allah Almighty says, "The son of Ādam has denied Me and he has no right to do that. He has abused Me and he has no right to do that. He denies Me by claiming that I cannot bring him back as he was. He abuses Me by saying that I have a child. I am too glorious to take a consort or child."'

The word word *subḥāna* (Glory be) mean 'to declare free of' and 'to disconnect'. It declares the impossibility of their statement that Allah has a son. Allah is unique in His Essence, One in His attributes. He has not had a child, obviating the need for him to have a consort: *'How could He have a son when He has no wife.'* (6:101) He was not born, obviating the need for something to have existed before Him. He is greatly exalted above what the wrongdoers and deniers say. A child is always of the same genus as his parent and so how could Allah – glory be to Him! – have a son among His creatures when nothing is like Him? The nature of a child is to be of the same species and in-time while timelessness necessitates oneness and permanence. He is Timeless, Pre-eternal, One, Unique. Alone, the Everlasting Sustainer of all. No one is comparable to Him.

Everything in the heavens and earth belongs to Him

There is nothing which He did not originate and bring into existence.

Everything is obedient to Him.

Qānit (obedient) means submissive and compliant. All creatures are subjected to Allah. The obedience of inanimate things is in the manifestation of the work done on them and by them. *Qunūt* means obedience as well as meaning silence. Zayd ibn Arqam said, 'We used to speak in the prayer, a man speaking to the man at his side, until it reached: *"Stand in obedience to Allah."* (2:238) We were commanded to be silent and forbidden to talk.' *Qunūt* is the prayer. As-Suddī and others said that it means that everyone will stand in obedience to Him on the Day of Rising. Al-Ḥasan said that it means that everyone undertakes to testify that they are His slave. *Qunūt* linguistically means standing, as az-Zajjāj said. The *āyah* means: creatures are obedient, undertake slavehood, either by conscious admission or, if they do not consciously obey, the effect of Allah's action becomes clear on them. It is also said that the root meaning is 'obedience'.

بَدِيعُ ٱلسَّمَٰوَٰتِ وَٱلْأَرْضِ وَإِذَا قَضَىٰٓ أَمْرًا فَإِنَّمَا يَقُولُ لَهُۥ كُن فَيَكُونُ ﴿١١٧﴾

117 The Originator of the heavens and earth. When He decides on something, He just says to it, 'Be!' and it is.

The Originator of the heavens and earth.

The form used for the name 'the Originator' is one that gives extra emphasis to the meaning. To originate something is to bring it into existence without any prior model. This means that Allah brought the heavens and the earth into existence and fashioned them without any previous model. Anyone who makes something not previously thought of is called an originator. The verb is the source of the term *bid'ah* which means innovation. It is called that because the one who does it innovates something which was not previously done or enunciated by any qualified imam.

No innovation issuing from a creature can have a basis in the Sharī'ah. If it has any basis at all it may fall under the category of recommended actions. If it is praiseworthy, even if it has no precedent, like some type of generosity or other good deed, it may well be a praiseworthy action, even if no one has done it before. This is supported by the words of 'Umar regarding the *tarāwīḥ* prayer, 'This is an excellent innovation', since it was a good and praiseworthy action. The Prophet ﷺ prayed it, and then left it and did not continue doing it and people did not gather for it. 'Umar reinstated it and people gathered for it and he recommended it to them as an innovation, but a praiseworthy one.

Anything which is contrary to what Allah and His Messenger commanded is categorically repudiated and blameworthy and this is what is being referred to by the Messenger of Allah ﷺ when he said in his *khuṭbah*, 'The worst of matters are the new ones, and every innovation (*bid'ah*) is misguidance,' meaning anything which is not in keeping with the Book or the *Sunnah* or the practice of the Companions. The matter is made even clearer by the words of the Prophet ﷺ: 'Anyone who innovates a good sunnah in Islam has its reward and the reward of whoever does it after him without that decreasing his reward in any way. Anyone who innovates a bad sunnah in Islam bears its burden and the burden of whoever acts by it after him without that decreasing his burden in any way.' So innovations can be good or bad, and this is the basic principle regarding this matter. Protection and success are by Allah. There is no Lord but Him.

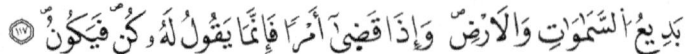

When He decides on something, He just says to it, 'Be!' and it is.

This means that, when He desires to complete something and make it perfect in accordance with His perfect knowledge of it, He says to it, 'Be!' Ibn 'Arafah said, 'Allah's decision on a thing entails perfecting it, carrying it out and finishing it. That is why a judge is called a *qāḍī*, because, when he decides on a judgment, the quarrel is ended.' Al-Azharī said that the verb *qaḍā* (decide) has various meanings. Its root meaning means to finish something and complete it.

Our scholars say that *qaḍā* is a word with various meanings. It can mean 'to create' as in Allah's words: *'...He determined* (qaḍāhunna*) them as seven heavens'* (41:12), meaning 'created them'. It can mean 'to inform' as in: *'We decreed* (qaḍaynā) *for the tribe of Israel in the Book'* (17:4), and it can mean to command as in: *'Your Lord has decreed* (qaḍā) *that you should worship none but Him.'* (17:23) It can mean to force a judgment to be carried out which is why a judge is called a *qāḍī*. It can mean to settle a right in full as in: *'When Mūsā had fulfilled* (qaḍā) *the appointed term'* (28:29), and it can also mean 'to will', meaning 'to decide or want' as in: *'When He decides on* (qaḍā) *something, He just says to it, "Be!" and it is.'* (40:67) Ibn 'Aṭiyyah says it means 'determine'. According to the people of the Sunnīs, the *āyah* has both meanings: He determined it before time and then carried it out. According to the Mu'tazilites: He determined when He created and brought into existence.

The word translated here as 'something' (*amr*), which generally means a command or a matter, is used in the Qur'an in different ways to mean various things: Islam: '*Until the truth came and Allah's command prevailed*' (9:48), meaning here the *dīn* of Islam; word: '*When Our command comes*' and '*they argued among themselves about the matter.*' (20:62); punishment: '*When the affair is decided*' (14:22) meaning the punishment becomes mandatory; the Prophet 'Īsā: Allah says: '*When He decides on something*' (3:47) meaning, in this instance, 'Īsā, whom He knew would be born without having had a father; the killing of the unbelievers at Badr: Allah says: '*When Allah's command comes*' (40:78), meaning the killing which would take place at Badr. And again: '*So that Allah could settle a matter whose result was preordained*' (8:42) referring to the killing of the unbelievers of Makkah; the conquest of Makkah: Allah says: '*Wait until Allah brings about His command*' (9:24), meaning the Conquest of Makka; the killing of the Jewish tribe of Qurayẓah and the nobles of the tribe of an-Naḍīr: Allah says: '*Pardon and overlook until Allah gives His command*' (2:109), referring to the Jewish enemies of the Muslims in Madīnah; the Day of Rising: Allah says: '*Allah's command is coming.*' (16:1); the Decree: Allah says: '*He directs the whole affair*' (10:3), meaning what He has decreed; Revelation: Allah says: '*He directs the whole affair from heaven to earth.*' (32:5) Revelation descends from heaven to earth. And He says: '*The Command descending down through all of them*' (65:12), meaning Divine Revelation; command over creation:

Allah says: '*Indeed all matters return eventually to Him*' (42:53), meaning the affairs of every creature; victory: Allah says: '*They say, "Do we have any say in the affair at all?"*' (3:154), meaning victory. '*The affair belongs entirely to Allah*' (3:154), meaning victory; wrong action: Allah says: '*They tasted the evil consequences of what they did* (amrihim)' (65:9), meaning the repayment for their wrong actions; action: Allah says: '*Pharaoh's command was not rightly guided*' (11:97); and He says: '*Those who oppose His command should beware*' (24:63), meaning the action of the Prophet ﷺ.

The Divine command '*kun*' (Be!) is what is meant by the words of the Prophet ﷺ, 'I seek refuge in the complete Word (or Words) of Allah from the evil of what He created.' This is also indicated in what is related by Abū Dharr from the Prophet ﷺ that Allah said in a *ḥadīth qudsī*: 'My gift is words and My punishment is words.' At-Tirmidhī transmitted it in a long hadith. So 'word' can mean 'words', but when one word is used for different matters at different times, it becomes words, even if it goes back to one word.

Depending on how the grammar is taken, there are two possible ways of looking at the phrase *fa-yakūnu* ('and it is'). The first is that the thing comes into being after the command. Even if it was non-existent, it has the same status as something existent, because Allah already 'knew' it as will be explained. According to the second view, the thing comes into being simultaneously with the command, and aṭ-Ṭabarī preferred that. He said, 'His command to the thing does not have prior or later existence.' The thing commanded to exist only exists by the command, and there is nothing which exists except that it has been commanded to exist, as will be explained. He said, 'It is like when people rise from their graves. Allah's summons (30:25) is neither earlier nor later, it is at the moment when He calls them.' Ibn 'Aṭiyyah says this is weak and incorrect in respect of the meaning because it would necessitate the word to be accompanied by bringing into being and existence.

To summarise what is deduced from this *āyah*: Allah Almighty continues to command non-existent things to come into existence. He decrees and can delay decreed things and He is All-Knowing and can delay known things. The entire *āyah* demands futurity, required by the things commanded, since temporal things come into being after they were not. All depends on Allah's Power and Knowledge. He is timeless and continues forever. The meaning of the Divine command 'Be!', however, is timeless and connected to the Essence.

Al-Māwardī says, 'It might be asked, "In what state were the things to which He said *'"Be" and it is'* – non-existence or existence? If it was in a state of non-existence, it is impossible that He command other than what is commanded, as it is impossible for the command to issue from other than the One who commands.

If it is the state of its existence, that state cannot have existence or temporality commanded for it because it is already a temporal existent?" There are three answers to this question:

'One is that it is a report from Allah regarding the carrying out of His commands in His existing creation, as when He commanded the tribe of Israel to become apes, in which case it is not about bringing something non-existent into existence.

'The second is that Allah knows every being before it is and so the things which do not yet actually exist are already in His prior knowledge of them. So they are similar to what exists and it is permissible to say, "Be!" to them and to command them to emerge from the state of non-existence to the state of existence, since He has conceived of them and has knowledge of them in the state of non-existence.

'The third is that it is a general report from Allah about what He brings into being and forms when He desires to create it and bring it into being. It is His Decree which is designated by the word "Be!", even if it is not an actual word.'

وَقَالَ الَّذِينَ لَا يَعْلَمُونَ لَوْلَا يُكَلِّمُنَا اللَّهُ أَوْ تَأْتِينَا آيَةٌ كَذَٰلِكَ
قَالَ الَّذِينَ مِن قَبْلِهِم مِّثْلَ قَوْلِهِمْ تَشَابَهَتْ قُلُوبُهُمْ قَدْ بَيَّنَّا
الْآيَاتِ لِقَوْمٍ يُوقِنُونَ ﴿١١٨﴾

118 Those who do not know say, 'If only Allah would speak to us, or some sign come to us!' just like those before them who said the same as they say. Their hearts are much the same. We have made the Signs clear for people who have certainty.

Ibn 'Abbās said that '*those who do not know*' are the Jews while Mujāhid said that it is the Christians who are being referred to, which aṭ-Ṭabarī prefers because they are mentioned immediately before this *āyah*. Ar-Rabī', as-Suddī and Qatādah say that it is the Arab idolaters who said these words, claiming that they would become believers if this were to happen. '*Their hearts are much the same*' as the hearts of those before them in respect of obstinacy, brashness and lack of faith. Al-Farrā' said that it is because they agree in disbelief.

إِنَّا أَرْسَلْنَاكَ بِالْحَقِّ بَشِيرًا وَنَذِيرًا وَلَا تُسْأَلُ عَنْ أَصْحَابِ الْجَحِيمِ ﴿١١٩﴾

119 We have sent you with the Truth, bringing good news and giving warning. Do not ask about the inhabitants of the Blazing Fire.

Do not ask about the inhabitants of the Blazing Fire.

Muqātil said that the Prophet ﷺ said, 'If Allah were to send down His violent force on the Jews, they would have faith,' and then Allah revealed this. It is said that the reason for this was that the Prophet was asked about the state of his ancestors and this *āyah* was revealed.

There are two readings of the word 'ask'. Nāfi' has it as *tas'al*, the apocopate form as a prohibition, meaning 'Do not ask'. The others have it as *tus'alu*, 'You will not be asked'. There are two aspects to the Nāfi' reading. One is that it forbids asking about the living person who has disobeyed Allah and disbelieved because their state might change and they might still becomes believers and obedient. The second, which is most likely, is that it forbids asking about those who have died in disbelief and disobedience, making their circumstances grave. It is as you say, 'Do not ask about so-and-so! He is worse than you can imagine!'

وَلَن تَرْضَىٰ عَنكَ ٱلْيَهُودُ وَلَا ٱلنَّصَٰرَىٰ حَتَّىٰ تَتَّبِعَ مِلَّتَهُمْ قُلْ إِنَّ
هُدَى ٱللَّهِ هُوَ ٱلْهُدَىٰ وَلَئِنِ ٱتَّبَعْتَ أَهْوَآءَهُم بَعْدَ ٱلَّذِى جَآءَكَ مِنَ ٱلْعِلْمِ
مَا لَكَ مِنَ ٱللَّهِ مِن وَلِىٍّ وَلَا نَصِيرٍ ﴿١٢٠﴾

120 The Jews and the Christians will never be pleased with you until you follow their religion. Say, 'Allah's guidance is the true guidance.' If you were to follow their whims and desires, after the knowledge that has come to you, you would find no protector or helper against Allah.

The Jews and the Christians will never be pleased with you until you follow their religion.

Allah is telling His Messenger that it is not the goal of the Jews and Christians to gain faith by their queries about the *āyahs*. Even if he were to bring them everything they asked for, they would still not be pleased with him. They will not be pleased until he abandons Islam and follows them. The word *millah* (religion) means what Allah has prescribed for His slaves in His Books and on the tongues of His Messengers and so *millah* and Sharī'ah are very similar in meaning. There is a difference between the words *dīn*, *millah* and sharī'ah. *Millah* and sharī'ah designate what Allah orders His slaves to do and *dīn* is what the slaves actually make of Allah's commands to them.

A group of scholars, including Abū Ḥanīfah, ash-Shāfi'ī, Dāwūd and Aḥmad ibn Ḥanbal, hold the view that, according to this *āyah*, all disbelief constitutes one religion since the Almighty says: *'your religion'*, which is singular, and He says: *'You have your* dīn *and I have my* dīn' (109:6) and the Prophet ﷺ said, 'The people of two religions do not inherit from one another.' What is meant is Islam as the Prophet ﷺ also said, 'A Muslim does not inherit from an unbeliever.' Mālik and Aḥmad in another transmission believe that disbelief consists of several different religions and so a Jew does not inherit from a Christian and neither of them inherit from a Magian, taking the hadith of the Prophet ﷺ literally. The word *millah* here means a multiplicity of beliefs, even though it is singular.

Say, 'Allah's guidance is the true guidance.'

This means: 'O Muḥammad, what you have of the true guidance of Allah, which He places in the heart of whomever He wishes, is the true guidance, not what these people claim.'

If you were to follow their whims and desires,

There are two aspects to the use of the second person here. One is that it is addressed to the Messenger ﷺ alone; and the second is that while it is addressed to the Messenger ﷺ, it is his Community that is meant. According to the first aspect, it means to discipline Community since their position is less than his. The reason for the *āyah* was that the idolaters were asking for a truce while continuing to attack the Prophet ﷺ and Islam. So Allah informed him that they would not be pleased until he followed their religion and He commanded jihād against them.

after the knowledge that has come to you,

Aḥmad ibn Ḥanbal was asked about the one who says that the Qur'an is created. He said, 'He is an unbeliever.' It was asked, 'On what basis is he an unbeliever?' He said, 'By the *āyahs* of the Book of Allah: *"If you were to follow their whims and desires after the knowledge that has come to you."* This shows that the Qur'an is part of Allah's knowledge and so whoever claims it is created is an unbeliever.'

ٱلَّذِينَ ءَاتَيْنَٰهُمُ ٱلْكِتَٰبَ يَتْلُونَهُۥ حَقَّ تِلَاوَتِهِۦٓ أُو۟لَٰٓئِكَ يُؤْمِنُونَ بِهِۦ ۗ وَمَن يَكْفُرْ بِهِۦ
فَأُو۟لَٰٓئِكَ هُمُ ٱلْخَٰسِرُونَ ﴿١٢١﴾

121 Those to whom We have given the Book, who recite it in the way it should be recited, such people believe in it. As for those who reject it, they are the losers.

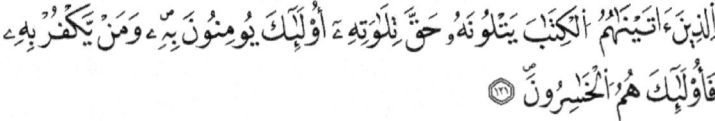

يَا بَنِي إِسْرَائِيلَ اذْكُرُوا نِعْمَتِيَ الَّتِي أَنْعَمْتُ عَلَيْكُمْ وَأَنِّي فَضَّلْتُكُمْ
عَلَى الْعَالَمِينَ ﴿١٢٢﴾ وَاتَّقُوا يَوْمًا لَا تَجْزِي نَفْسٌ عَنْ نَفْسٍ شَيْئًا وَلَا يُقْبَلُ مِنْهَا عَدْلٌ
وَلَا تَنْفَعُهَا شَفَاعَةٌ وَلَا هُمْ يُنْصَرُونَ ﴿١٢٣﴾

122 Tribe of Israel! remember the blessing I conferred on you, and that I preferred you over all other beings. 123 Have fear of a Day when no self will be able to compensate for another in any way, and no ransom will be accepted from it, and no intercession benefit it, and they will not be helped.

Those to whom We have given the Book,

Qatādah said that they are the Companions of the Prophet ﷺ and the Book is the Qur'an. Ibn Zayd said, 'They are those of the tribe of Israel who became Muslim, and so the Book is the Torah.' The *āyah* is, in fact, general.

who recite it in the way it should be recited,

There is disagreement about the meaning of the *āyah*. It is said that it means they follow the Book as it should be followed by obeying its commands and avoiding its prohibitions, observing the *ḥudūd* and the unlawful and in general acting according to what it contains, as 'Ikrimah said. 'Ikrimah also said, 'In the words of Allah Almighty: *"The moon when it follows it"* (91:2), the word *talā* – which in the *āyah* means "recite" – means "to follow", and that is what Ibn 'Abbās and Ibn Mas'ūd said.' Ibn 'Umar said that these words of Allah mean, 'They follow it as it should be followed.' According to al-Khaṭīb Abū Bakr Aḥmad, its *isnād* contains more than one unknown transmitter, but its meaning is sound. Abū Mūsā al-Ash'arī said, 'If someone diligently studies the Qur'an, it will bring him into the meadows of Paradise.'

'Umar ibn al-Khaṭṭāb said, 'They are those who, when they read an *āyah* of mercy, ask Allah for it, and when they read an *āyah* of punishment, seek refuge from it.' This understanding was reported in connection with the Prophet ﷺ. It was said of him that when, in the course of his recitation, he recited an *āyah* of mercy, he asked for it and when he recited an *āyah* of punishment, he sought refuge from it. Al-Ḥasan said, 'They are those who know its *āyahs* of judgment, believe its ambiguous *āyahs*, and entrust what is unclear in them to the Knower.' It is said that it means 'they recite it properly', but this is unlikely, unless it means they pronounce its phrases slowly and understand its meanings. One understands meanings by following them.

وَإِذِ ٱبْتَلَىٰٓ إِبْرَٰهِـۧمَ رَبُّهُۥ بِكَلِمَـٰتٍ فَأَتَمَّهُنَّ ۖ قَالَ إِنِّى جَاعِلُكَ لِلنَّاسِ إِمَامًا ۖ
قَالَ وَمِن ذُرِّيَّتِى ۖ قَالَ لَا يَنَالُ عَهْدِى ٱلظَّـٰلِمِينَ ﴿١٢٤﴾

124 Remember when Ibrāhīm was tested by his Lord with certain words which he carried out completely. He said, 'I will make you a model for mankind.' He asked, 'And what of my descendants?' He said, 'My contract does not include the wrongdoers.'

Remember when Ibrāhīm was tested by his Lord with certain words which he carried out completely.

Since the Ka'bah and qiblah are shortly going to be mentioned, this section is linked to Ibrāhīm who is the one who built the House. Part of the duty of the Jews, who are the descendants of Ibrāhīm, is not to tum away from his *dīn*. The 'testing' referred to was by commands and acts of worship. Ibrāhīm is a Syriac name, meaning 'merciful father' as al-Māwardī and Ibn 'Aṭiyyah mentioned. As-Suhaylī said, 'Often there is agreement between Syriac and Arabic, or the words are very similar.' Do you not see that Ibrāhīm was merciful to children? That is why he and his wife, Sārah, are entrusted with the care of the children of believers who die young until the Day of Rising? This is indicated by what al-Bukhārī transmitted about the long hadith of the vision reported from Samurah. In it the Prophet ﷺ said that Ibrāhīm was in the meadow surrounded by people's children.

Ibrāhīm was the son of Terath son of Nahor according to some commentators. The Revelation has: *'When Ibrāhīm said to his father, Āzar.'* (6:74) That is also what we find in *Ṣaḥīḥ al-Bukhārī*. There is no contradiction as we discuss later. According to as-Suhaylī, he had four sons: Ismā'īl, Isḥāq, Madyan and Madā'in.

The 'words' referred to are, in reality, the words of the Creator but they are considered to be the tasks which He imposed on Ibrāhīm. Since the means of their imposition was through words, they are called words, just as Jesus is also called a word since He issued from the word 'Be!' A thing can be called metaphorically by what it resulted from. Ibn al-'Arabī said that.

Scholars disagree about what is meant by these 'words' (*kalimāt*). One position is that they are the laws of Islam and that they entail thirty qualities:

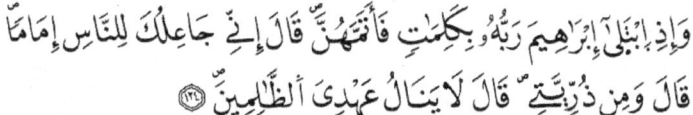

Ten are in *Sūrat at-Tawbah*: *'Those who make sincere repentance, those who worship, those who praise, those who fast, those who bow, those who prostrate, those who command what is*

known to be right, those who forbid what is recognised as wrong, those who preserve the limits of Allah: give good news to the believers.' (9:112)

Ten are in *Sūrat al-Aḥzāb*: *'Men and women who are Muslims, men and women who are believers, men and women who are obedient, men and women who are truthful, men and women who are steadfast, men and women who are humble, men and women who give* ṣadaqa, *men and women who fast, men and women who guard their private parts, men and women who remember Allah much: Allah has prepared forgiveness for them and an immense reward.'* (33:35)

And ten are in *Sūrat al-Mu'minūn*: *'It is the believers who are successful: those who are humble in their prayer; those who tum away from worthless talk; those who pay zakāt; those who guard their private parts except from their wives, or those they own as slaves, in which case they are not blameworthy – but those who desire anything more than that are people who have gone beyond the limits – those who honour their trusts and their contracts; those who safeguard their prayer.'* (23:1-9)

Ibn 'Abbās said, 'Allah did not test any person who fulfilled every one of these qualities except for Ibrāhīm. He was tested by Islam and fulfilled it completely. Allah exonerated him and said: *"Ibrāhīm who paid his dues in full."* (53:37)' Some said that it means the command and prohibition. Another said that the test was sacrificing his son. Yet another said it means carrying out the Message. The ideas are close to one another. Mujāhid said, 'It refers to the words of the Almighty to Ibrāhīm. Ibrāhīm said, "Will You make me a model for mankind?" "Yes," He said. He asked, "And what of my descendants?" He said, "My contract does not include the wrongdoers." Ibrāhīm asked, "Will You make the House a place of return for people?" "Yes," He answered. He asked, "And a sanctuary?" "Yes," He said. He said, "Will You show us our rites of worship and turn towards us?" "Yes," He answered. He asked, "Will You provide its inhabitants with fruits?" "Yes," He said. So according to this position, Allah Almighty is the one who carried out His own words.'

Sounder than this is what Ṭāwus reported that Ibn 'Abbās said about this matter: 'Allah tested him by acts of purification: five connected with the head and five with the body. They are, in respect of the head trimming the moustache, rinsing the mouth, snuffing water up the nose, using the *siwāk*, and parting the hair; and in respect of the body they are clipping the nails, shaving the pubes, circumcision, plucking the underarms, and washing the site of faeces and urine with water.' According to this position, the one who carried out the words was Ibrāhīm. It is the literal meaning of the Qur'an.

Maṭar related from Abu-l-Jald that there are ten although there is a difference: instead of parting the hair, there is washing the knuckles, and instead of washing the site of faeces and urine there is shaving the pubes with a razor. Qatādah said that they are the practices of the *Ḥajj*. Al-Ḥasan said that they are six things: rejecting first the planets, then the moon, then the sun, being thrown into the fire, emigration and circumcision. Az-Zajjāj said that these reports are not contradictory because all of them are part of what Ibrāhīm was tested with.

We see in the *Muwaṭṭā'* and elsewhere that Sa'īd ibn al-Musayyib was heard to say, 'Ibrāhīm was the first to be circumcised, the first to give hospitality, the first to make a mosque, the first to clip his nails, the first to trim the moustache, and the first to have white hair. When he saw the white hair, he asked, "What is this?" Allah answered, "Gravity." He said, "Lord, increase me in gravity!"' Abū Bakr ibn Abī Shaybah mentioned from Sa'īd ibn Ibrāhīm that his father said, "The first to give a *khuṭbah* on a minbar was Ibrāhīm, the Friend of Allah." Someone else said that he was the first to make a meat stew, the first to strike with a sword, the first to use *siwāk*, the first to use water in the lavatory and the first to wear trousers. Mu'ādh ibn Jabal reported that the Prophet ﷺ said, 'If I adopt a minbar, my father Ibrāhīm adopted it. If I take a staff, my father Ibrāhīm used it.' All these things will be dealt with in their proper place.

Scholars agree that Ibrāhīm was the first to be circumcised. There is disagreement about the age at which the circumcision took place. In the *Muwaṭṭā'* Abū Hurayrah is reported in a *mawqūf* report as stating that he was 120 and lived for eighty years after that. Something like this would not be stated based on mere opinion. Al-Awzā'ī related it *marfū'* from Yaḥyā ibn Sa'īd from Sa'īd ibn al-Musayyib. Abū 'Umar mentioned it. Others relate that it was done at the age of eighty and was carried out with an adze.

Scholars disagree about the legal status of circumcision. The majority say that it is a confirmed *sunnah* and part of the natural patterning of Islam which men should not abandon. A group say that it is obligatory since Allah says: *'Follow the religion of Ibrāhīm, a man of pure natural faith.'* (2:123) Qatādah said that that refers to circumcision and some Mālikīs believe that. That is the view of ash-Shāfi'ī. Some of our people argue on the basis of what al-Ḥajjāj ibn Arṭa'ah related from Abu-l-Maliḥ from his father from Shaddād ibn Awas that the Messenger of Allah ﷺ said, 'Circumcision is sunnah for men, and honour for women.' Al-Ḥajjāj is not someone who is used as authority.

Part of what is considered authoritative about this matter is the hadith of Abū Hurayrah that the Prophet ﷺ said, 'The natural form (*fiṭrah*) consists of five: circumcision…' Abū Dāwūd related from Umm 'Aṭiyyah that a woman used to circumcise women in Madīnah. The Prophet ﷺ told her, 'Do not cut a lot. That is better for the woman and more liked by her husband.' Abū Dāwūd said that this hadith is weak. It contains someone unknown. A boy born with no foreskin is spared circumcision. Al-Maymūnī said, 'I said to Aḥmad, "This is a man who was born circumcised. He is very grieved about it." He said, "Allah has spared him the burden. What is he unhappy about?"'

Abū al-Faraj al-Jawzī said that Ka'b al-Aḥbār said, 'Thirteen Prophets were created circumcised: Ādam, Shīth, Idrīs, Nūḥ, Sām, Lūṭ, Yūsuf, Mūsā, Shu'ayb, Sulaymān, Yaḥyā, 'Īsā and the Prophet ﷺ.' Muḥammad ibn Ḥabīb al-Hāshimī said that there were fourteen: Ādam, Shīth, Nūḥ, Hūd, Ṣāliḥ, Lūṭ, Shu'ayb, Yūsuf, Mūsā, Sulaymān, Zakariyyā, 'Īsā, Ḥanẓalah ibn Ṣafwān (the Prophet of the people of ar-Rass) and the Prophet ﷺ.

There are differing reports about the Prophet ﷺ. Ḥāfiẓ Abū Nu'aym said in *Kitāb 'l-ḥilyah* with an *isnād* that the Prophet ﷺ was born uncircumcised. In *at-Tamhīd* Abū 'Umar has an *isnād* from Aḥmad ibn Muḥammad ibn Aḥmad from Muḥammad ibn 'Īsā from Yaḥyā ibn Ayyūb al-'Allāf from Muḥammad ibn Abī as-Sariyy al-'Asqallānī from al-Walīd ibn Muslim from Shu'ayb from 'Aṭā' al-Khurāsāni from 'Ikrimah from Ibn 'Abbās that 'Abd al-Muṭṭalib circumcised the Prophet ﷺ on the seventh day, prepared a feast for him and named him 'Muḥammad'. Abū 'Umar said that it is a hadith with a strange *isnād*. Yaḥyā ibn Ayyūb said, 'I looked for this hadith and did not find it with any of the people of hadith I met except for Ibn Abī as-Sariyy.' Abū 'Umar remarked that it is said that the Prophet ﷺ was born uncircumcised.

There is disagreement about when a boy should be circumcised. It is confirmed in reports from a group of scholars that Ibrāhīm circumcised Ishmael at the age of thirteen and circumcised his son Isaac at the age of seven days. It is related from Fāṭimah that she circumcised her son on the seventh day. Mālik objected to that and said that it is part of Jewish practice. Ibn Wahb mentioned it from him. Al-Layth ibn Sa'd said, 'A child is circumcised between the age of seven and ten.' Ibn Wahb related the like from Mālik. Aḥmad said, 'I have not heard anything about this.' We find in al-Bukhārī that Sa'īd ibn Jubayr said, 'Ibn 'Abbās was asked, "What were you like when the Messenger of Allah ﷺ died?" He said, "I was still uncircumcised that day."' He said, 'They used not to circumcise a male until he had reached puberty, or shortly before.'

Scholars recommend that an adult male should be circumcised. 'Aṭā' used to say that a man's Islam is not complete until he is circumcised, even if he is eighty. It is related that al-Ḥasan allowed an old man who becomes Muslim to not be circumcised and he saw no harm in him, his testimony, slaughtering, ḥajj and prayer. Ibn 'Abd al-Barr said, 'This is what most of the people of knowledge believe. The hadith of Buraydah about the ḥajj of an uncircumcised man is not confirmed.' It is related from Ibn 'Abbās, Jābir ibn Zayd and 'Ikrimah that the animals slaughtered by someone uncircumcised are not eaten and his testimony is not accepted.

With regard to clipping the nails, Mālik said, 'It is recommended for women to clip their nails and shave their pubes just as it is for men.' Al-Ḥārith ibn Miskīn and Saḥnūn mentioned it from Ibn al-Qāsim. At-Tirmidhī mentioned in *Nawādir al-uṣūl* from 'Umar ibn Ibn 'Umar from Ibrāhīm ibn al-'Alā' az-Zubaydī that 'Umar ibn Bilāl al-Fazārī heard 'Abdullāh ibn Bishr al-Māzinī that the Messenger of Allah ﷺ said, 'Cut your nails and bury the clippings. Clean your knuckles. Cleans your gums of food and brush your teeth. Do not visit me stinking.'

Trimming the moustache involves cutting it back a little so that the edge of the lip appears but not removing it completely, which constitutes self-mutilation according to Mālik. Ibn 'Abd al-Ḥakam reported that he said, 'I think that someone who shaves off his moustache should be disciplined.' Ashhab said that Mālik said about shaving it, 'It is an innovation and I think that the one who does it should be beaten.' Ibn Khuwayzimandād said that Mālik said, 'I think that someone who shaves should be painfully beaten.' This seems to be because he viewed it as self-mutilation. The same is true about plucking it out. It is better to trim it than shave.

It is related that the Prophet ﷺ used to trim his nails and moustache before he went to Jumu'ah. Aṭ-Ṭaḥāwī said, 'We did not find any text from ash-Shāfi'ī on that. His companions whom we saw, namely al-Muzanī and ar-Rabī', used to trim their moustaches. That indicates that they took that from ash-Shāfi'ī.' He said that the school of Abū Ḥanīfah, Zafar, Abū Yūsuf and Muḥammad was that it was better to trim the hair and moustache close than to shorten it. Ibn Khuwayzimandād mentioned that the school of ash-Shāfi'ī was to shave the moustache as was the school of Abū Ḥanīfah. Abū Bakr al-Athram said, 'I saw that Aḥmad ibn Ḥanbal trimmed his moustache a lot. I heard him being asked about the sunnah of trimming the moustache and he said, "It is trimmed as the Prophet ﷺ said, 'Trim the moustache.'"'

Abū Bakr said that there are two basic principles here: one is trimming, which is a word subject to interpretation, and the other is shortening it, which is explanatory. That which is explained trumps that which is subject to interpretation. That was the practice of the people of Madīnah, and it is the most appropriate thing that is said about this topic. At-Tirmidhī related that Ibn 'Abbās said, 'The Messenger of Allah ﷺ used to shorten his moustache and said, "Ibrāhīm, the Beloved of the All-Merciful, used to do this.'" He said that it is a *ḥasan gharīb* hadith. Muslim transmitted from Abū Hurayrah that the Prophet ﷺ said, 'The natural form consists of five: circumcision, shaving the pubes, shortening the moustache, clipping the nails and plucking the armpits.' Regarding that, Ibn 'Umar said that the Messenger of Allah ﷺ said, 'Be different to the idolaters. Trim the moustache and let the beard be full.' The Persians used to shorten their beards and let their moustaches grow, or let them both grow. This is contrary to beauty and cleanliness. Razīn mentioned from Nāfi' that Ibn 'Umar used to trim his moustache until the skin showed, and he cut what was between the moustache and the beard. We find in al-Bukhārī: 'Ibn 'Umar used to cut off of his beard what was more than a handful when he went on ḥajj or *'umrah.* At-Tirmidhī related from 'Abdullāh ibn 'Amr ibn al-'Āṣ that the Messenger of Allah ﷺ used to cut some of his beard on the sides and end. He said that it is a *gharīb* hadith.

The sunnah for armpits is to pluck them as the sunnah for the pubes is to shave them. If the reverse is done, that is permitted because cleanliness is achieved, but the first is more appropriate since it is the custom.

The hair is parted. The Prophet ﷺ used to part his locks. One describes 'parting' the hair when it is not left to grow however it will. An-Nasā'ī related from Ibn 'Abbās that the Prophet ﷺ used leave his hair to hang down and the idolaters used to part their hair. He liked to be in conformity with the People of the Book when he had not been commanded anything specific. Then after that he ﷺ parted his hair. Al-Bukhārī and Muslim transmitted it from Anas. Qāḍī 'Iyāḍ said that in reference to the hair, *sadl* is to let it grow freely. What is meant by scholars here is to let the hair fall on the forehead and to put it into a lock. Parting the hair is sunnah because it is that to which the Prophet ﷺ reverted. It is related that when 'Umar ibn 'Abd al-'Azīz left the *Jumu'ah* prayer, he put guards at the door of the mosque to cut off the forelock of everyone who had not parted his hair. It is said that parting was part of the sunnah of Ibrāhīm ﷺ. Allah knows best.

Regarding white hair, it is a light and it is disliked to pluck it out. We find in an-Nasā'ī and Abū Dāwūd from 'Amr ibn Shu'ayb from his grandfather that the Prophet ﷺ said, 'Do not pluck out white hair. There is no Muslim who has become white-haired in Islam but that it will be a light for him on the Day of Rising and a good deed will be will be written for him and an error dropped.' It is also disliked to dye it black, but permitted to use other colours as is reported in the hadith in which Abū Quḥāfah was brought to the Prophet ﷺ and his beard was white like wormwood. The Prophet ﷺ said, 'Change this, but avoid black.'

He said, 'I will make you a model for mankind.'

The word *imām* here means a model. It is used for a builder's measure and also for a road because it directs the traveller. It means: 'We will make you an imam for people, whom they will imitate in these qualities, and the righteous will follow you.' So He made him an imam for the people who obey Him. That is why all the nations agree that he was rightly guided, and Allah knows best.

He asked, 'And what of my descendants?'

This is a kind of supplication which consists of asking for information from Allah, meaning, 'Lord, will You place this right guidance among my descendants?' This is asking for information or it may be a simple question. Allah informed him that the disobedient and wrongdoers among them are not entitled to be models.

The word for 'descendants' is *dhuriyyah*. That is because Allah brought them out from the loins of Adam like atoms (*dharr*) when He made them bear witness against themselves. It is also said that it is derived from *dhara'a*, when Allah created them.

He said, 'My contract does not include the wrongdoers.'

There is disagreement about what is meant by *'ahd* (contract) here. Ibn 'Abbās said that it refers to Prophethood as did as-Suddī. Mujāhid said it refers to the imamate; Qatādah that it refers to faith; 'Aṭā' that it refers to mercy; and aḍ-Ḍaḥḥāk that it refers to the *dīn* of Allah. It is said that Allah's contract is His command and that the usage of *'ahd* is found elsewhere in the Qur'an, as in *'Allah made a **contract** with us'* (3:183), meaning 'commanded us'. Allah says: *'Did I not make a contract with you, tribe of Ādam?'* (36:60) It means 'command' because the contract of Allah consists of His commands. So this *āyah* means: 'It is not possible for them to be in the same position as those accept the commands of Allah since the wrongdoers do not establish them.' Ma'mar related that Qatādah also said that it means: 'My contract concerning the Next World does not include the wrongdoers. As for in this world, it is possible wrongdoers may obtain it.' Az-Zajjāj said, 'This is a good view. It means that the hopes of the wrongdoers will not be realised: they are not safe from Allah's punishment.' Sa'īd ibn Jubayr said that 'wrongdoer' means 'idolater'.

A group of scholars use this *āyah* as evidence that the imam must be one of the people of justice, good and excellence and have the ability to fulfill the task of leadership. This is borne out by the command of the Prophet ﷺ: 'Do not dispute power with its people.' The people of iniquity, injustice and wrong cannot be considered its people because of this *āyah*. This was the reason for the rebellion of Ibn az-Zubayr and that of al-Ḥusayn, the rebellion of the virtuous people and scholars of Iraq against al-Ḥajjāj, and the rebellion of the people of Madīnah against the Umayyads at the Battle of al-Ḥarrah when Muslim ibn 'Uqbah attacked it.

Most scholars take the view that perseverance in obedience to an unjust ruler is better than rebellion because the consequence of resisting him and rebelling against him is to replace security with fear, shed blood, give free rein to foolish people, attack the Muslims and corrupt the earth. The other is a position of a group of Mu'tazilites and the position of the Khārijites.

Ibn Khuwayzimandād said, 'No wrongdoer can be a Prophet or judge or mufti or leader of the prayer. If such a thing occurs then what he relates of the Sharī'ah is not accepted and his testimony is not accepted in judgment, although he is not dismissed for his iniquity until those entitled to appoint and dismiss do so. His judgments that accord with what is correct are carried out. Mālik stated this about the Khārijites and the rebels: their judgments are not declared void when they entail some form of *ijtihād* and do not violate the consensus or oppose texts and this was the consensus of the Companions. That is because the Khārijites rebelled in their time but it is not transmitted that the imāms criticised their judgments or anulled any of them or repeated their collection of *zakāt* or objected to their carrying out the *ḥudūd* punishments when they had done it. That indicates that, when they use proper *ijtihād*, their rulings are not attacked.'

Ibn Khuwayzimandād said, 'As for taking stipends from unjust leaders, there are three possibilities. If everything in their possession has been gathered according to the just demands of the Sharī'ah, it is permitted to take the stipend, and the Companions and *Tābi'ūn* took it from al-Ḥajjāj and others. If the lawful and unjust are mixed, as is the case of rulers today, it is scrupulous to forgo it, but it is permitted for the needy to take it. In this case the ruler is like a thief who has both stolen property and lawful property in his possession and gives something as charity to someone. The recipient is permitted to accept it as *ṣadaqah* even though it is possible that it might be part of the stolen property. The same is true if such a ruler buys or sells: the contract is binding although it is more scrupulous to avoid it. If, however, everything that is in his possession is clearly unlawful, then it is not permitted to accept his *ṣadaqah*. If the property in their possession is usurped and it is not known who is its owner and there is no claimant, then it is like what is found in the possession of thieves and highwaymen and is put in the treasury to await a claimant. If there is no one to claim it, the ruler spends as seems best in the best interests of the Muslims.

وَإِذْ جَعَلْنَا ٱلْبَيْتَ مَثَابَةً لِّلنَّاسِ وَأَمْنًا وَٱتَّخِذُوا۟ مِن مَّقَامِ إِبْرَٰهِـۧمَ مُصَلًّى ۖ
وَعَهِدْنَآ إِلَىٰٓ إِبْرَٰهِـۧمَ وَإِسْمَـٰعِيلَ أَن طَهِّرَا بَيْتِىَ لِلطَّآئِفِينَ وَٱلْعَـٰكِفِينَ
وَٱلرُّكَّعِ ٱلسُّجُودِ ﴿١٢٥﴾

125 And when We made the House a place of return, a sanctuary for mankind, and they took the Maqām of Ibrāhīm as a place of prayer. We contracted with Ibrāhīm and Ismā'īl: 'Purify My House for those who circle it, and those who stay there, and those who bow and who prostrate.'

And when We made the House a place of return, a sanctuary for mankind,

The House is the Ka'bah. *Mathābah* (place of return) is the form of the noun used for place, derived from the verb *thāba*, 'to return'. It is called that because people return to it year after year. The use of the word 'sanctuary' in this *āyah* was taken by Abū Ḥanīfah and a group of *fuqahā'* as evidence for not imposing the *ḥadd* punishment in the Ḥaram when an adulterer or thief takes refuge there. In making that ruling they also rely on the words of Allah: *'All who enter it are safe.'* (3:97) The sound position is that the *ḥudūd* punishments are carried out in the Ḥaram and that this *āyah* is abrogated although there is agreement that the killing does not take place in the House but outside of it. The disagreement is about killing inside the Ḥaram. If someone violates a *ḥadd* there, he is punished there. If someone attacks in it, he is fought and killed where he is. Abū Ḥanīfah says that the one who seeks refuge in the Ḥaram is not killed or pursued and remains confined in it until he dies or leaves. We kill him with the sword and Allah kills him by hunger and constriction, thus condemning him to a worse death. The fact that it is a sanctuary reinforces the command to face the Ka'bah in the prayer because Jerusalem does not have this virtue and people do not make *ḥajj* to it.

and they took the Maqām of Ibrāhīm as a place of prayer.'

There are two readings of the verb 'to take' in this phrase. Nāfi' and Ibn 'Āmir recite it as *ittakh**a**dhū*, making it a report about those of the followers of Ibrāhīm who prayed there, added to *'We made'* and so it reads: 'they took the Maqām of Ibrāhīm as a place of prayer.' Or it means 'when We made' and 'when they took'. The second reading is *ittakh**i**dhū* in the imperative mood so the meaning is a command and the phrase reads: 'Take the Maqām of Ibrāhīm as a place of prayer.' According to the first, there is one sentence, and according to the second, there are two sentences. The majority read it with a *kasrah* as a command and disconnect it from the first sentence.

Ibn 'Umar reported that 'Umar said, 'I coincided with my Lord on three occasions: regarding the Maqām of Ibrāhīm, the ḥijāb and the captives of Badr.' Muslim and others transmitted it. A similar report comes from al-Bukhārī. He suggested praying behind the Maqām and then this was revealed. He suggested the ḥijāb and 33:53 was revealed.

The word *maqām* means a place where you stand. There are various statements about the *Maqām*. The soundest is that it is the stone which people recognise today and behind which they pray the two *rak'ah*s after completing the *Ṭawāf* of Arrival. This is the position of Jābir ibn 'Abdullāh, Ibn 'Abbās, Qatādah and others. In *Ṣaḥīḥ Muslim*, in a long hadith, Jābir said, 'When the Prophet ﷺ saw the House, he greeted the Corner and then trotted three circuits and walked four. Then he went to the Maqām Ibrāhīm and recited, *"they took the Maqām of Ibrāhīm as a place of prayer,"* and prayed two *rak'ah*s in which he recited *Sūrat al-Ikhlāṣ* and *Sūrat al-Kāfirūn*.' This indicates that the two *rak'ah*s of *ṭawāf* and other prayers are better for the people of Makkah. In another transmission, as will be mentioned, it indicates that *ṭawāf* is better for non-resident visitors.

In al-Bukhārī it states that it is the stone which Ibrāhīm climbed on when he was too weak to lift up the stones which Ismā'īl handed him when they were building the House and his feet sank into it. Anas said, 'In the Maqām I saw the trace of his fingers and heels and the hollows of his feet. But that disappeared when people continued to wipe it with their hands.' Al-Qushayrī mentioned it. As-Suddī said, 'The Maqām is the stone which Ismā'īl's wife placed under Ibrahim's feet when she washed his head.' Ibn 'Abbās, Mujāhid, 'Ikrimah and 'Aṭā' said that the Maqām is all of the ḥajj. 'Aṭā' said that it is 'Arafah, Muzdalifah and the *jamrah*s. Ash-Sha'bī said that. An-Nakha'ī said that all of the Ḥaram is the Maqām of Ibrāhīm. Mujāhid said that.

The sound position about the Maqām is the first statement since it is confirmed in the *Ṣaḥīḥ*. Abū Nu'aym transmitted from Muḥammad ibn Sūqah from Muḥammad ibn al-Munkadir that Jābir said, 'The Prophet ﷺ looked at a man between the corner and the Maqām — or the door and the Maqām — making supplication. He was saying, "O Allah, forgive so-and-so." The Prophet ﷺ asked him, "What is this?" He said, "A man charged me to supplicate for him in this Maqām." He said, "Return. Your companion is forgiven."' It has further paths of transmission.

We contracted with Ibrāhīm and Ismā'īl: 'Purify My House

'We contracted' (*'ahidnā*) here means 'We commanded' or 'We revealed to'. The Kufans say that 'purify' means to clear it of idols, as Mujāhid and az-Zuhrī said. 'Ubayd ibn 'Umayr and Sa'īd ibn Jubayr said that it means to purify it of evil things and doubt. It is said that it means from unbelievers. As-Suddī said, 'They built it and founded it on purity and with the intention of purity and so it is connected to the words of the Almighty: *"Founded on* taqwā." (9:108) By saying "My House" Allah ascribes it to Himself to honour it. It is like the relationship of a creature to the Creator and a slave to his Master.' He says, 'My House' to honour it. When Allah says: *'Purify My House'*, He means all mosques, and so its ruling is that of cleanliness and purification. The Ka'bah is mentioned because it was the only mosque at that time or because it is the most respected House. The first view is more likely, and Allah knows best. We read in the Revelation: *'In houses which Allah has permitted to be built.'* (24:36)

'Umar ibn al-Khaṭṭāb related that he heard the noise of a man in the mosque. He said, 'What is this? Do you know where you are?' Ḥudhayfah said that the Prophet ﷺ said, 'Allah revealed to me, "Brother of the warners! Brother of the Messengers! Warn your people to only enter one of My houses with sound hearts, truthful tongues, clean hands and pure private parts. One should not enter one of My houses as long as he has an injustice on his head. I will curse him as long as he stands before Me until that injustice is restored to its people. Then I am his hearing with which he hears and his sight with which He sees, and he is one of My friends and chosen ones. He goes with the Prophets, truthful, martyrs and righteous."'

Those who circle it,

The word used here is *ṭā'ifīn* and its apparent meaning is to circumambulate it, as 'Aṭā' says. Sa'īd ibn Jubayr says that it means 'strangers who come to Makkah'. That is somewhat unlikely.

and those who stay there,

This is also said to mean those who live in its vicinity, or even, as Ibn 'Abbās states, those who pray there. It is said that it means 'those who sit there without doing *ṭawāf*'.

and those who bow and who prostrate.'

Bowing and prostrating refer to praying towards the Ka'bah in the Ḥaram. These two things are mentioned because they are the states in which the one who prays is closest to Allah. Ash-Shāfi'ī Abū Ḥanīfah, ath-Thawrī and a group of the

Salaf used this *āyah* as evidence for the permission to pray both the *farḍ* and *nāfilah* prayers inside the House. Ash-Shāfi'ī said that if you pray inside it and face one of its walls, then your prayer is allowed. If you pray towards the open door, your prayer is invalid. That also applies to someone who prays on top of it because he does not face anything. Mālik said, 'You may not pray a *farḍ* or *sunnah* in it, but you may pray *nāfilah* prayers inside. If someone prays the *farḍ* prayer there, he must repeat it if it is still within the time of that prayer.' Aṣbagh said he must always repeat it, even outside the time.

This is sound according to what Muslim related from Ibn 'Abbās. He said, 'Usāmah ibn Zayd told me that when the Prophet ﷺ entered the House, he made supplication in all its corners but did not pray until he had come out. When he came out, he prayed two *rak'ahs* facing the Ka'bah and said, "This is the *qiblah*."' Al-Bukhārī related that Ibn 'Umar said, 'The Messenger of Allah ﷺ entered with Usāmah ibn Zayd, Bilāl, and 'Uthmān ibn Ṭalḥah al-Ḥajabī and they locked the door behind them. When they opened the door, I was the first to enter and met Bilāl. I asked him, "Did the Messenger of Allah ﷺ pray?" "Yes," he answered, "between the two pillars on the right."' Muslim transmitted it. It says in it: 'He had two pillars on his left, a pillar on his right and three pillars behind him.' At that time the House had six pillars. It is possible that 'pray' means to make supplication as Usāmah said, and it is also possible that it is the normal prayer.

Ibn al-Mundhir and others related that Usāmah said, 'The Messenger of Allah ﷺ saw some images in the Ka'bah. I brought some water in a bucket with which he washed them off.' Abū Dāwūd aṭ-Ṭayālisī transmitted from Ibn Abī Dhi'b from 'Abd ar-Raḥmān ibn Mahrān from 'Umayr, the freedman of Ibn 'Abbās, that Usāmah ibn Zayd said, 'I went in to the Messenger of Allah ﷺ in the Ka'bah and he saw some images. He called for a bucket of water. I brought it to him and he began to wash them off, saying, "May Allah fight a people who make images of what they did not create!"' It is possible that the Prophet ﷺ prayed while Usāmah had gone to look for water and Bilāl saw him but Usāmah did not. Affirming it is more proper than denying it. Usāmah himself said, 'People took what Bilāl said and left what I said.' Mujāhid related that 'Abdullāh ibn Ṣafwān said, 'I asked 'Umar ibn al-Khaṭṭāb, "How did the Messenger of Allah ﷺ pray when he entered the Ka'bah?" "Two *rak'ahs*," he replied.'

This is possible for *nāfilah* prayers. We do not know of any disagreement between scholars on the validity of *nāfilah* prayers in the Ka'bah. That is not the case with *farḍ* prayers because Allah Almighty specified direction when He says: *'Turn your face, therefore, towards the Masjid al-Ḥaram.'* (2:144) When he said, 'This is the qiblah' when he came out, he specified it as Allah had specified it. If the *farḍ* prayer had been valid inside it, he would not have said, 'This is the qiblah.' This is a sound manner of combining the two hadiths.

There is also disagreement about praying on top of it. Ash-Shāfi'ī said what we mentioned. Mālik said, 'Whoever prays on top of it should repeat the prayer within the time.' Some of Mālik's people said that it should always be repeated. Abū Ḥanīfah says that one who prays there does not owe anything.

They also disagree about which is better: praying at the House or *ṭawāf* of it. Mālik said that *ṭawāf* is better for the people of other places and that prayer is better for the people of Makkah. That is mentioned from Ibn 'Abbās, 'Aṭā' and Mujāhid. The majority say that the prayer is better. We find in a report: 'If it had not been for humble men, bowing old men, suckling babes, and grazing animals, We would have poured the punishment on you.' Abū Bakr Aḥmad ibn 'Alī ibn Thābit the Khaṭib said that 'Abdullāh ibn Mas'ūd said that the Messenger of Allah ﷺ said, 'If it had not been that among you are humble men, grazing animals and suckling babes, the punishment would have poured down on the sinners.' Abū Dharr said, 'The prayer is best, so do a lot of it,' Al-Ajurrī transmitted it. There are many reports that attest to the excellence of the prayer and prostration. Allah knows best.

وَإِذْ قَالَ إِبْرَٰهِيمُ رَبِّ ٱجْعَلْ هَٰذَا بَلَدًا ءَامِنًا وَٱرْزُقْ أَهْلَهُۥ مِنَ
ٱلثَّمَرَٰتِ مَنْ ءَامَنَ مِنْهُم بِٱللَّهِ وَٱلْيَوْمِ ٱلْءَاخِرِ ۖ قَالَ وَمَن كَفَرَ فَأُمَتِّعُهُۥ
قَلِيلًا ثُمَّ أَضْطَرُّهُۥٓ إِلَىٰ عَذَابِ ٱلنَّارِ ۖ وَبِئْسَ ٱلْمَصِيرُ ﴿١٢٦﴾

126 And when Ibrāhīm said, 'My Lord, make this a place of safety and provide its inhabitants with fruits – all of them who believe in Allah and the Last Day,' He said, 'I will let anyone who becomes an unbeliever enjoy himself a little but then I will drive him to the punishment of the Fire. What an evil destination!'

And when Ibrāhīm said, 'My Lord, make this a place of safety and provide its inhabitants with fruits –

This means Makkah. He prayed for his descendants and others to have security and ample livelihood there. It is related that when he made this supplication, Allah commanded Jibrīl to uproot the town of Ṭā'if from Syria and he then carried it around the Ka'bah for a week, which is why it is called Ṭā'if. Then he set it down in Tihāmah. Makkah and what was around it was a desert without water or plants. Allah blessed the area around it like Ṭā'if and other places and plants grew.

Scholars disagree about whether Makkah became a *ḥaram* by Ibrāhīm's supplication or whether it was one before that. One view is that it has always been a *ḥaram*, protected from tyrants, earthquakes and other such things that happen to other lands. Rebellious people feel respect for it so that its people alone enjoy security. In it Allah has placed the great symbol of His Unity. Its special status is shown by game which go into it. Dogs and game meet in it and the dogs do not attack the game. But, when the game animal leaves the *ḥaram*, the dogs run after it. Ibrāhīm asked his Lord to protect it from drought, famine and attacks and to provide its people with fruits. He did not, as some people think, refer to shedding blood in it when that was necessary. That was not what he intended so that someone might say that he asked Allah to forbid the killing of those who sought refuge in it. This is very unlikely.

The second view is that it was not a *ḥaram* before the prayer of Ibrāhīm and was like any other place and that it only became a *ḥaram* when he made his supplication, as Madīnah became one when the Messenger of Allah ﷺ made it one. The people of the first position use as evidence the hadith of Ibn 'Abbās in which the Messenger of Allah ﷺ said on the Day of the Conquest, 'This city (Makkah) was made a *ḥaram* the day when Allah created the heavens and the earth and so will remain sacred by Allah's making it sacred until the Day of Rising. It was not lawful for anyone to fight in it before me and it was only lawful for me for one hour of one day. It will remain sacred because Allah has made it so until the Day of Rising. Its thorns should not be cut, its game should not be hunted and something dropped should not be picked except by someone who announces that he has found it.' Ibn 'Abbās said, 'Messenger of Allah, except for idhkhir-herb for our goldsmiths and houses.' He said, 'Except for *idhkhir*-herb.' Muslim and others transmitted something similar from Shurayḥ.

In *Ṣaḥīḥ Muslim*, 'Abdullāh ibn Zayd ibn 'Āṣim reported that the Messenger of Allah ﷺ said, 'Ibrāhīm made Makkah a *ḥaram* and prayed for its people. I made Madīnah a *ḥaram* as Ibrāhīm made Makkah a *ḥaram* and I prayed for its *ṣā'* and *mudd* in the same way that Ibrāhīm prayed for the people of Makkah.' Ibn 'Aṭiyyah said that there is no conflict between the two hadiths because the first one reports about the prior knowledge and decree of Allah for it and that it was sacred in the time of Ādam and the time when those with belief lived there, and the second reported about Ibrāhīm renewing its inviolability after it had fallen away. The first statement of the Prophet ﷺ reports about the huge importance of the inviolability of Makkah for the believers by making that inviolability go back to Allah. Mentioning Ibrāhīm when he made Madīnah a *ḥaram* is providing a model. It is not impossible that the inviolability of Madīnah also came from Allah, and was the carrying out of His Decree and by His prior knowledge. Aṭ-Ṭabarī said, 'Makkah was a *ḥaram*, but Allah did not make people worship by that until Ibrāhīm asked him for it and so He made it inviolable.'

He said, 'I will let anyone who becomes an unbeliever enjoy himself a little

Scholars disagree about whether this statement was made by Ibrāhīm or Allah. Ubayy ibn Ka'b, Ibn Isḥāq and others said, 'That is from Allah Almighty'. Six readings have ***u****matti'uhu* ('I will let enjoy') while Ibn 'Āmir has ***nu****matti'uh'* ('We will let enjoy') as well as 'We will drive him'. Ibn 'Abbās, Mujāhid and Qatādah said that the statement was made by Ibrāhīm. They read it as *amti'hu* in the imperative, and so it is a supplication made by Ibrāhīm against them: "Let him enjoy..." Ibn 'Abbās said, 'Ibrāhīm prayed for those who believed in particular and Allah informed him that He would provide for those who disbelieved as well as those who believed and that He would let them enjoy themselves a little and then force them to the punishment of the Fire.' Abū Ja'far said that Allah says: '*We sustain each one, the former and the latter, through the generous giving of your Lord'* (17:20) and He also says: *'There are nations to whom We will give enjoyment.'* (11:48) Abū Isḥāq said, 'Ibrāhīm knew that there would be unbelievers among his descendants and so he singled out the believers.

وَإِذْ يَرْفَعُ إِبْرَٰهِيمُ ٱلْقَوَاعِدَ مِنَ ٱلْبَيْتِ وَإِسْمَٰعِيلُ رَبَّنَا تَقَبَّلْ مِنَّآ إِنَّكَ أَنتَ
ٱلسَّمِيعُ ٱلْعَلِيمُ ١٢٧

127 And when Ibrāhīm laid the foundations of the House with Ismā'īl: 'Our Lord, accept this from us! You are the All-Hearing, the All-Knowing.

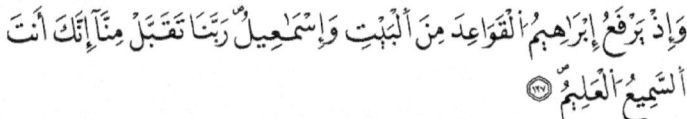

The word *qawā'id* (foundations) mentioned here is the subject of some discussion. Abū 'Ubaydah and al-Farrā' say it means foundations but al-Kisā'ī says it means walls. Its usual meaning however, is foundations. In a report we find: 'When the House was demolished, huge stones from it were brought, and Ibn Az-Zubayr said, "These are the foundations (*qawā'id*) which Ibrāhīm laid."' It is said that the foundations had been demolished and Allah informed Ibrāhīm about them. Ibn 'Abbās said, 'The House was set on foundations which existed a thousand years before this world was created.' The singular of *qawā'id* is *qā'idah.*

People disagree about who first built the House and its foundations. It is said that it was the angels. It is related that Ja'far ibn Muḥammad said, 'While I was present, my father was asked about the initial creation of the House. He said, "When Allah said, *'I am putting a caliph on the earth'* (2:30), the angels said, *'Why put on it one who will cause corruption on it and shed blood when we glorify You with praise and proclaim Your purity?'* He became angry with them and they sought refuge with His Throne and circled it seven times, seeking to please their Lord so that He might be pleased with them. He told them, 'Build for Me a House on the earth at which those of the sons of Ādam with whom I am angry might seek refuge and circumambulate it as you did of my Throne. I will be pleased with them as I am pleased with you.' So they built this House."'

'Abd ar-Razzāq mentioned from Ibn Jurayj from 'Aṭā', Ibn al-Musayyab and others that they reported that Allah revealed to Ādam, 'When you go down to the earth, build me a House. Then go around it as you saw the angels going around My Throne in heaven.' 'Aṭā' said, 'People claim that it was built from five mountains: Ḥirā', Sinai, Lebanon, al-Jūdī and Mt. Zayta. Its *rubḍ* was from Ḥirā'.' Al-Khalīl said that the meaning *rubḍ* in this context is the circular foundation of the House which is made of stone. One also calls the outskirts of Madīnah *rubḍ.*

Al-Māwardī mentioned from 'Aṭā' that Ibn 'Abbās said, 'When Ādam descended to earth from the Garden, he was told, "Ādam, go and build a House for Me. Circumambulate it and remember Me at it as you saw the angels doing around My Throne." Ādam went forward and traversing the earth was shortened for him. Every place on which his foot fell flourished until he reached the site of the Sacred House. Jibrīl was striking the earth with his wings and uncovered a firm foundation on the ground of the lowest earth. The angels threw stones to him and one of the stones could not be lifted by thirty men.' He built it from five mountains as we mentioned.

It is related in some reports that Ādam brought down one of the tents of the Garden and set it up at the site of the Ka'bah so that he could live in it and circumambulate it. It remained there until Allah took Ādam and then it was removed. This is reported from Wahb ibn Munabbih. One version has: 'A House came down with him, and he did *ṭawāf* of it as did his believing children. That was how it was until the time of the Flood. Then Allah removed it to heaven. It is what is called "the Inhabited House".' This is related from Qatādah. Al-Ḥalīmī mentioned it in *Kitāb minhāj 'd-dīn.* He said, 'It is possible that what Qatādah said about it descending with him was the measure of the Inhabited House in height, width and thickness. Then he was told to build according to those measurements and to position it opposite it. So the position of the Ka'bah is opposite it and he built it there. As for the tent, it could have descended and been set up in the location of the Ka'bah. When he was commanded to build it, he built it and it was around the Ka'bah, giving peace of mind to Ādam as long as he lived. Then it was removed.' So these reports agree. This was the building of Ādam and then Ibrāhīm rebuilt it.

It is related from 'Alī ibn Abī Ṭālib that when Allah commanded Ibrāhīm to build the House, he set out from Syria with his son Ismā'īl and Ismā'īl's mother Hajar. The *Sakīnah* was sent with him with a tongue by which it spoke. Ibrāhīm went with it morning and evening until it brought him to Makkah. Then it told Ibrāhīm, 'Build the foundation where I am.' He and Ismā'īl raised the House until it reached the height of the Corner. He told his son, 'My son, look for a stone to set in place as a marker for people.' He brought a stone, but he did not like it and said, 'Look for another.' He began to look and brought it but he had already brought the corner stone and put it in its place. He asked, 'Father, who brought you this stone?' He answered, 'One who was not letting me rely on you.'

Ibn 'Abbās reported that [Mount] Abū Qubays said, 'Ibrāhīm! Friend of the All-Merciful! You have a deposit with me. Take it.' It was a white stone from the rubies of the Garden. Ādam brought it down with me from the Garden. When Ibrāhīm and Ismā'īl raised the foundations of the House, a square cloud with a face came and called out: 'Raise it on my square.' This is the structure of Ibrāhīm.

It is related that when Ibrāhīm and Ismā'īl finished building the House, Allah gave them horses as a reward for raising the foundations of the House. Al-Ḥakīm at-Tirmidhī related from 'Umar ibn Abī 'Umar from Nu'aym ibn Ḥammād from 'Abd al-Wahhāb ibn Hammām, the brother of 'Abd ar-Razzāq from Ibn Jurayj from Ibn Abī Mulaykah that Ibn 'Abbās said, 'Horses were wild like other wild animals. When Allah allowed Ibrāhīm and Ismā'īl to raise the foundations, Allah Almighty said, "I will give you a treasure that I have stored up for you." Then He revealed to Ismā'īl: "Go out to Ajyad and call. Your treasure will come to you." He went to Ajyad which was a dwelling, not knowing what the supplication was nor what the treasure was. He inspired him and there was no horse on the face of the earth in the land of the Arabs that did not come to him. He was able to take their forelocks and they were subject to him. He rode them and foddered them. They are good fortune and the legacy of your father Ismā'īl. They are called "*faras*" [whose root means "perception"] in Arabic because Ismā'īl was commanded to make supplication and it came to him.'

'Abd al-Mun'im ibn Idrīs related that Wahb ibn Munabbih said, 'Shīth was the first to build using mud and stones. The structures of Quraysh are known and the report about the serpent in connection with that has been mentioned. It stopped them from destroying it until Quraysh gathered at the Maqām and cried out, "Our Lord! Do not be alarmed! We want to honour and adorn Your House if You are pleased with that. Otherwise do what seems best to You!" They heard the sound of the wings of a heavy bird in the sky and saw a bird larger than an eagle with a black back and white belly and two legs. It sunk its talons in the neck of the serpent and then left with it while its tail was dragging, being greater than such-and-such and took it towards Ajyad.

'So Quraysh demolished it and began to rebuild it with the stones of the wadi which Quraysh carried on their backs. They raised it upwards to the level of twenty cubits. The Prophet ﷺ was carrying stones from Ajyad. He was wearing a striped garment and it was tight on him. He went to put the garment on his shoulder and his private parts could be seen because of the smallness of the garment. There was a call: "Muḥammad! Cover your private parts!" He was not seen naked after that.' There were five years between building the Ka'bah and the descent of Revelation and fifteen years between his leaving and its rebuilding. 'Abd ar-Razzāq mentioned it from Ma'mar from 'Abdullāh ibn 'Uthmān from Abu-ṭ-Ṭufayl.

It is mentioned from Ma'mar from az-Zuhrī: 'When they had built it and reached the place of the Cornerstone, Quraysh argued about the Cornerstone and which tribe should raise it and it became an open quarrel. They said, "Let the first one who comes to us from that door be the arbiter between us!" They agreed on that and the Messenger of Allah ﷺ, who was a young man wearing a striped garment, entered and they had him judge. He commanded that the stone be placed on a robe and then told the leader of each tribe to take a corner of the robe. They raised it up and the Prophet ﷺ put it in place.'

Ibn Isḥāq said: 'I was told that Quraysh found a document written in Syriac in a corner. They could not understand it until a Jewish man came and read it for them. It said: "I am Allah, the Lord of Bakkah. I created it on the day that I created the heavens and the earth, and formed the sun and moon, and I surrounded it with seven pure angels. It will remain as long as its two mountains remain, a blessing to its people with water and milk."' Abū Ja'far Muḥammad ibn 'Alī said, 'In the time of the Amalekites, Jurhum and Ibrāhīm, the door of the Ka'bah was on the ground until Quraysh rebuilt it.' Muslim transmitted that 'Ā'ishah said, 'I asked the Messenger of Allah ﷺ whether the wall was part of the House. "Yes," he answered. I asked, "Then why do they not include it in the

House?" He said, "Your people did not have sufficient funds." I asked, "Why is its door elevated?" He said, "Your people did that so that they could admit whomever they wished and deny whomever they wished. If it had not been that your people were very recently in the time of the Jāhilyyah and I feared that their hearts would be averse, I would have incorporated the wall into the House and brought the door down to the ground."'

He transmitted that 'Abdullāh ibn az-Zubayr said, 'My aunt ('Ā'ishah) told me that the Prophet ﷺ said, "'Ā'ishah, if it had not been that your people were recently idolaters, I would have destroyed the Ka'bah and made it level with the earth and given it two doors: an eastern door and a western door, and would have included in it six cubits of the Ḥijr. Quraysh made it smaller when the Ka'bah was built."' 'Urwah related his father that 'Ā'ishah said, 'The Messenger of Allah ﷺ said to me, "If it had not been that your people were recently unbelievers, I would have demolished the Ka'bah and built it on the foundations of Ibrāhīm. When Quraysh built the Ka'bah, they made it smaller, and I would have given it a back door." Al-Bukhārī has that Hishām ibn 'Urwah said, 'He meant a door.' Al-Bukhārī also has 'two doors'. This was the structure of Quraysh.

When the Syrians attacked 'Abdullāh ibn az-Zubayr and the Ka'bah was weakened by being burned, Ibn az-Zubayr demolished it and then rebuilt it based on what 'Ā'ishah had told him. He added to it five cubits from the Ḥijr so that he exposed its foundation and people looked at it. Then he built it on it. The height of the Ka'bah was eighty cubits. When he added to it, it appeared to be small and so he added ten cubits to its height. He gave it two doors: one by which to enter and one by which to leave. That is what is stated in Muslim, although the wording of reports varies.

Sufyān mentioned from Dāwūd ibn Shābūr that Mujāhid said, 'When Ibn az-Zubayr wanted to demolish the Ka'bah and rebuild it, he said to the people, "Demolish it." They refused to demolish it, fearing that punishment would descend on them. We went out to Minā and stayed there for three days, awaiting the punishment. Ibn az-Zubayr climbed up the wall of the Ka'bah himself. When they saw that nothing happened to him, they were bold enough to undertake that and they demolished it. When he rebuilt it, he gave it two doors: one by which to enter and one by which to leave. He added six cubits on the side of the Ḥijr and added nine cubits to its height.'

Muslim said in his hadith: 'When Ibn az-Zubayr was killed, al-Ḥajjāj wrote to 'Abd al-Malik ibn Marwān to inform him that Ibn az-Zubayr had rebuilt it on the foundations that had been seen by reputable people of Makkah. 'Abd al-Malik wrote to him, "We are not concerned with any of the mess of Ibn az-Zubayr. As for what he added of the Ḥijr, return it as it was. Block off the door which he opened." So he demolished it and restored it as it was.' One version has: "Abd al-Mālik said, "I do not think that Abu-l-Khubayb (i.e. Ibn az-Zubayr) heard from 'Ā'ishah what he claimed that he heard." Al-Ḥārith ibn 'Abdullāh interjected, "Yes, I heard it from her." He demanded, "What did you hear her say?" He said, "She said, 'The Messenger of Allah ﷺ said, "Your people reduced its size. If it had not been that your people were recently idolaters, I would have restored what they left of it. It may occur to your people to build it. Come and I will show you what they left out of it."' He showed her about seven cubits."' One variant says that 'Abd al-Mālik said, 'If I had heard it before I demolished it, I would have left it as Ibn az-Zubayr rebuilt it'. This is what has been reported about building the Ka'bah.

It is related that Hārūn ar-Rashīd mentioned to Mālik ibn Anas that he wanted to demolish what al-Ḥajjāj had built of the Ka'bah and to restore it to what Ibn az-Zubayr had built based on what was reported from the Prophet ﷺ and which Ibn az-Zubayr followed. Mālik said to him, 'I beseech you by Allah, Amīr al-Mu'minīn, do not make this House a toy for kings. Then they will all want to reduce the House and rebuild it. Then the awe that people have for it will leave their hearts.' Al-Wāqidī mentioned from Ma'mar that Hammām ibn Munabbih heard Abū Hurayrah say, 'The Messenger of Allah ﷺ forbade cursing As'ad al-Ḥimyarī, who was Tubba', and was the first to put a covering over the House. He was the last Tubba'.' Ibn Isḥāq said, 'It was covered with Egyptian linen and then with a striped cloth. The first to use brocade was al-Ḥajjāj.'

One should not take any of the kiswah of the Ka'bah. It is a gift to it. It should not be decreased at all. Sa'īd ibn Jubayr disliked taking any of the scent of the Ka'bah for medicinal purposes.

The name Ismā'īl in Syriac means 'Listen, O God!' *'Īl'* in Syriac means 'God'.

رَبَّنَا وَاجْعَلْنَا مُسْلِمَيْنِ لَكَ وَمِن ذُرِّيَّتِنَآ أُمَّةً مُّسْلِمَةً لَّكَ وَأَرِنَا
مَنَاسِكَنَا وَتُبْ عَلَيْنَآ إِنَّكَ أَنتَ التَّوَّابُ الرَّحِيمُ ﴿١٢٨﴾

128 Our Lord, make us both Muslims submitted to You, and our descendants a Muslim community submitted to You. Show us our rites of worship and tum towards Us. You are the Ever-Returning, the Most Merciful.

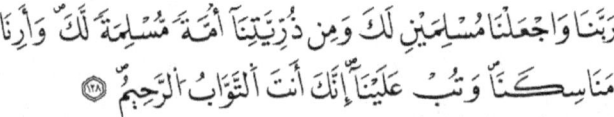

Our Lord, make us both Muslims submitted to You,

'Muslims' here means both in terms of faith and in terms of action, as Allah says: '*The* dīn *with Allah is Islam.*' (3:19). Those who say that Islam and faith are one and the same use this as evidence. This is also supported by another *āyah*: '*We brought out all the believers who were there but found in it only one house of Muslims.*' (51:35-36)

and our descendants a Muslim community submitted to You.

It is said that every Prophet only prayed for himself and his own community, except for Ibrāhīm who also prayed for this community as well as his own. It is said that He uses the partitive '*min*' because his descendants included wrongdoers. Aṭ-Ṭabarī reported that it means the Arabs in particular. As-Suhaylī says that it means the Arabs because they are the sons of Nabt ibn Ismā'īl or Tayman ibn Ismā'īl. It is also said that their ancestor was was Qaydar ibn Ismā'īl. The 'Adnānī Arabs are descended from Nabt, and the Qaḥṭānī from Qaydar or Tayman. Ibn 'Aṭiyyah said that this is weak because its claim appeared among the Arabs and those other than them who believe.

The word *ummah* (community) means a social grouping. It can refer to a single person since he is imitated in good, as Allah says: '*Ibrāhīm was a community in himself obedient to Allah*' (16:120). The Prophet ﷺ said about Zayd ibn 'Amr, 'He was sent as a community on his own' because he did not commit *shirk* in his religion. Allah knows best. The expression can also be used in other contexts to mean region, time, or stature or the face. That is found in the following *āyahs*: '*We found our fathers following an* ummah,' (43:22) meaning a religion; '*This* ummah *of yours is one* ummah' (21:92), which can mean a time; and '*remembering after an* ummah' (12:45), meaning 'a time'.

Show us our rites of worship

'Show' (*arinā*) is recited as *arnā* by 'Umar ibn 'Abd al-'Azīz, Qatādah, Ibn Kathīr, Ibn Muḥayṣin, as-Suddī, Rawḥ from Ya'qūb, Ruways and as-Sūsī.

The linguistic root of the word *manāsik* (rites of worship) is *nusk* and means 'washing'. In the Sharī'ah it is the term used for an act of worship. Scholars disagree about what rites are meant here. It is said that it means the practices and waymarks of *ḥajj* as Qatādah and as-Suddī said. Mujāhid, 'Aṭā' and Ibn Jurayj held the view that it refers to sacrificing. It is also said to mean all the acts of worship by which Allah is worshipped. *Nāsik* means a worshipper.

Zuhayr ibn Muḥammad said, 'When Ibrāhīm finished building the House, he said, "O Lord, I have finished, so show us our rites of worship!" So Allah sent

Jibrīl to him and he performed the *ḥajj* for him. When he returned from 'Arafah and the Day of Sacrifice came, Iblīs appeared before him and Jibrīl said, "Throw pebbles at him." So Ibrāhīm threw seven pebbles at him. That happened for the next two days. Then he went up Thabīr and called out, "Slaves of Allah, answer!" and his call was heard by those between the seas with an atom of faith in their heart and they said, "At Your service, O Allah! At Your service!" Were it not for the presence of Muslims, the earth and those on it would have been destroyed. The people of Yemen were the first to answer.'

Abū Miljaz said: 'When Ibrāhīm finished building the House, Jibrīl came to him and showed him how to do *ṭawāf* of the House (and I think he also said, 'of Ṣafā and Marwa'). Then they went to 'Aqabah and Shayṭān confronted them. Jibrīl took seven pebbles and gave Ibrāhīm seven pebbles. He stoned him, saying the *takbīr*. Then he told Ibrāhīm, "Stone and say the *takbīr*." He did so with every pebble until Shayṭān retreated. Then they went to the middle Jamrah and Shayṭān confronted them. Jibrīl took seven pebbles and gave Ibrāhīm seven pebbles. He stoned him, saying the *takbīr*. Then he told Ibrāhīm, "Stone and say the *takbīr*." He did so with every pebble until Shayṭān retreated. Then they went to the furthest *jamrah* and Shayṭān confronted them. Jibrīl took seven pebbles and gave Ibrāhīm seven pebbles. He stoned him, saying the *takbīr*. Then he told Ibrāhīm, "Stone and say the *takbīr*." He did so with every pebble until Shayṭān retreated. Then he took him to Jam' and said, "Here the people join the prayers." Then he took him to 'Arafāt and said, "Do you recognise (*'arafta*)?" "Yes," he answered. That is why it is called 'Arafāt.' It is also related that he repeated the question three times and it means Minā, Jam' and this ('Arafāt).

Khuṣayf ibn 'Abd ar-Raḥmān reported that Mujāhid said, 'When Ibrāhīm said, *"Show us our rites"*, it means Ṣafā and Marwah, which are the 'waymarks of Allah' mentioned in the text of the Qur'an.' Then Jibrīl took him out. When he passed by the Jamrat 'l-'Aqabah, Iblīs was on it and Jibrīl told him, 'Say the *takbīr* and stone him.' Then Iblīs went on top of the middle one and Jibrīl told him, 'Say the *takbīr* and stone him.' Then the same thing happened with the furthest Jamrah. Then he took him to the Mash'ar al-Ḥarām and then to 'Arafāt. He asked him, 'Do you recognise (*'arafta*) what I have shown you?' 'Yes,' he answered. That is why it is called 'Arafāt. Then he told him, 'Announce the ḥajj to people.' He asked, 'What do I say?' The answer was, 'Say: "People! Respond to your Lord!" three times.' He did so and they said, 'At Your service, O Allah, at Your service!' Whoever answered on that day was a ḥājjī. Another variant said that he turned in a circle so that he called in every direction and the people in and the east and the west responded. The mountains bowed so that the sound went a great distance.

Muḥammad ibn Isḥāq said, 'When Ibrāhīm, the Friend of Allah, finished building the Sacred House, Jibrīl came to him and said, 'Go around it seven times.' So he and Ismā'īl went around it seven times, greeting all the corners on every circuit. When they finished the seven, they prayed two *rak'ahs* at the Maqām. Jibrīl rose and showed them all the rites: Ṣafā and Marwah, Minā and Muzdalifah.' He continued, 'When he entered Minā and descended from 'Aqabah, Iblīs appeared to him...'

Ibn Isḥāq said, 'I heard that Ādam used to greet all of the corners before Ibrāhīm.' He said that Isḥāq and Sārah performed ḥajj from Syria. Ibrāhīm used to perform ḥajj every year on Burāq and the Prophets and nations after him performed ḥajj.

Muḥammad ibn Sābiṭ related that the Prophet ﷺ said, 'When the nation of one of the Prophets was destroyed, he would go to Makkah and worship there along with those who believed with him until they died. Nūḥ, Hūd and Ṣāliḥ died there and their graves are between Zamzam and the Ḥijr.' Ibn Wahb mentioned that Shu'ayb died in Makkah with the believers with him. Their graves are located in the western part of Makkah between the Dār an-Nadwah and the Banū Sahm. Ibn 'Abbās said, 'There are only two graves in the Masjid al-Ḥarām: that of Ismā'īl and of Shu'ayb. Ismā'īl's grave is in the Ḥijr and Shu'ayb's is opposite the Black Stone. 'Abdullāh ibn Ḍamrah as-Salūlī said, 'Between the Corner and the Maqām are the graves of ninety-nine Prophets who came on ḥajj and were buried there.

and turn towards Us.

There is disagreement about what this means since both Ibrāhīm and Ismā'īl were Prophets protected from wrong action. A group say that they were asking for constancy and continuance, not for forgiveness from wrong actions. This is good but even better than that is the interpretation which maintains that, when they had learned the practices and built the House, they wanted to make that clear to people and acquaint them with the rites they had to perform and inform them that this place of standing and those places are places for intercession for wrong actions and seeking repentance. It is said that it means: 'Turn towards the wrongdoers among our community.'

رَبَّنَا وَٱبۡعَثۡ فِيهِمۡ رَسُولٗا مِّنۡهُمۡ يَتۡلُواْ عَلَيۡهِمۡ ءَايَٰتِكَ وَيُعَلِّمُهُمُ ٱلۡكِتَٰبَ
وَٱلۡحِكۡمَةَ وَيُزَكِّيهِمۡۚ إِنَّكَ أَنتَ ٱلۡعَزِيزُ ٱلۡحَكِيمُ ١٢٩

129 Our Lord, raise up among them a Messenger from them to recite Your Signs to them and teach them the Book and Wisdom and purify them. You are the Almighty, the All-Wise.'

Our Lord, raise up among them a Messenger from them

Khālid ibn Mad'ān related that a group of the Companions of the Prophet ﷺ said, 'Messenger of Allah, tell us about yourself.' The Prophet ﷺ replied, 'Indeed, I am the supplication of my father Ibrāhīm and the good news of 'Īsā?' The word *rasūl* (Messenger) means someone who is sent and comes from the verb *arsala* meaning to send out.

and teach them the Book and Wisdom

The 'Book' is the Qur'an and the 'Wisdom' (*hikmah*) is recognition and acceptance of the *dīn*, grasping its interpretation and understanding it, which is by an innate faculty and light from Allah. Mālik stated that and Ibn Wahb related it from him. Qatādah said that the 'Wisdom' is the *Sunnah* and clarification of the laws of the Sharī'ah. It is said that it refers to the judgments and rulings derived from it. The meanings are close. Teaching is ascribed to the Prophet ﷺ since he gives the commands which are followed and taught us how to look at the Revelation Allah gave him. It is said that the 'Book' means the meaning of the words and the 'Wisdom' refers to the judgments derived from it. Allah means the unrestricted and restricted, detailed and general, ambivalent and specific.

and purify them

...from the filth of idolatry, as Ibn Jurayj and others said. *Zakāh* is purification. It is said that the Signs are the recitation of the words, the Book is the meaning of the words, and Wisdom is judgment. It is what Allah means in the address of undefined and defined, explained and unexplained, general and specific. Allah knows best.

You are the Almighty, the All-Wise.'

The Almighty (*al-'Azīz*) is the One whom no one can overpower. Ibn Kaysān said that it means the One whose power extends to everything as evinced by Allah's words: *'Allah cannot be withstood in any way, either in the heavens or on earth.'*

(35:44) It is also said that it means the One Who has no like, the Incomparable. Al-Kisā'ī said that it means the Conqueror as seen in His words: *'He got the better of me* ('azzanī) *with his words.'* (38:23) It is said that it is the One Who has no like.

وَمَن يَرْغَبُ عَن مِّلَّةِ إِبْرَٰهِـۧمَ إِلَّا مَن سَفِهَ نَفْسَهُۥ وَلَقَدِ ٱصْطَفَيْنَٰهُ فِى ٱلدُّنْيَا
وَإِنَّهُۥ فِى ٱلْءَاخِرَةِ لَمِنَ ٱلصَّٰلِحِينَ ﴿١٣٠﴾

130 Who would deliberately renounce the religion of Ibrāhīm except someone who reveals himself to be a fool? We chose him in this world and in the Next World he will be one of the people of right action.

Who would deliberately renounce the religion of Ibrāhīm except someone who reveals himself to be a fool?

This question is in fact a rebuke and a negative answer to it is implied, such as: 'No one would.' It is also an expression which tends to distance the reader from doing such a thing. *Millah* means religion and law. The 'someone who reveals himself to be a fool' is said by Qatādah to be the Jews and Christians who renounced the religion of Ibrāhīm and adopted Judaism and Christianity, which were innovations that did not come from Allah. Az-Zajjāj said that *safiha* (to be a fool) means 'to be ignorant of a matter because of not thinking about it'. Abū 'Ubaydah says that it means 'destroys himself'. Ibn Baḥr says, 'It means that it refers to someone having no self-knowledge and no grasp of the evidence and proofs within himself, which indicate that he has an incomparable Creator, thus failing to recognize Allah's unity and power.'

Az-Zajjāj said, 'He reflects about his hands with which he strikes, his feet with which he walks, his eyes with which he sees, his ears with which he hears, his tongue with which he speaks, his molars which grow when he has no need to suckle and needs to masticate the food he eats, his stomach which processes his nourishment, his liver which detoxifies, his veins and passageways which reach the limbs, his intestines where the dregs of food settle and then emerge from the bottom of his body. He uses this as evidence that He has an All-Powerful, All-Knowing Wise Creator. This is the meaning of His words: "*in yourselves as well. Do you not see?*" (51:21)' Al-Khaṭṭābī indicated this.

This *āyah* is used as evidence by those who say that the Sharī'ah of Ibrāhīm is the same as our Sharī'ah except for those aspects of it which have been abrogated as He says: *'the religion of your forefather Ibrāhīm'* (22:78) and *'Follow the religion of Ibrāhīm.'* (16:123)

We chose him in this world

This means: 'We chose him to bear Our Message and purified him.' The word *iṣṭafā* (chose) is derived from *ṣafwah* which means to be pure and to choose the best.

and in Next World he will be one of the people of right action

The 'people of right action' in the Next World are those who are successful and will enter the Garden. Arabic scholars say three things about the phrasing in this *āyah*. One is: 'He will be righteous in the Next World'. The second is that '*in the Next World'* is connected to something elided, i.e. 'his righteousness is in the Next World.' The third is that *ṣāliḥīn* does not mean 'those who do right action' here but is simply a designation like 'man'. There is also a fourth view which states that it means: 'He is one of the righteous in respect of the actions of the Next World.' Al-Ḥusayn ibn al-Faḍl said, 'There is a change in the normal order of words. It implies: "We chose in this world and in the Next World, and he is one of the people of right action."' Ḥajjāj ibn Ḥajjāj (who is Ḥajjāj al-Aswad and Ḥajjāj al-Aḥwal, known as Ziqq 'l-'Asal) said that he heard Mu'āwiyah ibn Qurrah say, 'O Allah, You made the righteous righteous and provided them with actions in obedience to You so that You are pleased with them. O Allah, as You made them righteous, make us righteous. As You provided them with actions in obedience to You, provide us with actions in obedience to You. Be pleased with us!'

إِذْ قَالَ لَهُۥ رَبُّهُۥٓ أَسْلِمْ قَالَ أَسْلَمْتُ لِرَبِّ ٱلْعَٰلَمِينَ ﴿١٣١﴾

131 When his Lord said to him, 'Become a Muslim!' he said, 'I am a Muslim who has submitted to the Lord of all the worlds.'

This *āyah* is connected to the previous one and the implication is, 'We chose him when his Lord said to him, "Become a Muslim and submit."' Allah said this to Ibrāhīm after He had tested him with the stars, the moon and the sun (cf. 6:76-84). Ibn Kaysān and al-Kalbī said it means: 'Make your *dīn* sincere for Allah through *tawḥīd*.' It is said that it means: 'Be humble and submitted.' Ibn 'Abbās said, 'Allah said that to him when he abandoned the customs of his people.' Islam here entails all its various aspects. In Arabic the word 'Islam' implies submission and obedience to the one submitted to. Not everyone's Islam entails faith but everyone's faith entails Islam because whoever believes in Allah necessarily submits to and obeys Allah. Not everyone who submits to Allah believes in Him because his submission may be out of fear of the sword and that is not faith.

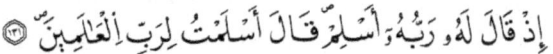

The Qadariyyah and Kharijites hold a contrary view saying that Islam is synonymous with faith and that every Muslim is a believer and every believer a Muslim based on Allah's words: *'The* dīn *in the sight of Allah is Islam'* (3:19). This indicates that Islam is the *dīn* and that whoever is not a Muslim is not a believer. Our evidence is found in His words: *'The desert Arabs say, "We believe." Say: "You do not believe. Say rather: 'We have become Muslim.'"'* (49:14) Allah reported that not every one who becomes Muslim is a believer and so it indicates that not every Muslim is a believer. When Sa'd ibn Abī Waqqāṣ said, 'Give to so-and-so. He is a believer,' the Prophet ﷺ said to him, 'Or a Muslim.' Muslim transmitted it. It indicates that faith and Islam are not the same. Faith is internal and Islam is external. This is clear. 'Faith' can be used to mean Islam and Islam can be used to mean 'faith' since they are connected. It is as if Islam were the fruit of faith and an indication of its soundness. Success is by Allah.

وَأَوْصَىٰ بِهَآ إِبْرَٰهِـۧمُ بَنِيهِ وَيَعْقُوبُ يَـٰبَنِىَّ إِنَّ ٱللَّهَ ٱصْطَفَىٰ لَكُمُ
ٱلدِّينَ فَلَا تَمُوتُنَّ إِلَّا وَأَنتُم مُّسْلِمُونَ ﴿١٣٢﴾

132 Ibrāhīm directed his sons to this, as did Ya'qūb: 'My sons! Allah has chosen this dīn for you, so do not die except as Muslims.'

Ibrāhīm directed his sons to this, as did Ya'qūb:

'This' may refer to 'the religion' or to the words, 'I submit to the Lord of the worlds.' The latter view is more correct because it was the last thing mentioned. Some readings have *waṣṣā* for 'directed' whereas the people of Madīnah and Syria read *awṣā*.

Ismā'īl and Isḥāq were the sons of Ibrāhīm. The elder was Ismā'īl and his mother was Hajar the Copt. There are three positions regarding the age of Ismā'īl at the time Ibrāhīm took him to Makkah: as a baby, as a two year old infant or as a fourteen year old youth. The first is considered the soundest. He was born fourteen years before his brother Isḥāq and died when he was one hundred and thirty-seven or one hundred and thirty years old. He was eighty years old when Ibrāhīm died. According to one statement, he was the son Ibrāhīm was commanded to sacrifice. Isḥāq's mother was Sārah, and he was the sacrifice according to another statement, which seems sounder. We will deal with this when we examine the story in *Sūrat aṣ-Ṣāffāt* (37:102-109). From him descend the Romans, Greeks and Armenians and those like them and the sons of Israel. Isḥāq lived to the age of one hundred and eighty and died in the Holy Land. He was buried with his father

Ibrāhīm. When Sārah died, Ibrāhīm married Qanṭūrā (Keturah) bint Yaqṭan the Canaanite and she bore him Madyan, Madāyin, Nahshān, Zimrān, Nashīq and Shuyūkh. He died about 2600 years before the birth of the Prophet ﷺ. The Jews lessen this by 400 years.

Ya'qūb gave the same directive to his other sons. Al-Kalbī said, 'When Ya'qūb looked at the people in Egypt, he saw them worshipping idols, fire and cows, so he collected his sons and alerted them, asking, "What will you worship after me?"' He was called Ya'qūb because he was the second of twins and was born holding onto the heel of his brother (*'aqib*). He lived to the age of one hundred and forty-seven and died in Egypt. He instructed that he should be transported to the Holy Land and buried with his father, Isḥāq. Yūsuf transported him and buried him there.

'My sons! Allah has chosen this dīn for you, so do not die except as Muslims.

The *dīn* is Islam. This means: 'Cling to Islam and persevere in it and do not part from it until you die.' This contains an admonition and a reminder of death. That is because everyone knows that they will die but they do not know when. So the command is that death should not come upon you when you are not following the *dīn*. It is a constant, continuing command.

أَمْ كُنتُمْ شُهَدَآءَ إِذْ حَضَرَ يَعْقُوبَ ٱلْمَوْتُ إِذْ قَالَ لِبَنِيهِ مَا تَعْبُدُونَ مِنۢ بَعْدِى قَالُوا۟ نَعْبُدُ إِلَٰهَكَ وَإِلَٰهَ ءَابَآئِكَ إِبْرَٰهِـۧمَ وَإِسْمَٰعِيلَ وَإِسْحَٰقَ إِلَٰهًا وَٰحِدًا وَنَحْنُ لَهُۥ مُسْلِمُونَ ١٣٣

133 Or were you present when death came to Ya'qūb and he said to his sons, 'What will you worship when I have gone?' They said, 'We will worship your God, the God of your forefathers, Ibrāhīm, Ismā'īl and Isḥāq – one God. We are Muslims submitted to Him.'

This is addressed to the Jews and Christians who, by following Judaism and Christianity, falsely attribute to Ibrāhīm something for which he gave no authority. Allah refuted their words and rebuked them here. He says that they are forging lies. Ismā'īl is included because the uncle is counted with the father.

تِلْكَ أُمَّةٌ قَدْ خَلَتْ لَهَا مَا كَسَبَتْ وَلَكُم مَّا كَسَبْتُمْ وَلَا تُسْـَٔلُونَ عَمَّا
كَانُوا يَعْمَلُونَ ١٣٤

134 That was a community which has long since passed away. It has what it earned. You have what you have earned. You will not be questioned about what they did.

This *āyah* indicates that a person's actions and earnings, good or evil, are ascribed to him, even though it is Allah who gives him the power to do what he does. If it is good, it is by Allah's favour. If it evil, it is by His justice. This is the school of the People of the *Sunnah*. There are many *āyahs* in the Qur'an which express this. A person earns his actions since the power connected to the action was created for him and there is a clear difference between a movement he makes by his own choice and, for instance, an involuntary movement such as a shiver. That capacity is the core of accountability. The Jabrites negate any possibility of personal responsibility and say that people are like plants which move whichever way the wind blows. The Qadarites and Mu'tazilites take the opposite position that a person creates his own actions. No one will be punished for the actions of another.

وَقَالُوا كُونُوا هُودًا أَوْ نَصَارَىٰ تَهْتَدُوا قُلْ بَلْ مِلَّةَ إِبْرَاهِيمَ حَنِيفًا وَمَا
كَانَ مِنَ الْمُشْرِكِينَ ١٣٥

135 They say, 'Be Jews or Christians and you will be guided.' Say, 'Rather adopt the religion of Ibrāhīm, a man of natural pure belief. He was not one of the idolaters.'

Each claims that what they have is the real truth but Allah refuted that. The *āyah* means: 'Say, O Muḥammad, "We follow the one religion."' This is why the word "*millah*" (religion) is in the accusative case. It is said that it means: 'Follow the religion of Ibrāhīm.' It implies: 'Guidance is a religion,' or 'Our religion is that of Ibrāhīm.' Az-Zajjāj said that. Ibrāhīm is called a *ḥanīf* because he inclined to the *dīn* of Allah, which is Islam. *Ḥanf* means 'inclination'. A man who is *aḥnaf* (clubfooted) has his feet turn toward each other. *Ḥanf* means 'going straight' as well. Ibrāhīm is called a *ḥanīf* because he went straight.

قُولُوٓا۟ ءَامَنَّا بِٱللَّهِ وَمَآ أُنزِلَ إِلَيْنَا وَمَآ أُنزِلَ إِلَىٰٓ إِبْرَٰهِـۧمَ وَإِسْمَـٰعِيلَ وَإِسْحَـٰقَ
وَيَعْقُوبَ وَٱلْأَسْبَاطِ وَمَآ أُوتِىَ مُوسَىٰ وَعِيسَىٰ وَمَآ أُوتِىَ ٱلنَّبِيُّونَ مِن
رَّبِّهِمْ لَا نُفَرِّقُ بَيْنَ أَحَدٍ مِّنْهُمْ وَنَحْنُ لَهُۥ مُسْلِمُونَ ١٣٦

136 Say, 'We believe in Allah and what has been sent down to us and what was sent down to Ibrāhīm and Ismā'īl and Isḥāq and Ya'qūb and the Tribes, and what Mūsā and 'Īsā were given, and what all the Prophets were given by their Lord. We do not differentiate between any of them. We are Muslims submitted to Him.'

Al-Bukhārī transmitted that Abū Hurayrah said, 'The People of the Book used to recite the Torah in Hebrew and explain it in Arabic to the people of Islam. The Messenger of Allah ﷺ said, "Neither believe nor deny the People of the Book. Say, 'We believe in Allah and what has been revealed.'"' Muḥammad ibn Sīrīn said, 'When you are asked, "Are you a believer?" recite this *āyah*.' Many of the Salaf disliked anyone saying, 'I am truly a believer.' The reason for that will be explained in *Sūrat al-Anfāl*, Allah willing. One of the early people was asked about a man who was asked, 'Do you believe in the Prophet so-and-so?' and gave a name he did not know. If he said that he did, it is possible that it was not a Prophet and he was attesting to the Prophethood of someone who was not a Prophet. If he said that he did not, perhaps it was actually a Prophet and he was denying one of the Prophets. So what should he do? The reply was that he should say, 'If he is a Prophet, I believe in him.'

This *āyah* is addressed to this community to instruct them in faith. Ibn 'Abbās said, 'A group of Jews came to the Prophet ﷺ and asked him about which of the Prophets he believed in and this *āyah* was revealed. When he mentioned 'Īsā, they said, "We do not believe in 'Īsā or in anyone who does believe in him."'

and the Tribes,

Asbāṭ (the Tribes) are from the twelve sons of Ya'qūb. A nation sprang from each of them. They are called *asbāṭ*, which comes from *sabṭ*, which means succession, and so it was as if they followed one another. *Sabṭ* is the term used for the tribes descending from Ya'qūb as *qabīlah* is used for Arab tribes. It is also said that the word is derived from *sabaṭ*, which means a tree. The singular is *sabaṭah*. Abū Isḥāq az-Zajjāj said that this in clear in what Muḥammad ibn Ja'far al-Anbārī related from Abū Nujayd ad-Daqqāq from al-Aswad ibn ʿĀmir from Isrāʾīl from Simāk from ʿIkrimah that Ibn ʿAbbās said, ʿAll the Prophets were from the tribe of Israel except for ten: Nūḥ, Shuʿayb, Hūd, Ṣāliḥ, Lūṭ, Ibrāhīm, Isḥāq, Yaʿqūb, Ismāʿīl and Muḥammad ﷺ. None of them had two names except for ʿĪsā and Yaʿqūb.' *Sibṭ* denotes a group or tribe who come from a single ancestor.

We do not differentiate between any of them,

This means 'We do not believe in some and reject others like the Jews and Christians do.'

فَإِنْ ءَامَنُوا۟ بِمِثْلِ مَآ ءَامَنتُم بِهِۦ فَقَدِ ٱهْتَدَوا۟ ۖ وَّإِن تَوَلَّوْا۟ فَإِنَّمَا هُمْ فِى شِقَاقٍ ۖ فَسَيَكْفِيكَهُمُ ٱللَّهُ ۚ وَهُوَ ٱلسَّمِيعُ ٱلْعَلِيمُ ﴿١٣٧﴾

137 If their faith is the same as yours then they are guided. But if they turn away, they are entrenched in hostility. Allah will be enough for you against them. He is the All-Hearing, the All-Knowing.

If their faith is the same as yours then they are guided.

This is addressed to Muḥammad ﷺ and his community. It means that if they believe as you believe and affirm what you affirm, they are guided. So similarity can occur between two faiths. Baqiyyah related from Shuʿbah from Abū Ḥamzah that Ibn ʿAbbās said, 'Do not say, "If they believe in the like of what you believe." Allah has no like. Rather say, "in that in which you believe."' ʿAlī ibn Naṣr al-Jahḍamī corroborate it from Shuʿbah. Al-Bayhaqī mentioned it. It is also said to mean that if they believe in your Prophet and all the Prophets without differentiating between them, then they are guided.

But if they turn away, they are entrenched in hostility.

If they refuse to do anything except differentiate between them, then they veer from the *dīn* to hostility. Zayd ibn Aslam said that the expression 'entrenched in hostility' (*fī shiqāq*) means 'in contention'. It is said to be quarrelling, opposition and hostility. It is derived from *shaqq*, which is the side of a chasm, so it is as if each was one of two sides. It is said that it is derived from a verb meaning to be difficult and hard and so it is as if it means that each side wants to make things difficult for the other side.

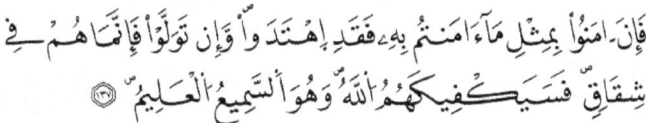

Allah will be enough for you against them.

Allah will protect His Messenger against his enemies. This is a promise from Allah to His Prophet ﷺ that He would protect him from those who were hostile to him and opposed him. He carried out that promise. That was when the Banū Qaynuqā‘ and the Banū Qurayẓah were killed and Banū 'n-Naḍīr were expelled. It was this *āyah* on which ‘Uthman's blood spilled when he was murdered as the Prophet ﷺ had foretold about him. It is related that Abū Dulāmah visited al-Manṣūr wearing a tall hat, a cloak on the back of which was written: *'Allah will be enough for you against them. He is the All-Hearing, the All-Knowing'*, and a sword girded around his waist. Al-Manṣūr had commanded the army to dress in that garb. He asked him, ‘How are you, Abū Dulāmah?’ ‘Bad, Amīr al-Mu'minīn,’ he answered. ‘Why is that?’ he inquired. He said, ‘What would you think of man whose face is on his waist, whose sword in on his bottom, and he has thrown the Book of Allah behind his back?’ Al-Manṣūr laughed at him and immediately ordered that the manner of dress be changed.

صِبْغَةَ ٱللَّهِ وَمَنْ أَحْسَنُ مِنَ ٱللَّهِ صِبْغَةً وَنَحْنُ لَهُۥ عَٰبِدُونَ ﴿١٣٨﴾

138 The dye of Allah – and what dye could be better than Allah's? It is Him we worship.

Al-Akhfash and others said that ‘the dye of Allah’ is the *dīn* of Allah and is an appositive for *'millah'*, and so it implies: ‘Follow it’. Shaybah related that Qatādah said, ‘The Jews used to baptise their sons as Jews and the Christians baptised their sons as Christians. The baptism of Allah is Islam.’ Mujāhid said that it is the natural form on which people are created. Az-Zajjāj says, ‘This statement of Mujāhid refers to Islam because the natural form ever since the beginning of creation has been Islam.’ Mujāhid, al-Ḥasan, Abū al-‘Āliyah and Qatādah said that the ‘dye’ is the *dīn*. This also derives from immersion in water. Ibn ‘Abbās said that Christians baptised their children when they were seven days old to replace circumcision, which is purification. When they do this, they say, ‘Now he is truly a Christian.’ Allah refuted them by saying that the dye of Islam is better. It is Islam. Calling the *dīn* this is a metaphor since the effect of it in actions can be seen in a person in the same way that dye can be seen in a garment. It is said that it refers to the *ghusl* taken by someone who wants to become Muslim which replaces Christian baptism. Al-Māwardī said that.

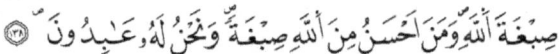

Because one meaning of ‘dye of Allah’ is the ‘washing (*ghusl*) of Allah’ it is said that washing when you become Muslim is an obligatory practice. The evidence for this in the Sunnah comes from Qays ibn 'Aṣim and Thumāmah ibn Athāl who both had a *ghusl* when they became Muslims. Abū Ḥātim al-Bustī said in a sound transmission that Abū Hurayrah said that Thumāmah al-Ḥanafī was captured and one day the Prophet ﷺ passed by him and he became Muslim. He sent him to the garden of Abū Ṭalḥah and told him to have a *ghusl*. He did so and prayed two *rak'ahs*. The Prophet ﷺ said, 'The Islam of your companion is good.' It is also transmitted that Qays ibn 'Āṣim became Muslim and the Prophet ﷺ told him to have a *ghusl* with water and lote-leaves. An-Nasā'ī mentioned it and Abū Muḥammad 'Abd al-Ḥaqq said that it is sound. It is said that an act by which one draws near to Allah is called 'dye'. Ibn Fāris related that in *al-Mujmal*. Al-Jawharī said that 'the dye of Allah' is His *dīn*. It is also said that it is circumcision.

قُلْ أَتُحَآجُّونَنَا فِي ٱللَّهِ وَهُوَ رَبُّنَا وَرَبُّكُمْ وَلَنَآ أَعْمَٰلُنَا وَلَكُمْ
أَعْمَٰلُكُمْ وَنَحْنُ لَهُۥ مُخْلِصُونَ ﴿١٣٩﴾

139 Say, 'Do you argue with us about Allah when He is our Lord and your Lord? We have our actions and you have your actions. We act for Him alone.'

Al-Ḥasan said, 'Their argument is that they say, *"We are more entitled to Allah than you because we are the sons of Allah and those He loves."*' (cf. 5:18) It is said that it was because of 'our ancestors and books and because we did not worship idols.' So the meaning of the *āyah* is: 'Ask them, Muḥammad,' – meaning those Jews and Christians who claim that they are the sons of Allah and those He loves and claim that they are more entitled to Allah than you because of their ancestors and Books – 'Where is your argument when the Lord is One and everyone will be repaid for his actions? What advantage will precedence in the *dīn* give you?' *'About Allah'* means 'about His *dīn*'.

We act for Him alone.'

This means: 'We are sincere in our worship.' This contains a sense of rebuke, implying, 'You are not sincere so how can you claim that you are more entitled?' The reality of sincerity (*ikhlāṣ*) is to purify the action in question from taking any account of creatures. The Prophet ﷺ said, 'Allah Almighty says, "I am the best associate. Anyone who associates a partner with Me, belongs to his associates. O people, make your actions sincere for Allah Almighty. Allah Almighty does not accept other than what is done sincerely for Him alone. Do not say, "This is for

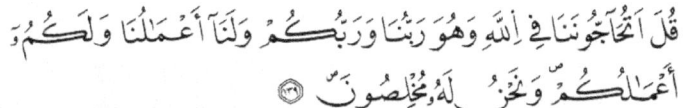

Allah and my relatives." If it is for your relatives, none of it is for Allah. Do not say, "This is for Allah and your sakes." Then it is for your sakes and none of it is for Allah.' Aḍ-Ḍaḥḥāk ibn Qays al-Fihrī related it and ad-Dāraquṭnī transmitted it.

Ruwaym said, 'Sincerity in action is that the person who does something does not want any recompense or return for it in either this world or the Next.' Al-Junayd said, 'Sincerity is a secret between Allah and the slave. An angel cannot know it so as to record it, nor can a shayṭān corrupt it, nor can passion incline to it.' Al-Qushayrī reported that the Prophet ﷺ said, 'I asked Jibrīl about sincerity and what it was. He replied, "I asked the Lord of Might about what sincerity was and He said, 'A secret of Mine which I entrust in the heart of those I love among My slaves.'"'

وَلَكُمۡ أَعۡمَٰلُكُمۡ وَنَحۡنُ لَهُۥ مُخۡلِصُونَ ١٣٩ أَمۡ يَقُولُونَ إِنَّ
إِبۡرَٰهِـۧمَ وَإِسۡمَٰعِيلَ وَإِسۡحَٰقَ وَيَعۡقُوبَ وَٱلۡأَسۡبَاطَ كَانُواْ
هُودًا أَوۡ نَصَٰرَىٰۗ قُلۡ ءَأَنتُمۡ أَعۡلَمُ أَمِ ٱللَّهُۗ وَمَنۡ أَظۡلَمُ مِمَّن كَتَمَ
شَهَٰدَةً عِندَهُۥ مِنَ ٱللَّهِۗ وَمَا ٱللَّهُ بِغَٰفِلٍ عَمَّا تَعۡمَلُونَ ١٤٠

140 Or do they say that Ibrāhīm and Ismā'īl and Isḥāq and Ya'qūb and the Tribes were Jews or Christians? Say, 'Do you know better or does Allah? Who could do greater wrong than someone who hides the evidence he has been given by Allah? Allah is not unaware of what you do.

Or do they say that Ibrāhīm and Ismā'īl and Isḥāq and Ya'qūb and the Tribes were Jews or Christians?

Ḥamzah, al-Kisā'ī and 'Āṣim in the transmission of Ḥafṣ has 'Do you say?' with *tā'* which is a good reading. It is as if it means: 'Do you argue about Allah or say that the Prophets were following your *dīn*?' The other reading is with *yā'*, 'do they say'. This is, in either case, a rebuke to the claims of both the Jews and the Christians. Allah refutes them because He knows better than you.

Who could do greater wrong than someone who hides the evidence he has been given by Allah?

No one does greater wrong. The word 'evidence' (*shahāda*) here refers to the actions they have been commanded to do since the *dīn* of all the Prophets was Islam. It is also said to refer to their concealment of the description of Muḥammad ﷺ in their Revealed Books as Qatādah said, but the first explanation is more in keeping with the context.

Allah is not unaware of what you do.

This is a threat that they will not be spared and will have to pay for what they did. A heedless or unaware person (*ghāfil*) is someone who does not grasp things because he ignores them. It is derived from earth which is *ghufl*, which means there is no sign or trace of habitation on it. A camel which is *ghufl* has no markings. A man who is *ghufl* has no experience of matters.

تِلْكَ أُمَّةٌ قَدْ خَلَتْ لَهَا مَا كَسَبَتْ وَلَكُم مَّا كَسَبْتُمْ وَلَا تُسْـَٔلُونَ عَمَّا
كَانُوا يَعْمَلُونَ ١٤١

141 That was a community which has long since passed away. It has what it earned. You have what you have earned. You will not be questioned about what they did.

This is repeated (cf. 2:134 above) because it contains a threat. Since the Prophets, in spite of their excellence and imamate, will be repaid for their actions, how much more will that be the case with you!

TABLE OF CONTENTS FOR *ĀYATS*

Sūrat al-Fātiḥah

1 Praise 22
The Lord of all the Worlds 26
2 The All-Merciful, Most Merciful 28
3 The King of the Day of Repayment 29
4 You alone we worship and You alone we ask for help 32
5 Guide us on the Straight Path 33
6 The Path of those whom You have blessed 34
7 not of those with anger on them nor of the misguided 35

Sūrat al-Baqarah

1 Alif. Lam. Mim. 39
2 That is the Book… 42
3 those who believe in the Unseen… 46
4 those who believe in what has been sent down to you… 60
5 They are the people guided by their Lord… 61
6 As for those who disbelieve… 61
7 Allah has sealed up their hearts… 63
8 Among the people there are some who say, 'We believe in Allah… 68
9 They think they deceive Allah and those who believe… 71
10 There is a sickness in their hearts… 72
11 When they are told, 'Do not cause corruption on the earth,'… 75
12 No indeed! They are the corrupters, but they are not aware of it… 75
13 When they are told, "Believe in the way that the people believe," … 76
14 When they meet those who believe, they say 'We believe.' … 77
15 But Allah is mocking them… 77
16 Those are the people who have sold guidance for misguidance… 79
17 Their likeness is that of people who light a fire… 80
18 Deaf, dumb, blind. They will not return… 81
19 Or that of a storm-cloud in the sky… 82
20 The lightning all but takes away their sight… 84
21 Mankind! worship your Lord, Who created you… 86
22 It is He who made the earth a couch for you… 87
23 If you have doubts about what We have sent down to Our slave… 89

24 If you do not do that – and you will not do it – then fear the Fire…	91
25 Give the good news to those who believe and do right actions…	92
26 Allah is not ashamed to make an example of a gnat …	94
27 Those who break Allah's contract after it has been agreed…	96
28 How can you reject Allah, when you were dead …	98
29 It is He who created everything on the earth for you…	100
30 When your Lord said to the angels, 'I am putting a caliph…	107
31 He taught Ādam the names of all things…	119
32 They said, 'Glory be to You! We have no knowledge except…	123
33 He said, 'Ādam, tell them their names.' …	125
34 We said to the angels, 'Prostrate to Ādam!'…	127
35 We said, 'Ādam, live in the Garden, you and your wife…	131
36 But Shayṭān made them slip up by means of it…	138
37 Then Ādam received some words from his Lord…	146
38 We said, 'Go down from it, every one of you!…	148
39 But those who disbelieve and deny Our Signs…	149
40 Tribe of Israel! remember the blessing I conferred on you…	150
41 Believe what I have sent down, confirming what is with you…	151
42 Do not mix up truth with falsehood and knowingly hide the truth…	157
43 Establish the prayer and pay *zakāt* and bow with those who bow…	159
44 Do you order people to piety and forget yourselves…	178
45 Seek help in steadfastness and the prayer…	182
46 those who are aware that they will meet their Lord…	185
47 Tribe of Israel! remember the blessing I conferred on you…	185
48 Have fear of a Day when no self will be able to compensate…	185
49 Remember when We rescued you from the people of Pharaoh…	188
50 And when We parted the sea for you and rescued you…	191
51 And when We allotted to Mūsā forty nights…	195
52 Then We pardoned you after that…	197
53 Remember when We gave Mūsā the Book and discrimination…	198
54 And when Mūsā said to his people, 'My people…	199
55 And when you said, 'Mūsā, we will not believe in you until…	200
56 Then We brought you back to life after your death…	201
57 And We shaded you with clouds and sent down manna and quails…	202
They did not wrong Us; rather it was themselves they were wronging…	202
58 Remember when We said, 'Go into this town. And eat from it…	204
59 But those who did wrong substituted words…	207
60 And when Mūsā was looking for water for his people…	208
61 And when you said, 'Mūsā, we will not put up with…	210

62 Those who believe, those who are Jews, and the Christians... 215
63 Remember when We made the covenant with you... 216
64 Then after that you turned away... 216
65 You are well aware of those of you who broke the Sabbath... 219
66 We made it an exemplary punishment for those there then... 222
67 And when Mūsā said to his people, 'Allah commands you... 223
68 They said, 'Ask your Lord to make it clear to us... 225
69 They said, 'Ask your Lord to make it clear to us what colour... 225
70 They said, 'Ask your Lord to make it clear to us... 226
71 He said, 'He says it should be a cow not trained to plough... 227
72 Remember when you killed someone... 228
73 We said, 'Hit him with part of it!'... 229
74 Then your hearts became hardened after that... 235
75 Do you really hope they will follow you in faith... 236
76 When they meet those who believe, they say, 'We believe.'... 237
77 Do they not know that Allah knows what they keep secret... 237
78 Some of them are illiterate, knowing nothing of the Book... 238
79 Woe to those who write the Book with their own hands... 240
80 They say, 'The Fire will only touch us for a number of days.'... 241
81 No indeed! Those who accumulate bad actions... 243
83 Remember when We made a covenant with the tribe of Israel... 243
84 And when We made a covenant with you... 247
85 Then you are the people who are killing yourselves... 248
86 Those are the people who trade the Next World for this world... 249
87 We gave Mūsā the Book ... 250
88 They say, 'Our hearts are uncircumcised.'... 251
89 When a Book does come to them from Allah... 252
90 What an evil thing they have sold themselves for... 253
91 When they are told, 'Believe in what Allah has sent down,'... 254
92 Mūsā brought you the Clear Signs... 254
93 Remember when We made a covenant with you... 255
94 Say, 'If the abode of the Next World with Allah is for you alone... 256
95 But they will never ever long for it because of what they have done... 256
96 Rather you will find them the people greediest for life... 257
97 Say, 'Anyone who is the enemy of Jibrīl should know... 257
98 Anyone who is the enemy of Allah and of His angels... 258
99 We have sent down Clear Signs to you... 259
100 Why is it that, whenever they make a contract... 259
101 When a Messenger comes to them from Allah... 259

102 They follow what the shayṭāns recited in the reign of Sulaymān... 260
103 If only they had believed and been godfearing!... 269
104 You who have faith! do not say, '*Rā'inā*,' say, '*Unẓurnā*,'... 269
105 Those of the People of the Book who disbelieve... 272
106 Whenever We abrogate an *āyah* or cause it to be forgotten... 273
107 Do you not know that Allah is He to Whom the kingdom... 277
108 Or do you want to question your Messenger... 278
109 Many of the People of the Book would love it if... 278
110 Establish the prayer and pay *zakāt*... 279
111 They say, 'No one will enter the Garden except for Jews... 282
112 Not so! All who submit themselves completely to Allah... 282
113 The Jews say, 'The Christians have nothing to stand on,'... 283
114 Who could do greater wrong than someone who bars access... 283
115 Both East and West belong to Allah... 286
116 They say, 'Allah has a son.' Glory be to Him!... 290
117 The Originator of the heavens and earth... 292
118 Those who do not know say, 'If only Allah would speak to us... 295
119 We have sent you with the Truth, bringing good news... 295
120 The Jews and the Christians will never be pleased with you... 296
121 Those to whom We have given the Book... 297
122 Tribe of Israel! remember the blessing I conferred on you... 298
124 Remember when Ibrāhīm was tested by his Lord... 299
125 And when We made the House a place of return... 307
126 And when Ibrāhīm said, 'My Lord, make this a place of safety... 311
127 And when Ibrāhīm laid the foundations of the House... 313
128 Our Lord, make us both Muslims submitted to You... 318
129 Our Lord, raise up among them a Messenger from them... 322
130 Who would deliberately renounce the religion of Ibrāhīm... 323
131 When his Lord said to him, 'Become a Muslim!'... 324
132 Ibrāhīm directed his sons to this, as did Ya'qūb... 325
133 Or were you present when death came to Ya'qūb... 326
134 That was a community which has long since passed away... 327
135 They say, 'Be Jews or Christians and you will be guided.'... 327
136 Say, 'We believe in Allah and what has been sent down to us... 328
137 If their faith is the same as yours then they are guided... 329
138 The dye of Allah – and what dye could be better than Allah's?... 330
139 Say, 'Do you argue with us about Allah... 331
140 Or do they say that Ibrāhīm and Ismā'īl and Isḥāq... 332
141 That was a community which has long since passed away... 333

Glossary

Abū Qubays: a mountain located to the east of the Masjid al-Ḥarām.

adhān: the call to prayer.

Ajyad: an area in Makkah, south of the Ḥarām.

Āmīn: 'Ameen', a compound of verb and noun meaning 'Answer our prayer' or 'So be it'.

Amīr al-Mu'minīn: 'the Commander of the Believers', the caliph.

Anṣār: the "Helpers", the people of Madīnah who welcomed and aided the Prophet ﷺ.

'āqilah: the paternal kinsmen of an offender who are liable for the payment of blood money.

'Arafah: a plain 15 miles to the east of Makkah. One of the essential rites of the ḥajj is to stand on 'Arafah on the 9th of Dhū 'l-Ḥijjah.

'arāyā: plural of *'arīyah.*

'arīyah: a kind of sale by which the owner of an *'arīyah* is allowed to sell fresh dates while they are still on the palms by means of estimation, in exchange for dried plucked dates.

'aṣabah: male relatives on the father's side.

'Āshūrā': the 10th day of Muḥarram, the first month of the Muslim lunar calendar. It is considered a highly desirable day to fast.

'Aṣr: the mid-afternoon prayer.

awliyā': the plural of *walī.*

āyah: a verse of the Qur'an.

Āyat al-Kursī: the Throne Verse, 2:255.

'ayn: ready money, cash.

Ayyūb: the Prophet Job.

Badr: a place near the coast, about 95 miles to the south of Madīnah where, in 2 AH in the first battle fought by the newly established Muslim community, the 313 outnumbered Muslims led by the Messenger of Allah overwhelmingly defeated 1000 Makkan idolaters.

Banū: lit. sons, meaning a tribe or clan.

Baqī' al-Gharqad: the cemetery of Madīnah.

barakah: blessing, any good which is bestowed by Allah, and especially that which increases, a subtle beneficent spiritual energy which can flow through things or people.

basmalah: the expression 'In the name of Allah, the All-Merciful, the Most Merciful'.

Bu'āth: a battle between Aws and Khazraj two years before the Hijrah.

Burāq: the mount on which the Prophet ﷺ made the Night Journey.

ḍammah: the Arabic vowel 'u'.

Dār an-Nadwah: a house built by Qusayy next to the Ka'bah were tribal meetings took place.

Dāwud: the Prophet David.

dhikr: lit. remembrance, mention. Commonly used, it means invocation of Allah by repetition of His names or particular formulae.

dhimmah: obligation or contract, in particular a treaty of protection for non-Muslims living in Muslim territory.

dhimmī: a non-Muslim living under the protection of Muslim rule.

Dhu-l-Ḥijjah: the twelfth month of the Muslim calendar, the month of the hajj.

Dhu-l-Qa'dah: the eleventh month of the Muslim calendar.

dīn: the life-transaction, lit. the debt between two parties, in this usage between the Creator and created.

Ditch: the Battle of the Ditch (or Trench), which took place in 627 CE/5 AH in which the combined forces of Quraysh and their allies unsuccessfully laid siege to Madīnah for thirty days.

Fajr: the dawn prayer.

farḍ: an obligatory act of worship or practice of the *dīn* as defined by the Sharī'ah.

faqīh: pl. *fuqahā'*, a man learned in knowledge of **fiqh** who by virtue of his knowledge can give a legal judgment.

al-Fārūq: a name for the second caliph, 'Umar ibn al-Khaṭṭāb, It means someone who makes a distinction between truth and falsehood, or between cases.

fatḥah: the Arabic vowel 'a'.

Fātiḥah: "the Opener," the first sūrah of the Qur'an.

fatwa: an authoritative statement on a point of law.

fiqh: the science of the application of the Sharī'ah. A practitioner or expert in **fiqh** is called a faqih.

fuqahā': plural of *faqīh*.

ḥadd: Allah's boundary limits for the lawful and unlawful. The *ḥadd* punishments are specific fixed penalties laid down by Allah for specified crimes.

gharīb: a hadith which has a single reporter at some stage of the *isnād*.

Ghaṭafān: a very large tribal grouping who lived east of Madīnah and Makkah in the land between the Hijaz and the Shammar mountains.

ḥadīth: reported speech of the Prophet ﷺ.

ḥadīth qudsī: those words of Allah on the tongue of His Prophet ﷺ which are not part of the Revelation of the Qur'an.

hady: sacrificial camel.

ḥāfiẓ: pl. ḥuffāẓ, someone who has memorised the Qur'an.

hajj: the annual pilgrimage to Makka which is one of the five pillars of Islam.

ḥāl: In Arabic grammar, a circumstantial adverb in the accusative case which describes something happening at the same time as the action or event mentioned in the main clause.

ḥalāl: lawful in the Sharī'ah.

hamzah: the character in Arabic which designates a glottal stop.

ḥarām: unlawful in the Sharī'ah.

Ḥaram: Sacred Precinct, a protected area in which certain behavior is forbidden and other behaviour necessary. The area around the Ka'bah in Makkah is a Ḥaram, and the area around the Prophet's Mosque in Madīnah is a Ḥaram. They are referred to together as al-Ḥaramayn, 'the two Ḥarams'.

ḥarbī: as belligerent.

ḥarf: (plural *aḥruf*) one of the seven modes or manners of recitation in which the Qur'an was revealed.

al-Ḥarrah: a stony tract of black volcanic rock east of Madīnah where a terrible battle took place in 63 AH (26 August 683) between the forces of Yazīd I and 'Abdullāh ibn az-Zubayr which ended in Madīnah being sacked and plundered.

Hārūn: the Prophet Aaron, the brother of Mūsā.

Hārūt and Mārūt: the two angels mentioned in the Qur'an (2: I02) in Babel from whom people learned magic. Some commentators state that they are two kings rather than two angels (*malik* rather than *malak*).

ḥasan: good, excellent, often used to describe a hadith which is reliable, but which is not as well authenticated as one which is *ṣaḥīḥ*.

Ḥawwā': Eve, the first woman.

ḥijāb: a partition which separates two things; a curtain; in modern times used to describe a form of women's dress.

Hijaz: the region along the western seaboard of Arabia in which Makkah, Madīnah, Jidda and Ta'if are situated.

al-Ḥijr: the unroofed portion of the Ka'bah which at present is in the form of a semi-circular compound towards the north of the Ka'bah.

Hijrah: emigration in the way of Allah. Islamic dating begins with the Hijrah of the Prophet Muḥammad ﷺ from Makkah to Madīnah in 622 AD.

ḥimā: a place of pasturage and water prohibited to the public. It was used for animals paid as zakat and mounts for jihad.

Ḥirā': a mountain two miles north of Makkah where the Prophet ﷺ used to go into retreat before he received the Revelation.

Hūd: the Prophet sent to the people of 'Ād.

Ḥudaybīyah: a well-known place ten miles from Makkah on the way to Jiddah where the Homage of ar-Riḍwān took place.

ḥudūd: plural of *ḥadd*.

Iblīs: the personal name of the Devil. He is also called Shayṭān or the 'enemy of Allah'.

Ibrāhīm: the Prophet Abraham.

'Īd: a festival, either the festival at the end of Ramadan or at the time of the Hajj.

iḍāfah: a possessive construction in Arabic in which the first noun is indefinite and the second usually definite. It is used to indicate possession. The first word is called '*muḍāf*' and the second is '*muḍāf ilayhi*'.

'iddah: a period after divorce or the death of her husband for which a woman must wait before re-marrying.

Idrīs: a Prophet, possibly Enoch.

ijtihād: to exercise personal judgment in legal matters.

imam: Muslim religious or political leader; leader of Muslim congregational worship.

īmān: belief, faith.

'īnah: a transaction in which the price in paid in advance based on the description of the goods purchased.

iqāmah: the call which announces that the obligatory prayer is about to begin.

'Īsā: the Prophet Jesus.

'Ishā': the obligatory evening prayer.

Isḥāq: the Prophet Isaac.

ishbā': lengthening a vowel.

Ismā'īl: the Prophet Ishmael.

isnād: a hadith's chain of transmission from individual to individual.

Jāhiliyyah: the Time of Ignorance before the coming of Islam.

Jam': another name for Muzdalifah.

jamrah: lit. a small walled place, but in this usage a stone-built pillar. There are three *jamrah*s at Minā. One of the rites of hajj is to stone them.

Jamrat al-'Aqabah: the largest of the three *jamrah*s at Minā.

janābah: major ritual impurity requiring a ghusl: caused by intercourse, sexual discharge, menstruation, childbirth.

Jibrīl: the angel Gabriel.

jihad: struggle, particularly fighting in the way of Allah to establish Islam.

jinn: inhabitants of the heavens and the earth made of smokeless fire who are usually invisible.

jizyah: a protection tax payable by non-Muslims living under Muslim rule as a tribute to the Muslim ruler.

Jumu'ah: the day of gathering, Friday, and particularly the Jumu'ah prayer which is performed instead of *Ẓuhr* by those who attend it.

Jurhum: an old Arab tribe, originally from Yemen, who moved to Makkah. They gave protection to Hajar and Ismā'īl.

Ka'bah: the cube-shaped building at the centre of the Ḥaram in Makkah, originally built by the Prophet Ibrāhīm ﷺ. Also known as the House of Allah.

kalām: 'theology' and dogmatics. Kalām starts with the revealed tradition and employs rationalistic methods in order to understand it and resolve contradictions.

Karrāmites: a sect with anthropomorphist views on Allah, founded by Muḥammad ibn Karrām.

kasrah: the Arabic vowel i.

Khārijites: the earliest sect, who separated themselves from the body of the Muslims and declared war on all those who disagreed with them, stating that a wrong action turns a Muslim into an unbeliever.

Khaybar: Jewish colony to the north of Madinah which was laid siege to and captured by the Muslims in the seventh year after the Hijrah because of the Jews' continual treachery.

khuṭbah: a speech, and in particular a standing speech given by the imam before the Jumu'ah prayer and after the two 'Īd prayers.

kufr: disbelief, to cover up the truth, to reject Allah and refuse to believe that Muhammad ﷺ is His Messenger. A person who does this is a *kāfir*.

kunyah: a respectful but intimate way of addressing people as "the father of so-and-so" or "the mother of so-and-so."

Lā ḥawla walā quwwata illā billāh: 'There is no power nor strength except in Allah.'

Lā ilaha illā 'llāh: 'There is no god but Allah.'

lawth: strong suspicion based on strong circumstantial evidence.

Lūṭ: the Prophet Lot.

Maghrib: the sunset prayer.

maḥram: a male relative with whom marriage is forbidden.

Maqām of Ibrāhịm: the place of the stone on which the Prophet Ibrāhīm stood while he and Ismā'īl were building the Ka'bah, which marks the place of the two *rak'ah* prayer following *ṭawāf* of the Ka'bah.

marfū': 'elevated', a narration from the Prophet ﷺ mentioned by a Companion, e.g. "The Messenger of Allah ﷺ said..."

Maryam: Mary, the mother of 'Īsā.

Masjid al-Ḥarām: the great mosque in Makkah.

Mathānī: lit. 'the often recited', said to be the first long *sūrah*s, or the *Fātiḥah* and also various other things.

mawqūf: 'stopped', a narration from a Companion without mentioning the Prophet ﷺ.

Minā: a valley five miles on the road to 'Arafah where the three *jamrah*s stand. It is part of the hajj to spend four or possibly three nights there over the course of the hajj.

mu'adhdhin: someone who calls the *adhan* or call to prayer.

Mufassal: the *sūrah*s of the Qur'an starting from *Sūrat al-Hujurāt* (49) or *Sūrat Qāf* (50) to the end of the Qur'an.

mufti: someone qualified to give a legal opinion or fatwa.

Muhājirūn: Companions of the Messenger of Allah ﷺ who accepted Islam in Makkah and made hijrah to Madīnah.

Muḥarram: the first month of the Muslim lunar year.

munkar: "denounced", a narration reported by a weak reporter which goes against another authentic hadith.

munqati': a hadith whose *isnād* has a link which is omitted.

mursal: a hadith where a man in the generation after the Companions quotes directly from the Prophet without mentioning the Companion from whom he got it.

Mūsā: the Prophet Moses.

mutakallimūn: those who study the science of *kalām*, the science of investigating theological doctrine.

mutashābih: intricate, unintelligible, referring to a word or text whose meaning is not totally clear.

mutawātir: a hadith which is reported by a large number of reporter: at all stages of the *isnād.*

Mu'tazilite: someone who adheres to the school of the Mu'tazilah which is rationalist in its approach to existence. Originally they held that anyone who commits a sin is neither a believer nor an unbeliever. They also held the Qur'an to be created.

muzābanah: a forbidden sale in which something whose number, weight, or measure is known is sold for something whose number, weight or measure is not known.

Muzdalifah: a place between 'Arafah and Minā where the pilgrims returning from 'Arafah spend a night in the open between the ninth and tenth day of Dhū 'l-Ḥijjah after performing Maghrib and 'Ishā' there.

An-Naḍīr: a Jewish tribe in Madīnah.

nāfilah: (plural *nawāfil*): supererogatory act of worship.

Najrān: a region in the southern Arabian peninsula which birders Yemen.

Nūḥ: the Prophet Noah.

People of Hadith: 'the adherents of Hadith', the movement who considered only the Qur'an and hadith to be valid sources of fiqh.

People of Opinion (*ra'y*): a term used to describe those who use personal opinion to deduce judgment. It was a term used particularly to describe the early Ḥanafīs.

Qadariyyah: sect who said that people have power (qadar) over their actions and hence free will.

qāḍī: a judge, qualified to judge all matters in accordance with the Sharī'ah and to dispense and enforce legal punishments.

qasāmah: an oath taken by fifty members of a tribe or locality to refute or establish accusations of complicity in unclear cases of homicide.

Qaynuqā': one of the Jewish tribes of Madīnah.

qiblah: the direction faced in prayer – towards the Ka'bah in Makkah.

qirāḍ: wealth put by an investor in the trust of an agent for use for commercial purposes, the agent receiving no wage, but taking a designated share of the profits after the capital has been paid.

Qubā': a village on the outskirts of Madīnah (originally about 5 km/3 miles outside the city) where the first mosque in Islam was built, also known as the Masjid at-Taqwā (Mosque of Fear of God).

Quraysh: one of the great tribes of Arabia. The Prophet Muḥammad ﷺ belonged to this tribe, which had great powers spiritually and financially both before and after Islam came. Someone from this tribe is called a Qurayshī.

Qurayẓah: one of the Jewish tribes of Madīnah.

Rajab: the seventh month of the Muslim calendar.

rak'ah: a unit of the prayer consisting of a series of standings, bowing, prostrations and sittings.

Ramadan: the month of fasting, the ninth month in the Muslim lunar calendar.

rūḥ: (plural *arwāḥ*) the soul, vital spirit.

rukū': the bowing position in the prayer.

ṣadaqah: charitable giving in the Cause of Allah.

sadd adh-dharā'i': the blocking of a means which might lead to undesired consequences.

Ṣafā and Marwah: two hills close to the Ka'bah.

Ṣaḥīḥ: 'the Sound', the title of the hadith collections of al-Bukhārī and Muslim.

sajdah: prostration.

Sakīnah: calmness, tranquility, the Shekhinah.

Salaf: the early generations of the Muslims.

salām: the expression, '*as-salāmu 'alaykum*,' or 'Peace be upon you,' used as a greeting and to end the prayer.

Ṣāliḥ: the Prophet sent to the people of Thamūd.

Sha'bān: the eighth month in the Muslim calendar

shahādah: bearing witness, particularly bearing witness that there is no god but Allah and that Muhammad is the Messenger of Allah. It is one of the pillars of Islam. It is also used to describe legal testimony in a court of law.

Sharī'ah: The legal modality of a people based on the revelation of their Prophet. The final Sharī'ah is that of Islam.

Shawwāl: the tenth month of the Muslim calendar.

Shayṭān: devil, particularly Iblīs, one of the jinn.

shirk: the unforgiveable wrong action of worshipping something or someone other than Allah or associating something or someone as a partner with Him.

Shu'ayb: the Prophet Jethro.

shūrā: consultation, especially used for the council of six Companions who met after the death of 'Umar to choose the next Caliph.

Sīrah: biography, particularly biography of the Prophet ﷺ.

siwāk: a small stick, usually from the arak tree, whose tip is softened and used for cleaning the teeth.

Ṣuffah: a verandah attached to the Prophet's Mosque where the poor Muslims used to sleep.

suḥūr: pre-dawn meal before a day of fasting.

suknā: designating the use of a dwelling for a poor person for a certain period of time.

sukūn: a diacritic mark that means that there is no sound after a consonant.

Sulaymān: the Prophet Solomon.

sunan: the plural of *sunnah.*

Sunnah: the customary practice of a person or group of people. It has come to refer almost exclusively to the practice of the Messenger of Allah ﷺ.

sūrah: a chapter of the Qur'an.

Tābi'ūn: the second generation of the early Muslims who did not meet the Prophet Muhammad ﷺ but learned the *dīn* of Islam from his Companions.

tafsīr: commentary or explanation of the meanings of the Qur'an.

taḥrīm: a term used for entering a state of worship in which certain other actions are forbidden. The *taḥrīm* of the prayer is saying, *'Allahu akbar'* to start it.

Ṭā'if: a walled town south of Makkah known for its fertility. It was the home of the tribe of Thaqīf.

takbīr: saying *'Allāhu Akbar,'* 'Allah is greater'.

takbīr al-iḥrām: the *takbīr* which begins the prayer.

Ṭālūt: Saul.

tanwīn: nunation.

taqwā: awe or fear of Allah, which inspires a person to be on guard against wrong action and eager for actions which please Him.

tasbīḥ: glorification of Allah by saying *'Subhāna'llāh'*.

tashahhud: lit. to pronounce the *shahādah.* In the context of the prayer, it is a formula which includes the *shahādah* and is recited in the final sitting position of each two *rak'ah* cycle.

taslīm: giving the Islamic greeting of *'as-salāmu 'alaykum,'* 'Peace be upon you.' The prayer ends with a *taslīm.*

ṭawāf: circumambulation of the Ka'bah, done in sets of seven circuits.

tawḥīd: the doctrine of Divine Unity.

tawjīh: orientation, a supplication formula recited before starting the prayer.

tayammum: purification for the prayer with clean dust, earth, or stone, when water for *ghusl* or *wuḍū'* is unavailable or would be detrimental to health.

Uḥud: a mountain just outside of Madīnah where five years after the Hijrah, the Muslims lost a battle against the Makkan idolaters. Many great Companions, and in particular Ḥamzah, the uncle of the Prophet, were killed in this battle.

Umm al-Kitāb: literally 'Mother of the Book'. It has a number of meanings, one of which is the celestial prototype of the Qur'an. It is also used for the Fātiḥah.

umm walad: a slavegirl who has had a child by her master.

'umrah: the lesser pilgrimage to the Ka'bah in Makkah performed at any time of the year.

ūqiyyah: unit of weight equal to forty dirhams.

'ushr: land tax of one tenth of the produce if naturally watered and one twentieth if artificially irrigated.

'Uzayr: Ezra.

walī: (plural *awliyā'*) someone who is a 'friend' of Allah, thus possessing the quality of *wilāyah.*

witr: literally 'odd', a single *raka'h* prayed after the *shaf'* which makes the number of sunnah prayers uneven.

wuḍū': ritual washing to be pure for the prayer.

Yaḥyā: the Prophet John the Baptist, the son of Zakariyyā.

Ya'qūb: the Prophet Jacob, also called Isrā'īl (Israel).

Yathrib: the ancient name for Madīnah.

Yūnus: the Prophet Jonah.

Yūsuf: the Prophet Joseph.

zakat: a wealth tax, one of the five pillars of Islam.

Zamzam: the well in the Ḥaram of Makkah.

zandaqah: heresy. This is an Arabicised Persian word. The term had been used for heterodox groups, especially Manichaeans, in pre-Islamic Persia, and hence it was originally applied to Magians.

az-Zaqqūm: a tree with bitter fruit which grows at the bottom of the Fire. Its fruit resembles the heads of devils.

zindīq: a term used to describe a heretic whose teaching is a danger to the community or state.

zuhd: making do with little of this world and leaving what you do not need.

Ẓuhr: the midday prayer.

www.ingramcontent.com/pod-product-compliance
Lightning Source LLC
Chambersburg PA
CBHW080724230426
43665CB00020B/2610